T0383944

Energy Efficiency and Robustness of Advanced Machine Learning Architectures

Machine Learning (ML) algorithms have shown a high level of accuracy, and applications are widely used in many systems and platforms. However, developing efficient ML-based systems requires addressing three problems: energy-efficiency, robustness, and techniques that typically focus on optimizing for a single objective/have a limited set of goals.

This book tackles these challenges by exploiting the unique features of advanced ML models and investigates cross-layer concepts and techniques to engage both hardware and software-level methods to build robust and energy-efficient architectures for these advanced ML networks. More specifically, this book improves the energy efficiency of complex models like CapsNets, through a specialized flow of hardware-level designs and software-level optimizations exploiting the application-driven knowledge of these systems and the error tolerance through approximations and quantization. This book also improves the robustness of ML models, in particular for SNNs executed on neuromorphic hardware, due to their inherent cost-effective features. This book integrates multiple optimization objectives into specialized frameworks for jointly optimizing the robustness and energy efficiency of these systems.

This is an important resource for students and researchers of computer and electrical engineering who are interested in developing energy efficient and robust ML.

Chapman & Hall/CRC
Artificial Intelligence and Robotics Series

Series Editor: Roman Yampolskiy

For more information about this series please visit:
https://www.routledge.com/Chapman--HallCRC-Artificial-Intelligence-and-Robotics-Series/
book-series/ARTILRO

Energy Efficiency and Robustness of Advanced Machine Learning Architectures

A Cross-Layer Approach

Alberto Marchisio and Muhammad Shafique

CRC Press
Taylor & Francis Group
Boca Raton London New York

CRC Press is an imprint of the
Taylor & Francis Group, an **informa** business

A CHAPMAN & HALL BOOK

First edition published 2025
by CRC Press
2385 Executive Center Drive, Suite 320, Boca Raton, FL 33431

and by CRC Press
4 Park Square, Milton Park, Abingdon, Oxon, OX14 4RN

CRC Press is an imprint of Taylor & Francis Group, LLC

ISBN: 978-1-032-85550-9 (hbk)
ISBN: 978-1-032-87013-7 (pbk)
ISBN: 978-1-003-53045-9 (ebk)

DOI: 10.1201/9781003530459

Contents

Authors

Alberto Marchisio received his B.Sc. and M.Sc. degrees in Electronic Engineering from Politecnico di Torino, Turin, Italy, in October 2015 and April 2018, respectively. He received his Ph.D. degree in Computer Science from the Technische Universität Wien (TU Wien) Informatics Doctoral College Resilient Embedded Systems, Vienna, Austria, in September 2023. Currently, he is a Research Group Leader with the eBrain Lab, Division of Engineering, New York University Abu Dhabi (NYUAD), United Arab Emirates. His main research interests include hardware and software optimizations for machine learning, brain-inspired computing, VLSI architecture design, emerging computing technologies, robust design, and approximate computing for energy efficiency. He (co-)authored 30+ papers in prestigious international conferences and journals. He received the honorable mention at the Italian National Finals of Maths Olympic Games in 2012, and the Richard Newton Young Fellow Award in 2019.

Muhammad Shafique (M'11 - SM'16) received his Ph.D. degree in Computer Science from the Karlsruhe Institute of Technology (KIT), Germany, in 2011. Afterwards, he established and led a highly recognized research group at KIT for several years as well as conducted impactful collaborative R&D activities across the globe. Besides co-founding a technology startup in Pakistan, he was also an initiator and team lead of an ICT R&D project. He has also established strong research ties with multiple universities in worldwide, where he has been actively co-supervising various R&D activities and student/research Theses since 2011, resulting in top-quality research outcome and scientific publications. Before KIT, he was with Streaming Networks Pvt. Ltd. where he was involved in research and development of video coding systems several years. In October 2016, he joined the Institute of Computer Engineering at the Faculty of Informatics, Technische Universität Wien (TU Wien), Vienna, Austria as a Full Professor of Computer Architecture and Robust, Energy-Efficient Technologies. Since Sep.2020, Dr. Shafique is with the New York University (NYU), where he is currently a Full Professor and the director of eBrain Lab at the NYU-Abu Dhabi in UAE, and a Global Network Professor at the Tandon School of Engineering, NYU-New York City in USA. He is also a Co-PI/Investigator in multiple NYUAD Centers, including Center of Artificial Intelligence and Robotics (CAIR), Center of Cyber Security (CCS), Center for InTeractIng urban nEtworkS (CITIES), and Center for Quantum and Topological Systems (CQTS).

Dr. Shafique has demonstrated success in obtaining prestigious grants, leading team-projects, meeting deadlines for demonstrations, motivating team members to peak performance levels, and completion of independent challenging tasks. His experience is corroborated by strong technical knowledge and an educational record (throughout Gold Medalist). He also possesses an in-depth understanding of various video coding standards and machine learning algorithms. His research interests are in AI & machine learning hardware and system-level design, brain-inspired computing, neuromorphic computing, approximate computing, quantum machine learning, cognitive autonomous systems, robotics, wearable healthcare, AI for healthcare, energy-efficient systems, robust computing, machine learning secrity and privacy, hardware security, emerging technologies, electronic design automation, FPGAs, MPSoCs, embedded systems, and quantum computing. His research has a special focus on cross-layer analysis, modeling, design, and optimization of computing and memory systems. The researched technologies and tools are deployed in application use cases from Internet-of-Things (IoT), Smart Cyber-Physical Systems (CPS), and ICT for Development (ICT4D) domains.

Dr. Shafique has given several Keynotes, Invited Talks, and Tutorials at premier venues. He has also organized many special sessions at flagship conferences (like DAC, ICCAD, DATE, IOLTS, and ESWeek). He has served as the Associate Editor and Guest Editor of prestigious journals like IEEE Transactions on Computer Aided Design (TCAD), IEEE Design and Test Magazine (D&T), ACM Transactions on Embedded Computing (TECS), IEEE Transactions on Sustainable Computing (T-SUSC), and Elsevier MICPRO. He has served as the TPC Chair of several conferences like CODES+ISSS, IGSC, ISVLSI, PARMA-DITAM, RTML, ESTIMedia and LPDC; General Chair of ISVLSI, IGSC, DDECS and ESTIMedia; Track Chair at DAC, ICCAD, DATE, IOLTS, DSD and FDL; and PhD Forum Chair of ISVLSI. He has also served on the program committees of numerous prestigious IEEE/ACM conferences including ICCAD, DAC, MICRO, ISCA, DATE, CASES, ASPDAC, and FPL. He has been recognized as a member of the ACM TODAES Distinguished Review Board in 2022. He is a senior member of the IEEE and IEEE Signal Processing Society (SPS), and a professional member of the ACM, SIGARCH, SIGDA, SIGBED, and HIPEAC. He holds one US patent and has (co-)authored 7 Books, 20+ Book Chapters, 350+ papers in premier journals and conferences, and over 100 archive articles.

Dr. Shafique received the prestigious 2015 ACM/SIGDA Outstanding New Faculty Award, the AI-2000 Chip Technology Most Influential Scholar Award in 2020, 2022 and 2023, the ATRC's ASPIRE Award for Research Excellence in 2021, six gold medals in his educational career, and several best paper awards and nominations at prestigious conferences like CODES+ISSS, DATE, DAC and ICCAD, Best Master Thesis Award, DAC'14 Designer Track Best Poster Award, IEEE Transactions of Computer "Feature Paper of the Month" Awards, and Best Lecturer Award. His research work on aging optimization for GPUs featured as a Research Highlight in the Nature Electronics, Feb.2018 issue. Dr. Shafique was named in the NYU's 2021 Faculty Honors List. His students have also secured many prestigious student and research awards in the research community.

CHAPTER 1

Introduction

Among Machine Learning (ML) systems, Deep Neural Networks (DNNs) have emerged as an established milestone for several applications, such as computer vision, medicine, finance, and robotics. This led to the need to deploy the DNN inference workload across various devices, including embedded systems with constrained resources. However, the current trends in the ML community are projected in the other direction since the newer networks tend to be deeper and more complex. For instance, Capsule Networks (CapsNets) are peculiar types of DNNs based on capsules, which are arrays of neurons, to learn high-level features with better capabilities than traditional DNNs. As a result, the next generation of computing platforms executing advanced DNNs would exhibit high complexity and consume high energy, thus challenging their feasible implementations in resource-constrained devices.

On the other hand, Spiking Neural Networks (SNNs) emerged as an efficient computation infrastructure for elaborating event-based DNNs, which represent a closer manner to our current understanding of the human brain's functionality. This led to the development of the neuromorphic computing paradigm, whose hardware architectures support the execution of energy-efficient event-based SNNs.

Another fundamental aspect to consider when deploying advanced Deep Learning (DL) architectures is security. The system requires high robustness against various vulnerability threats when dealing with safety-critical applications. An adversary can threaten the integrity of the DL system through attacks at different levels, including the hardware and software stacks, and perturbing the inputs, the memory, or the computational engine. As a result, defensive countermeasures in different abstraction layers of the system must be applied, which typically require some energy and computation overhead. Moreover, while the security of traditional DNNs has been extensively studied, investigating the security of advanced DL systems offers unique opportunities to exploit their peculiar features.

Besides these constraints and requirements, the constantly evolving market has imposed enormous pressure on delivering optimized end-to-end systems in a timely manner. Therefore, the optimizations for speeding up the design process are crucial to sustaining these time-to-market demands.

1.1 OPTIMIZATION OBJECTIVES FOR DNN MODELS AND ARCHITECTURES

1.1.1 Energy-Efficiency

Advanced DNNs are massively resource-hungry, requiring large memories and expensive computation engines. Moreover, due to the stringent constraints of real-time systems, the outputs must be generated with a fast response. To enable the usage of fast and high-accurate DNNs in resource-constrained portable devices, several optimization techniques can be applied to improve the energy efficiency of DNNs' execution.

At the software level, compression techniques like pruning [79][154][51] and quantization [96][275] significantly reduce the resources needed to process a DNN workload. However, these methods typically incur some accuracy loss or require high re-training overhead to partially restore the original accuracy.

Another prominent research direction for finding energy-efficient DNNs is represented by hardware-aware neural architecture search (NAS) methods. Hardware-aware NAS methodologies [239] jointly search for DNNs' accuracy and efficiency of their execution on a target hardware platform. However, due to the large search space and since DNN training and hardware measurements are very costly operations, the exploration time tends to explode.

At the hardware level, to efficiently perform the most common DNN operations, which are convolutional layers and fully connected layers (i.e., generic matrix multiplications, GEMM operations), several application-specific hardware designs have been proposed. The most widely adopted architectures are based on a Processing Element (PE) array [29][100] to exploit the row stationary dataflow. More flexible dataflows can be supported by configurable architectures [144][116][31]. Moreover, the need for supporting the software-level compression optimizations, like pruning and quantization, and other specialized architectures have been designed for efficiently processing sparse DNNs [77][203] and flexible bit-widths [244].

On the other hand, the breakthrough of event-based computation led to the design of neuromorphic architectures [170][40], whose aim is to perform computations asynchronously, only when events are present. Therefore, these systems achieve extremely low energy consumption when the scenes are captured by event-based cameras, such as Dynamic Vision Sensors (DVS). However, the development of the tools and algorithms for designing and training event-based SNNs is still immature, and SNN-based implementations in neuromorphic hardware incur an inevitable accuracy loss compared to the correspondent DNN implementations on conventional hardware.

1.1.2 Robustness

Despite the great success and popularity of DL-based systems in the last few years, recent works have demonstrated that DNNs have intrinsic weaknesses, which undermine their trustworthiness. At the hardware level, the DNN systems' misfunctioning can be caused by permanent faults appearing during the device fabrication process or by transient faults such as soft errors, aging, and process variations. Moreover, since the chip supply chain comprises several third-party facilities, malicious hardware Trojans can be inserted into the design. When their triggering conditions are met, the Trojan is activated, and its effect may alter the correct behavior of the system.

Toward fault tolerance, traditional fault-mitigation methods are based on redundancy [195]. However, they are inefficient since the redundant hardware/execution consists of a considerable overhead for real-time ML-based systems. Hence, different types of techniques need to be employed. Fault-Aware Pruning and Training techniques [287] are effective for mitigating permanent faults, while Range Restriction methods [89][32] can mitigate transient faults. Moreover, recent methods [238] proposed to integrate the fault tolerance property in the optimization goals of the NAS by minimizing the DNN model sensitivity to bit-flips. To mitigate against hardware Trojans, detection methods [49] can be employed. They aim to monitor the systems' operation and detect any suspect functionality violations.

At the software level, adversarial security threads [67] are emerging. The scope of such attacks is to apply minor modifications to the DNNs' inputs to induce the system's misfunctioning. If an adversary takes control of a given DNN model's behavior, the security and integrity of the system are threatened, and it can affect the environment around it as well. Moreover, privacy threats are concerning when dealing with large databases. By analyzing private information at a large scale, confidential information can be leaked during the DNNs' processing flow.

To increase the robustness, various defensive approaches can be used. The most common technique is known as adversarial training [148], which consists of augmenting the input data with adversarial examples to force the training model to learn to behave correctly also in the presence of attacks. Other defense techniques include quantization [132] and noise filtering [125], which aim at reducing the impact of the adversarial perturbation.

To preserve privacy, different methodologies have been proposed. The differential privacy [2] is based on introducing randomization during the learning process. The multi-party computation approach is based on distributing the training and testing data on different devices, simultaneously performing computations using a specific privacy-preserving protocol [173]. Homomorphic encryption-based mechanisms [62] maintain data confidentiality by executing the computations in the ciphertext domain. However, these techniques significantly increase the system's computational requirements. Therefore, achieving cost-effective robustness is challenging and an open research question.

1.2 SUMMARY OF THE STATE-OF-THE-ART CHALLENGES AND RESEARCH GOALS

Advanced DNN systems employ a set of compute-intensive and memory-intensive operations to provide high accuracy for their predictions. Moreover, several applications require fast responses in real time. While general-purpose hardware platforms are slow and inefficient in computing DNN workloads, deploying such resource-hungry algorithms on edge devices is prohibitive. Therefore, a complete design flow comprising software-level optimizations, such as compression, specialized hardware designs, and mapping, is required.

Moreover, safety-critical applications demand DNN systems to be highly robust in adverse conditions. There are several scenarios where an adversary agent can undermine the system's integrity. Hence, it is worth investigating such conditions from various perspectives and elaborating on defensive methodologies that can mitigate the effect of these threats.

1.2.1 Limitations of the State-of-the-Art

1. *Excessive hardware and re-training overhead*: Several techniques require non-negligible hardware overhead or extensive (re-)training overhead, which makes the ML algorithms' execution less convenient, despite the advantages. Lightweight methodologies (i.e., which do not incur large overhead) have not yet been studied successfully.

2. *Lack of automation in the design space exploration*: An extremely manual-intensive design effort has been conducted in the optimization design. More systematic design space exploration methodologies need to be developed to efficiently explore the space of the solutions.

3. *Combining multiple optimization objectives*: The integration of different optimization techniques has not been studied in detail yet. Combining more aspects as multiple optimization objectives is extremely important for developing an integrated framework that can improve the efficiency and robustness of DNNs beyond the capability of individual techniques.

4. *Lack of specialized optimizations for advanced DL models*: Different optimization methodologies have been proposed for traditional DNNs, but they are typically not very efficient on advanced DL models, such as CapsNets and SNNs. Specialized optimizations for such complex DL models have not been systematically studied yet.

5. *Combining multiple techniques for resilient DL*: Different techniques have been proposed to mitigate the effects of hardware-induced faults or software-level attacks. However, their combined effects on the DNNs' energy efficiency have not been investigated.

1.2.2 Scientific Objectives and Goals

Due to several limitations of the related work and the heterogeneity of the advanced DL models, providing cross-layer optimizations for their energy efficiency and robustness is challenging. We breakdown the main research objectives into the following scientific goals:

1. **Identifying potential performance/energy bottlenecks of executing ML tasks**
   The state-of-the-art advancements in complex DL models [291][220] are mainly focused on maximizing the accuracy, while their hardware implementations might not be optimized, due to the potential discrepancies between the algorithmic workload and the hardware architectures.

   Goal: This objective focuses on studying the execution of advanced DL models on existing hardware and reporting the breakdowns. Afterward, we study whether these analyses can be leveraged to focus the designs and optimizations on mitigating the found bottlenecks. The key focus is exploring optimization techniques that significantly improve the most inefficient parts of the computations.

2. **Analyzing different types of vulnerability threats and their resiliency**
   Due to the wide variety and heterogeneity of vulnerability threats for DNNs, the design and deployment of trustworthy ML-based systems are challenging [242]. The state-of-the-art techniques and optimizations for DNN resiliency are focused on simplified objectives, while other more complex vulnerability scenarios might still threaten the systems.

   Goal: This objective focuses on analyzing the DL-based systems' robustness by investigating the problem from previously unexplored perspectives and combining multiple types of vulnerability threats. The identification of these threats will contribute to providing more solid and cost-effective techniques to mitigate these vulnerabilities.

3. **Investigating and designing resource-efficient optimizations for improving the performance and energy consumption of advanced DL models**
   The state-of-the-art optimizations for DNN energy-efficiency [22] are tailored for traditional DNNs, which are composed of convolutional and fully-connected layers. Therefore, the software-level techniques and hardware architectures might not be optimized for a different type of workload in advanced DL models, such as CapsNets [236].

   Goal: This objective focuses on designing novel frameworks for improving the efficiency of training and inference of complex DL models. Moreover, it is possible to design specialized hardware architectures and optimization tools that significantly improve their efficiency. By systematically exploring the design space, it is possible to identify Pareto-optimal design solutions which leverage the tradeoffs between different optimization objectives (e.g., accuracy, energy, latency, area, memory).

4. **Investigating and designing cost-effective optimizations for improving the robustness against adversarial attacks**
   The state-of-the-art defenses against adversarial attacks on DL models [241] are tailored for traditional DNNs, while they might not be as efficient or applicable

to different types of encoding and communication of the information between layers, as is the case for SNNs. Hence, different methodologies need to be employed to improve their robustness.

Goal: This objective focuses on analyzing the application-specific behavior of advanced DL models to propose and evaluate cost-effective defenses against adversarial attacks. Moreover, the evaluations can be conducted for various vulnerability threat models.

5. **Designing application-specific optimization techniques**
   An in-depth analysis of the types of operations involved in the advanced DL algorithms and the specialized hardware architectures for accelerating their execution allows leveraging the knowledge for further improving their efficiency.

   Goal: This objective focuses on analyzing application-specific optimizations for efficiently executing advanced DL systems on specialized hardware. This study proposes optimizations to improve the accuracy and the memory energy efficiency without affecting the execution time.

6. **Studying the interaction between different optimization objectives when exploring the space of the solutions**
   The state-of-the-art optimization techniques for DL inference effectively improve the DNN energy efficiency but might expose the DL system to vulnerability threats. On the other hand, the state-of-the-art techniques for improving the DL robustness often incur hardware overhead and significant energy consumption. Moreover, their interactions have not been studied so far.

   Goal: This objective focuses on exploring the interaction of different optimization techniques for the energy efficiency and robustness of DL systems. This will help in building frameworks for integrating multiple optimization objectives and efficiently exploring the space of the solutions.

1.3 BOOK CONTRIBUTIONS

This book aims at achieving high energy efficiency and high robustness in advanced DL systems, enabling cost-effective resiliency for several application domains. This book presents novel techniques at both the hardware architecture and software levels, such that these optimizations significantly reduce energy consumption while maintaining high robustness. As illustrated in Figure 1.1, this book is composed of the following contributions:

- **HW Designs and SW-Level Optimizations for Energy-Efficiency of Advanced DL Architectures**
  DATE '19 [155], *DATE '20* [157], *'20* [150], *JCNN 20* [149][168], *TVLSI '21* [159], *TCAD '21* [158], *IJCNN '21* [271], *ISLPED '22* [151], *IROS '22* [272]
  It consists of the complete optimization flow for designing efficient CapsNet hardware, which includes the design of efficient hardware architecture, the

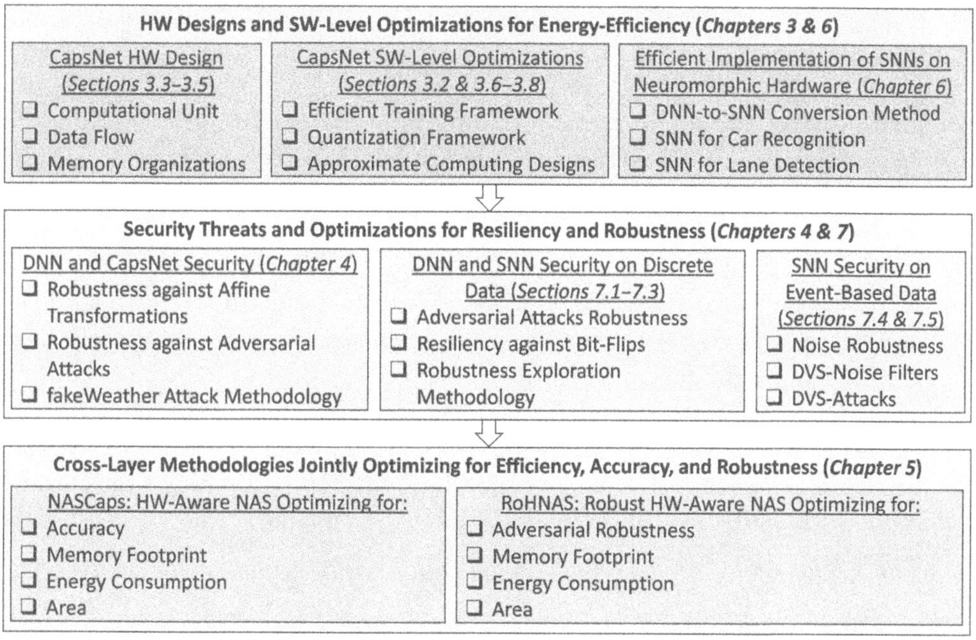

HW Designs and SW-Level Optimizations for Energy-Efficiency (*Chapters 3 & 6*)		
CapsNet HW Design (*Sections 3.3–3.5*) ❑ Computational Unit ❑ Data Flow ❑ Memory Organizations	CapsNet SW-Level Optimizations (*Sections 3.2 & 3.6–3.8*) ❑ Efficient Training Framework ❑ Quantization Framework ❑ Approximate Computing Designs	Efficient Implementation of SNNs on Neuromorphic Hardware (*Chapter 6*) ❑ DNN-to-SNN Conversion Method ❑ SNN for Car Recognition ❑ SNN for Lane Detection

Security Threats and Optimizations for Resiliency and Robustness (*Chapters 4 & 7*)		
DNN and CapsNet Security (*Chapter 4*) ❑ Robustness against Affine Transformations ❑ Robustness against Adversarial Attacks ❑ fakeWeather Attack Methodology	DNN and SNN Security on Discrete Data (*Sections 7.1–7.3*) ❑ Adversarial Attacks Robustness ❑ Resiliency against Bit-Flips ❑ Robustness Exploration Methodology	SNN Security on Event-Based Data (*Sections 7.4 & 7.5*) ❑ Noise Robustness ❑ DVS-Noise Filters ❑ DVS-Attacks

Cross-Layer Methodologies Jointly Optimizing for Efficiency, Accuracy, and Robustness (*Chapter 5*)	
NASCaps: HW-Aware NAS Optimizing for: ❑ Accuracy ❑ Memory Footprint ❑ Energy Consumption ❑ Area	RoHNAS: Robust HW-Aware NAS Optimizing for: ❑ Adversarial Robustness ❑ Memory Footprint ❑ Energy Consumption ❑ Area

Figure 1.1: Overview of this book.

exploration of different configurations of computational units, data flow, and memory organizations. The hardware-level techniques are coupled with software-level methodologies that improve the system's efficiency in both training and inference stages through a specialized quantization framework and approximate computing designs. Moreover, it includes design methodologies and optimization techniques for deploying efficient SNNs on neuromorphic hardware. Targeting the Loihi computing platform, multiple SNN designs have been implemented and mapped on Loihi for different applications.

- **Security Threats and Optimizations for Resiliency and Robustness of Advanced DL Architectures**
  UDL @ ICML '19 [162], *IJCNN '20* [163][270], *DATE '21* [47], *IJCNN '21* [165], *IROS '21* [166], *IJCNN '22* [152], *MICPRO '23* [164], *IJCNN '23* [153]

  Exploiting the inherent features of advanced DL architectures, it is possible to devise attack algorithms or defensive countermeasures tailored for these networks. This book systematically compares the robustness of DNNs and CapsNets against affine transformations and adversarial attacks. It also analyzes their robustness against newly-designed attacks that fake the effect of weather conditions on the captured images. Moreover, various security threats are investigated for SNNs. For the analyses on discrete data, the adversarial robustness and bit-flip resiliency for DNNs and SNNs are investigated, and a robustness exploration methodology is proposed to fine-tune the inherent structural parameters of SNNs and achieve high robustness. Concerning event-based data analyses, after studying the impact of random noise, various attack algorithms are generated, and DVS-noise filters are employed as a defense mechanism toward higher robustness.

- **Cross-Layer Methodology Jointly Optimizing for Efficiency, Accuracy, and Robustness of Advanced DL Architectures**
  ICCAD '20 [156], *DyNN @ ICML '22* [160], *Access '22* [161]
  An HW-Aware NAS framework is proposed for designing Pareto-optimal DNNs based on Capsule layers. To reduce the gigantic training time and search space, an analytical model is designed to estimate the memory, energy, and latency of DNNs executed on specialized hardware accelerators. The design space exploration is conducted through a multi-objective evolutionary algorithm. Moreover, toward conjoint optimizations for robustness and hardware efficiency, a systematic analysis is conducted to select the adversarial perturbation values to employ in the NAS. In this way, the proposed framework finds Pareto-optimal DNNs w.r.t. memory, energy, latency, and adversarial robustness.

1.4 BOOK OUTLINE

Chapter 2 describes the basic concepts of DNNs and discusses the background information about CapsNets and SNNs. Afterward, it presents an overview of the vulnerability threats for DL systems. Moreover, it discusses the current trends and related works employed for optimizing the energy efficiency and robustness of DL systems while also highlighting the challenges and limitations of state-of-the-art techniques.

Chapter 3 discusses the proposed design flow of software and hardware optimizations for CapsNets. It includes SW-level optimizations for training and inference, hardware designs of CapsNet inference accelerators and memory systems, and post-training optimizations like quantization and approximations. The implementations and outputs of the integrated framework are used in the security analyses of Chapter 4 and in the proposed cross-layer methodology of Chapter 5.

Chapter 4 investigates the security vulnerabilities of advanced DL models such as DNNs and CapsNets. It performs a comparative analysis of their robustness against affine transformations and adversarial attacks. Moreover, novel adversarial attack algorithms are proposed and evaluated for DNNs and CapsNets.

Chapter 5 discusses the proposed integrated frameworks for multi-objective optimizations of advanced DNNs. First, it presents a NAS methodology for jointly optimizing the accuracy, memory, energy, and latency of DNNs and CapsNets. Afterward, it discusses a framework that also includes adversarial robustness as a joint optimization objective.

Chapter 6 presents efficient design methodologies and optimizations for deploying SNNs on the Intel Loihi neuromorphic processor. After providing an overview of the Loihi architecture, it discusses the design and optimizations of SNNs for different applications. Following an analysis to optimize the DNN-to-SNN conversion and a pre-processing technique for training event-based data in the DNN domain, efficient SNNs for gesture recognition are deployed and mapped on the Loihi chip. Afterward, toward autonomous driving applications, efficient SNN designs and implementations on the Loihi processor are proposed for car recognition and lane detection tasks.

Chapter 7 discusses the vulnerabilities of SNNs against security threats. After comparing the adversarial robustness between DNNs and SNNs, novel attack methodologies and defensive countermeasures are proposed. An attack threat is devised in which a specific adversarial noise pattern in the inputs triggers a hardware Trojan that generates bit-flips in the most vulnerable weight locations of DNNs and SNNs. Afterward, the inherent robustness of SNNs is investigated, and a methodology is proposed to explore different values of the SNNs' structural parameters. Toward event-based SNNs' security, a novel methodology employing DVS-noise filters is proposed for improving the SNNs' robustness against adversarial attacks. Moreover, a set of adversarial attacks for event-based SNNs is proposed and evaluated in the presence of such noise filters.

Finally, **Chapter 8** concludes this book and provides an outlook for potential future research directions.

CHAPTER 2

Background and Related Work

This book proposes cross-layer optimizations for advanced DL architectures, covering energy efficiency and resiliency perspectives. Besides the DNNs, a special focus is given to the advanced DL models such as CapsNets and SNNs. This chapter provides an overview of the DL systems' functionality and the challenges related to the specific goals. Section 2.1 discusses a general background on DNNs followed by the latest related work on hardware accelerators for DNNs and optimizations for energy efficiency. Section 2.2 provides an overview of the CapsNets, with a special focus on the differences compared to the traditional DNNs. Section 2.3 discusses the background information on SNNs, neuromorphic architectures, and event-based vision. Section 2.4 discusses the DL vulnerability threats and the notable related works optimizing security and resiliency.

2.1 DEEP NEURAL NETWORKS

The basic element of a neural network is the *neuron*, which attempts to mimic the behavior of the biological neuron. A biological neuron [52], shown in Figure 2.1, consists of the cell body (soma), the dendrites, and an axon. The dendrites carry input stimuli processed by the soma, while the axon transmits the neuron output signal to other neurons. On the other hand, the artificial neuron performs a weighted sum of its inputs (Equation (2.1)), to which an offset is added as the bias term b. Then, the neuron's output is obtained by applying a non-linear activation function σ (Equation (2.2)).

$$g(\mathbf{x}) = \sum_{n=0}^{N-1} \mathbf{x}[n]\mathbf{w}[n] \tag{2.1}$$

$$y = \sigma\left(g(\mathbf{x}) + b\right) \tag{2.2}$$

The neurons are organized in layers. In feedforward networks, each neuron of layer l receives inputs from layer $l-1$ and sends its activation to the neurons of layer $l+1$.

DOI: 10.1201/9781003530459-2

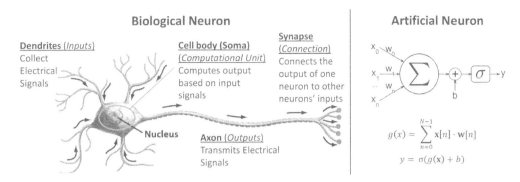

Figure 2.1: Comparison between a biological neuron (figure adapted from [52]) and an artificial neuron.

The number of stacked layers indicates the depth. A neural network is typically called a *Deep Neural Network* (DNN) [13] if there are more than three hidden layers.

2.1.1 Layers and Operations

The layers are categorized based on the types of connections. The following list contains the most common types of layers in DNNs.

- **Fully-Connected (FC) layers:** each neuron of layer l receives as inputs all the activations of layer $l-1$ (see Figure 2.2a). Since all the connections are present, the number of parameters of an FC layer is potentially huge. However, in practice, it is not always necessary for an output neuron to receive information from all the input neurons. For this reason, the convolutional layers have been designed.

- **Convolutional (Conv) layers:** the neurons are organized in a 2D grid, i.e., a *feature map*, and every neuron of layer l does not receive all the activations of the layer $l-1$, but it is connected to a small receptive field [118] (see Figure 2.2b). The receptive field size, which corresponds to the weight matrix, is commonly called *kernel size* and the stride parameter S defines the distance between

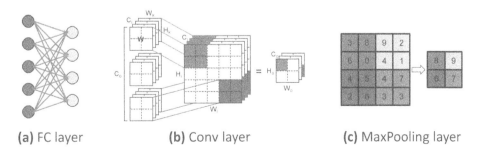

(a) FC layer   (b) Conv layer   (c) MaxPooling layer

Figure 2.2: **(a)** Example of an FC layer. **(b)** Example of a Conv layer. **(c)** Example of a MaxPooling layer.

adjacent receptive fields. In Conv layers with shared weights, all the neurons of layer l have the same matrix of weights and detect the same feature in different locations of layer $l - 1$. To detect multiple features, a Conv layer has multiple channels, i.e., there are multiple feature maps.

- **Pooling layers:** similar to Conv layers, Pooling layers have receptive fields. For the group of neurons in each receptive field, their output is a single value that contains a statistic of the group, e.g., the maximum or the average value. An example of a MaxPooling layer is shown in Figure 2.2c. The stride parameter is typically set equal to the dimension of the receptive field to have non-overlapping windows. Pooling layers reduce the number of activations of a layer and consequently decrease the memory requirements and the number of computations while achieving invariance to small local translations. Pooling layers down-sample the Conv layer outputs, whose values heavily depend on the position of the input. Hence, Pooling layers make DNNs more robust to minor input variations.

- **Normalization layers:** the input activations are usually preprocessed to have a normal distribution, i.e., zero mean and unit variance. The normalization is beneficial since it keeps different inputs within the same range of values to ease the computations and avoids saturating the non-linear activation functions. Typically, Normalization layers are inserted between Conv and FC layers. Moreover, the activations' normalization speeds up the training since the layers do not need to adapt to different distributions at each training step. The most common type of normalization is the *Batch Normalization* [94].

- **Activation functions:** without a non-linear activation function, the DNN would be a simple cascade of linear algebra operations. To solve complex non-linear problems, different non-linear functions are applied to the weighted sum of a neuron. In the first developments of DNNs, the Sigmoid and Hyperbolic Tangent functions were adopted, but their usage was reduced over the years due to their computational complexity. The most common function is the *Rectified Linear Unit (ReLU)*, which forces the activations to be greater than or equal to zero. Its newer variants, such as Leaky-ReLU and Exponential Linear Unit (ELU), aim at introducing a negative slope for negative values. Moreover, the *Softmax* function is typically used in output layers of DNNs for classification since it bounds the values in the range $(0, 1)$ to represent the probabilities associated with the output classes.

2.1.2 Training and Inference

DNNs learn how to perform a specific task by properly determining its parameters (weights and biases), which are continuously updated during the *training* phase. Afterward, during the *inference* phase, the parameters are kept constant, and the DNN makes the prediction. The dataset is typically split into training, validation, and testing sets. The training set is used for updating the parameters, while the validation set is used to fine-tune the hyperparameters. The inference is conducted on the testing set, which contains previously unseen data. There are different approaches for training DNNs:

- **Supervised learning:** A set of labeled input-output pairs is required. In supervised learning, the DNNs' parameters are updated to minimize the differences between the output labels and the DNN predictions. This approach is widely used nowadays in many applications due to its good performance. A common supervised learning algorithm for training DNNs is the *gradient backpropagation*. The DNN's outputs are compared with the labels, and a *loss* score is calculated with a *loss function*, such as the Euclidean distance or the Mean Squared Error (MSE). The parameters are updated accordingly by an amount proportional to the partial derivative (i.e., the gradient) of the loss w.r.t. the parameters. The gradients are computed through the backpropagation algorithm, which is based on the *chain rule* of calculus. The actual update is done with an *optimization algorithm*, such as the gradient descent or the Adam [110]. A common problem when training DNNs is *overfitting*, i.e., high performance on the train set and low performance on the test set. The techniques used to overcome this issue include L1 and L2 regularization [188], which add a regularizing term to the loss function, and dropout [256], which randomly removes some neurons in the DNN.

- **Unsupervised learning:** When only non-labeled data are available, the goal is to find common patterns or data grouping without any guidance. The most popular unsupervised learning approaches are based on clustering, a data mining technique that groups unlabeled data based on attribute similarities or differences. Common DNNs that apply unsupervised learning are autoencoders and Generative Adversarial Networks (GANs).

- **Reinforcement learning:** Reinforcement learning is the third primary type of learning. Similar to unsupervised learning, it does not need labeled data. It is based on autonomous agents who decide to travel across states in a given environment. The agent gets a reward in case of success but will not receive any reward in case of failure. Hence, the agent learns how to maximize the reward from the environment.

2.1.3 DNN Models

In recent years, many DNN models have been proposed to achieve high performance on a given task. For instance, the ILSVRC competition has driven researchers to develop high accurate DNNs for the ImageNet dataset [43]. *Along with higher accuracy, the DNN models are growing over the years in depth and complexity, thus making them challenging to deploy in tiny embedded devices.* Historically, the most popular DNN models are included in the following list.

- **LeNet [118] (1998)**: it is one of the first CNN trained with backpropagation, designed for learning the grayscale handwritten digit recognition task. It consists of a sequence of two Conv layers followed by three FC layers.

- **AlexNet [113] (2012)**: it is the first deep CNN designed and trained for the ImageNet dataset, significantly outperforming other non-convolutional models that have won the ILSVRC in previous years. It also introduced the ReLU activation function. To ease its training, the computation was split into two GPUs.

- **VGG [251] (2014)**: starting from the structure of the AlexNet, it furtherly increases the number of Conv layers. Its success was supported by the availability of hardware resources that support heavy training computations. However, a very deep sequence of layers is challenging due to the vanishing gradient problem. As the magnitude of the gradient drastically reduces with the depth of the network, the earlier layers might have small gradients that hinder the correct training.

- **ResNet [84] (2015)**: to overcome the vanishing gradient problem, the Residual Networks (ResNets) employ skip connections in parallel to a series of Conv layers. Hence, this structure significantly deepens the network up to 200 layers. Moreover, the batch normalization layers are introduced as a regularization strategy.

- **MobileNet [93] (2017)**: it is a model based on depthwise separable convolutions. Its structure allows a faster execution compared to DNNs with traditional convolutions. Hence, it is suited for implementation on mobile devices.

- **NasNet [291] (2018)**: it is one of the first DNN model obtained through neural architecture search (NAS). It initiated a common trend of determining the architecture of the DNN model through solving an optimization problem in which the goal is to maximize the accuracy.

2.1.4 DNN Hardware Architectures

DNNs are a class of algorithms with intrinsic parallelism that can be exploited using parallel computations for efficient implementations [23]. At the hardware level, the architectures are based on many *Processing Elements (PEs)* that perform operations in parallel. They can be classified as spatial and temporal architectures [262]. An overview of their basic functionality is shown in Figure 2.3. In temporal architectures, the control is centralized, as the PEs can only access data from the central memory without inter-PE connections. On the contrary, in spatial architectures, each PE can also have local memory cells and its control logic. Most importantly, the PEs in spatial architectures are interconnected to exchange data, thus forming a PE array.

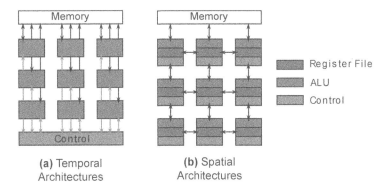

Figure 2.3: Overview of **(a)** Temporal architectures and **(b)** Spatial architectures.

2.1.4.1 Temporal Architectures

Temporal architectures are commonly employed in general-purpose processors, such as CPUs and GPUs. CPUs can be realized as vector processors, capable of working with multiple data elements simultaneously. Vector processors have several Arithmetic and Logic Units (ALUs) that synchronously perform an instruction on vector data. Therefore, vector processors adopt the Single-Instruction-Multiple-Data (SIMD) paradigm. GPUs are manycore architectures specifically designed for parallel computation with thousands of cores. Similar to vector CPUs, GPUs adopt the Single-Instruction-Multiple- Thread (SIMT) paradigm. First introduced by Nvidia, the SIMT model simultaneously executes a single instruction on multiple cores. Each core receives different data belonging to multiple threads running in parallel. GPUs are the common platforms for training large and complex DNNs, thanks to the support of popular ML frameworks like PyTorch [204] and TensorFlow [1] to execute on Nvidia GPUs. At the back end, cuDNN [34] is an optimized library for mapping DNNs onto GPUs. In high-end Nvidia GPUs, the traditional CUDA cores are combined with Tensor Cores [167], which are specifically designed for large matrix operations.

2.1.4.2 Spatial Architectures

Spatial architectures are tailored and optimized for specific tasks, which offer less flexibility, as they are commonly implemented on FPGAs or ASICs. DNNs are suitable for such implementation since the sequence of operations is known at design time. The computations are based on simple multiply-and-accumulate (MAC) operations performed at a large scale. Hence, the memory accesses to fetch the inputs and store the results of the MACs become the performance bottleneck. Moreover, state-of-the-art DNN accelerators exhibit large DRAM access energy consumption compared to the MAC energy consumption [262]. Due to the high DRAM cost, DNN accelerators have focused on exploiting *data reuse*, i.e., optimizing the architecture and dataflow for reusing the weights and feature maps when they are stored in on-chip register files or buffers, thus minimizing the DRAM accesses. The different techniques for exploiting data reuse are associated with the dataflow classified by the taxonomy proposed in [30] (see Figure 2.4).

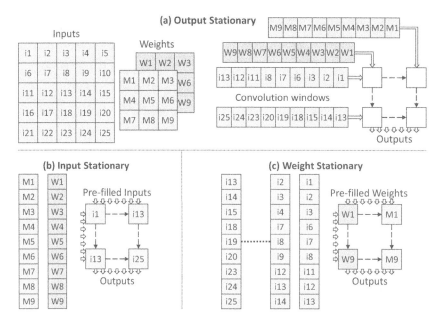

Figure 2.4: Different dataflows for a DNN spatial architectures. ((**a**) Output Stationary. (**b**) Input Stationary. (**c**) Weight Stationary.

- **Weight Stationary**: It exploits the weight reuse to minimize the energy consumption for fetching the weights from the DRAM. Since the weights are kept stationary in the PEs, the inputs and the partial sums are coordinately moved through the PE array to optimize the data movement. A weight stationary dataflow is characterized by spatial unrolling operations, in which the *for* loops are replaced by *parallel for* loops. This mapping operation is equivalent to a loop reordering transformation from the software perspective. An example of weight stationary dataflow is represented by the Tensor Processing Unit (TPU) [100], where the stationary weights are stored in the PEs, the input feature maps are horizontally forwarded, and the partial sums are accumulated along the vertical dimension.

- **Output Stationary**: It minimizes the data movement necessary to store and load the partial sums from the global buffer (GLB). While using the weight stationary dataflow the partial sum of a single output value must be stored and reloaded to/from the GLB several times, in the output stationary dataflow each PE is modified for locally accumulating the results of the MACs. Hence, each PE computes all the required operations to obtain an output feature map since the partial sums are accumulated into a single register. A popular architecture using the output stationary dataflow is the ShiDianNao [46], where each PE of the 2D array computes the value of a single output feature map. On the other hand, the weights are broadcasted to all the PEs at every operation cycle, and the input feature maps are horizontally forwarded.

- **Row Stationary**: Its purpose is to maximize the reuse of inputs, weights, and partial sums jointly. In the row stationary dataflow, all the MACs performing a row of the convolution are mapped to a single PE. A PE has a register file to store a row of the weight kernel while the inputs are streamed in the PE using the sliding window mechanism. A 2D array of PEs is required to process a whole Conv layer, where each column of the array accumulates the partial sums that contribute to a row of the output feature map. An example of row stationary dataflow is designed in the Eyeriss architecture [29], where different types of reuse are obtained. In fact, a row of PEs shares the same weights, the input pixels are reused diagonally, and the partial sums are vertically accumulated.

- **No Local Reuse**: It maximizes the storage area by removing register files from the PEs and allocating all the on-chip memory in the GLB. As a drawback, the traffic between the GLB and the PE array will be higher. Another critical aspect of this dataflow is that the global buffer size may not be sufficient to fully contain the input feature maps, kernel weights, and output feature maps. This issue is bypassed through the *loop tiling* method [285], which partitions the larger tensors into smaller tensors that can be contained in the buffer.

2.1.4.3 Memory Hierarchy

While algorithm-level optimizations and computational workload acceleration are fundamental to achieving high performance, inefficient memory management could lead to a bottleneck since, typically, the memory accesses dominate the energy consumption of a system [76]. Hence, memory organizations must be considered a high-priority concern at the earliest design stages. The required memory bandwidth is drastically different for the various DNN layers since the memory access patterns vary according to the type of layer and operations involved. For instance, an FC layer, where data reuse becomes practically impossible, requires enormous bandwidth. To compensate for this effect, it is crucial to devise an efficient DRAM mapping policy to optimize the DRAM accesses and different layer scheduling [213].

Traditional memory hierarchies of DNN accelerators [122] are composed of an off-chip DRAM and an on-chip SRAM, where for DNN applications, the on-chip memory is not a traditional cache, but a scratchpad memory. Though general-purpose approaches for memory design exist [200], application-specific design and optimizations are required to achieve high energy efficiency. *An efficient design of the memory hierarchy for a specialized application requires the exploration of several design parameters (like size, banks, partitions, etc.) for multiple levels, affecting each other, which makes it a very challenging problem. To address this challenge, the DESCNet methodology discussed in Section 3.4 systematically studies the design requirements (size, accesses, etc.), performance, and energy consumption, for different inference operations. A specialized multi-banked scratchpad memory architecture is designed considering the dataflow mapping and the corresponding memory access patterns of various operations. The memory is partitioned into multiple sectors to support fine-grained sector-level power-gating, thereby providing a higher potential for energy savings at run-time varying memory usage scenarios.*

TABLE 2.1: An overview of Hardware and Software optimizations for reducing the energy consumption of DNN inference.

Technique	References	Short Description	Key Pros	Key Cons
Pruning	[79][154][51]	It removes redundant parameters of a DNN, aiming at reducing the memory footprint and the computations required for DNN inference	Less computation and memory requirements	Accuracy loss or high re-training overhead
Quantization	[75][96][275][81]	It reduces the wordlength of the DNN weights and activations, and converting them from floating-point into fixed-point/integer format	Less memory requirements and less complex hardware operations	Accuracy loss or high re-training overhead
Approximate Computing	[288][26][80][180]	It employs approximate or simplified arithmetic hardware modules, aiming at reducing their complexity	Less energy, area, and/or latency	Accuracy loss or high re-training overhead
Hardware-Aware Neural Architecture Search	[263][4][280][98]	It automatically explores and finds optimal DNN architectures for a given application, executing on a given hardware platform	Joint optimization for accuracy and efficiency	Long exploration time, high training cost

2.1.5 DNN Optimizations for Energy-Efficiency

State-of-the-art DNNs are highly resource-hungry, requiring large memories and expensive computation engines. To enable the usage of high accurate DNNs in resource-constrained portable devices, several optimization techniques have been proposed, aiming at improving the energy efficiency of DNN execution. Table 2.1 provides an overview of the most effective methods proposed in recent years.

2.1.5.1 DNN Compression

Most DNNs are subject to redundancy concerning the weights. Consequently, it is possible to conduct lightweight optimizations and compression methodologies without affecting their accuracy much. The compression techniques include pruning and quantization methodologies, which can also be combined into an integrated framework [78][268]. The key goal is to minimize the memory footprint of DNNs, by skipping redundant connections (i.e., pruning) and lowering the bit-width (i.e., quantization), thus enabling larger DNN models to be implemented on resource-constrained devices. *When conducting compression, it is extremely challenging to find good tradeoffs between memory footprint and accuracy. In this regard, our Q-CapsNets framework discussed in Section 3.5 addresses this challenge by exploring different layer-wise and operation-wise arithmetic precisions for the quantized network, with a maximum accuracy tolerance and a memory budget specified as constraints to the framework.*

2.1.5.2 Approximate DNNs

The high DNN redundancy can also be exploited by employing approximate hardware modules to reduce the complexity and improve the efficiency. Due to the inherent relatively high resilience of DNNs to approximation errors [80], approximate components cause low accuracy degradation while significantly reducing the energy consumption. Since the more frequent operations are based on the Multiply-and-Accumulate (MAC) unit, the most common approaches propose approximate multipliers and adders [179]. Automated frameworks are proposed to selectively approximate DNNs based on their error tolerance [180]. All the above-discussed optimizations can lead to significant energy savings, but at the cost of some accuracy loss or high re-training overhead to recover the original accuracy.

2.1.5.3 HW-Aware NAS

Another prominent research direction can be identified as hardware-aware NAS. While traditional NAS methodologies [291] optimize only the DNN accuracy, a hardware-aware NAS [239] jointly searches for DNN accuracy and efficiency of its execution in specialized hardware, e.g., energy, latency, and area. However, due to the large search space, and since DNN training and hardware measurements are costly operations, the exploration time tends to explode when all the DNN hyper-parameters are considered. The heuristic search methods for exploring the space of the solutions can be grouped into evolutionary algorithms, reinforcement learning, and differentiable NAS. *However, even using one of these heuristic search methods, the massive variety of possible configurations explored to find an exhaustive set of Pareto-optimal solutions is prohibitive. In addition, complete detailed post-synthesis hardware measurements are unfeasible for this search due to their long simulation times. These limitations challenge the applicability of such an exploration in real-case HW/SW co-design searches, with stringent time-to-market constraints. To address these challenges, our NASCaps framework discussed in Section 5.2 employs analytical models of the functional behavior of a given specialized accelerator to quickly obtain accurate estimations of memory usage, energy consumption, and latency when different DNN models are executed. Moreover, the training time while exploring multiple solutions is reduced by evaluating the accuracy of partially-trained DNNs. The number of training epochs to employ in the search is chosen based on the tradeoff between training time and Pearson correlation coefficient w.r.t. fully-trained DNNs.*

2.2 CAPSULE NETWORKS

Among advanced DL models, Capsule Networks (CapsNets) [236] have become popular in recent years, due to their high learning capabilities and improved generalization skills, compared to the traditional DNNs. The ability to learn hierarchical information of different features (e.g., position, orientation, and scaling) in a single capsule achieves high accuracy in ML vision applications, e.g., MNIST [118] and Fashion-MNIST [284] classification, as well as effective applicability to other

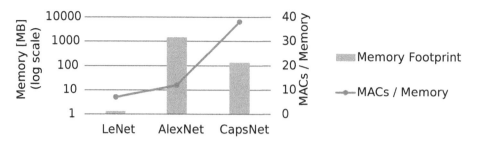

Figure 2.5: Comparison of Memory footprint and (Multiply-and-Accumulate operations vs. memory) ratio (MACs/Memory) between the LeNet [118], AlexNet [113], and CapsNet [236].

ML application domains, such as speech recognition [281], natural language processing [290], and healthcare [175]. Indeed, CapsNets can encapsulate the hierarchical and spatial information of the input features in a closer manner to our current understanding of the human brain's functionality.

However, the capsule-based layers introduce an additional dimension compared to the matrices of the Conv and FC layers of the traditional DNNs, significantly increasing the computational and communication workload of the underlying hardware. Therefore, a key challenge in deploying CapsNets is their extremely high complexity. They require intense computations due to the multiplications in the matrices of capsules and the iterative dynamic routing-by-agreement algorithm for learning the cross-coupling between capsules. Figure 2.5 compares the CapsNet [236] with the LeNet [118] and the AlexNet [113], in terms of their memory footprints and the total number of MAC operations needed to perform an inference pass. The MACs/memory ratio is a good metric to show the computational complexity of the models, thus demonstrating the higher compute-intensive nature of CapsNets, compared to traditional DNNs.

2.2.1 Traditional DNNs vs. CapsNets

As discussed in [86], among the major drawbacks of traditional DNNs, which are based on Conv operations, there are two key issues:

1. DNNs have too few structural levels. Thus, they cannot handle different viewpoints on the same object.

2. Pooling layers are too naive forms of information encoding since they make DNNs translation-invariant rather than equivariant.

To overcome these problems, the CapsNets are designed. The key differences w.r.t. traditional DNNs are summarized in Figure 2.6.

Inspired by the concept of inverse graphics, in [86] the neurons are grouped into vectors to form the so-called *capsules*. A capsule encodes both the instantiation parameters (i.e., *pose*, like width, skew, rotation, and other spatial information) and its length (i.e., its Euclidean Norm) is associated with the instantiation probability

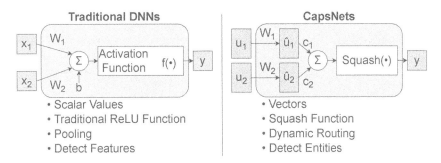

Figure 2.6: Summary of key differences between traditional DNNs and CapsNets.

of the entity. In this way, from the image pixels, the CapsNets encode the pose of low-level features, and from the pose of the "parts", it is possible to understand the pose of the "whole", i.e., the high-level entities, to make a better prediction. The CapsNets use the *Squash* activation function, a multidimensional non-linear function that efficiently fits the prediction vector that forms the capsule.

Moreover, the concept of routing is introduced to tackle the problem that DNNs are not invariant to translations. The (Max) Pooling operation consists of collecting a group of adjacent neurons and selecting the one with the highest activity, thus discarding the spatial information provided by this group of neurons. For this reason, the pooling layers are responsible for the so-called Picasso problem, in which DNNs classify an image having a nose below the mouth and an eye below the nose as a face since they lose spatial relationships between features. To replace the pooling layers, an iterative routing procedure to determine the values of the coupling coefficients between a low-level capsule to higher-level capsules is proposed in [236]. It is an iterative process in which the agreements between the capsules of two consecutive layers are measured and updated for a certain number of iterations at runtime during the inference.

2.2.2 CapsNet Models and Applications

Hinton et al. [86] first showed the practical applicability of CapsNets, which adopt the *capsules* as basic blocks and can learn the image features in addition to its deformations and viewing conditions. A more detailed explanation of how poses and probabilities are computed to form a CapsNet is described in [236]. A capsule is a vector of neurons, where each element of the array represents an instantiation parameter of the entity and the instantiation probability is measured as the length of the vector. To represent such probability in the range $\{0, 1\}$, the *Squash* function is used. The iterative procedure for computing the coupling coefficients c_{ij} constitutes the Dynamic Routing-by-Agreement, as shown in Algorithm 1. The coupling coefficient determines to which extent the lower-level capsule i sends its activation to all the higher-level capsules. In other words, c_{ij} represents the prior probability that an entity detected by a lower-level capsule i belongs to the higher-level entity of capsule j. To satisfy the property that the sum of these coefficients must be unitary, the *Softmax* function is applied (see line 8 of Algorithm 1). The activation v_j of the capsule j is obtained by applying the *Squash* function to the pre-activation s_j (line 14). The last step, consisting of updating the logits b_{ij}, is used in the following iteration by computing the agreement through the scalar product between the input prediction votes $\hat{u}_{i|j}$ and the activation v_j (line 18).

Algorithm 1: Dynamic Routing-by-Agreement in CapsNets.

Input: Prediction Votes $\hat{u}_{i|j}$; Number of Iterations r; Layer l
Output: Activation Vectors v_j

1 **for** Capsule i in Layer l **do**
2   **for** Capsule j in Layer $(l+1)$ **do**
3   Logits Initialization: $b_{ij} \leftarrow 0$;
4   **end**
5 **end**
6 **for** r Iterations **do**
7   **for** Capsule i in Layer l **do**
8   **Softmax:** $c_{ij} \leftarrow \texttt{softmax}\,(b_{ij}) = \frac{e^{b_{ij}}}{\sum_k e^{b_{ik}}}$;
9   **end**
10   **for** Capsule j in Layer $(l+1)$ **do**
11   **Sum:** $s_j \leftarrow \sum_i c_{ij} \cdot \hat{u}_{i|j}$;
12   **end**
13   **for** Capsule j in Layer $(l+1)$ **do**
14   **Squash:** $v_j \leftarrow \texttt{squash}\,(s_j) = \frac{||s_j||^2}{1+||s_j||^2} \frac{s_j}{||s_j||}$;
15   **end**
16   **for** Capsule i in Layer l **do**
17   **for** Capsule j in Layer $(l+1)$ **do**
18   **Update:** $b_{ij} \leftarrow b_{ij} + \hat{u}_{i|j} \cdot v_j$;
19   **end**
20   **end**
21 **end**

The first CapsNet model [236], using the vector capsules and the dynamic routing, is shown in Figure 2.7. A Conv layer with kernel 9×9, stride 1 and 256 output channels is followed by the PrimaryCaps layer, in which the neurons are grouped into 8D vectors, organized in 32 output channels, and form a Conv capsule layer of kernel size 9×9 and stride 2, using the *Squash* activation function. In the last ClassCaps layer, each of the 10 capsules is dedicated to recognizing the output classes. The *Dynamic Routing* analyzes the features encoded by the 1152 8D capsules of the PrimaryCaps layer to generate the 10 16D activations of the ClassCaps layer. For training purposes, a decoder network (i.e., a cascade of three FC layers) is built for obtaining the image reconstruction and then combining the *reconstruction loss* with the *margin loss* (i.e., computed from the instantiation probabilities of the output activations) to form the loss function. Despite being applied mainly to relatively simple tasks, like MNIST [118] and Fashion-MNIST [284] classification, this architecture developed by

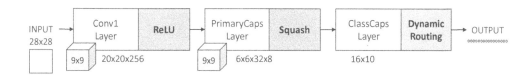

Figure 2.7: Architectural model of the ShallowCaps [236].

the Google Brain's team has been extensively analyzed and studied by the community. Hence, in the following, we consider it the Google's CapsNet, simply CapsNet, or ShallowCaps, in contrast to the deeper CapsNet models.

A major limitation of the ShallowCaps is that it is highly compute-intense and requires many parameters to perform similarly to traditional DNNs for complex tasks. To overcome these issues, the DeepCaps architecture [220] has been proposed. As shown in Figure 2.8, besides increasing the depth, the DeepCaps exploits 3D Conv capsule layers and 3D dynamic routing, thus significantly reducing the number of parameters. Moreover, the decoder employs deconvolutional layers that capture more spatial relationships than FC layers.

2.2.3   Summary of Challenges for Capsule Networks

As comprehensively discussed in this section, one of the CapsNets' main challenges is their high complexity due to the computations involving vector capsules and complex operations like the Squash and the Dynamic Routing-by-Agreement. State-of-the-art specialized hardware architectures accelerate the execution of traditional Conv, FC, and pooling layers. Consequently, they do not support (or support an inefficient implementation of) the operations involving CapsNets. *To address these challenges and bridge the gap between the high learning capability of CapsNets and their relative execution inefficiency, Chapter 3 presents a design flow for improving the energy efficiency of CapsNets executed on hardware. It involves optimizations for speeding up the training and the hardware design of a specialized accelerator for running CapsNet inference.*

Moreover, the execution patterns of different CapsNet layers and operations, including both the computational requirements and memory accesses, are significantly different compared to the patterns observed from traditional DNNs, thus making their efficient dataflow challenging. Hence, *detailed analyses monitoring the memory*

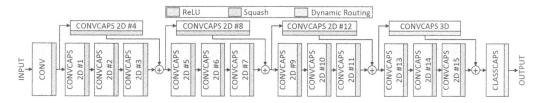

Figure 2.8: Architectural model of the DeepCaps [220].

access patterns and resiliency for different layers and operations lead to designing advanced memory architectures that can be coupled with CapsNet accelerators, and further lightweight optimizations involving quantization and approximate computing, as will be discussed in Chapter 3.

2.3 SPIKING NEURAL NETWORKS

Spiking Neural Networks (SNNs) have recently demonstrated great success due to their high performance and low energy consumption, making them suitable for being implemented on embedded devices, such as neuromorphic chips. Inspired by the principles of neural computation in nature, neuromorphic architectures have emerged as high-performance and low-power computing platforms. SNNs are models that simulate the asynchronous event-based decision-making process of the human brain. As shown in Figure 2.9, the SNNs receive trains of spikes as inputs. Their associated time at which they occur, their magnitude, and their shape can be used to encode numerical information. The event-driven computations performed by neurons and synapses propagate the spiking information from the input to the output. SNNs can be programmed to learn and execute complex tasks in real time and consume low energy. Considered the third generation of neural networks [147], the SNNs follow the wave of success of the DNNs to perform complex ML tasks. While conventional DNNs process continuous values, SNNs process discrete spike trains, mimicking the information processing behavior of the neurons in the human brain. The key advantage of SNNs, besides the biological plausibility, is that they offer great potential for developing energy-efficient ML when co-designed with neuromorphic hardware due to the sparse nature of SNNs. Figure 2.9 shows the basic functionality of SNNs. The input spikes encode the information using spike trains. The neurons of the network integrate the incoming spikes, which contribute to increasing the neurons' membrane potential. In this way, the output spikes are generated when the membrane potential exceeds a threshold.

2.3.1 Spiking Neuron Models

A neuron is considered the simplest computational knob in an SNN. When a spike coming from a presynaptic neuron arrives at the input of the postsynaptic neuron, the spiking current injected into the neuron's body, associated with the synaptic weight, is integrated into the membrane, thus contributing to raising its membrane potential. Several neuron models have been proposed in the literature, and this section provides an on the most common models employed for SNNs.

The *McCulloch-Pitts neuron* [169] is the predecessor model for the neural networks. It simply computes the sum of the incoming spikes and emits the boolean output 1 (fires) if the sum is higher than its threshold or 0 otherwise. Its main drawback consists of its inability to learn. To overcome this issue, the *perceptron* model [230] was proposed. It introduces the concept of learnable weights that are multiplied by the boolean outputs of the McCulloch-Pitts neuron. A network of perceptrons represents the first generation of neural networks, while the second

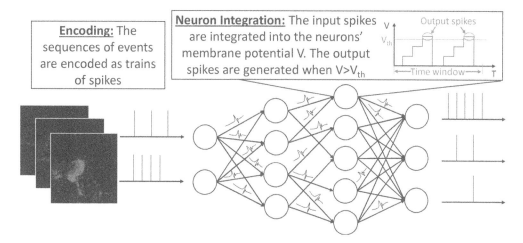

Figure 2.9: Functionality of an SNN, in which the events are encoded into spikes, and the neurons' output spikes are generated when the membrane potential exceeds the threshold voltage.

generation uses the same perceptron model but with a more complex activation function. For the third generation, which corresponds to the SNNs, different neuron models can be employed, leveraging the trade-off between biological plausibility and implementation cost:

- The *Hodgkin-Huxley model* [90] represents the most biologically plausible but also the most complex neuron model. It involves several differential equations, which make the development of large SNNs using this model impractical and inefficient.

- The *Izhikevich model* [95] can reproduce different spiking patterns as well as spike shapes of biological cortical neurons while being less compute-intensive than the Hodgkin-Huxley neuron. Its functionality is described through Equations (2.3) to (2.5), where v is the membrane potential, I is the input current, u is the membrane recovery variable, and a, b, c, d are constants that set the spike shape.

$$\frac{dv}{dt} = 0.04v^2(t) + 5v(t) + 140 - u(t) + I(t) \tag{2.3}$$

$$\frac{du}{dt} = a(bv(t) - u(t)) \tag{2.4}$$

$$\text{if } v \geq V_{th}, \text{then} \begin{cases} v \leftarrow c \\ u \leftarrow u + d \end{cases} \tag{2.5}$$

- The *Integrate-and-Fire (IF) model* [61] is the simplest model from the computational perspective. For this reason, it is widely used in the SNN community. The model is based on a resistance-capacitance (RC) circuit, similar to a low-pass filter. Equation (2.6) describes how the membrane potential of the postsynaptic neuron evolves over time, from which the time constant $\tau_m = RC$ can be derived as in Equation (2.7).

$$I(t) = \frac{v(t)}{R} + C\frac{dv}{dt} \tag{2.6}$$

$$\tau_m \frac{dv}{dt} = -v(t) + RI(t) \tag{2.7}$$

When the membrane potential reaches a certain threshold V_{th} at the firing time t_f, the postsynaptic neuron produces a spike $\delta(t - t_f)$, after which the membrane potential is reset to a value v_{rest} (often set to 0 as a common assumption [207]), obviously lower than V_{th}.

- The *Leaky-Integrate-and-Fire (LIF)* [278] is a modified version of the IF model that introduces the concept of refractory period. It represents the time period after a spike in which the membrane potential cannot increase even if a train of spikes is received at the input. The evolution over time of the membrane potential of a LIF neuron is described by Equation (2.8).

$$\tau_m \frac{dv}{dt} = -v(t) + \left(i_0(t) + \sum w_j i_j(t) \right) \tag{2.8}$$

A synaptic current $i_j(t)$ is generated when a spike is received. It is then modulated by its correspondent synaptic weight w_j and added to the bias current $i_0(t)$. Compared to the Hodgkin-Huxley model, the lower computational complexity of the LIF neuron comes at the price of a lower biological plausibility. The LIF model assumes that the shape of the action potentials is uniform for each spike. This assumption limits the ability to reproduce biological spike patterns and shapes. However, such a low complexity allows for creating large SNNs and their implementation on neuromorphic hardware.

2.3.2 Spike Coding Techniques

The input information of SNNs is represented and propagated to the output through spike trains. Different methods for encoding the information into spikes [210] are shown in Figure 2.10:

- *Rate Coding*: The intensity corresponds to the probability of firing a spike, which translates into the mean firing rate when multiple spikes are counted within an observation period. It is the most commonly used method due to its simplicity, but it might be power-consuming compared to other coding techniques due to the high spiking rate.

- *Inter-Spike-Interval (ISI) Coding*: The intensity is temporally coded as the precise delay between consecutive spikes.

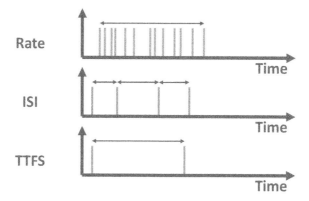

Figure 2.10: Comparison between Rate, Inter-spike interval (ISI), and Time to first spike (TTFS) encoding techniques.

- *Time-to-First-Spike (TTFS) Coding*: The intensity I is coded as the time difference Δt between the stimulus and the first spike of a neuron. Such delay can be either the inverse of the intensity ($\Delta t = 1/I$) or a linear relation, such as $\Delta t = 1 - I$. This encoding approach assumes that a neuron generates only one spike for any given stimulus. Hence, eventual subsequent spikes that follow from that neuron are simply ignored [199]. The main advantage is that the processing can proceed fast since the information is already transmitted when the first spike is received.

2.3.3 SNN Learning Techniques

Different methods for training SNNs can be adopted based on the topology of learning. For unsupervised learning, the possible approaches are based on Hebbian learning [235], the Spike-Driven Synaptic Plasticity (SDSP) [56], and the Spike-Time-Dependent Plasticity (STDP) [255]. The STDP, the most commonly used method in the community, is based on strengthening (or weakening) the synaptic weights depending on the degree of correlation between the presynaptic and postsynaptic neuronal spikes in spatial and temporal domains.

The supervised DNN learning methods, based on the gradient backpropagation, cannot be directly applied to SNNs since the spiking loss function is not differentiable [232]. The possible solutions to overcome this challenge are either (1) using DNN-to-SNN conversion after learning the weights in the DNN domain or (2) approximating the spiking derivative w.r.t. the loss function by using a surrogate gradient.

1. The *DNN-to-SNN conversion* approach is based on training the DNN with a common gradient backpropagation procedure and then converting the trained network into the SNN domain [234]. The accuracy loss during the conversion can be balanced by applying weight normalization and carrying out a single forward pass for SNN inference in multiple discrete timesteps. Another hybrid approach consists of training a DNN, converting it into SNN, and then incrementally

training the SNN with an approximated backpropagation [223]. *However, the DNN-to-SNN conversion approach can be applied only to static datasets since DNNs cannot be directly trained on event-based data. This challenge limits the applicability of this technique since most of the energy-efficiency gains achieved by the SNNs are due to using event data.*

2. The *surrogate gradient learning* [185] bypasses the non-differentiability issue of a LIF neuron by defining an approximate gradient during backward propagation. It allows for employing common SNN-based backpropagation methods, such as the Spatio-Temporal Back-Propagation (STBP) [283] or SLAYER [248]. Further modifications and approximations of the learning rule can be applied to achieve online learning on neuromorphic devices [227][257].

2.3.4 Neuromorphic Architectures

The recent ML breakthroughs have boosted the intelligence in edge devices. However, as modern ML technologies and algorithms are maturing, the limitations of their conventional computing infrastructures are emerging. While DNNs can scale to solve complex problems, these gains are ensured by high computational power and memory-intense cost. Neuromorphic computing represents a fundamental redesign principle of the computer architecture, inspired by the mechanisms of the biological brain. The roadmap of neuromorphic computing departs from the abstraction layers and algorithms of conventional computing with the scope of unlocking orders of magnitude gains in efficiency and performance compared to conventional architectures. The conventional architectures, varying from standard desktop processors to the most advanced AI accelerators, consume higher power than neuromorphic architectures, whose power consumption is comparable to or lower than the biological brain of a human. The following paragraphs briefly present the most popular neuromorphic chips, while the Intel Loihi [40] is comprehensively discussed in Section 6.1.

TrueNorth [170] is a digital chip designed and implemented by IBM in a 28nm CMOS technology. The chip organization consists of a tiled array of 4096 neurosynaptic cores. Each core has 12.75 KB of local SRAM memory, which stores the synapse states, the neuron states, and the parameters of up to 256 LIF neurons. The spike-based communication and asynchronous routing infrastructure enable the integration of multiple TrueNorth chips into larger systems.

SpiNNaker [55] is a digital system designed to simulate large SNNs in real-time designed by the University of Manchester. Its basic blocks are ARM9 cores that can access a small amount of local memory, while some additional memory is shared across one multi-core chip. Eighteen processor cores are grouped to form a chip, while the system can scale when multiple chips are assembled on a board and multiple boards are connected. The second version, named SpiNNaker 2 [134] integrates more cores per chip and linear algebra accelerators to execute more efficiently sparse deep learning algorithms. Its software stack facilitates the SNN deployment using python-based simulators, such as PyNN [41]. Its interface supports standard neuron models such as LIF and Izhikevich neurons, and common learning algorithms such as the STDP.

BrainScaleS [237] is a hybrid system that combines analog neurons with digital communication networks. It supports the adaptive exponential IF neuron model, which can be configured through a parameter to adapt to different spiking behaviors. A single chip supports up to 512 neurons and 14 000 synapses per neuron. Larger networks can be built by connecting multiple chips directly on the silicon wafer.

NeuroGrid [16] is a platform that employs analog/digital mixed-signal circuits to implement large SNN models in real-time. A NeuroGrid board is composed of 16 CMOS NeuroCore chips, and each chip contains an array of 256×256 two-compartmental neurons. The full NeuroGrid board can scale up to one million neurons and billions of synapses thanks to its asynchronous multicast tree routing digital infrastructure.

DYNAP-SE [178] is a chip fabricated by INI Zurich in a 180nm CMOS technology node. The chip has four cores, with 256 neurons each, and supports $64k$ synapses. The asynchronous digital connectivity between neurons can be re-programmed at runtime, enabling flexible SNN model implementations, including recurrent networks.

ODIN [53] is a 28nm CMOS digital neuromorphic chip designed by the Catholic University of Louvain. A core is composed of 256 neurons, which can be configured with the LIF model or the Izikevich model. The parameters of the neurons are stored in a 4 KB SRAM array, and the 64k synapses are implemented as a 32 KB SRAM array.

μBrain [259] is a digital event-based neuromorphic chip implemented in a 40nm CMOS technology. The architecture is fully asynchronous, without a clock. Due to its ultra-low power consumption (a few tens of μW), it is more suitable for IoT applications.

2.3.5 Event-Based Cameras

Event-based sensors, also called dynamic vision sensors (DVS), take inspiration from the functionality of the human eye's retina. In traditional frame-based sensors the image recording of a scene consists of stacking a series of frames at a specific temporal rate. On the contrary, the information recorded by event-based sensors is directly related to the light variations in the scene. More specifically, when a pixel changes its brightness, the camera triggers an event with this information:

- x, y: the coordinates of the pixel;

- t: the timestamp of when the event occurred;

- p: the polarity of the brightness variation, which is ON or 1 for higher brightness, and OFF or 0 for lower brightness.

Thus, the brightness changes in the scene are recorded asynchronously and independently for every pixel as a variable data rate sequence. As shown in fig. 2.11, for each pixel, the brightness (measured as log intensity) is recorded when an event is triggered and continuously monitored for a (positive or negative) change of sufficient magnitude, compared to the previously memorized value.

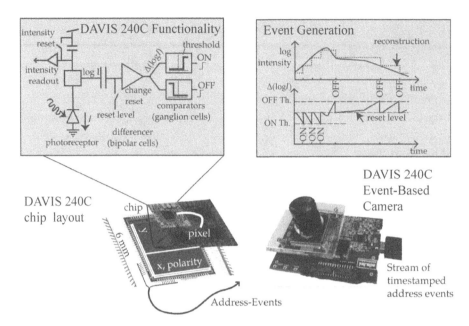

Figure 2.11: Functionality of the DAVIS240C camera [18], showing a simplified circuit diagram of the DAVIS pixel and the DVS operation of converting light into events. Figure adapted from [57].

The events are transmitted with the asynchronous address event representation (AER) protocol. Thanks to their structure, the spikes generated by a DVS camera can directly feed the SNNs' inputs without any manipulation. Recently, due to their increased popularity and demand, different high-tech. companies, including iniVation [18], Prophesee [50], CelePixel [28], and Samsung [261], have specialized in the commercialization of event-based sensors.

In summary, compared to the frame-based sensors, the event-based cameras offer the following improvements:

- *High resolution in time*: multiple events can be recorded with a time resolution of a few microseconds. Hence, common frame-based issues such as oversampling, undersampling, and motion blur are avoided. These improvements make event-based sensors suitable for high-speed or low-latency operations.

- *Adaptive data rate → less power and memory usage*: the data is recorded only when a bright variation is detected in the scene. Therefore, no information is recorded in the absence of light changes. Hence, almost zero power consumption and efficient information storage are achieved when the events are sparse.

- *High dynamic range* (up to $140dB$): the large range (compared to $\approx 60dB$ of the frame-based sensors) enables using DVS cameras also in extreme conditions, e.g., with very low light.

2.3.6   Example of Event-Based Datasets

Event-based SNNs are well suited for high-dynamics applications deployed in extremely low-power systems. Existing applications cover wide ranges such as industrial automation, IoT, smart mobility, healthcare, and robotics [57]. A key feature that boosts the research and development of optimized algorithms and computation mechanisms is the availability of open-source datasets which third parties can easily access. Among the open-source event-based datasets, a few are analyzed in more detail.

- The IBM **DvsGesture** dataset [8] is a fully event-based gesture recognition dataset. Each gesture is recorded with a *DVS128* camera [128] with a resolution of 128 × 128 pixels, providing in total 1 342 samples divided into 122 trials. In each trial, a subject executes the 11 different gestures in sequence. A total of 29 subjects under 3 different light conditions compose the whole dataset. Each gesture has an average duration of 6 seconds and is composed of a collection of all the events (positive and negative) recorded by the DVS camera whenever a (positive or negative) light variation is detected.

- The **N-CARS** dataset [252] is a recording of 80 minutes with an *ATIS* camera [211], a sensor that has a resolution of 304 × 240 pixels and it is mounted behind the windshield of a car. For recognition purposes, the outgoing events are converted into grey-scale images. These are processed with a state-of-the-art object detector [226] to extract the bounding boxes of size 120 × 100 pixels automatically. The dataset composed of multiple samples lasting 100 milliseconds is split into 7 940 car and 7 482 background training samples, and 4 396 car and 4 211 background testing samples.

- The **DET** [33] is the first dataset for the lane detection task recorded by a DVS camera. The streams are recorded by the *CeleX V* sensor [28], which is one of the event-based cameras with a high spatial resolution of 1 280 × 800 pixels. The dataset is composed of 5 424 samples split into 2 716 training, 873 validation, and 1 835 testing samples. The streams derive from 5 hours of recording in Wuhan city, and then they are accumulated into grey-scale raw images delayed from each other by 30 milliseconds.

2.3.7   Summary of Challenges for SNNs

One of the main challenges of SNNs is that they are still in the earliest development stages and are not yet mature. Hence, most of the common neuromorphic devices are only used for research purposes, and they have not been commercialized yet. As previously discussed, due to its incompatibility, the DNN-to-SNN conversion technique cannot be directly applied to event-based input. *To address this challenge, Section 6.2 proposes a pre-processing technique for enabling DNN training of event-based data. Moreover, autonomous driving implementations on neuromorphic devices are unexplored, and mapping an SNN onto an advanced neuromorphic chip like the Intel Loihi requires dedicated optimizations to adapt the architecture of the SNN and its parameter to the constrained hardware resources. To this regard, Section 6.3 and Section 6.4 propose event-based SNN implementations on Loihi for the "car vs. background" classification and for the lane detection tasks, respectively.*

2.4 VULNERABILITIES OF DL SYSTEMS

In light of their recent groundbreaking performances, DL systems are expected to be reliable against multiple security threats [241]. Several studies highlighted that one of the most critical challenges is represented by the adversarial attacks, i.e., small and imperceptible input perturbations that cause misclassifications. Moreover, as shown in Figure 2.12, also other DL vulnerabilities cause serious concerns questioning the deployment of DL models in safety-critical applications. Therefore, the community analyzed and proposed several attack methodologies and defensive countermeasures [242]. While the attacks and defenses for DNNs have been extensively studied, the security of advanced DL models such as CapsNets and SNNs is still in its emerging phase and needs more thorough investigations.

As shown in Figure 2.12, DL-based systems are vulnerable to different types of security and reliability threats, which can span from maliciously-injected perturbations, such as adversarial attacks, hardware Trojans, or injected faults, to natural misfunctioning of the system, like permanent faults generated during chip fabrication, aging, and process variations. Moreover, the leakage of sensitive and confidential data, including the intellectual property of the ML model (e.g., architecture and parameters) and training dataset, have raised several privacy issues. This section provides an overview of these vulnerability threats.

2.4.1 Privacy Threats

Due to the massive performance and computational power of high-end DL workstations, it is possible to perform advanced tasks using an enormous amount of data on a large scale. If such data is collected from users' private information, such

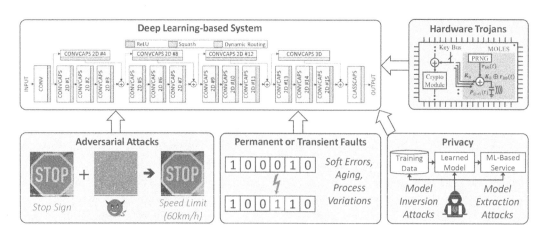

Figure 2.12: Vulnerability threats for DL-based systems, their manifestation and impact on their functionality.

as personal images, interests, web searches, and clinical records, the DL deployment toolchain will access sensitive information that could be mishandled. The privacy attacks for DL can be classified into two categories: Model Inversion Attacks and Model Extraction Attacks. While an attack in the former category aims to extract sensitive features of the training data, an attack in the latter category aims to extract private information of the DL model (e.g., model parameter, model architecture).

- *Model Extraction Attacks:* The goals of the adversary are to duplicate the parameters and hyperparameters of the DL model and to compromise the DL algorithms' confidentiality and intellectual property of the service provider [267][274].

- *Model Inversion Attacks:* The adversary aims at inferring sensitive information from the training data. Membership inference attacks [247] can infer whether a sensitive record belongs to the training set when the ML model is overfitted, While Property Inference Attacks [58] infer specific properties that only hold for a subset of the training data.

There are currently four possible categories of techniques that can be applied to avoid these leakages of sensitive information:

- *Differential Privacy:* The goal is to prevent the adversary from inferring whether specific data was used to train the target model, such that the DL algorithm learns to extract features of the training data without disclosing sensitive information about individuals. The privacy is guaranteed through a randomization mechanism, which could be either based on injecting noise into the stochastic gradient descent process (Noisy SGD [2]) or through the Private Aggregation of Teacher Ensembles (PATE) method [202], in which a "student" model receives the knowledge transferred from an ensemble of "teacher" models.

- *Homomorphic Encryption:* It is an encryption scheme $x \rightarrow y$, in which the ML computations are conducted on ciphertexts y, and the decrypted output in plaintext x matches the result that would have been computed without encryption. The data remains confidential as long as the decryption key is unknown to the adversary. Since the Fully Homomorphic Encryption (FHE) system [60] dramatically increases the computational complexity of the ML algorithm, a partial homomorphic encryption system [196] which supports only certain operations in the ciphertext domain, such as additions or multiplications, is more suited for complex computations. In the context of DL, CryptoNets [62] performs DNN inference on encrypted data, while Nandakumar et al. [184] extends the encryption support to the whole DNN training process.

- *Secure Multi-Party Computation:* The basic idea consists of distributing the training/testing data across multiple servers and training/inferring the DL model together, while each server does not have access to the training/testing data of the other servers. Different privacy-preserving DL protocols have been proposed, including SecureML [173], MiniONN [135], DeepSecure [231], Gazelle [101], and SecureNN [273].

- *Trusted Execution Environment:* Additional hardware is used to create a secure and isolated computation environment in which the DL algorithms are executed [137]. In this way, the data integrity and the confidentiality of the codes loaded inside the protected regions are guaranteed.

However, these privacy-preserving methods significantly increase the computational overhead and require customization for specific DL models at the software and hardware levels to improve the computation efficiency.

2.4.2 Fault Injection and Hardware Trojans

The hardware-level security vulnerabilities for DL systems include fault injection techniques (e.g., bit-flips) and the injected hardware Trojans into DL accelerators. Generically speaking, an adversary can flip the bits of data stored into the DRAM and SRAM memory cells through Row-Hammer attacks [107] or laser injection [5].

- *Fault Injection Attack Methodologies* aim at finding the most sensitive locations in which to inject faults [138]. The Bit-Flip Attack [221] finds the most vulnerable bits of the DL model parameters using a progressive bit search method, while the Practical Fault Attack [19] injects faults into DL activations.

- *Hardware Trojans* are maliciously-introduced hardware injected during chip fabrication that only activate when triggered. They represent critical threats when the hardware devices are manufactured in off-shore fabrication facilities, thus increasing the risk of facing untrusted supply chains. In the context of DL accelerators, Clements et al. [36] designed hardware Trojans for the DL activation function. A carefully designed input pattern triggers the hardware Trojan.

The defensive countermeasures to mitigate against the above-discussed vulnerabilities are based on improving the resiliency of DL accelerators and memory systems and detecting Trojans.

- *Fault tolerance methods*, similarly to the soft error mitigation methodologies, aim at improving the resiliency of DL architectures. Such defensive techniques are based on hardware redundancy [195], range restriction [32], or weight reconstruction [123]. More specifically, the algorithm-based fault tolerance (ABFT) method [289] detects and corrects errors in the Conv layers.

- *Trojan detection methods* are based on runtime monitoring [49] of the DL accelerator. The operations executed in the hardware device are constantly monitored, and any suspected functionality violation due to an inserted hardware Trojan or other reasons can be immediately detected and notified.

2.4.3 Reliability Threats

Unlike the vulnerability threats that malicious adversaries intentionally inject, DL systems are subjected to reliability threats that undermine their correct functionality.

The continuous technology node underscaling in which the chips are fabricated has significantly increased the probability that hardware circuits are affected by permanent or transient faults and has accelerated the aging process.

- *Permanent Faults:* These process variations represent imperfections generated during the fabrication of integrated circuits [219]. High rates of such process variations result in permanent faults, which dramatically decrease the yield of the fabricated wafer.

- *Transient Faults:* Soft errors are bit-flips caused by high-energy particle strikes or induced by radiation events [11]. They are categorized as transient errors since the faulty cells are not permanently damaged, but those faults vanish once new data is written into the same locations.

- *Aging:* The electronic circuits gradually degrade over time [103], due to various physical phenomena, like Bias Temperature Instability (BTI), Hot Carrier Injection (HCI), and Electromigration (EM). These effects can manifest as an increase in the transistors' threshold voltage, which causes timing errors and permanent faults over time.

Conventional fault mitigation techniques such as Dual Modular Redundancy (DMR) [269], Triple Modular Redundancy (TMR) [146], and Error-Correcting Codes (ECC) [212] can be applied, but they incur huge overheads, which makes them impractical for DL applications. Therefore, ad-hoc cost-effective mitigation techniques need to be used.

- *Permanent faults mitigation:* To mitigate permanent faults due to process variations in DL accelerators, different techniques have been proposed. Fault-Aware Training (FAT) and Fault-Aware Pruning (FAP) [287] incorporate the information of faults into the training process and bypass the faulty components. To avoid the re-training overhead, Fault-Aware Mapping techniques such as SalvageDNN [82] are based on mapping the least significant weights on the faulty units.

- *Soft error mitigation:* To mitigate transient faults, generic fault-tolerant methods like Ranger [32] and ABFT [289] can be applied. Moreover, FT-ClipAct [89] uses clipped activation functions mapped into pre-specified values within a range with the lowest impact on the output, and Sanity-Check [194] protects FC and Conv layers of DL models employing spatial and temporal checksums that exploit the linearity property.

- *Aging mitigation:* The effects of timing errors that occur in the computational units of DL accelerators can be mitigated with ThUnderVolt [286] and GreenTPU [201]. The NBTI aging of on-chip SRAM-based memory cells in DL accelerators is mitigated with the DNN-Life framework [83] that employs read and write transducers to balance the duty-cycle in each SRAM cell.

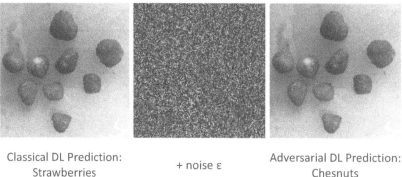

Figure 2.13: Example of adversarial attacks' functionality, where adding noise leads to a misclassification. Figure adapted from [67].

2.4.4 Adversarial Security Threats

Given a DL model M, an input x, and its output prediction label y_{true}, the goal of classical DL is to make a correct prediction, i.e., the predicted output $y = M(x)$ is equal to y_{true}. On the contrary, an adversarial attack method aims at generating a misclassification by introducing a small noise ε to the input, such that the adversarial example $x' = x + \varepsilon$ is incorrectly classified $(M(x') \neq y_{true})$. The common functionality of adversarial attacks is depicted in Figure 2.13. Due to the wide variety of adversarial attack typologies and threat models, it is important to define a common way for their categorization. Toward this, four different features of adversarial attacks are shown in Figure 2.14.

- *Attacker Knowledge:* It refers to the threat model in which the adversary operates and the accessible data and features. In white-box attacks, the adversary has full knowledge of the DL model, its parameters, the training algorithm, and the training data. On the contrary, black-box attacks assume no knowledge about the DL model. Hence the adversary can only craft an adversarial example by sending a series of queries and analyzing the vulnerability based on the corresponding outputs. Moreover, in the literature, different attacker knowledge assumption models are referred to as grey-box attacks, in which the adversary knows more features than black-box attacks but does not have full access like under the white-box assumption.

- *Adversarial Goal:* It refers to the scope of the attack algorithm. If the goal is simply a misclassification, the attack is untargeted, where any class different from the correct one can be the prediction of the adversarial example. On the other hand, in a targeted attack, the adversary produces adversarial examples that force the output of the DL model to predict a specific class.

- *Phase of the DL Flow:* It refers to the stage of the DL development in which the adversary operates. In training attacks, the adversary poisons the training data by injecting carefully designed samples to force the DL model to learn wrong

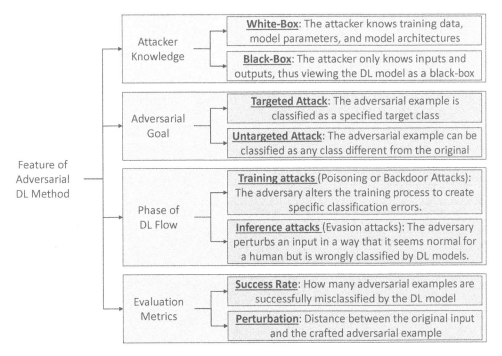

Figure 2.14: Categorization of different types of adversarial attack methods based on their features.

features that can later be used to generate specific misclassifications. On the contrary, in evasion attacks that operate at the inference stage, the adversary tries to evade the system by crafting malicious samples that force the DL model to make false predictions.

- *Evaluation Metrics:* These refer to the quantitative methods for measuring the strengths of the attacks and easily accessible comparison metrics. To evaluate the robustness of the attack, the success rate measures the number of adversarial examples that the DL model misclassifies. Since a well-designed attack needs to be imperceptible, i.e., hardly distinguishable from the original input by a human eye, the perturbation measures the distance between the adversarial example and the original (clean) input.

Due to their high accuracy on many tasks, DL models are prime candidate algorithms to be applied to safety-critical applications. However, several defensive countermeasures need to be applied due to the security vulnerabilities that undermine their correct functionality. An overview of adversarial attacks and defenses used in the DL design flow is shown in Figure 2.15.

2.4.4.1 *Adversarial Attacks*

As previously discussed, adversarial attacks can be categorized into different types based on the adversary's knowledge, goal, and phase of the ML flow. Due to the

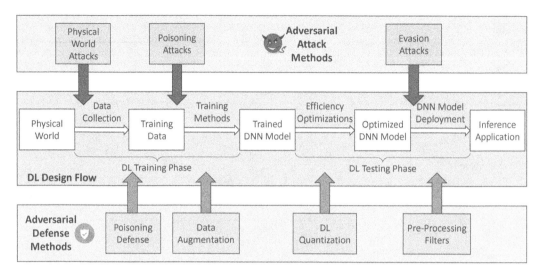

Figure 2.15: Adversarial attacks and defenses applied in different stages of the DL design flow.

mainstream usage of DL systems, several attack methodologies have been proposed. The following list discusses the most prominent ones:

- *Poisoning Attacks:* At the training stage, the training data can be poisoned with contaminated inputs. Based on the principles of Genetic Adversarial Networks (GANs), Goodfellow et al. [66] devised a procedure to generate samples similar to the training set, having almost identical distribution. This method inspired many of the successive adversarial attack methodologies. Poisoning Attacks [240] alter the training dataset to modify the decision boundaries of the DL classifiers. Backdoor Attacks [71] aim at training the DL model for a carefully crafted noise pattern (acting as a backdoor) while maintaining high accuracy on its intended task. However, a targeted misclassification is achieved when such a backdoor trigger is present at the network's input.

- *Evasion Attacks:* Different evasion attack methodologies were proposed. In white-box settings, gradient-based attacks like the Fast Gradient Sign Method (FGSM) [67] and its iterative version, the Projected Gradient Descent (PGD) [148] exploit the gradient of the DL output predictions w.r.t. the inputs to craft the adversarial perturbations as imperceptible noise that make the DL classifier cross the decision boundary. In black-box settings, the One Pixel Attack [260] demonstrated to misclassify DL models by changing only one pixel intensity. Decision-based attacks [20] are a subset of evasion attacks in which the adversary does not have access to the output probabilities but only to the prediction. For instance, the FaDec attack [104] jointly optimizes the number of queries and the perturbation distance between the adversarial example and the clean example to fool DNNs.

- *Attacks in the Physical World:* While the aforementioned attacks mainly make modifications in the experimental settings, the adversarial attacks can also be applied in real life by introducing physical modifications [115]. Examples of physical world attacks have been showcased in the context of road sign classification by adding stickers [48], in the context of object detection by adding adversarial patches [265], or in face detection using eyeglasses with special frames [243].

2.4.4.2 Adversarial Defenses

The large variety of adversarial attacks led to the design of several types of defenses, which can be summarized and grouped into the following categories:

- *Poisoning Defenses:* To mitigate against poisoning attacks, several defensive countermeasures have been proposed. Outlier detection-based defenses [206] filter out training sample outliers, which most likely correspond to poisoned samples. Since typically backdoor attacks exploit the sparsity of DL models, the Fine-Pruning method [136] defends against backdoor attacks by eliminating the neurons that are dormant for clean inputs in the backdoor network.

- *Data Augmentation:* The basic principle of Adversarial Training [148] is to extend the training example with the adversarial examples, for instance, generated with the PGD attack. In this way, the DNN models achieve higher robustness against such perturbations. This method is considered very effective in defending against adversarial attacks, but its high computation overhead pushes the community to search for efficient optimization of this procedure, such as the AccelAT framework [189].

- *Quantization:* The optimization techniques employed to improve the energy efficiency of DL accelerators can also achieve higher robustness against adversarial attacks. The Defensive Quantization method [132] demonstrated that the adversarial noise magnitude remains contained in quantized DNNs. The QuSecNets method [105] selects the quantization levels based on the DL resiliency and computes the appropriate quantization threshold values based on an optimization function. Other approaches, such as Defensive Approximation [72] are promising, but the work of Siddique et al. [249] demonstrated that approximate computing should not be referred to as a universal defensive technique against adversarial attacks.

- *Pre-Processing Filters:* Another common technique to improve the DL robustness against adversarial attacks is to employ pre-processing filters. The basic idea of this approach is to view the adversarial perturbation as a noise added to the input, which can be filtered out at runtime. Methods based on Sobel filters [6] and randomized smoothing [37] demonstrated that the pre-processing filters have a smoothing effect and significantly reduce the adversarial success rate.

2.4.5 Vulnerability Studies for CapsNets

Recent works showed that CapsNets are vulnerable to security threats differently than traditional DNNs [69]. Michels et al. [172] analyzed the CapsNets' robustness against common adversarial attacks, such as the Carlini-Wagner Attack [24], the Boundary Attack [20], the DeepFool Attack [177] and the Universal Attack [176]. Gugglberger et al. [73] applied the FGSM method [67] on CapsNets. Frosst et al. [54] presented an efficient method to detect the crafted images during the reconstruction stage. Qin et al. [217] investigated the detection of adversarial examples on CapsNets with the reconstruction network and proposed a successful deflection algorithm [216]. Gu et al. [68] proposed a novel CapsNet that further improves its robustness against affine transformations. Concurrently, the CapsNets security has been analyzed from different perspectives. The Vote Attack [70] is a technique that directly perturbs the CapsNets by manipulating the votes from primary capsules.

However, all the above-discussed works are at their earliest development stage and did not thoroughly analyze the effect of black-box attacks and affine transformations on CapsNets and DNNs. Moreover, before employing CapsNets in safety-critical applications, a challenging research question consists of analyzing their robustness in practical use-case scenarios, e.g., investigating applications where the CapsNets' classification accuracy is on par or better than the state-of-the-art DNNs, and when robust defenses like adversarial training are adopted. These challenges are addressed in Chapter 4.

2.4.6 Vulnerability Studies for SNNs

For SNNs, adversarial attacks and defenses can take advantage of different properties. For input spike sequences based on discrete data, white-box attacks [10] and black-box attacks [205] are generated and deployed. The work of [245] demonstrated that, after generating the adversarial examples in the DNN domain, the SNN generated through DNN-to-SNN conversion can be fooled by the same adversarial examples generated in the DNN domain. Moreover, the work of [126] proposed an attack algorithm that perturbs the SNN inputs based on the gradient computed both in the spatial and temporal domains. The SpikeAttack [111] impacts the performance efficiency and energy consumption of the SNNs by increasing their spiking activity.

In HIRE-SNN [114], a robust training method is designed based on adversarial training, where the input perturbation during training is generated through adversarial attacks. The work of Liang et al. [127] proposed a certification training of SNNs based on the defined input boundary. Besides the conventional defense methodologies, the work of [246] studied the impact of discrete input encoding and non-linear activations, i.e., the leak factor in LIF neurons, on the SNNs' adversarial robustness. It demonstrated that it is possible to fine-tune the SNNs' structural parameters to improve their robustness. *However, the impact on the SNNs' robustness due to other structural parameters, such as the LIF neuron's firing voltage thresholds and time window boundaries, remains unexplored.*

To mitigate against privacy issues, in the PrivateSNN framework [109] the DNN-to-SNN conversion is followed by weight encryption with spike-based training on synthetic data for privacy-preserving SNNs.

Fault injection attacks in SNNs are also becoming a hot topic in recent years. Nagarajan et al. [182] studied the practical fault injection scenarios in SNN accelerators. The enpheeph framework [38] flexibly allows for investigating SNN fault models and optimizes their simulated execution on CPUs and GPUs. Toward fault-tolerant SNNs, Spyrou et al. [254] proposed a technique for mitigating faults in SNNs by applying dropout and recovering the correct values in the hidden layers. The ReSpawn framework [214] proposed fault-aware mapping techniques to mitigate permanent memory faults in SNN accelerators. The SoftSNN methodology [215] proposed to bound the weight values to protect the neurons from soft errors.

Recently, different spike encoding techniques have drawn attention regarding their impact on the SNN robustness. Nomura et al. [190] studied the robustness of SNNs that use the TTFS coding. Guo et al. [74] analyzed different types of neural coding and their impact on the SNN robustness. According to Kim et al. [108], the rate coding turns out more robust against faults and adversarial attacks.

Since event-based sensing with dynamic vision sensors (DVS) is suitable for being deployed with high efficiency on low-power neuromorphic hardware, recent works demonstrated their applicability in safety-critical applications, such as autonomous driving, recognition, and tracking [99]. Therefore, it is key to analyze the security aspects of event-based SNNs. Toward this, the work of [21] modified existing DNN adversarial example generation algorithms to be applied to event series. The work of [120] generated event-based adversarial examples on 3D point clouds.

While the noise filters for neuromorphic sensors [133] have been initially designed for protecting against thermal noise and junction leakage fluctuation, their application to the input of neuromorphic computing engines as a defense mechanism against adversarial attacks is yet to be demonstrated. To address the above-discussed challenges, Chapter 7 presents security analyses for SNNs on both discrete and event-based data.

2.5 SUMMARY OF BACKGROUND AND RELATED WORK

This chapter has discussed the background information to a level of detail necessary to understand the rest of the book. After discussing the basic functionality of DNNs, an overview of the most prominent hardware architectures and the optimizations to achieve high energy efficiency has been presented. Moreover, this chapter contains an overview of the state-of-the-art CapsNets, SNNs, security vulnerabilities that affect DL systems, and the most common countermeasures. This chapter also describes the limitations of the related works with references to how they will be addressed in the following chapters.

CHAPTER 3

Hardware and Software Optimizations for Capsule Networks

This chapter discusses the SW-level optimizations for CapsNet training and inference, the hardware designs of the PE array, and the memory organizations for CapsNet inference, integrated with post-training optimizations such as quantization and approximate designs. Figure 3.1 shows the proposed design flow that contributes to designing efficient CapsNets.

The details of each contribution composing the flow are described in the rest of the chapter. In Section 3.1, a framework for efficiently training CapsNets is proposed. Note that, while the remaining sections focus on optimizations for CapsNets inference, the training methodology is key for achieving high accuracy in a reasonable training time, which is also beneficial for Chapter 4 and Chapter 5. Section 3.2 presents an efficient hardware accelerator for CapsNets inference, while a more comprehensive design space exploration (DSE) of the architecture based on PE arrays is discussed in Section 3.3. In Section 3.4, a DSE and design flow for the memory organizations in CapsNet accelerators are discussed. Section 3.5 presents a quantization framework for obtaining compact CapsNets models in a constrained memory budget. Further energy efficiency can be achieved by approximating the hardware designs of the PE array, as discussed in Section 3.6, or approximating the most compute-intensive activation functions like Squash and Softmax, as presented in Section 3.7.

Major Contributions of the Chapter:

- **FasTrCaps framework design**: It integrates different optimizations for selecting learning rate policies and batch sizes, and reducing the number of parameters of CapsNets through weight sharing and reducing its decoder's size.

- **CapsAcc architecture design:** It is a specialized CMOS-based accelerator that performs inference of a given CapsNet. The PE array allows large matrix computations, while a specialized dataflow orchestrates the movement

DOI: 10.1201/9781003530459-3

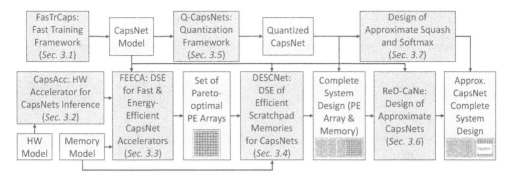

Figure 3.1: Overview of the design flow of this chapter.

of weights and activations across the architecture for different CapsNets' operations.

- **FEECA methodology design:** Given the CapsAcc architecture as a baseline, it explores the design space of different (micro-)architectural parameters of a given CapsNet accelerator. Using analytical models of the number of clock cycles and memory accesses required to execute CapsNets' operations, the proposed methodology employs an evolutionary algorithm to derive Pareto-optimal curves w.r.t. energy consumption, area, and performance.

- **DESCNet architecture design:** It is a specialized scratchpad memory architecture for CapsNet accelerators, partitioned into different sectors to support sector-level power management.

- **DESCNet methodology for design space exploration:** based on the sizes and accesses required for each operation of the CapsNets' inference, it explores different parameters of the DESCNet memory architecture to leverage the tradeoffs between memory, area, and energy consumption.

- **Q-CapsNets framework design:** Given a certain memory budget and accuracy tolerance, it automatically searches for the numerical precision for different CapsNets' layers and operations.

- **ReD-CaNe methodology design:** It analyzes the resiliency of CapsNets under approximation errors. The effect of having approximate components is modeled as a noise injection. The design space composed of approximations for different layers and operations is explored for designing approximate CapsNets while maintaining high accuracy.

- **Approximate Softmax and Squash designs:** Since these nonlinear operations are highly compute-intensive, specialized approximate architectures have been designed to execute these operations efficiently. Implementing different components leverage the tradeoffs between accuracy, area, power consumption, and delay.

3.1 FASTRCAPS: AN INTEGRATED FRAMEWORK FOR FAST YET ACCURATE TRAINING OF CAPSNETS

Recently, CapsNets have shown improved performance compared to the traditional Convolutional Neural Networks (CNNs), by encoding and preserving spatial relationships between the detected features in hierarchical capsules. However, one of the biggest hurdles in the broad adoption of CapsNets is their gigantic training time, primarily due to the relatively higher complexity of their new constituting elements that are different from CNNs.

In this section, we implement different optimizations in the training phase of CapsNets and investigate how these optimizations affect their training speed and accuracy. Toward this, we propose the novel *FasTrCaps* framework that integrates multiple lightweight optimizations and a novel learning rate policy called *WarmAdaBatch* (that jointly performs *warm restarts* and *adaptive batch size*), and appropriately steers them to provide high training-loop speedup at minimal accuracy loss. We also propose *weight sharing* for capsule layers. The objective is to reduce the hardware requirements of CapsNets by removing redundant/unused connections and capsules while keeping high accuracy through using different learning rate policies and batch sizes. The Pareto-optimal solutions generated by *FasTrCaps* can be leveraged to realize tradeoffs between training time and achieved accuracy.

3.1.1 System Overview

As shown in Figure 3.2, we present *FasTrCaps*, a framework that employs different optimization techniques for significantly reducing the training time and the number of parameters of CapsNets, while preserving or improving their accuracy.

The key contributions are:

- Different learning rate policies (like *one-cycle policy* or *warm restarts*) are tailored to specialize them for the CapsNet structure, and their efficiency in the CapsNet training loop vs. the corresponding training time is analyzed.

- A novel training framework, *FasTrCaps*, is proposed to accelerate the training of CapsNets by integrating different optimizations (like *warm restarts*, *adaptive batch size* and *weight sharing*) in an automated fashion specialized to the

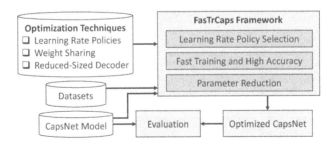

Figure 3.2: An overview of our novel contributions in this section relative to the FasTrCaps framework.

structure and training flow of the CapsNets (i.e., considering the capsules and the coupling between capsule layers).

- The parameter reduction is achieved via *weight sharing* and reducing the size CapsNets' decoder by removing its unused connections. Those optimizations reduce the number of parameters by more than 15%.

- The FasTrCaps framework is evaluated on the MNIST and Fashion-MNIST datasets to remain compliant with the experimental setup [236].

3.1.2 Overview of Learning Rate Policies

The learning rate (LR) is a key hyperparameter for a fast convergence during the training loop of a neural network. With a large learning rate, the optimization process may stop at a local minimum or diverge. In contrast, a low learning rate can lead to a very slow convergence [9][14]. Given the difficulty of choosing the best value for a constant learning rate, a dynamic learning rate policy is often adopted. It consists of varying the learning rate during the training [282].

One-Cycle Policy (OCP) [253]: This method consists of three phases of training. In phase 1, the learning rate linearly increases from a minimum to a maximum value in an optimal range. In phase 2, the learning rate symmetrically decreases. In phase 3, the learning rate must anneal to a very low value in a small fraction of the last steps. Equation (3.1) reports the formulas of the three phases of the *one-cycle policy*, where ts represents the training step, TS is the total number of steps in the training epochs, lr_{min} and lr_{max} are the boundaries of the learning rate range. Saddle points slow down the training flow since the gradients in these regions have smaller values. Increasing the learning rate helps to traverse the saddle points faster.

$$\begin{cases} lr = lr_{min} + ts \cdot \frac{lr_{max} - lr_{min}}{0.45 \cdot TS} & 0 < ts < 0.45 \cdot TS & \text{phase-1} \\ lr = lr_{min} + (ts - 0.9 \cdot TS) \cdot \frac{lr_{min} - lr_{max}}{0.45 \cdot TS} & 0.45TS < ts < 0.9TS & \text{phase-2} \\ lr = lr_{min} - 9 \cdot \frac{lr_{min}}{TS} \cdot (ts - 0.9 \cdot TS) & 0.9 \cdot TS < ts < TS & \text{phase-3} \end{cases} \quad (3.1)$$

Warm Restarts (WR): In the Stochastic Gradient Descent with Warm Restarts [141] (shortly called *warm restarts*), after initializing the learning rate to a maximum value, it is decreased with cosine annealing until the lower bound of a chosen interval is reached. Afterward, it is set again to its maximum value, realizing a step function. Equation (3.2) describes the cosine annealing function, where ts is the training step, lr_{min} and lr_{max} are the learning rate range boundaries, T_i is the number of training steps for every cycle. When $ts = Ti$ and $ts = 0$, the cycle starts again. This process is repeated iteratively during the whole training time, in which the cycle period needs to be properly set to optimize accuracy and training time. Gradually Increasing the learning rate emulates a warm restart cycle and encourages the network to step out from potential local minima or saddle points.

$$lr = lr_{min} + \frac{1}{2}(lr_{max} - lr_{min})\left(1 + cos\left(\pi \cdot \frac{ts}{T_i}\right)\right) \quad (3.2)$$

Adaptive Batch Size (AdaBatch): Training a DNN with a small batch size can provide faster convergence, while a larger batch size allows higher data parallelism and high computational efficiency. Therefore, many researches have investigated methods to increase the batch size with fixed policies or following an adaptive criterion, with the so-called *Adaptive Batch Size* [44]. Starting with a small batch size allows fast convergence in early epochs, and progressively increasing the batch size at selected epochs improves the performance due to the larger workload available per processor in later epochs.

3.1.3 Analysis of Learning Rate Policies on CapsNets

The above-discussed techniques have been tailored for improving the performance of traditional CNNs in terms of accuracy and training time. In this section, we aim at customizing different learning rate policies and batch size selection for training the CapsNets, and to studying whether and how effective these policies are, considering the multidimensional capsules and their cross-coupling. *Since the traditional neurons of the CNNs are replaced by capsules, the number of CapsNets' trainable parameters (weights and biases) is huge.*

For this reason, we implemented different state-of-the-art learning rate policies for the training loop of the CapsNet, such that *these techniques are enhanced for the capsule structures and relevant parameters of the CapsNet.* Table 3.1 shows how the accuracy of the LeNet5 and CapsNet for the MNIST dataset varies according to different optimization techniques.

From this analysis, we derive the following **key observations**:

1. The *warm restarts* technique is the most promising because it allows for reaching the same accuracy (99.37%) as the CapsNet with a fixed learning rate while reducing the training time by 79.31%.

TABLE 3.1: A table summarizing the comparative differences between the LeNet5 and the CapsNet, when the same learning rate policies are applied, but considering appropriate functional enhancements (without violating their optimization function and flow) are required to employ these policies for CapsNets. For each network, different columns of the table show the maximum reached accuracy, training epochs needed to reach the maximum accuracy, and the training epochs needed to reach the same accuracy of the network when using a fixed learning rate policy.

	LeNet5			CapsNet		
	Max Accuracy	Epoch of Max Accuracy	Epochs to Reach Accuracy of Fixed LR	Max Accuracy	Epoch of Max Accuracy	Epochs to Reach Accuracy of Fixed LR
Fixed	98.86%	17	17	99.37%	29	29
Exp. Decay	99.24%	28	6	99.40%	12	7
OCP	99.22%	30	19	99.38%	24	23
WR	99.23%	20	4	99.44%	11	6
AdaBatch	99.18%	19	5	99.41%	8	5

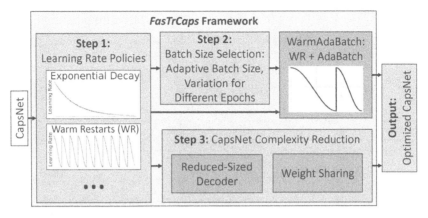

Figure 3.3: FasTrCaps processing flow: the CapsNet at the input goes through the different optimization stages to search for the right learning rate policy, batch size, and complexity reduction. It generates at the output the Optimized CapsNet, based on the optimization criteria chosen by the user.

2. A more extensive training with *warm restarts* leads to an accuracy improvement of 0.07%.

3. The *adaptive batch size* shows similar improvements in accuracy (99.41%) and training epochs.

4. The first epochs with smaller batch sizes execute relatively longer when compared to the ones with bigger batch sizes.

3.1.4 Overview of FasTrCaps Framework

Training CapsNets consists of a multi-objective optimization problem because our scope is to maximize the accuracy while minimizing the training time and the network complexity. A comprehensive processing flow of our *FasTrCaps* framework is shown in Figure 3.3. Before describing how to integrate different optimizations in an automated training methodology and how to generate the optimized CapsNet at the output, we present how these optimizations have been implemented with enhancements for the CapsNets, which is necessary to realize an integrated training framework.

3.1.4.1 Learning Rate Policies for CapsNets

The learning rate is the first parameter analyzed to improve the training process of CapsNets. The optimal learning rate range is evaluated within the range boundaries 0.0001 and 0.001. For our framework, we use the following parameters in these learning rate policies:

- **Fixed learning rate**: 0.001

- **Exponential decay**: starting value 0.001, decay rate 0.96, decay steps 2 000: $lr = lr_0 \cdot 0.96^{current\_step/2\,000}$

- **One cycle policy**: lower bound 0.0001, upper bound 0.001, annealing to 10^{-5} in the last 10% of training steps (see Algorithm 2)

- **Warm restarts**: lower bound 0.0001, upper bound 0.001, cycle length = one epoch (see Algorithm 3)

Algorithm 2: One Cycle Policy for CapsNets.

1   **Procedure** OneCyclePolicy($lr_{min}, lr_{max}, TotalSteps, Tcurr$)
2     $t_m \leftarrow 0.45 \cdot TotalSteps$;
3     $m \leftarrow \frac{lr_{max} - lr_{min}}{t_m}$;
4     $m_{ann} \leftarrow 9 \cdot \frac{lr_{min}}{TotalSteps}$;
5   **if** $Tcurr \leq t_m$ **then**
6 | $lr \leftarrow mx + lr_{min}$;
7   **else if** $t_m \leq Tcurr \leq 2t_m$ **then**
8 | $lr \leftarrow -m \cdot (x - 2t_m) + lr_{min}$;
9   **else**
10 | $lr \leftarrow -m_{ann} \cdot (x - 2t_m) + lr_{min}$;
11   **end**
12 **end**

Algorithm 3: Warm Restarts for CapsNets.

1   **Procedure** WarmRestarts($lr_{min}, lr_{max}, T_{curr}, T_i$)
2     $lr \leftarrow lr_{min} + \frac{1}{2}(lr_{max} - lr_{min})\left(1 + \cos \pi \frac{T_{curr}}{T_i}\right)$; // Learning rate update
3   **if** $T_{curr} = T_i$ **then** // Warm Restart after T_i training steps
4 | $T_{curr} \leftarrow 0$;
5   **else** // Current step update
6 | $T_{curr} \leftarrow T_{curr} + 1$;
7   **end**
8   **return** T_{curr};
9 **end**

3.1.4.2 Batch Size

To realize the *adaptive batch size*, the batch size is set to 1 for the first 3 epochs, and then increased 3 times every 5 epochs. That is, the user can choose a value P and the batch size will assume the values 2^P, 2^{P+1} and 2^{P+2} (see Algorithm 4).

3.1.4.3 Complexity of the CapsNet Decoder

The decoder is an essential component of the CapsNet. Indeed, the absence of a decoder would result in lower accuracy of the CapsNet. The outputs of the ClassCaps

---

Algorithm 4: AdaBatch for CapsNets.

---

1 **Procedure** AdaBatch($P, CurrentEpoch$)
2   **if** $CurrentEpoch \leq 3$ **then**
3 | $BatchSize \leftarrow 1$;
4   **else if** $4 \leq CurrentEpoch \leq 8$ **then**
5 | $BatchSize \leftarrow 2^P$;
6   **else if** $9 \leq CurrentEpoch \leq 13$ **then**
7 | $BatchSize \leftarrow 2^{P+1}$;
8   **else**
9 | $BatchSize \leftarrow 2^{P+2}$;
10   **end**
11 **end**

---

layer are fed to the decoder: the highest valued vector (capsule) at the output is left untouched, while the remaining 9 vectors are set to zero (Figure 3.4a). Thus, the decoder receives 10×16 values, where 9×16 are null. Therefore, we optimize the model using a reduced-sized decoder (Figure 3.4b) with only the 1×16 inputs linked to the capsule that outputs the highest probability. Overall, the original decoder has 1.4M parameters (weights and biases), while the reduced decoder provides a 5% reduction, with 1.3M parameters.

3.1.4.4 Complexity Reduction through Weight Sharing (WS)

Algorithm 5 illustrates how to share the weights between the PrimaryCaps and the ClassCaps layers by having a single tensor weight associated with all the 8-element vectors inside each 6×6 capsule. This method can reduce the total number of parameters by more than 15%, from 8.2 million to 6.7 million. However, the accuracy drops by almost 0.3% compared to the baseline CapsNet.

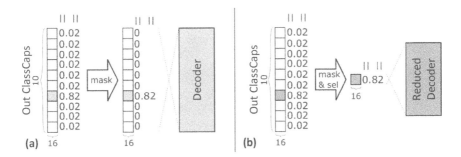

Figure 3.4: (a) All the ClassCaps outputs except the one with the highest magnitude are set to zero. Then the decoder receives 10×16 inputs. (b) Only the ClassCaps output with the highest magnitude is fed to a reduced decoder, with 1×16 inputs.

Algorithm 5: Weight Sharing for CapsNets, applied to the ClassCaps layer.

```
// BatchSize is the dimension containing single elements
// Input size is [BatchSize, 32, 36, 8]
```
1 **Procedure** ClassCaps(*input, BatchSize*)
```
    // Weight size is [BatchSize, 32, 1, 10, 16, 8]
```
2   *initialize weight*;
```
    // Bias size is [BatchSize, 1, 10, 16, 1]
```
3   *initialize bias*;
```
    // We move along the dimension with 36 elements
    // S here stands for Step
```
4   **for** $S = 1, 36$ **do**
```
        // Result size is [bs, 32, 36, 10, 16, 1]
        // We use the same weight, instead of cycling
```
5         $u[S] \leftarrow matrix\_multiply(weight[1], input[S])$;
6   **end**
```
    // Output size is [BatchSize, 1, 10, 16, 1]
```
7     $v \leftarrow routing(u, bias)$;
8   **return** v;
9 **end**

3.1.4.5 *WarmAdaBatch (WAB)*

Among the explored learning rate policies, the *warm restarts* guarantees the most promising results in terms of accuracy. On the other hand, the *adaptive batch size* provides a good tradeoff to obtain fast convergence. We propose the *WarmAdaBatch* (see Algorithm 6), a hybrid learning rate policy to expand the space of the solutions by combining the best of the two worlds. For the first three epochs, the batch size is set to 1. Then, it is increased to 16 for the remaining training time. The first cycle of the *warm restarts* policy lasts for the first three epochs, and the second cycle lasts for the remaining training epochs.

3.1.4.6 *Optimization Choices*

Our framework can automatically optimize CapsNets and its training depending on the parameters that a user wants to improve. For instance, using *WarmAdaBatch*, the accuracy and the training time are automatically co-optimized. The number of parameters can be reduced, at the cost of some accuracy loss and training time increase, by enabling *weight sharing*, along with the *WarmAdaBatch*.

3.1.5 Evaluation of the FasTrCaps Framework

3.1.5.1 *Experimental Setup*

We developed our framework using the PyTorch library [204], running on two Nvidia GeForce RTX 2080 Ti GPUs. We tested it on the MNIST [118] and

---

Algorithm 6: WarmAdaBatch training method for CapsNets.

---

1 **Procedure** WarmAdaBatch(lr_{min}, lr_{max}, $MaxEpoch$, $MaxStep$)

2 $\quad$ $T_{curr} \leftarrow 0$;

3 $\quad$ **for** $Epoch \in \{1, ..., MaxEpoch\}$ **do** // Batch size update

4 $\quad\quad$ AdaBatch($4.Epoch$);

5 $\quad\quad$ **if** $Epoch \leq 3$ **then**

6 $\quad\quad\quad$ $T_i \leftarrow 3 * 60,000$; // Steps in 3 epochs with batch size 1

7 $\quad\quad$ **else**

8 $\quad\quad\quad$ $T_i \leftarrow 27 * 3,750$; // Steps in 27 epochs with batch size 16

9 $\quad\quad$ **end**

10 $\quad\quad$ **for** $Step \in \{1, ..., MaxStep\}$ **do** // Learning Rate update

11 $\quad\quad\quad$ $T_{curr} \leftarrow WarmRestarts(lr_{min}, lr_{max}, T_{curr}, T_i)$;

12 $\quad\quad$ **end**

13 $\quad$ **end**

14 **end**

Fashion-MNIST [284] datasets. Both datasets are composed of $60,000$ samples for training and 10,000 test samples each. The MNIST is a collection of handwritten digits, while the Fashion-MNIST is a collection of grayscale fashion products. After each training epoch, a test is performed. At the beginning of each epoch, the training samples are randomly shuffled, while the testing samples are kept in the same order. The accuracy values are computed by averaging 5 training runs. Each training run lasts for 30 epochs, with the settings for each policy equal to the ones described in Section 3.1.4.1. The results are shown in Table 3.2 and Figure 3.5.

3.1.5.2 *Accuracy Results for the MNIST dataset*

Evaluating Learning Rate Policies: Among the state-of-the-art learning policies that we enhanced for CapsNets, the *warm restarts* are the most promising one, as the maximum accuracy improved by 0.074%. The CapsNet with *warm restarts* reaches the maximum accuracy of the baseline (with fixed learning rate) in 6 epochs rather than in 29 epochs as required by the baseline, thereby providing a training time reduction of 62.07%.

TABLE 3.2: Accuracy results obtained with CapsNet for the MNIST and Fashion-MNIST datasets, applying different proposed solutions.

Accuracy		Epochs to reach max accuracy		Parameters	Weight Sharing
FashionMNIST	*MNIST*	*FashionMNIST*	*MNIST*		
90.99%	99.37%	17	29	Fixed (Baseline)	No
91.47%	99.45%	27	8	WAB	No
90.47%	99.26%	17	26	Fixed (Baseline)	Yes
90.67%	99.38%	20	11	WAB	Yes

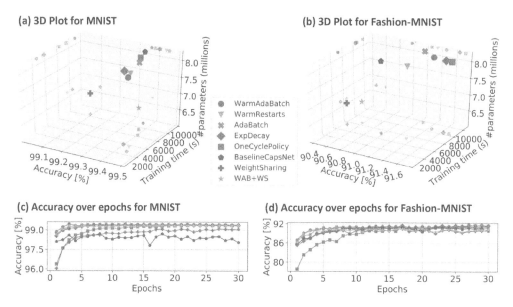

Figure 3.5: *The legend is common for all the figures.* **(a,b)** Comparison of different optimization types integrated in our *FasTrCaps* framework, on the basis of accuracy, training time and number of parameters. The training time is computed as the number of epochs to reach the maximum accuracy, multiplied by time (in seconds) per epoch. The abbreviated terms WAB and WS stand for *WarmAdaBatch* and *WeightSharing*, respectively, with *WeightSharing* including also the small-decoder optimization. **(c,d)** Accuracy improvements / changes over the training epochs for different optimization solutions. **(a,c)** Results for MNIST. **(b,d)** Results for Fashion-MNIST.

Evaluating Adaptive Batch Size: Different combinations of batch sizes in *adaptive batch size* algorithm have been tested since the smaller the batch size is, the faster the initial convergence. However, large batch sizes lead to slightly higher accuracy after 30 epochs and, most importantly, to a reduced training time. A CapsNet training epoch with batch size 1 lasts for 7 minutes, while with batch size 128, it lasts for only 28 seconds. Batch size 16 is a good tradeoff between fast convergence and short training time (i.e., 49 sec/epoch). The best results, applying *adaptive batch size*, are obtained using batch size 1 for the first three epochs and then increasing it to 16 for the remaining part of the training. With this parameter selection, the accuracy increases by 0.04% w.r.t. the baseline and the maximum baseline accuracy is reached in 5 epochs instead of 29 epochs as required by the baseline. However, the first three epochs take a longer time (88% longer) because of the reduced batch size. Hence, the *adaptive batch size* alone is not convenient. However, the total training time is reduced by 30% compared to the baseline.

Evaluating WarmAdaBatch: As for the batch, the first cycle of the learning rate lasts for 3 epochs and the second one for 27 epochs. Variations of batch size and learning rate cycles are synchronized. This solution allows a 0.088% gain in accuracy compared to the baseline CapsNet implementation, and the baseline maximum accuracy is reached by the CapsNet with the *WarmAdaBatch* in 3 epochs against 29 epochs. After the first three epochs, the batch size changes, and the learning rate is restarted. Hence, there is a drop in accuracy, which re-converges to the highest and most stable value in a few steps.

Evaluating Weight Sharing: By applying *weight sharing* to the ClassCaps layer, we can achieve a 15% reduction in the number of total parameters, decreasing from 8.2 million to 6.7 million. However, these reductions also lead to a slight decrease in the maximum accuracy, i.e., by 0.26%.

3.1.5.3 Comparison of Different Optimization Types

On the CapsNet model with the MNIST dataset, we also compare the different types of optimizations in terms of accuracy and based on the training time to reach the maximum accuracy and the number of parameters. As we can see in Figure 3.5a, we compare different optimization methods in a 3-dimensional space. This representation provides the Pareto-optimal solutions, depending on the optimization goals. We also compare, in Figure 3.5c, the accuracy and the learning rate evolution in different epochs, for *AdaBatch*, *WarmRestarts* and *WarmAdaBatch*. Among the space of the potential solutions, we discuss the following two Pareto-optimal choices in detail, i.e., the *WarmAdaBatch* and the combination of *WarmAdaBatch* and *weight sharing*, which we call WAB+WS.

WarmAdaBatch: This solution provides the optimal point in terms of accuracy and training time because it achieves the highest accuracy (99.45%) in the shortest time (3 epochs). Varying the batch size boosts the accuracy in the first epoch, and the restart policy accelerates the training.

WAB+WS: The standalone *weight sharing* reduces the number of parameters by 15%. By combining it with *WarmAdaBatch*, the accuracy loss is compensated (99.38% vs. 99.37% of the baseline). At the same time, the training time is shorter than the baseline (18 epochs vs. 29 epochs) but longer than the simple *WarmAdaBatch*. Our framework chooses this solution if the parameter reduction is also included in the optimization goals.

3.1.5.4 Accuracy Results for Fashion-MNIST

The results for the Fashion-MNIST dataset are shown in Table 3.2 and Figure 3.5b,d. However, while the combination WAB+WS is the most effective policy for reducing the network parameters while keeping a relatively high accuracy, the WAB policy, the ExpDecay policy, and the One-Cycle-Policy show good accuracy and training time results. The WAB policy can keep the same training time as the best policies but at the cost of a slight accuracy loss. Hence, even though Fashion-MNIST and MNIST require an equivalent CapsNet architecture (i.e., without any changes), our WAB policy for Fashion-MNIST is comparable to other learning policies.

3.1.6 Summary

The proposed FasTrCaps framework accelerates the training process of CapsNets by integrating multiple lightweight optimizations into the training loop. Different learning policies are analyzed and explored, and the novel *WarmAdaBatch* methodology is proposed. Other optimizations of the framework, such as reducing the complexity of the decoder and applying weight sharing, leverage the tradeoff between accuracy and training time. Such lightweight trained CapsNet models can be deployed into hardware accelerators to execute efficient CapsNets inference, as discussed in the following sections.

3.2 CAPSACC: AN EFFICIENT HARDWARE ACCELERATOR FOR CAPSNETS

Recently, CapsNets have overtaken traditional DNNs, because of their improved generalization ability due to the multi-dimensional capsules, in contrast to the single-dimensional neurons. Consequently, CapsNets also require extremely intense matrix computations, making it a tremendous challenge to achieve high performance. In this section, we propose *CapsAcc*, the first specialized CMOS-based hardware architecture to perform CapsNets inference with high performance and energy efficiency. Most State-of-the-art convolutional DNN accelerators do not work efficiently for CapsNets, as their designs do not account for critical operations involved in CapsNets, like squashing, dynamic routing, and multi-dimensional matrix processing. Our CapsAcc accelerator targets this problem and achieves significant improvements compared to an optimized GPU implementation. The CapsAcc exploits the massive parallelism by flexibly feeding data to a specialized PE array based on the operations required in different layers. It also avoids extensive on-chip memory load and store operations by reusing the data when possible. We synthesized the complete CapsAcc architecture using a 45nm CMOS technology using Synopsys design tools. This work enables highly-efficient CapsNets inference on embedded platforms.

3.2.1 Motivational Analyses of CapsNets Complexity and Execution Time

In this section, we analyze how CapsNet inference is performed on a high-end GPU, like the Nvidia GeForce RTX 2080 Ti GPU used in our experiments. First, we quantitatively analyze the number of trainable parameters per layer that must be fed from memory. Then, we benchmark our PyTorch-based CapsNet [236] implementation for the MNIST dataset to measure its inference performance on the GPU.

3.2.1.1 Trainable Parameters of the CapsNet

Table 3.3 shows quantitatively the number of parameters needed for each layer. As evident, most of the weights belong to the PrimaryCaps layer due to its 256 channels and 8D capsules. Even though the ClassCaps layer has FC behavior, it accounts for less than 25% of the total parameters of the CapsNet. Finally, the Conv1 layer

TABLE 3.3: Input size, number of trainable parameters, and output size of each layer of the CapsNet.

	Inputs	# parameters	Outputs
Conv1	784	20992	102400
PrimaryCaps	102400	5308672	102400
ClassCaps	102400	1474560	160
Coupling Coeff	160	11520	160

parameters and the coupling coefficients account for a tiny percentage of the total parameters. Based on that, we make a valuable observation for designing our hardware accelerator: *by considering 8-bit fixed point weights, we can estimate that an on-chip memory size of 8MB is large enough to contain every CapsNet's parameter.*

3.2.1.2 Execution Time Analyses of the CapsNet's Inference Operations

At this stage, we measure the required time for an inference pass on the GPU. Figure 3.6a shows the time consumed by the computations for each layer. The ClassCaps layer represents the computational bottleneck because it is around $10\times$ slower than the previous layers. To obtain more detailed indications, a specific analysis has been performed regarding each step of the routing-by-agreement process (Figure 3.6b). It is evident that *the squashing operation inside the ClassCaps layer is the most compute-intensive operation.* This analysis motivates us to *spend more effort optimizing routing-by-agreement and squashing* in our CapsNet accelerator.

3.2.1.3 Summary of Key Observations from our Analyses

From the previously discussed analyses, we derive the following key observations:

- The CapsNet inference performed on the GPU is more compute-intensive than memory-intensive due to *the bottleneck represented by the squashing operation.*

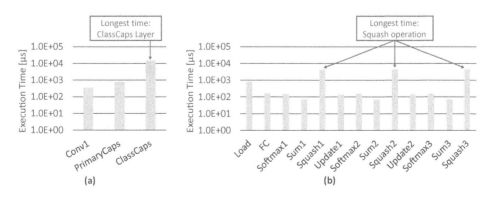

Figure 3.6: Execution time breakdown of the CapsNet [236] on the Nvidia GeForce RTX 2080 Ti GPU. (a) Layer-wise breakdown. (b) Operations in the dynamic routing.

- A massive parallel computation capability in the hardware accelerator is desirable to achieve a similar or better performance than the GPU.

- Since several parameters need to be stored in the memory, the buffers between the PEs and the on-chip memory are beneficial to maintain high throughput and mitigate the latency due to on-chip memory accesses.

3.2.2 CapsAcc Architecture Design

3.2.2.1 Overview

We designed the complete CapsAcc architecture and implemented it in hardware (RTL). The top-level architecture is shown in Figure 3.7a. The detailed schemes of different components of our accelerator are shown in Figure 3.7b and Figure 3.8. At the core, our CapsAcc architecture has a PE array responsible for all the matrix and vector operations in the CapsNets. The choice of PE arrays is based on the fact that they have demonstrated to be extremely efficient in processing Conv layers [100], which are also the initial layers of the CapsNets.

Moreover, our CapsAcc supports a specialized dataflow that allows us to exploit the computational parallelism for multi-dimensional matrix operations. The accumulator unit stores and properly adds together the partial sums. The activation unit performs different activation functions based on the required operations. The (Data, Routing, and Weight) buffers are essential to temporarily store the information to feed the PE array without frequently accessing the data and weight memories. The two multiplexers at the input of the PE array introduce the flexibility to process new data or reuse them according to the respective dataflow. The control unit coordinates all the operations at each stage of the inference.

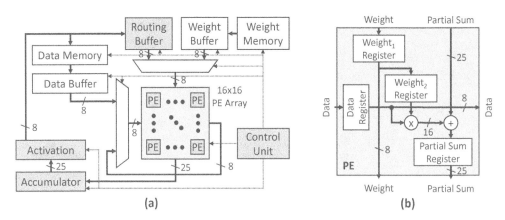

Figure 3.7: Hardware architecture of the CapsAcc accelerator. (a) Complete accelerator architecture. (b) Architecture of a PE.

3.2.2.2 Processing Element Array

The PE array of our CapsAcc architecture is composed of a 2D array of PEs, with 16 rows and 16 columns. The inputs are propagated toward the PE array outputs both horizontally (Data) and vertically (Weight and Partial sum). In the first row, the Partial sums inputs are zero-valued because each sum at this stage equals 0. Moreover, the Weight outputs in the last row are not connected since they are not used in the following operations.

Figure 3.7b shows the data path of a single PE. It has 3 inputs and 3 outputs: Weight, Data, and Partial sum. The PE is composed of a multiplier and an adder. It has 4 internal registers: (1) *Data Register* to store and synchronize the Data value coming from the left; (2) *Sum Register* to store the Partial sum before sending it to the neighbor PE below; (3) *Weight$_1$ Register* to synchronize the vertical transfer; (4) *Weight$_2$ Register* to store the value for data reuse. The latter is particularly useful for Conv layer operations, where the same filter weight must be reused across different input data. For FC operations, the second weight register introduces only one clock cycle latency without changing the throughput. The bit-widths of each signal have been designed as follows: (1) each PE computes the product of an 8-bit fixed-point Data and an 8-bit fixed-point Weight; (2) the sum is designed as a 25-bit fixed-point value. At full throttle, each PE generates one output-per-clock cycle, which also implies one output-per-clock cycle for every column of the PE array.

3.2.2.3 Accumulator

The Accumulator unit has a FIFO buffer to store the Partial sums from the PE array and add them up when needed. We designed the Accumulator to support 25-bit fixed-point data. Figure 3.8a shows the data path of our Accumulator. The multiplexer allows feeding the buffer with the data coming from the PE array or with the data coming from the internal adder of the Accumulator. In the overall CapsAcc architecture, there are as many Accumulators as the number of columns of the PE array.

3.2.2.4 Activation Unit

The Activation Units follow the Accumulators. As shown in Figure 3.8b, they perform different functions in parallel. The multiplexer selects the path to propagate the information toward the output. While the figure shows only one unit, in the complete CapsAcc architecture, there is one Activation Unit for each column of the PE array. The 25-bit data values coming from the Accumulators are reduced to 8-bit fixed-point values to reduce the computations at this stage.

The Rectified Linear Unit (ReLU) [183] is used for the first two layers of the CapsNet. It is implemented by connecting the input to the output through a multiplexer, which sets the output to zero if the input is negative.

We designed the **Normalization operator (Norm)** with a structure performing the Square-and-Accumulate operation, where, instead of a traditional multiplier, there is a *Power2* operator. Its data path is shown in Figure 3.8d. A register stores

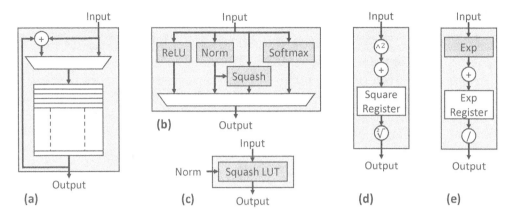

Figure 3.8: Hardware architectures of different components of the CapsAcc accelerator. (a) Accumulator. (b) Activation unit. (c) Squashing function unit. (d) Norm function unit. (e) Softmax function unit.

the partial sum, while the *Sqrt* operator produces the output. We designed the *Sqrt* operator as a Look-Up Table with 12-bit input and 8-bit output. The *Norm* operator produces a valid output every $n + 1$ clock cycle, where n is the length of the vector (or capsule dimension) for which we want to compute the Norm. Such an operator is either used to compute the classification prediction or as an input for the Squashing function, as illustrated in Figure 3.8b.

We designed and implemented the **Squashing function** as a Look Up Table, as shown in Figure 3.8c. The function takes the vector s_j (element-wise) and its norm $||s_j||$ as inputs. The Norm input comes from its respective unit. Hence, the Norm operation is not implemented again inside the Squash unit. The LUT takes a 6-bit fixed-point data and a 5-bit fixed-point norm as inputs to produce an 8-bit output. The first output of the vector is produced with just one additional clock cycle compared to the Norm. We decided to limit the bit-width to constrain the computational requirements at this stage, following the analysis performed in Section 3.2.1 shows the highest computational load for this operation. Such a design using a LUT significantly reduces the latency of the squashing operation. A pure logic-based implementation would have required complex mathematical operations that would not be efficient when implemented in hardware.

The **Softmax function** design is shown in Figure 3.8e. Initially, it computes the exponential function (8-bit Look Up Table) and accumulates the sum in a register, followed by a division. Overall, an array of n elements can compute the softmax function of the whole array in $2n$ cycles.

3.2.2.5 Control Unit

At each stage of the inference process, this unit generates different control signals for all the components of the accelerator, according to the operations needed. Its functionality is shown in Figure 3.9. The core of the control unit is a Finite State Machine (FSM), which generates at the output the control signals for the

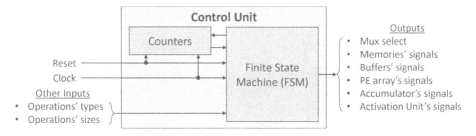

Figure 3.9: Functionality of the Control Unit of our CapsAcc architecture.

multiplexers, the memories, the buffers, and all the other components of the CapsAcc architecture. A set of counters interacts with the FSM to guarantee the correct timing of all the operations. For example, in a convolution operation, the number of clock cycles needed to process the data for a given set of weights is counted before the next set of weights is loaded onto the PE array. Therefore, the control unit is essential for correctly scheduling the operations of the accelerator.

3.2.2.6 Memory Hierarchy

Besides the registers embedded in the PE array and the activation unit, the memory hierarchy is organized as follows. For each operation, all the weights are stored in the on-chip weight memory, while the input data, which correspond to the pixel intensities of the input image, are stored in the on-chip data memory. As an interface between the memories and the accelerator, the data buffer and weight buffer work as a cushion for interacting with the PE array at high bandwidth and access rate. Moreover, the accumulator unit contains a buffer for storing the output partial sums, and the routing buffer is used to store the coefficients of the dynamic routing.

3.2.3 Dataflow Design

This section describes how to map the processing of different types of layers and operations onto our CapsAcc architecture. For ease of understanding, we illustrate the process with the help of a case study performing MNIST classification on our CapsAcc. Note that each stage of the CapsNet inference requires its mapping scheme.

3.2.3.1 Dataflow of the Conv1 Layer

The Conv1 layer has 256 channels and filters of size 9×9. First, we design a row-by-row mapping, and after the last row, we move to the next channel. Figure 3.10a shows how the dataflow is mapped onto our CapsAcc architecture. An illustrative example of mapping the weights onto the weight buffer is shown in Figure 3.11. To efficiently perform the convolutions, we hold the weight values in the PE array to reuse the filter across different input data.

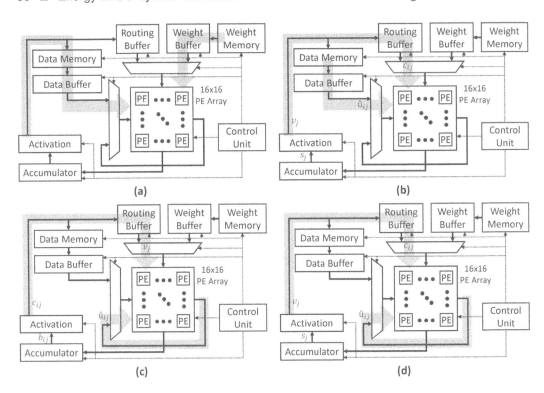

Figure 3.10: Dataflow of our CapsAcc for different case study scenarios. (a) Conv layer mapping. (b) Sum generation and squashing operation mapping for the first routing iteration. (c) Update and softmax operation mapping. (d) Sum generation and squashing operation mapping for all but the first routing iteration.

3.2.3.2 Dataflow of the PrimaryCaps Layer

The PrimaryCaps layer has one more dimension compared to the Conv1 layer, the capsule size (i.e., 8). However, we treat the 8D capsule as a Conv layer with 8 output channels. Thus, we map the parameters row-by-row, then move through different input channels, and only at the third stage we move on to the following output channel. This mapping procedure minimizes the accumulator size because our CapsAcc first computes the output features for the same output channel. Since

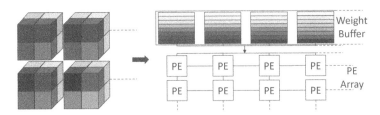

Figure 3.11: The procedure of mapping into the CapsAcc architecture is shown through an example of Conv filters mapped onto the weight buffer and the PE array.

this layer type is convolutional, the weight reuse dataflow is the same as the previous layer, as reported in Figure 3.10a.

3.2.3.3 Dataflow of the ClassCaps Layer

The mapping of the ClassCaps layer is described as follows. After mapping row-by-row, we consider input capsules and input channels as the third dimension. Output capsules and output channels represent the fourth dimension. Hence, in this way, the output feature map (OFMAP) reuse is achieved to minimize the energy consumption of the accumulators. However, recalling the procedure described in Algorithm 1, other types of computations, i.e., *sum, squash, update* and *softmax*, need to be performed in this layer. The input vectors for computing the *sum* and *update* operations are mapped column-by-column onto the PE array. This approach, having each vector mapped onto the same column of the PE array, simplifies the computations of the *squash* and *softmax* functions, which are performed by the activation units to avoid interdependence across different columns.

Then, we design the corresponding dataflow for each step of the routing-by-agreement process. It is a critical phase since a less efficient mapping can potentially impact the overall performance.

First, *we apply an algorithmic optimization on the routing-by-agreement algorithm*. During the first operation, instead of initializing b_{ij} to 0 and computing the *softmax*, we directly initialize the coupling coefficients c_{ij} to 0. This optimization can skip the *softmax* computation at the first routing iteration. In fact, in this operation, all the inputs are equal to 0, as they do not depend on the current data.

3.2.3.4 Dataflow of the Dynamic Routing

Regarding the dataflow of our CapsAcc, we identified three different scenarios during the dynamic routing algorithm:

1. **First sum generation and squash:** The predictions $\hat{u}_{j|i}$ are loaded from the Data Buffer, the coupling coefficients c_{ij} are coming from the Routing Buffer, the PE array computes the sums s_j, the Activation Unit selects and computes the Squash, and the outputs v_j are stored back in the Routing Buffer. This dataflow is shown in Figure 3.10b.

2. **Update and softmax:** The predictions $\hat{u}_{j|i}$ are reused through the horizontal feedback of the architecture, the outputs v_j are coming from the Routing Buffer, the PE array computes the updates for b_{ij}, and the Softmax at the Activation Unit produces the coefficients c_{ij} that are stored back in the Routing Buffer. Figure 3.10c shows the dataflow described above.

3. **Sum generation and Squash:** Figure 3.10d shows the dataflow for this scenario. Compared to the Figure 3.10b, the predictions $\hat{u}_{j|i}$ are coming from the horizontal feedback connection, thus exploiting data reuse also in this stage.

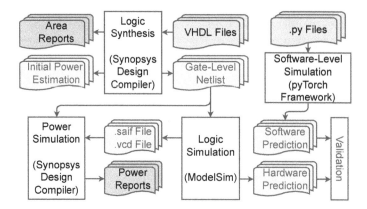

Figure 3.12: Synthesis flow and tool chain of our experimental setup.

3.2.4 Synthesis Evaluation of the Complete CapsAcc Architecture

3.2.4.1 Experimental Setup

We implemented the complete CapsAcc architecture design in RTL (VHDL), and evaluated it for the MNIST dataset *(to stay consistent with the original CapsNet paper)*. We synthesized the complete architecture in a 45nm CMOS technology using the ASIC design flow with the Synopsys Design Compiler. We did functional and timing validation through gate-level simulations using Mentor ModelSim and obtained the precise area, power, and performance of our design. The complete synthesis flow is shown in Figure 3.12.

Note that, since our hardware design is fully functionally compliant with the original CapsNet design of [236], we observed the same classification accuracy. Hence, we do not present any classification results in this section and only focus on the performance, area, and power consumption results, which are more relevant for an optimized hardware architecture.

3.2.4.2 Detailed Power and Area Breakdown

The details and synthesis parameters for conducting our design are reported in Table 3.4. Table 3.5 shows the absolute values for the area and power consumption of all the components of the synthesized CapsAcc. These values indicate that the buffers dominate the area and power contributions, and the PE array is less than 1/3 of the total budget.

3.2.4.3 Discussion on Comparative Results

The graph in Figure 3.13a shows the performance (execution time) results of the different layers of CapsNet inference on our CapsAcc, while Figure 3.13b shows the performance of every sequence of the routing process. Compared with the Nvidia GeForce RTX 2080 Ti GPU performance, we obtained a significant speedup for the overall computation time of a CapsNet inference pass (6×). *The main notable*

TABLE 3.4: Parameters of the synthesized CapsAcc.

Tech. node [nm]	45
Voltage [V]	1
Area [mm^2]	2.60
Power [mW]	427.44
Clk Freq. [MHz]	250
Bit width	8
On-Chip Mem. [MB]	8
Area [mm^2]	2.60
Power [mW]	427.44

TABLE 3.5: Area and power, for the different components of the CapsAcc architecture.

Component	Area [μm^2]	Power [mW]
PE Array	42 867	112.31
Accumulator	32 641	47.57
Activation	29 027	2.21
Data Buffer	136 222	199.31
Routing Buffer	32 598	47.56
Weight Buffer	11 961	17.46
Other	4 330	1.10

improvements are witnessed in the ClassCaps layer (12×) and in the Squashing operation (172×).

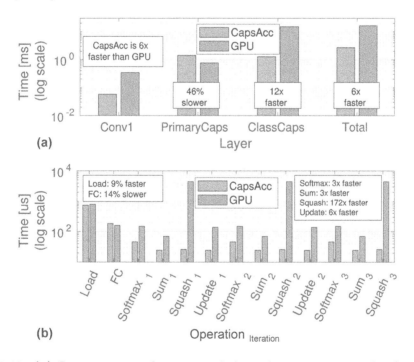

Figure 3.13: **(a)** Layer-wise performance of the inference pass on the CapsNet on CapsAcc, compared to the GPU. **(b)** Performance of the inference pass on each routing-by-agreement step on CapsAcc, compared to the GPU.

3.2.5 Summary

The proposed CapsAcc architecture is the first CMOS-based hardware accelerator for CapsNet inference. A significant performance speedup compared to the GPU execution is achieved by designing a flexible PE array with diverse dataflow patterns to exploit the parallelism across different operations of the CapsNets. The CapsAcc represents the first proof-of-concept for realizing CapsNet hardware and opens multiple directions for its high-performance inference deployments. In this regard, the following Section 3.3 discusses a novel methodology for exploring the design space of CapsNet accelerators and leveraging the tradeoff between area, latency, and energy consumption.

3.3 FEECA: A METHODOLOGY TO DESIGN A FAST, ENERGY-EFFICIENT CAPSNET ACCELERATOR

High-performance and energy-efficient designs of CapsNet accelerators require exploration of different design decisions (like the processing array size and configuration, and the structure of the PEs). Toward this, we propose *FEECA*, a novel methodology to explore the design space of the (micro-)architectural parameters of a CapsNet hardware accelerator. The FEECA methodology employs the Non-dominated Sorting Genetic Algorithm (NSGA-II) to explore the Pareto-optimal points w.r.t. area, performance, and energy consumption. It requires analytical modeling of the number of clock cycles needed to perform each operation of the CapsNet inference, and the memory accesses to enable a fast yet accurate design space exploration. We evaluated the architectures for the MNIST benchmark (as done by the original CapsNet paper from Google Brain's team) and for the German Traffic Sign Recognition Benchmark (GTSRB).

3.3.1 Overview of the FEECA Methodology

The FEECA methodology (Figure 3.14) requires a CapsNet and some optimization objectives (hardware parameters of a CapsNet accelerator) as inputs. The output of the methodology is a set of Pareto-optimal CapsNet accelerators.

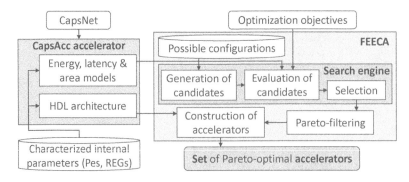

Figure 3.14: Our FEECA methodology for obtaining Pareto-optimal design configurations of the CapsNet accelerators w.r.t. the given optimization objectives.

The methodology works in general as follows. Given a generic configurable CapsNet accelerator (e.g., the CapsAcc) with a set of possible configurations (the search space for further optimizations), we construct analytical models to calculate the parameters of the accelerator for a given design, such as energy consumption, chip area, and delay (latency taken during the inference of one CapsNet input element). The analytical models use a set of pre-synthesized internal primitives such as PEs and registers. Then, a space-search engine is used to find the optimal configurations of a generic CapsNet accelerator. Since two or more optimization parameters are typically required, a multi-objective search algorithm is needed to find configurations that tradeoff all the parameters. In this work, we propose to deploy two different search algorithms, i.e., the brute-force and the NSGA-II algorithm, to reduce the search time.

The output of the search engine is a set of configurations. These configurations are applied to the generic CapsNet accelerator to get the final set of Pareto-optimal accelerators.

3.3.2 Optimization Problem

The CapsAcc architecture designed serves as a baseline to deploy our FEECA methodology, whose goal is to find Pareto-optimal sets of architectural parameters of the CapsNet accelerator to achieve a good tradeoff between our design objectives, which are area, energy, and performance. Since we focus on multiple objectives, standard optimization methods (e.g., branch and bound) are unsuitable for this task because they typically optimize only one objective and are exhaustive.

3.3.2.1 Problem Formulation

The optimization problem is defined as follows.

- We have as input k parameters $p_1 \in P_1$, $p_2 \in P_2$, ..., $p_k \in P_k$ of the accelerator where P_i is a set of possible values of parameter p_i.

- We define a set of configurations $C \subseteq P_1 \times P_2 \times \cdots \times P_k$.

- We are primarily interested in the configurations belonging to the *Pareto set* which contains the so-called *nondominated solutions*.

For example, if we consider two configurations c_1 and $c_2 \in C$, c_1 dominates c_2 if: (1) c_1 is not worse than c_2 in all objectives, and (2) c_1 is strictly better than c_2 in at least one objective.

3.3.3 Search Algorithms: Brute-Force vs. Heuristic Search

A straightforward approach uses a brute-force search. For the small test cases, evaluating all the configurations can be feasible. It is fundamental to use specialized algorithms to construct the Pareto front. In this work, we use an efficient construction algorithm based on binary space partitioning [64].

However, the enumeration of all the possible combinations may be time-consuming. To avoid that, we propose to use a multi-objective heuristic algorithm. The search algorithm uses a modified variant of the Non-dominated Sorting Genetic Algorithm (NSGA-II) [42]. It is a powerful and intelligent algorithm for multi-objective optimizations, significantly reducing the exploration time, despite finding solutions on the Pareto-front.

The NSGA-II algorithm [42] generates a set of offspring Q_t from the current population P_t. Each offspring is generated from two randomly picked individuals c_1, c_2 from P_t. Then, a crossover binary vector of length k is randomly generated. This vector specifies whether either c_1 or c_2 is used as a source for crossover. After that, one randomly selected configuration parameter (so-called gene) is mutated with a small probability ρ.

The individuals $P_t \cup Q_t$ are sorted into multiple fronts F_i, according to the dominance relation. The first front F_1 contains all the non-dominated solutions along the Pareto front. Each subsequent front $(F_2, F_3, \dots)$ is constructed by removing all the preceding fronts from the population and finding a new Pareto front. The first fronts (e.g., F_1 and F_2) are copied to the next population P_{t+1}. If any front must be split (e.g., F_3), a crowding distance is used to select individuals to P_{t+1}.

The algorithm runs iteratively for g generations (steps). Its pseudocode is reported in Algorithm 7, where the following procedures are used:

- $RandomConfigurations(X, n)$ randomly picks n configurations from a set X.

- $CrossoverAndMutate(X, n)$ generates n new offsprings from parents P by uniform crossover and mutation.

- $EstimateParameters(X)$ evaluate the new candidate solutions from a set X.

- $PickPareto(X)$ selects Pareto optimal solutions from a set X, and these solutions are removed from the set.

- $DistanceCrowding(X, n)$ returns n solutions from a set X.

The advantage of having a multi-objective algorithm is that it re-constructs the Pareto front in each generation and tries to cover all possible solutions. The output of the multi-objective algorithm is a set of non-dominated circuits.

3.3.4 Set of Internal Primitives

In contrast to the first version of the CapsAcc architecture, we propose a modified version of PEs with multiple pairs of weight and data inputs (n_{pe}) multiplied and reduced using a reduction tree.

Such types of PEs can be generated in a configurable manner, varying the following parameters:

- number of input pairs n_{pe} of bit-width b_{in};

- bit-width of the partial sum b_{out};

Algorithm 7: NSGA-II.

Input: search space S, sizes of population $|P|, |Q|$, number of generations g
Output: Pareto set $F \subseteq P_1 \times P_2 \times \cdots \times P_k$

1   $P_1 \leftarrow RandomConfigurations(S, |P|)$;
2   **for** $g = 1 \ldots g$ **do**
3      $Q_i \leftarrow CrossoverAndMutate(P_i, |Q|)$;
4      $T \leftarrow EstimateParameters(P_i \cup Q_i)$;
5      $P_{i+1} \leftarrow \emptyset$;
6   **while** $|P_{i+1} < |P|$ **do**
7         $F = PickPareto(T)$;
8   **if** $|P_{i+1}| + |F| \leq |P|$ **then**
9            $P_{i+1} \leftarrow P_{i+1} \cup F$;
10   **else**
11           $P_{i+1} \leftarrow P_{i+1} \cup DistanceCrowding(F, |P| - |P_{i+1}|)$;
12   **end**
13   **end**
14 **end**
15 **return** $PickPareto(P_g)$;

- number of stages of the pipeline n_{stg};

- number of rows of the PE array #ROWS;

- number of columns of the PE array #COLS.

The PEs are constructed to have a minimal logical depth $D = \lceil \log_2(n_{out} + 1) \rceil$, where n_{out} is the maximum number of outputs from the multiplier that must be added. We assume that $b_{out} \geq 2b_{in}$ because the output is the result of a sum of multiplications. Then, the bit-width of each adder in the tree structure has a depth value lower than or equal to b_{out}. Compared to the PE architecture of CapsAcc (recall Figure 3.7b), the PE in Figure 3.15 is a more generalized version. Hence, in the following experiments, we will use the latter version.

The longest computational paths of the tree can be reduced by inserting pipeline registers along the paths, i.e., by increasing the parameter n_{stg}. This modification may cause significant area and energy overhead because of the additional registers inserted in every wire at the same pipeline stage.

3.3.5 Estimation of the Parameters of the Accelerator

An essential aspect of the brute-force search, which is also valid for the heuristic space search, is the estimation of the HW parameters of the accelerator in a fast and accurate way. In this work, we focus on parameters of the HW accelerator that have no impact on the overall accuracy of the CapsNet. Hence, we focus on the parameters of the HW accelerator, which are area, delay, and energy consumption (considering the contributions of the PE array and the memory accesses).

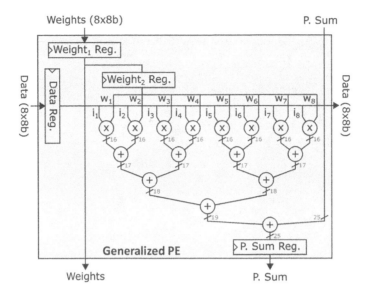

Figure 3.15: Example of a generalized PE with $n_{pe} = 8$ pairs, $b_{in} = 8, b_{out} = 25$ and $n_{stg} = 1$.

3.3.5.1 Area

The model to estimate the area of the PE array is simple yet accurate. We consider a modular approach where the estimation is built bottom-up. Since the PE array is a Cartesian grid of PEs, the area of the PE array can be estimated as a sum of values from a fully characterized set of primitives (PEs, Registers) for a given clock period T. Therefore, only the logic synthesis of the primitives is needed.

3.3.5.2 Delay

Modeling the delay, i.e., the computation latency of one inference pass of the CapsNet is the most critical step because it has to consider having different values of the internal primitives and different dataflows for each layer/operation of the inference. Therefore, we build one analytical model for each operation, which computes the number of clock cycles needed to process the inputs of the respective layer. It is parametrized by the internal primitives of the accelerator, i.e., n_{stg}, n_{pe}, #COLS, #ROWS. Therefore, for each layer, the delay is computed by multiplying the number of clock cycles by the clock period. The overall delay of the CapsNet inference is the sum of the delays for every single operation.

3.3.5.3 Energy Consumption

The energy consumption needed by the accelerator to complete one inference pass has two can be breakdown in two parts. The first one is the energy consumed by the PE array, i.e., the power consumption of the PE array (calculated in a similar way as for computing the area, summing the power consumption of a fully characterized set of primitives), multiplied by the delay. The second contribution is the energy required

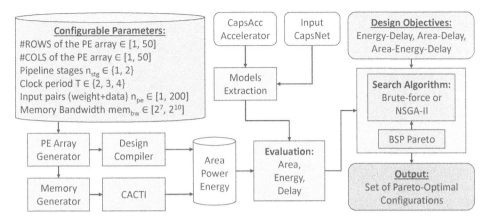

Figure 3.16: Experimental setup and toolflow for evaluating the FEECA methodology.

for the reading operations from the data and weight memories, assuming a maximum SRAM available of 8MB.

3.3.6 Evaluation of our FEECA Methodology

In this section, we show the ability of the proposed FEECA methodology to find Pareto-optimal configurations of the PE array of the CapsNet accelerator to efficiently perform inference of CapsNets. We conducted these experiments on the CapsNet model for the GTSRB dataset [92]. The experiments are divided into four parts. In the first experiment, the synthesis results of the internal primitives (PEs, registers, etc.) for selected n_{stg}, T, n_{pe}, b_{in} and b_{out} parameters are conducted. Then, two sets of Pareto-optimal configurations in terms of energy vs. delay and area vs. delay objectives are constructed and analyzed. The speedup and quality of the heuristic NSGA-II searching algorithm are analyzed and discussed. Finally, a three-dimensional Pareto front is constructed. The experimental setup and toolflow are shown in Figure 3.16. Here, the search algorithm explores different configurations to select Pareto-optimal solutions based on the design objectives. The evaluation is done based on the synthesized components (PEs and Regs.) and the models extracted from the baseline CapsAcc performing the inference of the input CapsNet.

3.3.6.1 Generator: Synthesis of Internal Primitives

First, we generate the design primitives for $b_{in} = 8$, $b_{out} = 25$, $n_{stg} \in \{1, 2\}$ and $n_{pe} \in [1, 400]$. The generated PEs have been synthesized using Synopsys Design Compiler in a 45nm technology node and clock periods $T \in \{2, 3, 4\}$. In Figure 3.17, the parameters of the designs for $n_{stg} \in \{1, 2\}$ are shown. Note that the constraint on the clock period limits the number of inputs n_{pe} because the depth of the reduction tree is larger, and the timing constraints are violated. For example, setting the clock period to $2ns$ limits $n_p e$ to 7. Therefore, the maximal n_{pe} is 7, 130 and 300 for $n_{stg} = 1$ and 7, 150 and 400 for $n_{stg} = 2$, respectively.

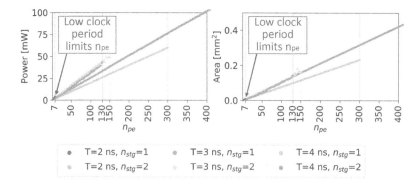

Figure 3.17: Power consumption and area of PEs with various bit-width of P.Sum (b_{out}) and $n_{stg} = 1$. The dotted lines show the maximal number of inputs n_{pe} that can be synthesized without violating the constraint for a given bit-width.

We also synthesize the designs where the computational path is divided into two clock cycles (registers are after the multipliers) in a pipelined fashion. The additional registers cause 28% power overhead compared to a single-cycle computation. The area overhead is 36%. To compute the energy consumption due to the memory accesses, we design the SRAM memory using the CACTI-P tool [124], considering the total size of 8MB and the block size of 128B. The results of area, energy for the read access, and leakage power, varying the memory bandwidth (mem_{bw}), are reported in Table 3.6.

3.3.6.2 Complete Accelerator Construction

The parameters of the CapsAcc are optimized using the proposed FEECA methodology, as discussed in Figure 3.16. We consider two pairs of objectives, which are energy vs. delay (E vs. D) and area vs. delay (A vs. D). Using a brute-force algorithm, our FEECA methodology finds 228 E vs. D Pareto-optimal configurations and 127 A vs. D Pareto-optimal configurations, as shown in Figure 3.18 (optimal points). Note that the Pareto-optimal solutions obtained by the brute-force highly overlap with the solutions generated with the NSGA-II algorithm, meaning that the latter is an efficient and fidelitous design space algorithm. Moreover, there is a relatively small area variation between the configurations. Note that there are different solutions with the same area but different delays. We also compared the Pareto-optimal solutions found by the NSGA-II-based FEECA methodology with a

TABLE 3.6: Parameters of the SRAM.

Bandwidth [bits]	128 (10^7)	256 (10^8)	512 (10^9)	1024 (10^{10})
Area [mm^2]	55.8	61.1	66.0	76.5
Read energy [nJ]	0.549	0.967	1.897	3.943
Leakage power [mW]	4272	4335	4385	4493

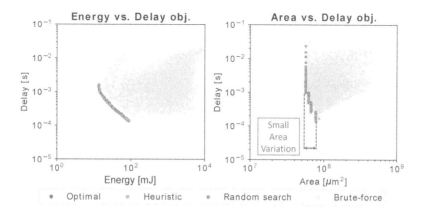

Figure 3.18: Pareto-optimal configurations found by the brute-force algorithm (optimal), NSGA-II algorithm (heuristic), random search, and the other Pareto-dominated solutions (brute-force), for (left) energy vs. delay and (right) area vs. delay objectives.

random search of the same number of candidate solutions. Compared to the Pareto-optimal points found by the random search (see the green points in Figure 3.18), the Pareto-optimal points found by the NSGA-II-based search exhibit $67\times$ and $146\times$ lower average normalized Euclidean distance to the optimal points for the E vs. D and A vs. D objectives, respectively.

For the E vs. D objectives, Figure 3.19 shows the energy consumption and delay of the configurations optimized (a) for the overall E vs. D and (b) for the E vs. D of each single layer. The *PrimaryCaps* layer has the biggest impact on the overall energy and delay. Thus, the layer-wise and the CapsNet-optimal configurations, in that case, fall almost on the same curve. On the other hand, the CapsNet-optimal configurations degrade the performance of the *Sum*, *Update* and mostly *Conv1* layers, but these layers participate on the overall objectives with a lower impact, compared to the *PrimaryCaps* layer. Indeed, an optimal solution for the whole CapsNet belongs only to the PrimaryCaps layer optimal, while it is not optimal for the other layers.

Another view on the optimal configurations is presented in Figure 3.20. This figure shows the distribution of the parameters of the CapsNet accelerator for different configurations. Note that if we consider all the objectives, better results are achieved when using $\#ROWS = 1$. Considering the E vs. D objectives, maximizing mem_{bw} is convenient. The highest contribution to the overall delay and energy consumption is due to the *PrimaryCaps* layer. It is convenient to choose the value of n_{pe} in the range between 1 and 7. However, considering the *Conv1* only, a better choice would have been $n_{pe} \in \{4.7\}$ and equal to 4 for the *ClassCaps* layer. The *Sum*, *Update* and *ClassCaps* layer prefer the size of the PE array equal to 32×1. On the other hand, the distribution of the optimal parameters for the A vs. D design objectives is different. Since the area strongly depends on mem_{bw}, all their values lead to some Pareto-optimal solutions.

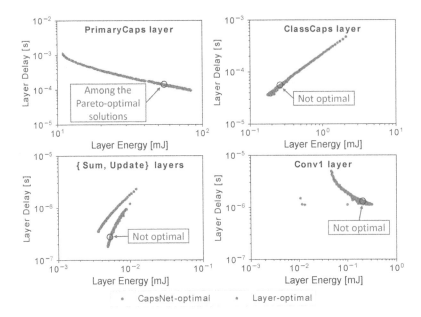

Figure 3.19: Energy and delay of the separate layers with configurations that are (blue dots) optimal for the whole CapsNet and (red dots) optimal for one layer only. The highlighted solution ($n_{stg} = 1$, $n_{pe} = 7$, #COLS = 12, #ROWS = 1, $mem_{bw} = 1024$, $T = 2$ ns) consumes approximatively 80% of the energy in the *PrimaryCaps* and *Conv1* layer, while the contributions for the other layer are significantly lower.

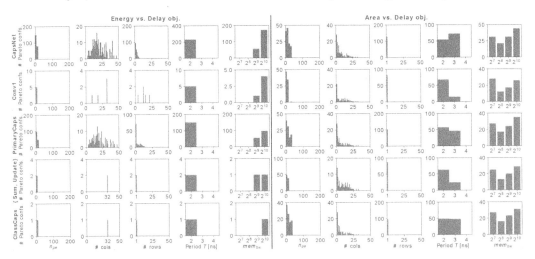

Figure 3.20: Distribution of n_{pe} and #COLS parameters for configurations that are Pareto optimal for E-L and A-L objectives. The blue bars show the distribution of the objectives of the whole CapsNet. The red bars show the configurations optimized for a single layer.

3.3.6.3 *Heuristic Search Algorithm*

The brute-force algorithm eventually finds the optimal solutions. However, it is very slow because all the possible solutions are explored. Therefore, we implement the heuristic NSGA-II algorithm to speed up the search process. For the E-L objectives, the NSGA-II runs for 1 000 iterations of the generation process, with a population size $|P| = |Q| = 50$, to find up to 50 Pareto-optimal configurations.

The NSGA-II algorithm needs only 50 050 evaluations (0.44% of the search space). Therefore, the exploration time has been decreased from 2.5 hours to 30 seconds compared to using brute force. The design for the E vs. D objective is not trivial because the optimal Pareto frontier consists of 228 configurations. Therefore, the initial settings $|P| = |Q| = 50$ allow us to find only a small subset of the optimal solutions, regularly distributed due to the distance crowding. However, almost all the found solutions belong to the optimal Pareto set, and the average normalized Euclidean distance (ANED) from the found solutions to the nearest optimal ones is $4 \cdot 10^{-5}$. However, the ANED from the optimal solutions to the nearest found solutions is 0.006. To reduce the distance from the optimal solutions, we increase the size of the population to $|P| = |Q| = 150$ (150 150 evaluations; 1.31% of the exploration time). With these settings, we found 150 solutions. Although such modification causes 3× more time for the design, the ANED from optimal to found solutions is decreased to 0.001, and each found solution belongs to the optimal Pareto set. The heuristic design for the A vs. D objective with $|P| = |Q| = 150$ allows us to find 97 of 127 configurations with an ANED from optimal to found solutions equal to $2 \cdot 10^{-4}$. The results are shown in Figure 3.18.

3.3.6.4 Multiobjective Optimization

By running the search algorithm on our benchmark, three objectives of the CapsNet accelerator are optimized: the area on the chip, the energy consumption for the inference of one input image, and the delay (i.e., the inference latency).

Figure 3.21 reports three different visualization perspectives of the results, where each couple of two objectives is combined into products, which are energy × delay (EDP), area × delay (ADP) and energy × area (EAP), respectively. By reducing the space dimension, only a smaller number of solutions remain in the Pareto-frontiers, shown by the grey lines. For example, the lowest-delay solution, which will be analyzed, as a case study, in the following section, is marked with grey circles in Figure 3.21. It lays on the Pareto-frontier only in the last two plots, i.e., the ADP vs. energy tradeoff and EAP vs. delay, while it is not Pareto-optimal for the other case. Indeed, if we consider the EDP, 75% of the configurations are Pareto-dominated. Similarly, considering the ADP and the EAP, more than 42% and 43% of the configurations are Pareto-dominated, respectively.

3.3.6.5 Case Study: Synthesis of a Pareto-Optimal Solution

As a case study, we synthesized the complete PE array of the selected solution (highlighted with a grey circle in Figure 3.21), using the Synopsys Design Compiler. The microarchitectural structure of the PE array is shown in Figure 3.22. Note, since the solution has one row, the structure of the PE differs from the generic PE (see Figure 3.15) in two aspects:

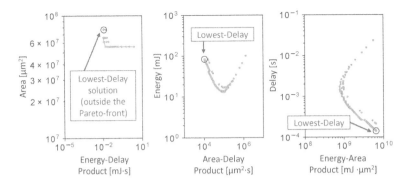

Figure 3.21: Pareto-set of configurations with three objectives in a figure (top) and combining two objectives as products (bottom). The highlighted lowest-delay solution has a configuration of $n_{stg} = 1$, $n_{pe} = 4$, #COLS $= 32$, #ROWS $= 1$, $T = 3\ ns$, $mem_{bw} = 1024$.

- Since there is only one row, the $Weight_1$ $Reg.$ is not needed because there is no reason to store the weight values for the subsequent rows.

- Since there is only one row, the input partial sums are null. Therefore, all the relative connections and additions are omitted.

The first row of Table 3.7 shows the results of the selected solution in Figure 3.21. The last two rows report the results of state-of-the-art designs of the baseline the architecture of CapsAcc (Section 3.2) and DESCNet (Section 3.4), while the rest of the rows show the results of a few other solutions, which have the same amount of multipliers as the solution in the first row.

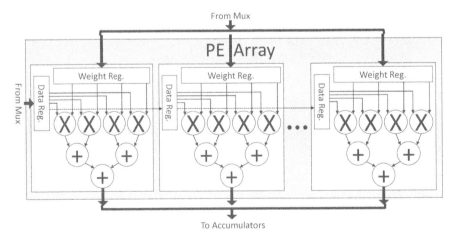

Figure 3.22: Microarchitecture of the PE array for the selected solution, which has $n_{pe} = 4$, #COLS $= 32$, #ROWS $= 1$.

3.3.6.6 Observations and Results Discussion

From the results in Table 3.7, we can derive that energy and delay significantly depend on the microarchitectural configurations of the accelerator. On the other hand, the area is strongly affected by the memory bandwidth. High memory bandwidth implies low delay but at the cost of higher energy consumption. The system's throughput can be derived as the inverse of the latency. **Key Observation:** Note that, despite the baseline design being 2D in terms of rows and columns of the PE array, *there exist solutions in the Pareto-front with only one row or only 1 column*. This is because the second dimension needed for accelerating the computation of matrix multiplication is embedded in the parameter n_{pe}, which is higher than 1. Hence, an efficient parallelism is guaranteed by the designed PE. It is remarkable that the selected solution, in the first row of Table 3.7, reduces the delay of a factor 7×, compared to the CapsAcc.

3.3.7 Summary

The FEECA methodology is proposed to explore the design space for specialized hardware accelerators computing CapsNet inference. To enable this methodology, the analytical models for the area, latency, and energy consumption as functions of the microarchitectural parameters of the PE array (such as the size and configuration

TABLE 3.7: Results for the PE array and estimated delay, area, and energy consumption for the whole CapsAcc architecture. The *fastest* (lowest delay) configuration of the CapsAcc is highlighted in green in the first row. In contrast, the original version of the CapsAcc, which was analyzed in Section 3.2, is reported in the second last row. All circuits have been synthesized with the clock period $T = 3\ ns$.

	Configuration			est. area $[mm^2]$	DeepCaps (est.)		CapsNet (est.)		PE array	
	mem_{bw}	n_{pe}	$c \times r$		energy $[mJ]$	delay $[ms]$	energy $[mJ]$	delay $[ms]$	area $[mm^2]$	power $[mW]$
Ours	1024	4	32×1	76.64	210.13	2.932	84.06	0.210	0.168	36.5
	512	4	32×1	66.13	203.78	3.247	81.70	0.392	0.168	36.5
	256	4	32×1	61.19	210.03	3.877	84.81	0.755	0.168	36.5
	128	4	32×1	55.93	241.23	5.137	98.88	1.482	0.168	36.5
Ours	1024	4	16×2	76.64	113.11	3.247	43.33	0.392	0.168	37.6
		4	2×16	76.64	54.23	8.021	21.37	3.086	0.168	38.2
		4	8×4	76.64	66.91	3.890	24.26	0.761	0.168	39.0
		4	4×8	76.64	49.05	5.215	17.52	1.514	0.168	39.1
		8	4×4	76.63	66.94	3.916	24.31	0.771	0.161	36.3
		8	8×2	76.63	112.91	3.254	43.32	0.395	0.161	35.8
		8	2×8	76.63	50.23	5.319	17.96	1.557	0.161	36.3
		16	4×2	76.63	112.53	3.267	43.29	0.400	0.158	35.2
		16	2×4	76.63	67.05	3.968	24.41	0.793	0.158	35.9
		16	1×8	76.63	52.72	5.528	18.93	1.646	0.158	35.3
		16	8×1	76.63	209.40	2.936	83.97	0.212	0.158	34.3
		32	2×2	76.63	111.85	3.293	43.23	0.411	0.163	35.3
		32	1×4	76.63	67.32	4.073	24.69	0.837	0.163	35.4
		32	4×1	76.63	208.46	2.942	83.86	0.215	0.163	35.0
		2	32×2	76.66	113.24	3.247	43.35	0.392	0.184	43.6
		2	2×32	76.66	86.11	13.425	39.20	6.143	0.184	44.1
		2	16×4	76.66	66.92	3.877	24.24	0.755	0.184	44.1
		2	4×16	76.66	50.54	7.812	19.89	2.999	0.184	44.9
CapsAcc	1024	1	16×16	76.86	479.8	103.1	40.12	8.621	0.434	112.3
DescNet	128	1	16×16	56.15	278.31	103.1	18.37	8.621	0.434	112.3

of the PE array and the structure of the PEs) are built. Through the exploration of the design space with the help of the genetic NSGA-II algorithm, the Pareto-optimal solutions are selected. Besides optimizing the computing hardware design, the memory architecture design and management are crucial for such hardware accelerators when considering energy reductions to the overall hardware design. Hence, investing further effort to analyze the possibilities and opportunities to employ an application-specific memory architecture can reduce the total memory energy, as demonstrated in Section 3.4.

3.4 DESCNET: DEVELOPING EFFICIENT SCRATCHPAD MEMORIES FOR CAPSNET HARDWARE

Compared to traditional DNNs, CapsNets have improved the generalization ability due to using multi-dimensional capsules and preserving the spatial relationship between objects. However, they pose high computation and memory requirements, making their energy-efficient inference a challenging task. In this section, we provide, for the first time, an in-depth analysis to highlight the design- and run-time challenges for the (on-chip scratchpad) memories employed in hardware accelerators that execute fast CapsNets inference. To enable high efficiency, we propose an application-specific memory architecture called DESCNet, which minimizes the off-chip memory accesses while efficiently feeding data to the hardware accelerator executing CapsNets inference. We analyze the corresponding on-chip memory requirement and leverage it to design a methodology that explores different scratchpad memory designs and their energy/area tradeoffs. Afterward, an application-specific power-gating technique for the on-chip scratchpad memory is devised to further reduce its energy consumption, depending upon the dataflow of the CapsNet and the utilization across different operations of its processing.

We integrated our DESCNet memory design with the CapsAc accelerator executing Google's CapsNet model for the MNIST dataset. We also enhanced the design to run the DeepCaps for the CIFAR10 dataset. The complete hardware is synthesized for a 45nm CMOS technology using the ASIC-design flow with Synopsys tools and CACTI-P, and detailed performance, area, and power/energy estimation is performed using different configurations. Our results for a selected Pareto-optimal solution demonstrate an energy reduction of 79% for the complete accelerator, including computational units and memories, compared to the state-of-the-art design.

3.4.1 Overview of DESCNet Methodology

The CapsAcc architecture described in Section 3.2 mainly focused on designing an efficient computational array and optimizing the dynamic routing algorithm. *However, the memory architecture design and management for the CapsNet accelerators are key aspects when considering energy reductions of the overall hardware system.* Moreover, memory optimizations for the traditional DNN accelerators do not operate efficiently as they do consider the distinct processing flow and compute patterns of the CapsNets algorithms. *This necessitates investigations for specialized memory architectures for the DNN accelerators executing CapsNets algorithms while exploiting their unique processing operations and memory access patterns to enable high energy efficiency.* Assuming a large on-chip memory is typically not applicable in resource-constrained embedded applications, e.g., deployed in the IoT-edge devices. Therefore, a memory hierarchy system with on-chip and off-chip memories is preferred in this scenario.

As will be demonstrated in Section 3.4.3, the energy consumption for both the on-chip and off-chip memories contributes to 96% of the total energy consumed by the CapsNet hardware architecture. Hence, it is crucial to investigate the energy-efficient design and management of an on-chip memory hierarchy for CapsNet hardware architectures. *The key to achieving high energy efficiency is to exploit the application-specific properties of CapsNets, which include the processing behavior of their unique computational blocks, mapped dataflow, and the corresponding memory access patterns.* Since the operations and memory access patterns of the CapsNet inference are distinct from those of the traditional DNNs, the existing memory architectures for the DNN accelerators might not be efficient when executing CapsNets inference. Therefore, to understand the corresponding design challenges and the optimization potential, we investigate the memory requirements in terms of size, bandwidth, and the number of accesses for every stage of the CapsNet inference when mapping it to the CapsAcc and to a traditional DNN accelerator like the TPU.

Traditional memory hierarchies in DNN accelerators are composed of an off-chip DRAM and an on-chip SRAM, where the on-chip memory is basically a scratchpad memory and not a traditional cache. Though general-purpose approaches for memory design exist [200], achieving high energy efficiency for CapsNets requires application-specific designs and optimizations, as discussed above. This application-specific design needs to consider the memory access behavior of different processing operations of the CapsNets and their respective dataflow on a CapsNet accelerator to explore the design space of different parameters of the memory hierarchy (i.e., size, number of banks, partitions) for multiple levels. For instance, intensive on-chip scratchpad memory (SPM) accesses lead to high energy and performance overhead, requiring a large on-chip memory coupled with CapsNet accelerators supporting efficient data reuse to alleviate the overhead of excessive off-chip memory accesses. However, a large SPM increases chip area and leakage power. Hence, besides efficient sizing and partitioning of the SPM, an application-specific power-gating control is also needed for further energy reduction under run-time scenarios of diverse memory usage influenced by different processing steps of the executing CapsNet algorithm, when considering the corresponding wakeup overhead. *Such an application-driven memory hierarchy design and power management of the SPM for CapsNet hardware architectures may provide significant energy reductions compared to the traditional memory architectures for DNN accelerators while keeping high throughput.*

3.4.1.1 Our Novel Contributions

Figure 3.23 provides an overview of our *DESCNet* memory architecture design methodology, showing the integration of our novel contributions with a CapsNet accelerator. In a nutshell, we propose:

1. **Memory Analysis of CapsNet Inference** to systematically study the design requirements (size, accesses), energy consumption and performance, for different operations of the CapsNet and DeepCaps inference.

2. *DESCNet*: **A Specialized Multi-Banked Scratchpad Memory Architecture for CapsNet Accelerators**, which is designed considering the dataflow and the corresponding memory access patterns of different operations of the CapsNet inference. The SPM is partitioned into different sectors to support fine-grained sector-level power-gating, thereby providing a higher energy savings potential under run-time varying memory usage. Since our SPM supports common input/output interfaces, it can be coupled with any accelerator that can execute CapsNet inference.

3. **Design Space Exploration (DSE)**, which is performed to automatically obtain the Pareto-optimal values of different key parameters of our *DESCNet* memory architecture. It leverages tradeoffs between memory, area, and energy consumption while exploiting the distinct processing behavior of different steps of the CapsNet inference.

4. **Application-Driven Memory Power Management:** it leverages the architectural parameters of the accelerator, the processing flow of the CapsNet inference, and the interfacing with memory, to devise a sector-level power-gating for reducing the static power.

5. **Hardware Implementation and Evaluation** of the complete CapsNet architecture with an integrated *DESCNet* memory in a 45nm CMOS technology using the ASIC-design flow with Synopsys tools and CACTI-P. We perform area and energy evaluations for 15 233 possible configurations of the on-chip memory architectures for the CapsNet and 215 693 for the DeepCaps, and benchmark them against the CapsAcc memory design.

3.4.2 Required Architectural Modification and Key Research Question

To overcome the limitation of having large on-chip memory in the baseline CapsAcc architecture (Figure 3.24a), and toward real-world edge implementations, we employ a modified architecture of CapsNet hardware that has a memory hierarchy consisting of an on-chip SPM and an off-chip DRAM, as shown in the blue boxes of Figure 3.24b, respectively.

Such a design can generalize the problem for diverse applications and CapsNet architectures. However, considering such a memory hierarchy, the challenge then lies in designing and managing the on-chip memory such that (i) the off-chip memory

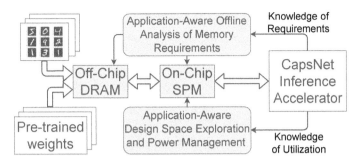

Figure 3.23: Overview of our *DESCNet* Memory Design Methodology.

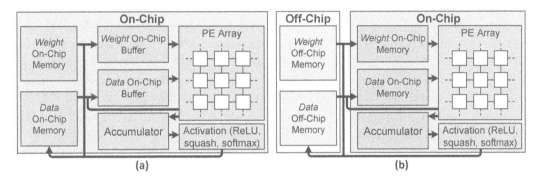

Figure 3.24: Architectural view of the CapsNet inference accelerator. **(a)** Baseline architecture in CapsAcc. **(b)** Modified architecture for this work with off-chip and on-chip memory partitioning, which is more practical for embedded implementations.

accesses are minimized, (ii) the reuse of intermediate data and weights stored in the on-chip memory is exploited at the maximal, and (iii) the unnecessary parts of the on-chip memory can be power-gated in some scenarios of varying memory accesses without reducing the performance of CapsNets processing. These problems have not been studied for the CapsNets hardware yet. *Toward this, we aim at investigating the following key questions when determining the memory sizes and the communication between off-chip and on-chip memories.*

1. How to minimize the off-chip memory accesses to reduce energy consumption? Every data is read from or written to the off-chip memory only once, while used once or multiple times in the on-chip memory.

2. How to keep the latency and throughput *similar/close* to the case of having all the memory on-chip, i.e., hiding the off-chip latency as much as possible? *This can be guaranteed by prefetching the data to the on-chip memory to mask the off-chip memory latency, assuming that the on-chip memory is large enough to contain all the necessary data.*

3. How to minimize the on-chip SPM size to reducing the leakage? What would be the appropriate design tradeoffs?

4. How can we design efficient power-gating for the on-chip SPM to save the leakage power for the unused sectors?

5. Can we exploit the unique processing and data reuse characteristics of CapsNets to optimize the corresponding memory access profiles?

Since the above-discussed challenges can pose contradicting requirements and constraints, in-depth analyses of the resource requirement and usage patterns of CapsNets processing are needed before making appropriate design decisions, which we discuss in the following Section 3.4.3.

3.4.3 Resource Analysis of CapsNet Inference

First, we investigate Google's CapsNet architecture [236] which performs MNIST [118] classification, using the architectural organization presented in Figure 3.24b. We analyze the performance and the on-chip memory requirements for different operations of the CapsNet inference, showing their on-chip read and write accesses. Afterward, we analyze the DeepCaps [220] for the CIFAR10 [112] classification, showing that the accumulators have the highest contributions in memory usage and accesses. Meanwhile, the energy breakdown analysis shows the respective contributions of the accelerator and the memories. Our experiments obtain the same classification accuracy as for the CapsNet on the MNIST dataset and for the DeepCaps on the CIFAR10 dataset, i.e., 99.67% and 92.74%, respectively.

3.4.3.1 *Performance and Memory Analyses for the Google's CapsNet on the MNIST Dataset*

Memory Usage Analysis: In Figure 3.25, we analyze the on-chip memory requirements for each operation of the CapsNet inference. The dashed lines represent their maximum values. Note, unique operations (like *ClassCaps*, *Sum*, *Squash*, *Update* and *Softmax*) of Google's CapsNet [236] inference mapped onto the *CapsAcc* accelerator exhibit different memory utilization profiles compared to when mapped to a memory architecture designed for the traditional DNNs like the TPU [100]. The overall size can be chosen by the operation that requires the largest amount of memory (i.e., the *PrimaryCaps* layer). For this configuration, the on-chip SPM is composed of the data, weight and accumulator memories. This analysis unleashes the available optimization potential for improving the memory energy efficiency when designing a specialized memory architecture for CapsNet accelerators.

Performance Analysis: Figure 3.26a presents the execution time (i.e., number of clock cycles) of different operations involved in the CapsNet inference. Note that the dynamic routing operations contribute to more than half of the execution time of the complete CapsNet inference. Overall, the performance is 116 frames-per-second (FPS) for the CapsAcc accelerator. Suppose we combine the results of Figures 3.25 and 3.26a. In that case, we notice that, potentially, a significant amount of leakage energy can be saved by the power-gating part of the on-chip memory when the utilization is below 100%. We leverage this observation to develop an

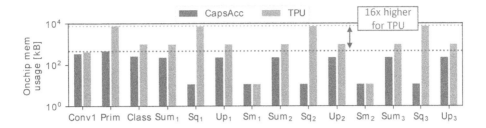

Figure 3.25: Memory utilization of Google's CapsNet inference, mapped on a specialized CapsNet accelerator (*CapsAcc*) and TPU. The bars represent the on-chip memory usage. The dashed lines show the maximum requirement.

application-specific power management policy for memories of the CapsNet Accelerators, as discussed in Section 3.4.4.

Memory Access Analysis: Figure 3.27a provides a detailed analysis for each memory component (i.e., data memory, weight memory and accumulators), which enables an efficient DSE of different architectural parameters of the *DESCNet*. Note that handling different memory components separately may enable efficient power management. Figure 3.27b and Figure 3.27c illustrate the read and write accesses, respectively, for each operation i of the CapsNet inference, i.e., *Convolutional1 (Conv1)*, *PrimaryClass (Prim)* and *ClassCaps-FullyConnected (Class)*. These values are required to compute the energy consumption of the memories in the subsequent sections.

The off-chip accesses, reported in Figure 3.28, can be computed using Equations (3.3) and (3.4), which are valid for the first three operations, are indicated

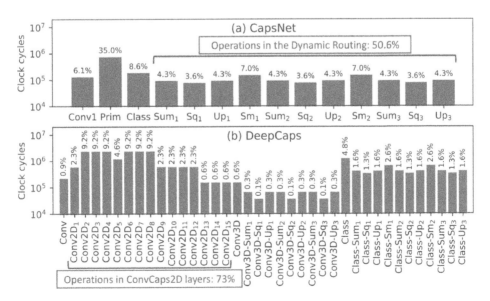

Figure 3.26: Clock cycles for different inference operations in (**a**) CapsNet for the MNIST dataset; (**b**) DeepCaps for the CIFAR10 dataset.

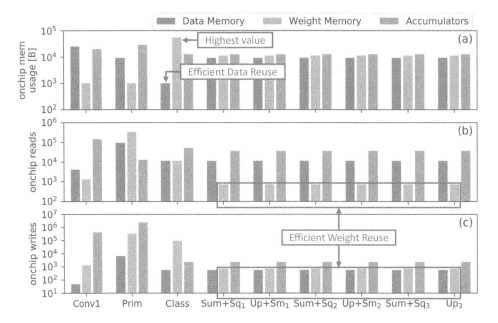

Figure 3.27: On-chip memory analyses for different operations of the CapsNet inference on the MNIST dataset. **(a)** On-chip memory usage. **(b)** On-chip reads. **(c)** On-chip writes.

with the index i. RD_{off} and WR_{off} indicate the SPM read and write accesses, while the subscripts $_D$ and $_W$ stand for on-chip data and weight memories, respectively. *In the dynamic routing, the off-chip memory is not accessed, except for the first and last operation, because all the values required during the dynamic routing are stored on-chip.*

$$(RD_{off})_i = (WR_D + WR_W)_i \tag{3.3}$$

$$(WR_{off})_i = (RD_D)_{i+1} \tag{3.4}$$

From the above analyses, we derive these key observations:

- For most operations, the accumulator's memory usage is more than the data and weight memories for each operation since it must store the temporary

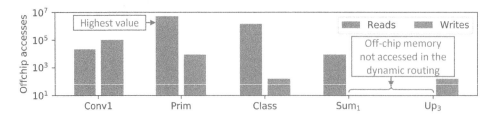

Figure 3.28: Off-chip accesses for the CapsNet inference.

partial sums of different output feature maps. However, the peak is visible in the weight memory of the *ClassCaps* layer, which is FC.

- Data and weight memory requirements vary significantly across different operations.

- In the first two layers, the weight memory usage is relatively low compared to the other stages because the architecture can efficiently reuse weights for the convolutions.

- In the *ClassCaps* layer, the data memory usage is low because the corresponding data reuse is efficient.

- Weight reuse is relatively more efficient in the last six operations (dynamic routing) compared to the first three.

- During the dynamic routing, the off-chip memory is not accessed, except for the read accesses in the first operation and write accesses in the last one, due to the efficient data and weight reuse in these operations.

3.4.3.2 Performance and Memory Analyses for the DeepCaps on the CIFAR10 Dataset

Similar analyses have also been carried on for deeper and more complex CapsNets such as the DeepCaps [220]. The performance in terms of clock cycles is shown in Figure 3.26b, and overall it is 9.7 FPS. Compared to the CapsNet, the DeepCaps shows a more distributed partition. Overall, we can notice that the most time-consuming operations are in the *ConvCaps2D* layers, which contribute to 73% of the execution time of the complete DeepCaps inference.

The on-chip memory usage reads and writes are shown in Figure 3.29. Similar to the case of the CapsNet, the accumulator's usage is higher than the data and weight memories. Moreover, the usage and accesses for the weight memory are low in the Conv layers but higher for the dynamic routing operations.

The off-chip accesses for the DeepCaps are shown in Figure 3.30. While reads and writes proportionally decrease by decreasing the sizes of the Conv layers, for the dynamic routing, the accesses are low, thanks to the efficient reuse. The peak is visible at the beginning of the *ClassCaps* layer due to the large number of weights in that operation.

3.4.3.3 Energy Breakdown Analysis

To compute the energy consumption of the complete architecture, we develop the following two different versions.

(a) Figure 3.24a: an accelerator (composed of NP array, activation unit and control unit), on-chip SPM buffers (data, weight and accumulator's memory), and an on-chip SPM (for data and weights). The total on-chip memory is of $8MiB$.

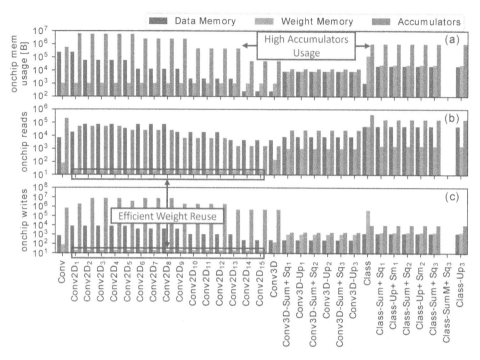

Figure 3.29: On-chip memory usage, reads and writes of different operations for the DeepCaps inference.

(b) Figure 3.24b: an accelerator with the same composition as above, but different architectures of on-chip and off-chip memories. The sizes are derived from the previous analyses.

The energy breakdown is shown in Figure 3.31. The results are obtained by synthesizing in a 45nm CMOS technology the CapsAcc accelerator executing the Google's CapsNet for the MNIST dataset. The on-chip and off-chip memory values are obtained using the CACTI-P tool [124] with the compatible technology parameters, as it is well-adopted by the memory community.

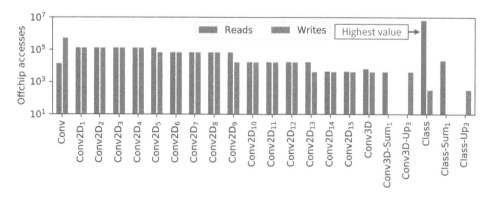

Figure 3.30: Off-chip accesses for the DeepCaps inference.

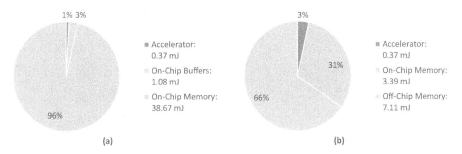

Figure 3.31: Energy breakdown of different components of the CapsNet Inference Architecture: considering **(a)** all on-chip, as employed in CapsAcc and **(b)** a memory hierarchy composed of on-chip and off-chip memories.

Our analysis shows that by designing a different memory hierarchy, we can save 73% of the total energy compared to CapsAcc. These savings can be attributed to the significantly reduced leakage energy due to the lower on-chip memory size. Moreover, the on-chip memory consumes 31% *of the total energy*, which corresponds to *the* 90% *of the on-chip energy* (i..e., accelerator and SPM). Hence, an application-driven memory power management can significantly impact the overall on-chip energy savings.

Note: the DeepCaps' execution for the CIFAR10 dataset does not fit in the $8MiB$ memory of CapsAcc. Hence, a comparison for executing the DeepCaps is not feasible. However, as we will demonstrate later in this section, our proposed DESCNet memory architecture enables the deployment of DeepCaps with low hardware resources.

3.4.3.4 *Summary of the Key Observations From Our Analyses*

Summarizing our analyses, we can leverage the following key observations to design an efficient memory sub-system for the CapsNet hardware.

- Most of the energy is consumed by the (on-chip and off-chip) memory, as compared to the computational array.

- An application-driven memory hierarchy, composed of an on-chip SPM and an off-chip DRAM, can save up to 73% of the energy on the Google's CapsNet model without compromising the throughput compared to having a fully on-chip memory organization. Note that the same throughput is guaranteed by prefetching the data for the next operation in an interleaved fashion with the processing of the current operation. Therefore, the off-chip memory latency can be hidden.

- The utilization of the on-chip memory is variable, depending upon the operation of the CapsNet inference. Thus, applying power-gating to the non-utilized sectors can further reduce its energy consumption.

- Partitioning the SPM into separate components (for data, weight, and accumulator) can be beneficial for storing values and efficiently feeding them to the accelerator.

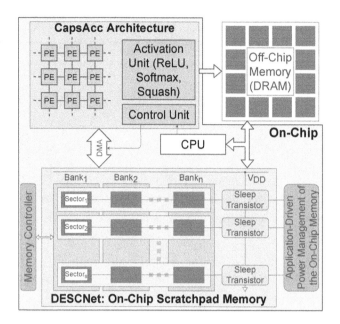

Figure 3.32: Architectural view of the complete CapsNet architecture, with a focus on our *DESCNet* SPM.

3.4.4 DESCNet: Scratchpad Memory Design

3.4.4.1 DESCNet Memory Architecture

The architecture of our *DESCNet* is depicted in Figure 3.32. It is connected to the CapsNet accelerator and to the off-chip memory through dedicated bus lines. The SPM is partitioned into B banks, where each bank consists of SC number of equally-sized sectors. Across different banks, all the sectors are connected through a power-gating circuitry (implemented with sleep transistors) to support an efficient sector-level power-management control at the cost of some area overhead. Our design has SC sectors, one for each bank, which share the same sleep signal. Note that we only consider ON and OFF modes as they came out to be beneficial in our designs, and we did not need state-retentive modes. Our application-driven memory power management unit determines the appropriate control signals (i.e., $ON \leftrightarrow OFF$) for the sleep transistors. Once the execution of the current operation is completed, the values in the SPM are discarded since, in our designs, we consider a deep-sleep OFF state, which is non-retentive. The transitions between sleep modes come at the cost of a certain wakeup energy and latency overhead that needs to be amortized by the leakage energy savings that depends upon the sleep duration and the number of sectors in the sleep mode. Note that our memory model can be generalized for different memory organizations supporting different sizes and levels of parallelism, including multi-port memories. *Toward this, we study the following three design options.*

(a) **Figure 3.33a—Shared Multi-Port Memory (SMP):** a shared on-chip memory with 3 ports for accessing the weights, input data and accumulator's storage in parallel.

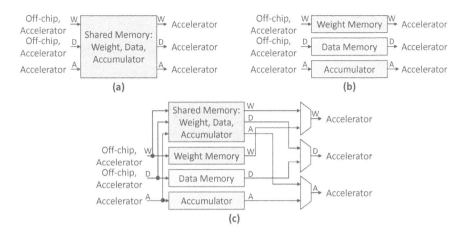

Figure 3.33: Different Architectural Design Options of the On-Chip SPM of the CapsNet Accelerator that are evaluated in our Application-Driven Memory DSE: (a) Shared Multi-Port Memory. (b) Separated Memory. (c) Hybrid Memory (Shared and Separated).

(b) **Figure 3.33b—Separated Memory (SEP):** weights, input data, and the accumulator's partial sums are stored in separate on-chip memories.

(c) **Figure 3.33c—Hybrid Memory (HY):** a combination of the above two design options, i.e., an *SMP* coupled with a *SEP* memory.

3.4.4.2 Application-Driven Memory Power Management

Our application-driven memory PMU determines the sleep signals according to the utilization profile of the memory, as observed in Figure 3.27a and Figure 3.29a. A simple schematic showing how a sleep transistor is connected to its memory sectors is depicted in Figure 3.34. The sleep request signal is followed by the acknowledge signal, to form a 2-way handshake protocol. The timing diagram of the complete sleep cycle ($ON \rightarrow OFF \rightarrow ON$) is shown in Figure 3.35. When exploiting the application-specific knowledge, it is known from the analysis presented in Section 3.4.3 which sectors need to be activated during the execution of different operations. Hence, *the wakeup latency overhead is transparently masked, i.e., the required sectors are pre-activated in advance, in such a way that they are active when needed.*

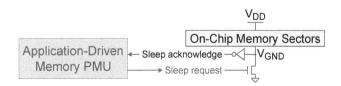

Figure 3.34: Circuit-level schematic of the power-gating circuit, using a footer sleep transistor connected to the PMU.

Figure 3.35: Timing diagram of a complete sleep cycle of a sector.

3.4.4.3 Application-Driven Design Space Exploration of the DESCNet Memory Designs

Considering the above memory models, we systematically determine their organization, sizes, the number of banks (B), and the number of sectors-per-bank (SC) through a DSE methodology. We explore different memory architecture configurations and evaluate their area and energy consumption. Different levels of abstraction of application-driven knowledge (i.e., architecture and utilization profiles specific to CapsNets) are employed. In the following equations and algorithms, we adopt these notations:

- i: index of the operations of the CapsNet inference.

- D_i, W_i, A_i: operation-wise memory usage of data memory, weight memory and accumulators, according to the analyses shown in Figure 3.27a and Figure 3.29a.

- $SZ_{\{S,D,W,A\}}$, $SC_{\{S,D,W,A\}}$, $B_{\{S,D,W,A\}}$: size, number of sectors, number of banks of {shared memory, data memory, weight memory, accumulators}, respectively.

- $\sigma(s)$: pool of available numbers of memory sectors for power-gating, given the memory size s, which are all the power of two values in the range $\left[2, \frac{s}{128}\right]$. Note, the latter value is due to a limitation of the CACTI-P [124] tool, which sets the limit for the ratio between memory size and sector size to be at least 128.

For all the memory designs, without loss of generality, the number of banks is chosen to be $B_D = B_W = B_A = B_S = 16$, as it corresponds to the number of rows and columns of the NP array of the *CapsAcc* architecture. To facilitate efficient data feeding to the accelerator, this parameter is not changed in our DSE.

For the *SMP* design, the size of the shared memory is derived from the operation-wise maximum memory usage scenario, as shown in Equation (3.5). Since only finite values of memory sizes are acceptable, when computing the $\max_i$ function, the memory size becomes the smallest acceptable size that is greater than or equal to the operation-wise maximum, and vice-versa for the $\min_i$.

$$\text{SMP}: SZ_S = \max_i(D_i + W_i + A_i) \tag{3.5}$$

For the *SEP* design, the sizes of the data memory, weight memory, and accumulator are set as in Equation (3.6), based on the operation-wise maximum memory usage of the separated components.

$$\text{SEP}:\begin{cases} SZ_D = \max_i(D_i) \\ SZ_W = \max_i(W_i) \\ SZ_A = \max_i(A_i) \end{cases} \tag{3.6}$$

Sizing the memories becomes a more complicated challenge for the *HY* design. Within the range allowed by Algorithm 8, the memory sizes considered in our design space have power-of-two values, with the addition of four randomly selected memory sizes (that are $25kiB$, $108kiB$, $450kiB$, and $460kiB$), to have more fine-grained results in the low-sized range. For every possible size of data memory, weight memory, and accumulators, the size of the shared memory is computed as the operation-wise worst-case that still guarantees the minimum memory usage required by each operation.

Algorithm 8: Exploration of hybrid memory sizes.

Input: Operation-wise memory usage D_i, W_i, A_i.
Output: Hybrid memory sizes SZ_S, SZ_D, SZ_W, SZ_A.
1 $ret \leftarrow \{\}$;
2 **for** $sz_d \leftarrow \min_i D_i$ **to** $\max_i D_i$ **do**
3   **for** $sz_w \leftarrow \min_i W_i$ **to** $\max_i W_i$ **do**
4   **for** $sz_a \leftarrow \min_i A_i$ **to** $\max_i A_i$ **do**
5          $sz_s \leftarrow \max_i(\max(0, D_i - sz_d) + \max(0, W_i - sz_w) + \max(0, A_i - sz_a))$;
6          $ret \leftarrow ret \cup \{(sz_s, sz_d, sz_w, sz_a)\}$;
7   **end**
8   **end**
9 **end**
10 **return** ret;

After finding the appropriate memory sizes, the power-gating technique can be applied. It directly affects the number of sectors in the memory designs, since a sleep transistor is connected to each sector to switch ON or OFF the whole sector. Hence, for the memory designs where the power-gating is not supported, the number of sectors is 1. When the power-gating is supported, the choice of the number of sectors directly influences the tradeoff between the reduction in the static power and the overhead of the power-gating circuitry overhead. Toward this, Algorithm 9 describes all the combinations of a valid number of sectors allowed by the function $\sigma(s)$ that are explored.

Following the above-discussed procedures, we have generated $15\,233$ *configurations of the DESCNet architecture for the CapsNet*, and $215\,693$ *configurations for the DeepCaps*, with different design options (*SMP*, *SEP*, *HY*), different sizes and number of sectors. Note that the *SMP* and *SEP* design options can also be considered as the boundary cases of the *HY* design option. On the one hand, a *HY* organization where SZ_D, SZ_W, and SZ_A are maximum is equivalent to the *SEP* because the corresponding SZ_S for the *HY* results to be null. On the other hand, if SZ_D, SZ_W and SZ_A of a *HY* organization are all equal to 0, its resulting

---

Algorithm 9: Exploration of the number of memory sectors.

    Input: Memory sizes sz_s, sz_d, sz_w, sz_a

    Output: Number of sectors SC_s, SC_d, SC_W, SC_A

1 $ret \leftarrow \{\}$;

2 **for** $sc_s \in \sigma(sz_s)$ **do**

3   **for** $sc_d \in \sigma(sz_d)$ **do**

4   **for** $sc_w \in \sigma(sz_w)$ **do**

5   **for** $sc_a \in \sigma(sz_a)$ **do**

6               $ret \leftarrow ret \cup \{(sc_s, sc_d, sc_w, sc_a)\}$;

7   **end**

8   **end**

9   **end**

10 **end**

11 **return** ret;

SZ_S would have the same value as the one for the SMP. Note that this particular solution, with $SZ_D = SZ_W = SZ_A = 0$, cannot be achieved for a HY solution, due to the minimum constraints given in Algorithm 8. However, it represents a hypothetical extreme case to discuss.

3.4.5 Our Methodology for the DSE of Scratchpad Memories

The flow of our methodology is depicted in Figure 3.36. The inputs are the CapsNet models and the hardware accelerators for CapsNets. At the output, for each design option, the values of memory organization (i.e., size, number of banks, and sectors), energy consumption, and area are generated. The key steps of our methodology are:

1. Extraction of the memory usage and memory accesses for each operation of the CapsNet inference. While the usage is needed for defining the design options and sizes, the read and write accesses, along with the operation-wise clock cycles, are used for computing the energy consumption.

2. Analysis of the design options (SMP, SEP, HY), and definition of the memory configurations, such as size and number of banks and sectors for the power-gating.

3. A DSE of the possible memory configurations under analysis, through an exhaustive search, to find and select the non-dominated solutions. The estimation of area and energy consumption, with and without the power-gating option, are conducted through the CACTI-P tool [124]. Note that we have performed an exhaustive search because, due to the practical limitations on the memory sizes and the number of sectors, the execution time of the search still results relatively low. We measured the times for executing a complete DSE, including the estimation of energy and area provided by CACTI-P, of 1.5 minutes Google's CapsNet and 22 minutes for DeepCaps, when running with a

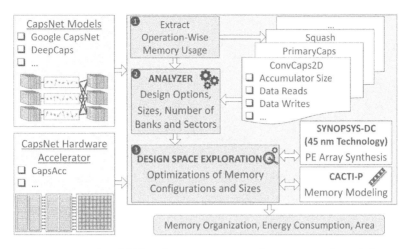

Figure 3.36: *DESCNet* design space exploration and tool flow.

single-thread application on an AMD Ryzen 5 CPU with 32GB RAM. However, if the search space increases or more sophisticated memory evaluations require longer computational time, a heuristic search algorithm can easily be integrated into our methodology to find a solution more quickly. Such a solution may be far from the optimal solution found by the exhaustive search.

3.4.6 Evaluation of the DESCNet Methodology

3.4.6.1 *Results for Google's CapsNet (Area and Energy of the On-Chip Memory)*

We evaluate different memory architectural options for area and energy consumption using the CACTI-P tool. The results of different *DESCNet* architectural designs of the scratchpad memory for the CapsNet on the MNIST dataset are discussed below.

Design Space Exploration Results and Selected Configurations (Figure 3.37): The figure shows the tradeoff between energy and area for 15 233 different *DESCNet* architectural configurations. For each design option (*SMP, SEP, HY*) and its corresponding version with power-gating (with the suffix *-PG*), the Pareto-optimal solutions with lowest-energy are selected. Note, while *SEP, SEP-PG* and *HY-PG* belong to the Pareto-frontier, *HY, SMP* and *SMP-PG* are dominated by other configurations. Their size and number of sectors are reported in Table 3.8.

Area Comparison (Figure 3.38a): The figure shows the area breakdown of different memory components of the *DESCNet*. We notice that, while the *SEP* organization has relatively larger memory sizes compared to the other architectures, their area is relatively smaller. This effect is due to having a single-port memory instead of a shared multi-ported design, where the latter requires more area for the complex interconnections. Indeed the area of the *HY* organization is lower than the *SMP*, due to a small-sized shared memory. Moreover, the power-gating circuitry also incurs additional area overhead (on average, 2.75% for equally-sized SPMs) due to the sleep transistors.

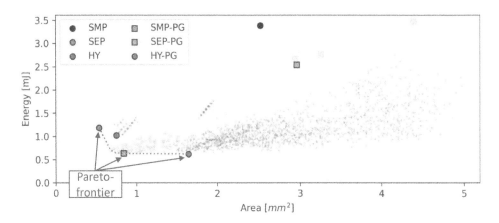

Figure 3.37: DSE results of the *DESCNet* memory configurations for the CapsNet.

Energy Breakdown at the Component Level (Figure 3.38b): The figure shows that the *HY-PG* design option is more energy-efficient than the others due to having higher flexibility and higher potential of power-gating a heterogeneous combination of sectors compared to other designs such as the *SEP-PG*, whose energy consumption is slightly higher. Note that despite having a smaller size than the weight memory, the shared memory of the *HY* organization consumes more energy due to the more complex internal architecture of a multi-ported memory.

Dynamic vs. Static Energy Consumption (Figure 3.38c): When comparing different architectural designs, the figure illustrates that: (1) moving from *SMP* to *SEP* and then to *HY*, the dynamic energy can be reduced progressively; (2) moving from *HY* to *HY-PG*, the static energy can be further reduced due to the benefits of the power-gating, and (3) the dynamic energy remains unchanged between *non-PG* and *-PG* organizations.

Besides this, we noticed that the wakeup latency overhead is negligible. Even though it is masked by preloading the necessary values, its value is very low ($0.072ns$) compared to the average computational time of an operation ($614\mu s$) where the sleep transistors driving their corresponding memory sectors are in a steady state, either *ON* or *OFF*. This behavior also explains why the contribution of the wakeup energy

TABLE 3.8: Selected memory configurations for the CapsNet.

Mem	Shared		Data		Weight		Acc	
	SZ	SC	SZ	SC	SZ	SC	SZ	SC
SEP	—	—	25 kiB	1	64 kiB	1	32 kiB	1
SEP-PG	—	—	25 kiB	2	64 kiB	8	32 kiB	2
SMP	108 kiB	1	—	—	—	—	—	—
SMP-PG	108 kiB	2	—	—	—	—	—	—
HY	25 kiB	1	8 kiB	1	32 kiB	1	16 kiB	1
HY-PG	32 kiB	2	25 kiB	2	25 kiB	4	32 kiB	2

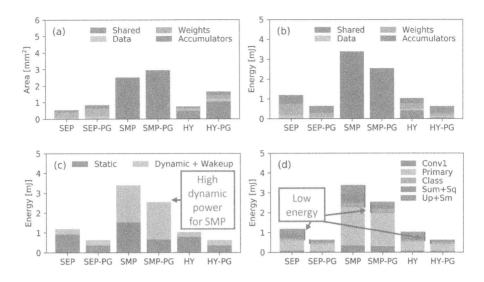

Figure 3.38: Google's CapsNet results for different components of the *DESCNet* memory configurations: (**a**) Area breakdown, (**b**) Energy breakdown, (**c**) Static vs. dynamic energy consumption, (**d**) Energy breakdown of the different operations of the CapsNet inference.

(on average $1.6nJ$), which appears during the transitions between *OFF* and *ON*, is low.

Energy Breakdown for the Different Operations of the CapsNet Inference (Figure 3.38d): Though the absolute values vary, the relative proportions of the energy consumption by different operations of the CapsNet inference remain approximately similar across different memory designs. The highest portion of energy comes from the *PrimaryCaps (Prim)* layer since it has a high memory utilization and frequent access to it. As it requires most of the available memory, the power-gating potential is limited. On the contrary, the energy consumed by the dynamic routing operations (i.e., *Sum+Squash, Update+Softmax*) is significantly lower for the *-PG* organizations.

3.4.6.2 *Results for DeepCaps (Area and Energy of the On-Chip Memory)*

Similarly to the above-discussed results for the Google's CapsNet, detailed evaluations are also conducted for the DeepCaps. Figure 3.39 shows the solutions in the area vs. energy space, for 215 693 different memory design organizations. The selected solutions with memory size and number of sectors are reported in Table 3.9. Note that the high-energy solutions have only 1 sector (i.e., the power-gating cannot be applied), the high-area solutions have the size of the shared memory equal to $8MiB$, while the solutions with a low area and low energy consumption have a shared memory with a size lower than or equal to $256kiB$. Compared to the CapsNet, the DeepCaps needs larger memory sizes to efficiently handle large-scale and more complex computations.

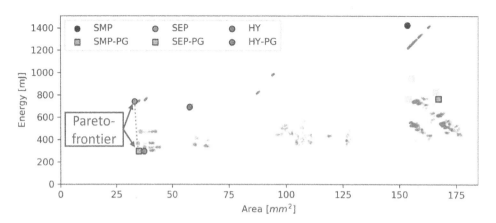

Figure 3.39: Design space exploration results of the *DESCNet* memory configurations for the DeepCaps.

As a consequence, although allowing to explore more different solutions, having larger memory sizes implies higher area and energy consumption; see results in Figure 3.40. Regarding the area, an interesting result is, as shown in Figure 3.40a, the lower area of the *HY-PG* compared to the *HY*, despite the power-gating circuitry. This is due to the different sizes of shared memory and accumulators, which are the most impactful memories between the two organizations.

The energy consumption for the *-PG* organization is significantly lower than the *non-PG* counterparts due to a heterogeneous usage of the memories across different operations of the DeepCaps. Hence, applying power-gating reduces the static energy not only for the dynamic routing operations but also for the ConvCaps2D computations, whose contribution is the highest, as shown in Figure 3.40d.

In a similar way as noticed for the Google's CapsNet, for the DeepCaps, the *HY-PG* is the solution with the lowest energy consumption, the *SEP* organization has the lowest area and the *SEP-PG* is another organization belonging to the Pareto-frontier.

TABLE 3.9: Selected memory configurations for the DeepCaps.

Mem	Shared		Data		Weight		Acc	
	SZ	SC	SZ	SC	SZ	SC	SZ	SC
SEP	—	—	256 kiB	1	128 kiB	1	8 MiB	1
SEP-PG	—	—	256 kiB	8	128 kiB	16	8 MiB	16
SMP	8 MiB	1	—	—	—	—	—	—
SMP-PG	8 MiB	8	—	—	—	—	—	—
HY	2 MiB	1	108 kiB	1	8 kiB	1	4 MiB	1
HY-PG	128 kiB	2	128 kiB	8	64 kiB	8	8 MiB	16
HY, P_S=1	4 MiB	1	256 kiB	1	8 kiB	1	2 MiB	1
HY-PG, P_S=1	4 MiB	8	256 kiB	8	128 kiB	16	2 MiB	4

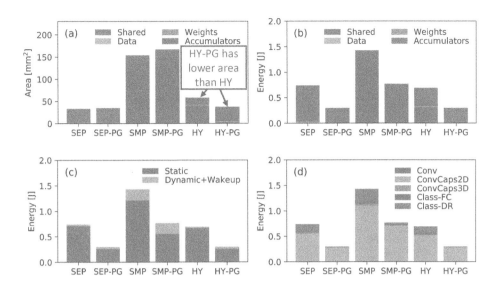

Figure 3.40: DeepCaps results for different components of the *DESCNet* memory configurations: **(a)** Area breakdown, **(b)** Energy breakdown, **(c)** Static vs. dynamic energy consumption, **(d)** Energy breakdown of the different operations of the DeepCaps inference.

3.4.6.3 DSE for the HY-PG Design Option With Size-Constrained Memory for DeepCaps

Motivated by the observation that the shared memory size significantly impacts the efficiency (see Figure 3.39), and since embedded systems might have size-constrained memory, we extend the analysis by exploring the HY-PG architectural organizations with a memory constraint. More specifically, we performed a DSE by constraining the maximum size of the shared memory. Moreover, the memory usage patterns and partitions show that the shared memory of the *HY* and *HY-PG* design options do not always require having three ports, because, for some solutions, the shared memory only needs to store one or two different types of values.

In this regard, in this analysis, we also explored the space of the *HY-PG* solutions with constrained shared memory ports (P_S). Figure 3.41 shows their tradeoffs between area and energy consumption, for 113 337 different memory configurations. The most efficient solutions in Figure 3.41a have a size of the 1-port shared memory equal to 2 *MiB* and 4 *MiB*. The worst results are obtained by combining a shared memory of 4 *MiB* with an accumulator memory of 8 *MiB*. Note, despite having a smaller-sized shared memory, the solutions with the 1-port shared memory of size 128 *kiB* and 256 *kiB* are relatively less efficient. It implies that such a size of the shared memory can couple more efficiently with the rest of the system to achieve overall a lower area and energy consumption. Moreover, as clearly visible from Figure 3.41b, the area and energy efficiency are improved by having a lower P_S. The detailed memory configuration for the *HY* and *HY-PG* lowest-energy solutions are shown in the respective lines of Table 3.9.

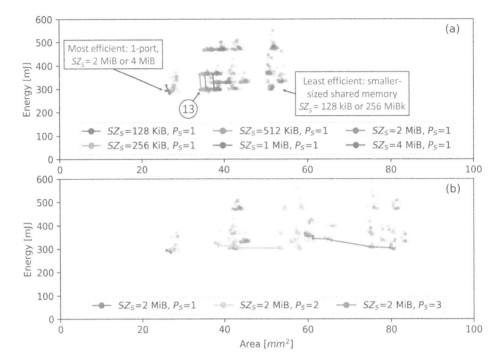

Figure 3.41: Design space exploration results for the *HY-PG DESCNet* memory configurations for the DeepCaps, having constraints on the size and number of ports of the shared memory.

3.4.6.4 *Impact of the Memory on the Complete CapsNet Accelerator Architecture*

Based on the evaluations performed in the previous sections, we select two Pareto-optimal *DESCNet* architectures for the CapsNet, which are *SEP* and *HY-PG*. The choice of these organizations is strategic because they represent the Pareto-optimal solutions with the lowest area and the lowest energy, respectively. Note that there is no performance loss compared to the CapsNet and DeepCaps executed on the baseline *CapsAcc*. We synthesize the complete architecture of the DNN accelerator executing CapsNets for the MNIST dataset and DeepCaps on the CIFAR10 dataset in a 45nm CMOS technology library, using the ASIC design flow with the Synopsys Design Compiler.

The detailed area and energy estimations of the complete on-chip architectures for the Google's CapsNet, comprising the accelerator and the on-chip memories with *SEP* and *HY-PG* organizations are shown in Figures 3.42 and 3.43, respectively.

When comparing the initial design as discussed in Figure 3.31 version (b) with the *SEP* (Figure 3.42a), the total on-chip memory energy is reduced by 65% and the on-chip memory area by 91%. Compared to version (a), our *DESCNet SEP* incurs 78% reduced energy and 47% reduced area for the complete accelerator.

Our proposed *DESCNet HY-PG* organization reduces the on-chip energy by 82% and the on-chip area by 35%, compared to the version (b) while reducing the total energy and the total area by 79% and 40% compared to version (a), respectively.

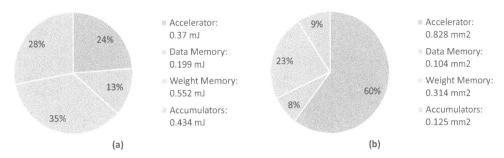

Figure 3.42: **(a)** Energy and **(b)** area breakdown of our CapsNet inference architecture using **SEP** memory.

Consequently, compared to version (a), which corresponds to the state-of-the-art design of CapsAcc, our proposed approach can provide total energy and area reductions, comprising accelerator, on-chip memory and off-chip memory, of up to 79% and 47%, respectively, without any performance loss.

Energy and area estimations of the complete on-chip architecture executing the DeepCaps, using the *SEP-PG* organization, are reported in Figure 3.44. The graphs show a clear dominance of the accumulator memory on both the on-chip area and the on-chip energy due to its large size. On the contrary, the *HY-PG*, P_S=1 organization results reported in Figure 3.45 show a relatively more balanced distribution of the energy and area between the accumulator and the shared memory. As discussed before, since the original baseline architecture of CapsAcc cannot execute the DeepCaps for the CIFAR10 dataset, we cannot compare their work with our *DESCNet* design deploying the DeepCaps. This also shows that our memory sub-system can indeed successfully support DeepCaps, enabling its memory-efficient acceleration, which is not possible for the original baseline CapsAcc.

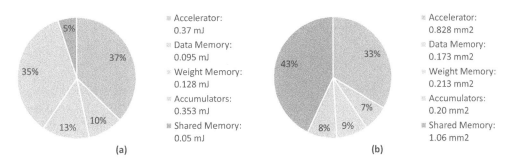

Figure 3.43: **(a)** Energy and **(b)** area breakdown of our CapsNet inference architecture using **HY-PG** memory.

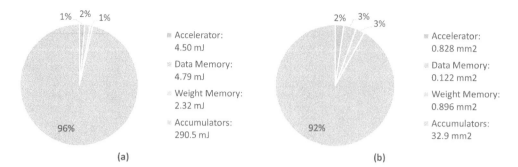

Figure 3.44: (a) Energy and (b) area breakdown of our DeepCaps inference architecture using **SEP-PG** memory.

3.4.6.5 Results Summary and Discussion

Table 3.10 shows the detailed results of the area and energy consumption for the different *DESCNet* architectures obtained by our DSE for the CapsNet and the DeepCaps. The following **key observations** can be derived from our analyses.

- Despite many efforts in optimizing the computational arrays of the DNN accelerators, more fruitful areas and energy savings are obtained when the optimizations are applied to the memory, as showcased in this section with the DNN accelerators executing both the Google's CapsNets and the DeepCaps.

- Having large and shared multi-port memories, where different values are stored, e.g., the *SMP* organization, is in general, a bad design choice, because of the resource-hungry hardware overhead for handling heterogeneous accesses, which are not necessary if we systematically study the application-driven memory resource requirements. Indeed, having $SZ_S \leq 256\ kiB$ can relatively jointly reduce the energy and the area, compared to other solutions with larger SZ_S.

- For a certain set of solutions belonging to the *HY* and *HY-PG* design options, the multi-port shared memory can be replaced by an equivalent single-port,

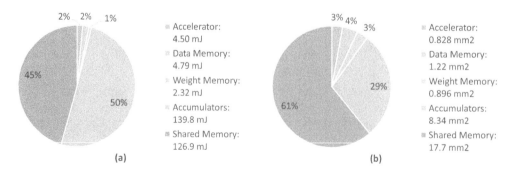

Figure 3.45: (a) Energy and (b) area breakdown of our DeepCaps inference architecture using **HY-PG, $P_S=1$** memory.

TABLE 3.10: Area and energy consumption results for different *DESCNet* architectural organizations.

NN	Mem	Shared Mem				Weight Mem				Data Mem				Accumulator Mem			
		Area [mm2]	Dynamic Energy [mJ]	Static Energy [mJ]	Wakeup Energy [nJ]	Area [mm2]	Dynamic Energy [mJ]	Static Energy [mJ]	Wakeup Energy [nJ]	Area [mm2]	Dynamic Energy [mJ]	Static Energy [mJ]	Wakeup Energy [nJ]	Area [mm2]	Dynamic Energy [mJ]	Static Energy [mJ]	Wakeup Energy [nJ]
CapsNet	SEP	—	—	—	—	0.314	0.051	0.501	—	0.104	0.011	0.188	—	0.125	0.196	0.238	—
	SEP-PG	—	—	—	—	0.469	0.053	0.135	0.041	0.173	0.012	0.083	0.048	0.200	0.205	0.148	0.064
	SMP	2.521	1.859	1.529	—	—	—	—	—	—	—	—	—	—	—	—	—
	SMP-PG	2.958	1.875	0.668	0.352	—	—	—	—	—	—	—	—	—	—	—	—
	HY	0.519	0.008	0.348	—	0.125	0.044	0.238	—	0.041	0.009	0.068	—	0.067	0.120	0.130	—
	HY-PG	1.061	0.004	0.046	0.080	0.213	0.045	0.083	0.032	0.173	0.012	0.083	0.048	0.200	0.205	0.148	0.064
DeepCaps	SEP	—	—	—	—	0.617	0.039	12.172	—	1.165	0.098	22.266	—	31.392	34.268	673.562	—
	SEP-PG	—	—	—	—	0.896	0.040	2.277	0.044	1.223	0.099	4.695	0.247	32.905	34.464	256.029	0.642
	SMP	153.474	213.961	1214.223	—	—	—	—	—	—	—	—	—	—	—	—	—
	SMP-PG	167.077	214.115	555.102	1.234	—	—	—	—	—	—	—	—	—	—	—	—
	HY	41.067	3.143	315.671	—	0.041	0.003	0.810	—	0.547	0.074	10.453	—	16.168	20.954	339.713	—
	HY-PG	3.293	0.125	1.211	0.464	0.469	0.019	1.619	0.041	0.816	0.079	3.898	0.064	32.905	34.464	256.029	0.642
	HY, $P_S=1$	16.168	6.108	339.713	—	0.041	0.003	0.810	—	1.165	0.098	22.266	—	8.949	11.037	173.698	—
	HY-PG, $P_S=1$	17.731	6.019	120.913	0.642	0.896	0.040	2.277	0.044	1.223	0.099	4.695	0.247	8.338	11.091	128.696	0.642

offering further energy and area reductions due to a more balanced memory breakdown between the accumulator and the shared memory.

- Employing efficient on-chip SPM memory organization architectures (e.g., *SEP*, *SEP-PG*, and *HY-PG*) significantly reduces the hardware resource requirements, thereby bearing the development of DNN accelerator executing complex operations such as the CapsNets in resource-constrained scenarios, which are typical for IoT-edge devices.

3.4.7 Summary

Motivated by the analyses showing that a significant amount of energy can be saved by designing a specialized memory design, the *DESCNet* SPM architecture is proposed. Different architecture designs are explored to minimize the off-chip memory accesses while efficiently feeding the data to the hardware accelerator executing CapsNets inference at high throughput. Its application-driven memory power management unit further reduces the leakage power. To enable the CapsNets deployment on even smaller resource- and memory-constrained edge devices, low-precision computations can be enabled by weight and feature map quantization, as demonstrated in Section 3.5.

3.5 Q-CAPSNETS: A SPECIALIZED FRAMEWORK FOR QUANTIZING CAPSNETS

CapsNets require intense computations and are difficult to be deployed in their original form on resource-constrained edge devices. This section presents *Q-CapsNets*, the first specialized framework for quantizing CapsNet models, to enable their efficient edge implementations. We evaluate our framework for several benchmarks. On the DeepCaps for the CIFAR10 dataset, the framework reduces the memory footprint by 6.2×, with only 0.15% accuracy loss. Our methodology is desirable for employing CapsNet inference at the edge, because it significantly reduces the computational workload and the CapsNet memory footprint, with minimal accuracy loss.

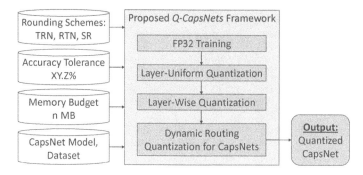

Figure 3.46: An overview of our quantization framework.

3.5.1 System Overview

Reducing the wordlength of weights and feature maps is extremely important for improving the energy efficiency. A too short wordlength lowers the accuracy of the CapsNets. It is typically an undesired outcome from the end-user perspective. To find an efficient tradeoff between the memory footprint, the energy consumption, and the classification accuracy, we propose the novel Q-CapsNets framework (see Figure 3.46). It explores different layer-wise and operation-wise arithmetic precisions to obtain the quantized version of a given CapsNet, with maximum accuracy tolerance and memory budget specified as constraints to the framework. Our approach optimizes in particular the dynamic routing, a peculiar feature of the CapsNets involving iterative and computationally expensive operations, with a significant impact on the energy consumption.

In this section, our novel contributions are:

- We propose a specialized framework for systematically quantizing CapsNets, given a certain accuracy tolerance (compared to the full-precision CapsNet) and a certain memory budget for storing the weights.

- Since an expensive part of CapsNets is the dynamic routing process, we further specialize in the search for the numerical precision for the operations of the dynamic routing. *A key advantage of using our framework*, compared to traditional DNN quantization methods, is that, as we will demonstrate in our experiments, *the number of bits for routing capsules can be further reduced* compared to the wordlengths of the other operations.

- We test our framework on the CapsNet model [236] on the MNIST and Fashion-MNIST datasets, and on the DeepCaps model [220] on the MNIST, FashionMNIST, and CIFAR10 datasets. For the latter dataset, the memory footprint is reduced by 6.2× with an accuracy loss of 0.15%.

3.5.2 Analysis of Area and Energy Consumption for Reduced Wordlength

Our overarching goal is to deploy CapsNets at the edge. The floating-point representation is abandoned by adopting a lighter fixed-point representation. Such

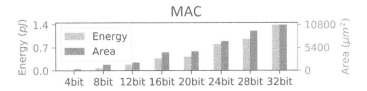

Figure 3.47: Energy consumption and area footprint for a fixed-point MAC unit with different wordlengths.

a wordlength reduction of the weights and activations of a CapsNet for computing the inference lightens the memory storage requirements. It might also significantly impact the energy consumption of the computational units. Therefore, we analyze energy consumption and area footprint of a MAC unit, which is the basic block of specialized CapsNet accelerators like the CapsAcc, and of hardware blocks that perform computationally complex operations, i.e., *squash* and *softmax*, which are needed during the CapsNet inference. Moreover, we design different versions of a MAC unit, a softmax module, and a squash module, varying their wordlength. We synthesize them in a 45nm CMOS technology with the Synopsys Design Compiler tool to measure their area and energy consumptions. Figure 3.47 shows that *the area and energy consumption of MAC units quadratically decrease w.r.t. the wordlength.* Such analyses motivate us to focus on minimizing the wordlength to reduce the energy consumption. The results shown in Figure 3.48 are obtained by varying the number of fractional bits while keeping a single bit for the integer part. As expected, *the softmax and the squash functions require more energy and area than a simple MAC operation.* The dependence on energy consumption and area footprint is related quadratically to the number of fractional bits. This effect further motivates us to reduce the number of bits used to execute the various operations of the CapsNet architectures.

3.5.3 Rounding Schemes

A fixed-point number has an integer part QI and a fractional part QF. Hence, it can be written as $\langle QI.QF \rangle$. The total number of bits, i.e., the wordlength N, is computed as $NI + NF$, which is the sum between the bits of the integer part and the fractional part. A fixed-point representation has precision $\epsilon = 2^{-NF}$, and its corresponding

Figure 3.48: Energy consumption and area footprint for fixed-point modules performing **(a)** the softmax and **(b)** the squash operations with different wordlengths.

range of representable numbers, in a two's complement format, is $[-2^{NI-1}, 2^{NI-1} - 2^{-NF}]$.

The *rounding operation* converts a floating-point or a large fixed-point number into a fixed-point number with shorter wordlength. Next, we present the most common rounding schemes.

The **Truncation (TRN)** simply removes all the extra digits from the fractional part, i.e., $x_q = \lfloor x \rfloor$. If we assume uniformly distributed numbers, the truncation introduces a negative average error (bias), defined as $x_q - x$.

The **Round-to-Nearest (RTN)** sets a rule for approximating those values which fall precisely halfway between the two representable numbers. In particular, half-up rounding consists of rounding up these values. Considering uniformly distributed numbers, rounding up halfway values introduces a negative average error, which is lower than introducing a simple truncation, as shown in Equation (3.7).

$$x_q = \lfloor x + \frac{\epsilon}{2} \rfloor \tag{3.7}$$

The **Stochastic Rounding (SR)** is defined as in Equation (3.8), where $P \in [0, 1)$ is a uniformly distributed random number. The SR scheme is unbiased, but the most compute-intensive from the hardware perspective because it requires the generation of random numbers.

$$\begin{cases} \lfloor x \rfloor & \text{if } P \geq \frac{x - \lfloor x \rfloor}{\epsilon} \\ \lfloor x + \frac{\epsilon}{2} \rfloor & \text{if } P < \frac{x - \lfloor x \rfloor}{\epsilon} \end{cases} \tag{3.8}$$

3.5.4 Q-CapsNets Framework

Our framework can progressively reduce the numerical precision of weights and activations in the CapsNet inference. In the first stage, we start with customizing the techniques for CapsNets, which are also applicable to traditional DNNs. Afterward, we employ a specialized approach for CapsNets, which is tailored for the loops of the dynamic routing. The inputs of our framework are:

- *A CapsNet architecture*, together with the training and test dataset, and its associated architecture-specific hyperparameters.

- *A library of rounding schemes* to employ when quantizing the data.

- Lowering the numerical precision reduces the accuracy reached by the model. Therefore, a tolerance acc_{TOL} on the loss of accuracy must be set to have a margin for quantizing the network. The target accuracy acc_{target} is computed in Equation (3.9).

$$acc_{target} = acc_{FP32} \cdot (1 - acc_{TOL}) \tag{3.9}$$

- *Maximum memory budget* that can be occupied for storing the quantized weights and biases.

Our Q-CapsNets framework aims at satisfying both requirements on memory usage and accuracy. An effective way to reduce a given model's memory usage is through aggressively quantizing the weights. We perform this operation in steps (1) and (2). Once the memory budget is satisfied, we reduce the numerical precision of the weights and activations if there is still some accuracy loss budget. Afterward, the framework returns the `model_satisfied`. Otherwise, if a solution that satisfies both the requirements of accuracy and memory usage cannot be found, our framework returns two sub-optimal solutions:

I `model_accuracy`: A quantized CapsNet model with the target accuracy and the minimum memory footprint (e.g., slightly higher than the budget);

II `model_memory`: A quantized CapsNet that satisfies the memory requirements and achieves the maximum accuracy (e.g., slightly lower than the target).

3.5.4.1 Step-by-Step Description of the Framework

As a preliminary step, a given input CapsNet is trained in full-precision (32-bits floating-point), whose accuracy is denoted as acc_{FP32}. From acc_{FP32} and the accuracy tolerance (acc_{TOL}, input of the framework), we compute the target accuracy (acc_{target}) as in Equation (3.9). The procedure followed for quantizing a given CapsNet (see Figure 3.49 and Algorithm 10) is composed of the following steps:

1) **Layer-Uniform Quantization of weights and activations**: We convert all weights and activations to fixed-point arithmetic, with a 1-bit integer part and Q_w-bit and Q_a-bit fractional parts, respectively. Afterward, we further reduce their precision in a uniform way (e.g., $Q_w = Q_a$). In this stage, only 5% of the acc_{TOL} is consumed. To find the correct wordlength of Q_w and Q_a, we use a binary search algorithm [121].

2) **Memory Requirements Fulfillment**: In this stage, we quantize only the CapsNet weights. Following the idea of Raghu et al. [218] that perturbations to

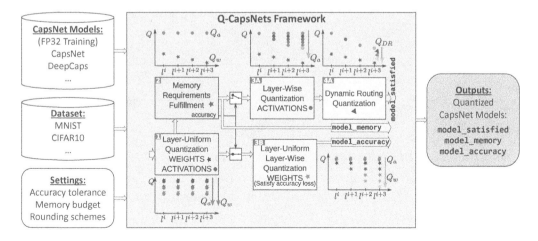

Figure 3.49: *Flow of Our Framework for Quantizing CapsNets.*

Algorithm 10: Pseudo-Code of Our Q-CapsNets Framework.

---

1 **Procedure** Q-CapsNets(acc_{TOL}, *memory_budget*)
    `/* Full Precision training                                */`
2   model, acc_{FP32} ← train(CapsNet);
3     $acc_{target} = acc_{FP32}(1 - acc_{TOL})$;
    `/* Step 1) Layer-Uniform Quantization of weights &`
       `activations                                       */`
4     $acc_{step1} = acc_{FP32}(1 - acc_{TOL} \cdot 0.05)$;
5   model, Q ← BinarySearch(model, (weights, act), $Q_{init} = 32$,
      $acc_{min} = acc_{step1}$);
6     $(Q_{w,s1})_l = Q$; $(Q_{a,s1})_l = Q \; \forall l$;
    `/* Step 2) Memory requirements fulfillment          */`
7     $[(Q_{w,mm})_0, ..., (Q_{w,mm})_L]$ ← Equation (3.10)(params P,
      memory_budget);
8   model_memory, acc_{mm} ← test(quant(model, weights ← $Q_{w,mm}$,
      act ← $Q_{a,s1}$));
9   **if** $acc_{mm} > acc_{target}$ **then**
        `/* Step 3A) Layer-Wise Quantization of activations    */`
10   model, Q_a ← LayerWise(model, act, $Q_{init} = Q_{a,s1}$,
        $acc_{min} = acc_{target} + 0.5(acc_{mm} - acc_{target})$);
        `/* Step4A) Dynamic Routing Quantization              */`
11   **for** *each layer l with dynamic routing* **do**
12   model, $(Q_a)_l$ ← DRquant(model, model.DRact$_l$, $Q_{init} = (Q_a)_l$,
            $acc_{min} = acc_{target}$);
13   **end**
14   **return** model_satisfied;
15   **else**
        `/* Step3B) Layer-Uniform and Layer-Wise Quantization of`
         `weights                                           */`
16   model, Q_w ← BinarySearch(model, weights, $Q_{init} = Q_{w,1}$,
        $acc_{min} = acc_{target}$);
17   model_accuracy, Q_w ← LayerWise(model, weights, $Q_{init} = Q_w$,
        $acc_{min} = acc_{target}$;
18   **return** model_memory, model_accuracy;
19   **end**
20 **end**

---

weights in the final layers can be more costly than perturbations in the earlier layers, we set for each layer l its respective Q_w such that $(Q_w)_{l+1} = (Q_w)_l - 1$. Afterward, we can compute the correct Q_w as the maximum integer value that satisfies Equation (3.10), where L is the total number of layers, M is the memory budget, and P^l is the number of parameters (weights) in the layer l.

$$\sum_{l=0}^{L-1} \left(P^l \cdot ((Q_w)_0 - l) \right) \leq M \tag{3.10}$$

With this rule, we can obtain a quantized CapsNet model, denoted as `model_memory`, which fulfills the memory requirements. Afterward, we test the accuracy of the `model_memory`, denoted as acc_{mm} and compare it to acc_{target}. Based on its results, the next stage can take two directions. If acc_{mm} is higher, we continue to (3A) for further quantization steps. Otherwise, it jumps to (3B).

3A) **Layer-Wise Quantization of activations**: To quantize the activations, we start from the initial Q_a, as computed during step (1). As shown in Algorithm 11, we proceed in a layer-wise fashion. First, each layer of the CapsNet (except the first one) is selected, and Q_a is decreased until the minimum value for which the accuracy remains higher than acc_{target}. Afterward, the wordlength of the first two layers is fixed, while we further reduce Q_a for all but the first layers. We repeat this step iteratively until the Q_a for the last layer is set.

Algorithm 11: Algorithm for Layer-wise Quantization

---

1   **Given**: Q_{init} initial number of quantization bits to start the algorithm, acc_{min} minimum value of accuracy that can be reached;

2   **Procedure** LayerWise(*model, params, Q_{init}, acc_{min}*)

3      $Q = [(Q)_0, (Q)_1, ..., (Q)_L], (Q)_l = Q_{init}$;

4      $StartL = 1$;

5   **while** $StartL < L$ **do**

6          $acc = 100$;

7   **while** $acc \geq acc_{min}$ **do**

8              $(Q)_l \leftarrow (Q)_l - 1, l \in [StartL, ...,L]$;

9   model, acc = test(quant(model, params $\leftarrow Q$));

10   **end**

11          $(Q)_l \leftarrow (Q)_l + 1, l \in [StartL, ...,L]$;

12          $StartL \leftarrow StartL + 1$;

13   **end**

14   **return** quant(model, params $\leftarrow Q$), Q;

15 **end**

4A) **Dynamic Routing Quantization**: The dynamic routing is computationally expensive due to the complex operations, such as *squash* and *softmax*, performed iteratively. Therefore, the wordlength of its arrays might be different compared to other CapsNet layers. This step only operates on the data involving the *squash* and *softmax* operations. As shown in Figure 3.50 and Algorithm 12, a specialized quantization process is performed in this step. The operators of

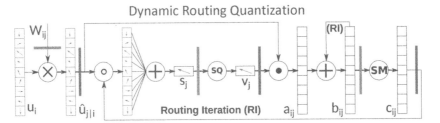

Figure 3.50: Quantization of a capsule layer with dynamic routing. The colored bars show the arrays that are rounded and quantized. In green, the weights are quantized with Q_w bits. In blue, the activations are quantized with Q_a bits. In red, data are more aggressively quantized with Q_{DR} bits. The precision is lowered before compute-intensive and complex functions (squash, softmax).

the dynamic routing may be quantized more than the other activations (i.e., with a wordlength lower than Q_a, which we call Q_{DR}). The quantized CapsNet model generated at the end of this step is denoted as `model_satisfied`.

Algorithm 12: Algorithm for Dynamic Routing Quantization

---

1 **Given**: Q_{init} initial number of quantization bits to start the algorithm,
   acc_{min} minimum value of accuracy that can be reached;
2 **Procedure** DRquant(*model, params, Q_{init}, acc_{min}*)
3    $Q = Q_{init}$;
4    $acc = 100$;
5   **while** $acc \geq acc_{min}$ **do**
6       $Q \leftarrow Q - 1$;
7   model, acc = test(quant(model, params $\leftarrow Q$));
8   **end**
9    $Q \leftarrow Q + 1$;
10   **return** quant(model, params $\leftarrow Q$), Q;
11 **end**

3B) **Layer-Uniform ad Layer-Wise Quantization of weights**: Starting from the step (1) outcome, we quantize the weights, first in a uniform and then in a layer-wise manner (as in step 3A) until reaching acc_{target}. The resulting CapsNet model (`model_accuracy`) is returned as the output of the framework, together with `model_memory`, as generated in step (2).

3.5.4.2 Rounding Scheme Selection

For every rounding scheme from the given library, its corresponding quantized model is generated. Hence, *our framework executes Algorithm 10 for each rounding scheme in parallel*. Due to different rounding errors, our framework may execute Path A for one rounding scheme, while it executes Path B for another scheme. After executing all branches, we select the best rounding scheme within the library using the following criteria, based on whether the algorithm has followed Path A or Path B.

A) **There are some models generated from Path A:**

1) Models from Path B are discarded.

2) The model with lower memory is selected.

3) With the same memory, the model with fewer bits used to represent activations is selected.

4) With the same memory and bits for the activations, the CapsNet model with the simplest rounding scheme is selected, e.g., with truncation, round-to-nearest-even, and stochastic rounding. Note that while the first one requires the deletion of the LSBs, the last one needs more complex operations to decide the direction of the rounding.

B) **There are models only from Path B:**

1) In this case, two models are returned. Selecting from `memory_model`, the model with the highest-possible accuracy is returned.

2) Selecting from `accuracy_model`, the model with the lowest-possible memory is returned.

3) If more than one model has the exact same highest accuracy and the lowest memory, the simplest rounding scheme is preferred to break the tie.

3.5.5 Evaluation of our Q-CapsNets Framework

3.5.5.1 Experimental Setup

We implement the Q-CapsNets framework in PyTorch [204], and we run it on two Nvidia GeForce RTX 2080 Ti GPUs. We test it on the Google's CapsNet model [236], i.e., the ShallowCaps, for the MNIST [118] and FashionMNIST [284] datasets, and on the DeepCaps model [220] for the MNIST, FashionMNIST and CIFAR10 [112] datasets. For the full precision training, the following data augmentation is executed:

- MNIST: the images are randomly shifted by a maximum of two pixels and rotated by 2 degrees;

- FashionMNIST: the images are randomly shifted by 2 pixels and horizontally flipped with a probability of 0.2;

- CIFAR10: the original images of size 32×32 are resized to 64×64 using bilinear interpolation to allow deeper networks, as reported in the original DeepCaps paper [220]. The images are also randomly shifted by 5 pixels, rotated by 2 degrees, and horizontally flipped with a probability of 0.5.

No data augmentation is conducted on the images for testing.

3.5.5.2 Quantized ShallowCaps for MNIST and FashionMNIST Datasets

The ShallowCaps architecture is trained in full precision (FP32) on the MNIST dataset for 100 epochs and batch size 100. We employ an exponential decay learning policy, with an initial learning rate of 0.001, 2 000 decay steps, and 0.96 decay rate. Its achieved test accuracy is 99.67%.

Afterward, the framework proceeds as described in Algorithm 10, intending to satisfy the memory and accuracy requirements concurrently. Since the algorithm has a conditional path, we present two examples that correspond to the execution of the different branches of the algorithm.

Test of the Path A: For the first set of experiments, we test the Path A of the framework, that is, when both the memory and accuracy constraints are satisfied. Since the memory requirement at FP32 is 217Mbit, we set the memory budget equal to 45Mbit, with an accuracy tolerance of 0.2%. The results in Figure 3.51 [Q1] show that the `model_satisfied` reduces the weights memory footprint by $4.11\times$ compared to the FP32 model and has an accuracy equal to 99.52%. Along with the reduction of the weight memory (W mem), we report the reduction of the activation memory (A mem). For `model_satisfied`, this memory footprint is reduced to $2.72\times$.

Test of the Path B: Since our framework executes Path B if it cannot find a solution that satisfies both requirements, for its testing purpose, we specify very low memory budgets as the input. The results of our experiments, shown in Figure 3.51, indicate that to satisfy the memory requirements, weights of `model_memory` [Q3] are set to very low wordlengths, causing an extreme reduction of accuracy. To satisfy the accuracy requirements in `memory_accuracy` [Q2], weights are reduced to the minimum possible wordlength.

Similar sequences of tests, with a set of accuracy tolerance and memory budget specifications, are performed on the ShallowCaps architecture for the FashionMNIST dataset. Our experiment results are reported in Table 3.11.

3.5.5.3 Quantized DeepCaps for MNIST, FashionMNIST, and CIFAR10 Datasets

Several tests are conducted on the DeepCaps architecture. We mainly focus on the results obtained with the SR scheme since it outperforms the other (simpler)

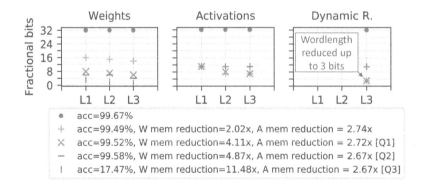

Figure 3.51: Q-CapsNets results of the ShallowCaps for the MNIST dataset.

TABLE 3.11: Q-CapsNet's accuracy results, weight (W) memory and activation (A) memory reduction for the ShallowCaps and for the DeepCaps on MNIST, Fashion-MNIST, and CIFAR10 datasets.

Model	Dataset	Accuracy	W mem reduction	A mem reduction
ShallowCaps	MNIST	99.58%	4.87×	2.67×
ShallowCaps	MNIST	99.49%	2.02×	2.74×
ShallowCaps	FMNIST	92.76%	4.11×	2.49×
ShallowCaps	FMNIST	78.26%	6.69×	2.46×
DeepCaps	MNIST	99.55%	7.51×	4.00×
DeepCaps	MNIST	99.60%	4.59×	6.45×
DeepCaps	FMNIST	94.93%	6.4×	3.20×
DeepCaps	FMNIST	94.92%	4.59×	4.57×
DeepCaps	CIFAR10	91.11%	6.15×	2.50×
DeepCaps	CIFAR10	91.18%	3.71×	3.34×

rounding schemes. The DeepCaps trained in full-precision on the MNIST dataset achieves 99.75% accuracy, on par with the accuracy obtained in the original DeepCaps paper [220], while on the FashionMNIST, it obtains a 95.08% accuracy. Table 3.11 reports some key results obtained with the Q-CapsNets framework on these two datasets. Figure 3.52 reports graphically some key results obtained with the Q-CapsNets framework on the DeepCaps for the CIFAR10 dataset.

3.5.5.4 Results Discussion

By considering the accuracy and the occupied weight memory as the evaluation metrics, we noticed that the `model_satisfied` is usually Pareto-dominated by the `model_accuracy`, like for Q1 and Q2 in Figure 3.51, and of Q4 and Q5 in Figure 3.52. However, since Q1 and Q5 have shorter wordlengths for the activations and the dynamic routing compared to Q2 and Q4, respectively, the potential energy efficiency gains for its computations using MAC operators, *squash* and *softmax* are huge, even with a slight change in the activation memory. Note that the wordlength for the

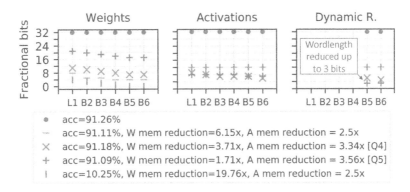

Figure 3.52: *Q-CapsNets results of the DeepCaps for CIFAR10 dataset.*

dynamic routing operations can be reduced up to 3 or 4 bits with minimal accuracy loss compared to the full-precision model. Such an outcome is due to a common feature of the dynamic routing. The operations of the coefficients (along with *squash* and *softmax*) are updated dynamically, thereby adapting to the quantization more efficiently than other layers like Conv Layer and PrimaryCaps. Therefore, these computations can tolerate a more aggressive quantization.

3.5.6   Summary

To enable efficient implementations of CapsNets on edge devices, the Q-CapsNets framework is proposed. It exploits the peculiar features of the CapsNets, including the operations involved in the dynamic routing, to enable precision reduction of the wordlength, based on user-defined accuracy and memory budgets. The obtained compact quantized CapsNet models can be deployed on target resource-constrained devices such as specialized CapsNet accelerators. As discussed in Section 3.6 and Section 3.7, further energy reductions in the execution of CapsNet inference can be achieved by approximating the computational hardware units.

3.6   RED-CANE: RESILIENCE ANALYSIS AND DESIGN OF CAPSNETS UNDER APPROXIMATIONS

Following the Approximate Computing trend of enabling energy-efficient designs, we conduct an extensive resilience analysis of the CapsNets inference subjected to approximation errors. Our methodology models the errors derived from the approximate components (like multipliers) and analyzes their impact on the classification accuracy of CapsNets. These analyses enable the selection of approximate components based on the resiliency of each operation of the CapsNet inference. We extend the TensorFlow framework to simulate the approximation noise injection (based on the models of the approximate components) at multiple computational operations of the CapsNet inference. Our results demonstrate that the CapsNets are more resilient to the errors injected in the computations involving the dynamic routing operations (the softmax and the update of the coefficients) rather than other stages like convolutions and activation functions. Our analysis is instrumental in designing efficient CapsNet hardware architectures with approximate components. To the best of our knowledge, it is the first proof-of-concept for designing approximations on the specialized CapsNet hardware.

3.6.1   System Overview

The proposed *ReD-CaNe* methodology, as shown in Figure 3.53, analyzes the resilience of CapsNets under approximations. First, we devise a noise injection model for simulating real scenarios of errors deriving from approximate hardware units like multipliers, which are very common within MAC operations for the matrix multiplications of capsules. Afterward, we analyze the error resiliency of the CapsNets by building a systematic methodology for injecting noise into the operations of the CapsNet inference and evaluating their impact on the accuracy. The outcome of

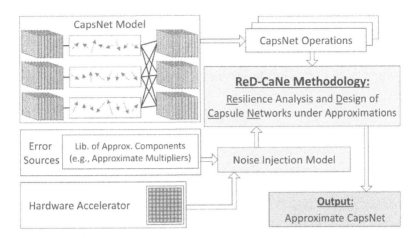

Figure 3.53: Overview of our ReD-CaNe methodology. The novel contributions are shown in blue boxes.

such investigations will produce guidelines for designing and selecting approximate components based on the resiliency of each operation. At the output, our methodology generates an approximated version of a given CapsNet, for achieving energy-efficient inference.

In a nutshell, our novel contributions are:

- We analyze and *model the noise injections* that can be generated by different approximate arithmetic components, e.g., multipliers.

- We devise *ReD-CaNe*, a novel methodology for analyzing the Resilience and Designing Capsule Networks under approximations, by systematically injecting noise into different operations of the CapsNet inference and by measuring the accuracy. The approximated components are chosen based on the resilience level of the different operations of the CapsNet inference.

- We test our methodology on the DeepCaps model for the CIFAR10, MNIST, and SVHN datasets, and on the CapsNet model for the MNIST and Fashion-MNIST datasets. Our results show that the least resilient operations are the convolutions in CapsLayers, while *the dynamic routing operations of the Caps3D and ClassCaps layers are relatively more resilient.*

3.6.2 Modeling the Errors as Injected Noise

3.6.2.1 *Error Sources*

In a generic DNN application, errors can occur due to different sources like hardware approximations (e.g., approximate multipliers), software approximations (e.g., quantization), transient faults (e.g., bit flips due to particle strikes), and permanent faults (e.g., stuck-at-one and stuck-at-zero). In this work, we focus on approximation errors as we target optimizations for energy efficiency.

If specialized hardware accelerators perform the CapsNet inference, a fixed-point representation is typically preferred, compared to the floating-point counterpart [96]. Therefore, a floating-point value x, represented in a b-bit fixed-point arithmetic, is mapped to a range $[0 : s^b - 1]$. The quantization function Q is defined in Equation (3.11).

$$Q(x) = \frac{x - \min(x)}{\max(x) - \min(x)} \cdot (2^b - 1) \tag{3.11}$$

In this work, we implement the CapsNets with floating-point arithmetic, but *the behavior of approximate fixed-point components is simulated by modifying their values according to the quantization effect*. Therefore, we focus on modeling the errors subjected to the employment of approximate components in CapsNet hardware accelerators.

3.6.2.2 Analysis of Different Operations in CapsNets

We investigate which hardware components have the highest impact on the total energy consumption of the CapsNets' computational blocks. Table 3.12 reports the number of operations occurring in the computational path of the DeepCaps inference and the energy consumption per operation. The latter has been evaluated by synthesizing the implementation with 8-bit fixed-point operations, in a 45nm CMOS technology node with the Synopsys Design Compiler tool. The last two columns also report the estimated total energy share for each operation and their respective percentage. The multipliers count for more than 96% of the total energy share of the computational path of the DeepCaps. The occurrences of the addition are also high, but they consume only 3% of the total energy share due to their reduced complexity compared to the multipliers. Hence, it is important to first explore the energy savings from approximating the multiplier operations, as we target in this work.

In the following, we investigate the energy optimization potential of employing approximate components. As a case study, we select the NGR approximate multiplier and the 5LT approximate adder from the EvoApprox8B library [179]. The results in Figure 3.54 demonstrates that approximating only the multipliers (XM) may save more than 28% energy compared to the accurate implementation (Acc). Due to the low energy share relative to the additions, the advantage of employing approximate

TABLE 3.12: Number of operations, unit, and total energy consumption of different basic operations of the DeepCaps.

OPERATION	# OPS	Unit Energy [pJ]	Total Energy [uJ]	%age
Addition	1.91 G	0.0202	38.57	3.22%
Multiplication	2.15 G	0.5354	1 153.5	96.37%
Division	4.17 M	1.0717	4.474	0.37%
Exponential	175 K	0.1578	0.0276	0.03%
Square Root	502 K	0.7805	0.3920	< 0.01%

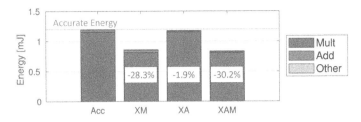

Figure 3.54: Optimization potential by applying approximate components in CapsNets.

adders (XA) or approximate adders and multipliers (XAM) is negligible compared to Acc and XM solutions, respectively.

Motivated by the above analyses, in the following, without loss of generality and for the ease of proof-of-concept development, *we focus our studies on the approximate multipliers since they have a high impact on the energy consumption, opening huge optimization potentials.*

3.6.2.3 Error Profiles for the Approximate Hardware Multipliers

We selected 35 approximate multipliers of the EvoApprox8B library [179] and analyzed the distributions of their erroneous products P' compared to the accurate product P of an 8-bit multiplier. The arithmetic error is computed in Equation (3.12), where a, b denote the inputs to the multipliers.

$$\Delta_{P'} = \{\forall a, b \in I : P'(a, b) - P(a, b)\} \tag{3.12}$$

The distributions of the arithmetic errors are computed considering to have a single multiplier, a sequence of 9 MAC units, and a sequence of 81 MAC units, with $|I| = 10^5$ random samples per each scenario. These studies are performed for estimating the accumulated error of a convolution with 3×3 and 9×9 filters, respectively. We selected these values since they reflect the size of the Conv kernels of the DeepCaps and CapsNet.

The majority of the components (i.e., 31 of 35) exhibit a Gaussian-like distribution of the arithmetic error Δ, with a mean value m and a standard deviation std. The error distributions of two approximated multipliers from the library are shown in Figure 3.55. Since the remaining 29 elements from the EvoApprox8B library with a Gaussian-like distribution show similar behaviors, we only report these two approximate multipliers.

Modeling a Gaussian noise Δ when employing b-bit fixed-point approximate components in a CapsNet with floating-point operations is an open research challenge. We propose to adjust the amount of noise w.r.t. the range R of values of a given array X. Therefore, we introduce the noise magnitude (NM) to indicate the standard deviation (std) of the noise Δ scaled w.r.t. $R(X)$, and the noise average (NA) to indicate the mean value (m) of the noise Δ scaled w.r.t. $R(X)$. The formulas for NM and NA are shown in Equation (3.13) and Equation (3.14), respectively.

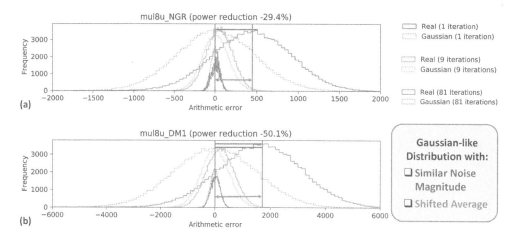

Figure 3.55: Artimetic error (w.r.t. accurate 8-bit multiplier) distributions and their interpolations w.r.t. Gaussian noise by having an approximate multiplier from the EvoApprox8B library. (a) Distribution for the NGR multiplier. (b) Distribution for the DM1 multiplier.

$$NM(\Delta_M) = \frac{stdev(\Delta_X)}{R(X)} \tag{3.13}$$

$$NA(\Delta_M) = \frac{m(\Delta_X)}{R(X)} \tag{3.14}$$

Since the inputs of the components (I) employed in CapsNets typically have specific distribution patterns, the NM of the approximate component depends on the application. This implies that the NM can significantly change for different CapsNet models and different datasets. Therefore, we show several experiments for different benchmarks in Section 3.6.4.

3.6.2.4 Noise Injection Modeling

Based on the above analysis, we model the error source deriving from approximate components as a Gaussian random noise added to the considered array X without loss of generality.

An error with specific values of NM and NA, associated with a given tensor X with shape s is modeled as in Equation (3.15). The noisy output is represented as X' in Equation (3.16).

$$\Delta_X = Gauss(s, (NM \cdot R(X))) + (NA \cdot R(X)) \tag{3.15}$$

$$X' = X + \Delta_X \tag{3.16}$$

$Gauss(s, std) + m$ is a function that generates a tensor of random numbers with shape s, which follows a Gaussian distribution with mean m and standard deviation std.

3.6.3 ReD-CaNe Methodology

Our methodology, shown in Figure 3.56, is composed of 6 steps. After having identified the list of arrays in which we want to inject noise, called *Groups*, we inject the noise, as described in Equation (3.16). By monitoring the impact on the accuracy of different operations, we identify the most and the least accurate operations in a given CapsNet. Hence, our ReD-CaNe methodology may provide useful guidelines for designing energy-efficient inference, demonstrating the potential to employ approximations to specific layers and operations (i.e., *the more resilient ones*) without sacrificing the accuracy much. The step-by-step flow of our methodology is discussed in the following:

1. **Group Extraction:** We divide the operations of the CapsNet inference into groups based on their type (e.g., MAC, activation function, softmax, or logits update). This step generates the *Groups*.

2. **Group-Wise Resilience Analysis:** We monitor the test accuracy drop by injecting noise into different groups.

3. **Mark Resilient Groups:** Based on the analysis performed in Step 2, we mark the more resilient groups. After that, there are two categories of Groups, the *Resilient* and *Non-Resilient* ones.

4. **Layer-Wise Resilience Analysis for Non-Resilient Groups:** For each non-resilient group, we monitor the accuracy drop by injecting noise at each layer.

5. **Mark Resilient Layers for Each Non-Resilient Group:** Based on the results of the analysis performed in Step 4, we mark the more resilient layers.

6. **Select Approximate Components:** For each operation, we select which approximate component to use from a given library based on the resiliency measured as the noise magnitude (NM).

Note that a step of resilience analysis consists of properly setting the input parameters of the noise injection mechanism, i.e., NM and NA, to add the noise to the selected CapsNet operations and monitoring the accuracy of the noisy CapsNet.

At the output, our methodology generates the approximated version of a given CapsNet, which is ready to execute in a specialized hardware accelerator for inference with approximate components. To save area and energy for each operation, we select the approximate components from a given library that correspond to their resiliency level. Therefore, more aggressive approximations are chosen for more resilient operations without significantly affecting the classification accuracy of the CapsNet inference.

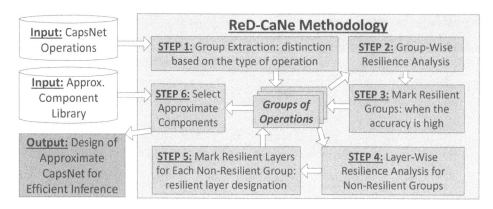

Figure 3.56: ReDCaNe: our methodology for resilience analysis and design of Approximate CapsNets.

3.6.4 Evaluation of the ReD-CaNe Methodology

3.6.4.1 Experimental Setup

We train each given CapsNet model for a given dataset using TensorFlow [1], running on two Nvidia GeForce RTX 2080 Ti GPUs. The trained model is an input to our ReD-CaNe methodology. The noise is injected into the arrays, and then the accuracy is monitored to identify the resilience of the operations.

We test our methodology on the DeepCaps [220] and the original CapsNet [236]. We use the CIFAR10 [112], SVHN [186], MNIST [118], and Fashion-MINST [284] datasets. The accuracy results obtained for different datasets are reported in Table 3.13. Table 3.14 shows the partition of the CapsNet operations into groups, which is then used in the group extraction step.

TABLE 3.13: Classification accuracy results using accurate multipliers.

Architecture	Dataset	Accuracy
DeepCaps	CIFAR10	92.74
	SVHN	97.56
	MNIST	99.72
CapsNet	Fashion-MNIST	92.88
	MNIST	99.67

TABLE 3.14: Grouping the operations of the CapsNet inference.

#	Group Name	Description
1	MAC Outputs	Outputs of the matrix multiplications
2	Activations	Output of the activation functions (Squash or ReLU)
3	Softmax	Results of the softmax (c coefficients in dynamic routing)
4	Logits Update	Update of the logits (b coefficients in dynamic routing)

The proposed methodology is implemented in TensorFlow [1]. First, the network is trained using standard techniques. We modified the computational graph in *protobuf* format by including our noise injection model in the *Graph tool*. We implemented a custom node for the noise injection, where the values of NA and NM may be specified as inputs to this node. Hence, for each node τ, a new set of nodes T is added to the graph. These nodes have the same shape as τ and they consist of adding a Gaussian noise with $std = NM \cdot R(\tau)$ and $m = NA \cdot R(\tau)$, given the range R of the node τ.

We use the EvoApprox8b library [179], which consists of 35 8-bit unsigned components. We select an 8-bit wordlength since it is accurate enough in the computational path of the CapsAcc.

3.6.4.2 Detailed Analysis for the CIFAR10 Dataset

As a case study, we report detailed results for the DeepCaps on the CIFAR10 dataset. We selected an $NM \in [0.5 \ldots 0.001]$. To analyze the general scenario of error resilience, we selected the average error $NA = 0$. In the experiment for **Step 2** of our methodology, we inject the same noise amount to every operation within a group while keeping the other groups accurate. From the results shown in Figure 3.57, we notice that the *Softmax* and the *Logits update* groups are more resilient than *MAC outputs* and *Activations* because the CapsNet accuracy starts decreasing with a relatively lower NM. Note that for low NM, the noise injection slightly increases the accuracy due to a regularization effect similar to the dropout [256].

3.6.4.3 Evaluating the Selection of Approximate Components

The selection of the approximate component for each operation depends on the level of NM that corresponds to a tolerable accuracy loss (typically null or very low). Recalling Equation (3.12), the parameters NM and NA are dataset-dependent since their values change accordingly to the input range R. In our case study (DeepCaps for CIFAR10), we select a subset of 10^6 elements from the inputs of every *Conv2D* layer of the DeepCaps, with their corresponding distributions (frequency of occurrence) shown in Figure 3.58a. The distribution is approximately Gaussian, but the peak between 40 and 50 in the input feature maps is caused by a specific distribution of

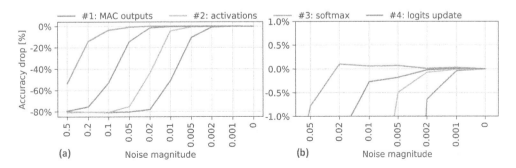

Figure 3.57: Group-wise resilience for the CIFAR10 dataset. (a) Complete results. (b) Zoomed view of the accuracy drop, centered at 0%.

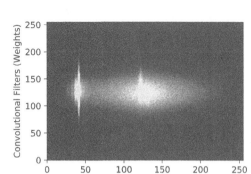
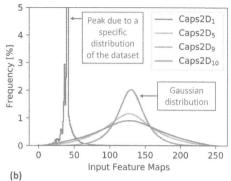

Figure 3.58: **(a)** Distribution of 10^6 random samples from the inputs of the convolutions in the DeepCaps for the CIFAR10 dataset. **(b)** A focus on some layers, showing the peak in the first Caps2D layer.

the input dataset. Indeed, such a peak occurs in the first Caps2D layer, as shown in Figure 3.58b.

Hence, in Table 3.15 we measure the NM and NA parameters of the selected multipliers in the library. We use two different input distributions, the *modeled* one that is based on random inputs generated with a uniform distribution, and the *real* one, which is based on the input distribution previously shown in Figure 3.58. Note that these values slightly differ because the NM and NA parameters are dataset-dependent. The major differences are due to our modeled distribution overestimating the NM and NA. Hence, the selection of approximate components based on our models may be systematically employed for designing approximate CapsNets.

3.6.4.4 Testing our Methodology on Different Benchmarks

We apply our methodology to other benchmarks. The results coming from the resiliency analysis of Step 2 are shown in Figure 3.59. A key property that we can notice is that MAC outputs and activations are less resilient than the other two groups. Meanwhile, we noticed that the logits update on the CapsNet for the MNIST dataset (Figure 3.59d) is slightly less resilient than the same group on the DeepCaps for the MNIST dataset (Figure 3.59b), because the CapsNet has only one layer that performs the Dynamic routing, while the DeepCaps has two.

3.6.4.5 Results Discussion

From our analyses, we derive that the CapsNets have interesting resilience properties. A key observation, noticed for every benchmark, is that the layers computing the dynamic routing (i.e., ClassCaps and Caps3D) and the corresponding groups of operations (i.e., softmax and logits update) are more resilient than others. Such an outcome is attributed to a common characteristic of the dynamic routing. The values of the involved coefficients (i.e., logits b and coupling coefficients c)

TABLE 3.15: Power, area, and noise magnitude, calculated with a modeled input dataset (with uniform distribution) and using a real input distribution I, for different approximated multipliers from the EvoApprox8B library. We have randomly selected 14 components representative of the complete library.

Multiplier mul8u_	Power μW	Area μm^2	Modeled Δ_X NA	NM	Real Δ_X NA	NM
1JFF	391 (-0%)	710 (-0%)	0.0000	0.0000	0.0000	0.0000
14VP	364 (-7%)	654 (-8%)	0.0000	0.0001	0.0000	0.0001
GS2	356 (-9%)	633 (-11%)	0.0004	0.0017	0.0001	0.0013
CK5	345 (-12%)	604 (-15%)	0.0000	0.0002	0.0000	0.0002
7C1	329 (-16%)	607 (-14%)	0.0011	0.0033	0.0007	0.0026
96D	309 (-21%)	605 (-15%)	0.0035	0.0077	0.0020	0.0051
2HH	302 (-23%)	542 (-24%)	-0.0001	0.0007	-0.0001	0.0007
NGR	276 (-29%)	512 (-28%)	0.0001	0.0008	0.0002	0.0009
19DB	206 (-47%)	396 (-44%)	0.0010	0.0019	0.0010	0.0021
DM1	195 (-50%)	402 (-43%)	0.0003	0.0025	0.0005	0.0025
12N4	142 (-64%)	390 (-45%)	0.0018	0.0054	0.0019	0.0056
1AGV	95 (-76%)	228 (-68%)	0.0027	0.0080	0.0026	0.0117
YX7	61 (-84%)	221 (-69%)	0.0484	0.0741	0.0268	0.0347
JV3	34 (-91%)	111 (-84%)	0.0021	0.0267	-0.0028	0.0301
QKX	29 (-93%)	112 (-84%)	0.0509	0.0736	0.0293	0.0350

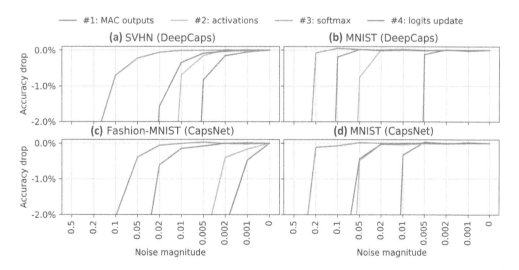

Figure 3.59: Group-wise resilience for different benchmarks. (a) DeepCaps for the SVHN dataset. (b) DeepCaps for the MNIST dataset. (c) CapsNet for the Fashion-MNIST dataset. (d) CapsNet for the MNIST dataset.

are dynamically updated, thereby adapting to the injected noise. Therefore, more aggressive approximations can be tolerated for these computations.

3.6.5 Summary

Following the recent trends of approximate computing, the ReD-CaNe methodology is proposed to trade off accuracy for energy efficiency by designing approximate CapsNets accelerators. Extensive analyses investigate the resiliency of the CapsNet inference subjected to approximation errors. Through error models due to the approximations, the ReD-CaNe methodology selects the approximation components to employ based on the resiliency level for every operation of the CapsNet inference. This work demonstrates significant energy reductions with minimal accuracy losses by applying approximate multipliers only. However, the CapsNets inference involves other compute-intensive operations such as squash and softmax. Toward this, the following Section 3.7 analyzes specialized hardware designs for approximating these complex functions.

3.7 APPROXIMATE SQUASH AND SOFTMAX DESIGNS

To enable the deployment of CapsNets on edge devices, we propose to leverage approximate computing for designing approximate variants of complex operations like squash and softmax. In our experiments, we evaluate tradeoffs between power consumption, area, critical path delay of the designs implemented with the ASIC design flow, and accuracy of the quantized CapsNets, compared to the exact functions.

3.7.1 System Overview

Despite their massive success, most advanced DNNs such as CapsNets exhibit high complexity due to their compute-intensive operations, which hinders their implementations on energy-constrained edge devices. Hence, several optimizations have been proposed for increasing the performance and reducing the energy consumption of complex DNNs on edge devices, such as quantization and pruning. In this section, we focus on leveraging approximate computing for optimizing CapsNets. Hence, our approach is orthogonal to other optimization methods, as we directly perform experiments on the quantized CapsNets.

In a nutshell, our novel contributions are:

- We analyze the state-of-the-art CapsNets models and the most advanced designs of approximate squash and softmax.

- We design specialized approximate softmax units using domain transformations.

- We design approximate squash units with piecewise approximations.

- We implement the approximate softmax and squash architectures in VHDL, synthesize them in a 45nm technology node with the ASIC design flow, and perform gate-level simulations to evaluate the area, power consumption, and critical path delay.

- We also integrate the functional approximations into the Q-CapsNets framework to compute the inference accuracy of state-of-the-art CapsNets using the proposed approximate units.

- Our proposed approximate *softmax-b2* design outperforms the related works, having −8% power, −11% area, −19% critical path delay, and comparable accuracy.

- Our proposed approximate *squash-exp* and *squash-pow2* have up to −36% critical path delay and up to −6% power consumption compared to the state-of-the-art while showing similar accuracy as having the exact squash function.

3.7.2 Approximate Computing for DNNs Nonlinear Operations

Approximate computing is a practical design methodology aiming to achieve low power consumption, high performance, and reduced chip area by relaxing the accuracy requirement in error-tolerant applications. Extensive research efforts have been dedicated to optimizing matrix multiplications in DNNs by proposing approximate designs for adders and multipliers. However, a key factor for achieving high computational efficiency in DNNs and CapsNets is the implementation of nonlinear functions, such as hyperbolic tangent, sigmoid, softmax, and squash.

Various techniques have been proposed to implement nonlinear functions in an approximate form and enable efficient hardware implementations with limited accuracy loss. The work in [7] proposed a piecewise linear approximation of the sigmoid function by saving the curve breakpoints in a look-up table and using linear interpolation.

Regarding the softmax function, the work in [59] proposed an approximate softmax architecture where the exponential function is computed using the Taylor series expansion and a look-up table. The work in [277] presented a hardware architecture exploiting a mathematical transformation into the logarithmic domain to simplify the division and approximates the logarithmic and exponential functions using linear fitting within a specific range.

For the squash function, the work in [25] described a set of approximations of the Euclidean norm to avoid the computation of square and square-root operations. The work in [63] introduced an approximate square-accumulate design with a self-healing mechanism suitable for computing the sum of the squared components in the Euclidean norm. *However, the previous works did not consider advanced methods, like piecewise approximations and domain transformations, which are possible due to the error tolerance of these functions inserted in the CapsNets computations, that we indeed exploit in this work.*

3.7.3 Approximate Softmax Designs

In the following, we discuss three approximate softmax architectures that describe the algorithmic approximations and the RTL implementations. The proposed approximations of the softmax function are referred to as *softmax-taylor*, *softmax-lnu* and *softmax-b2*, with names enclosing their key features.

The softmax function shown in Equation (3.17) is a probabilistic version of the argmax function that returns 1 for the highest input value and 0 for all the other values.

$$y_i = \frac{e^{x_i}}{\sum_{j=1}^{n} e^{x_j}} \quad (i = 1, ..., n) \tag{3.17}$$

The softmax computation involves three key operations: sum, division, and natural exponential. In the following approximate softmax designs, we focus on the approximate calculation of the division and the exponentiation, which are the most complex operations of the softmax function.

3.7.3.1 *Softmax-Taylor Design*

The *softmax-taylor* design is based on a specific softmax approximation [59] which exploits the Taylor series expansion approach for computing the exponential function and performs divisions in the logarithmic domain.

The natural exponential operation is simplified as in Equation (3.18) using the first-order Taylor polynomial approximation method. At the architecture level, the exponential unit consists of 2 look-up tables that implement the first two exponent contributions, a specialized bus arrangement to get $1 + c$ and a multiplier to compute the final product iteratively (see Figures 3.60a and 3.60b).

$$e^{x_i} = e^{a+b+c} \approx e^a \cdot e^b \cdot (1 + c) \tag{3.18}$$

The division is performed in logarithmic domain by exploiting the mathematical transformation in Equation (3.19).

$$\text{pow2}\left(\log_2\left(e^{x_i} / \sum_{j=1}^{n} e^{x_j}\right)\right) = \text{pow2}\left(w_1 + \log_2 k_1 - (w_2 + \log_2 k_2)\right)$$

$$\approx \text{pow2}\left(w_1 - w_2 + k_1 - k_2\right) = 2^{u_i + v_i} \approx 2^{u_i} \cdot (1 + v_i) \tag{3.19}$$

Here, $N_1 = e^{x_i}$ and $N_2 = \sum_{j=1}^{n} e^{x_j}$ are expressed as $2^{w_l} \cdot k_l$, with $w_l \in \mathbb{Z}$ and $k_l \in [1, 2)$ for $l = 1, 2$ and the base-2 logarithm of k_l is approximated by the linear fitting function $k_l - 1$. The argument of the power-2 operator is split into its integer and fractional parts, u_i and v_i, with $u_i \in \mathbb{Z}$ and $v_i \in [0, 1)$ and 2^{v_i} is estimated as $(1 + v_i)$.

The division unit has 2 base-2 logarithm units, a leading one detector (LOD) and a shift unit that computes the logarithm of the dividend and the divisor, a

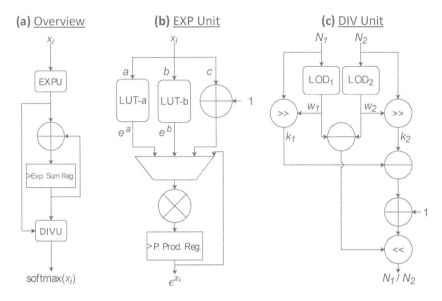

Figure 3.60: Architectures of the approximate Softmax-taylor design. (a) Overview of the Softmax-taylor architecture. (b) Softmax-taylor exponent unit. (c) Softmax-taylor division unit.

subtraction unit that performs the division in the logarithmic domain, and a power-2 unit (bus arrangement and shift unit) that computes the softmax output value (see Figure 3.60c).

To comply with the CapsNet models used in our experiments, the softmax architecture can process 10, 32, or 128 inputs.

3.7.3.2 Softmax-Lnu Design

The *softmax-lnu* design builds on a peculiar softmax approximation [277] that adopts a mathematical domain transformation involving natural exponential and natural logarithm operations (see Equation (3.20)).

$$\exp\left(\ln\left(e^{x_i} / \sum_{j=1}^{n} e^{x_j}\right)\right) = \exp\left(x_i - \ln\left(\sum_{j=1}^{n} e^{x_j}\right)\right) \tag{3.20}$$

The transformation into the logarithm domain allows performing the division by using a more straightforward subtraction. The exponentiation is needed to convert the softmax outputs from the logarithmic domain into the linear one. The architecture mainly consists of three computational units to calculate the natural exponential of the softmax inputs (EXPU), sum the exponentials, and evaluate the natural logarithm of the sum (LNU) required for the division (see Figure 3.61a).

The natural exponential operation is computed by using the mathematical transformation in Equation (3.21), with $u_i \in \mathbb{Z}$ and $v_i \in [0,1)$. At the architecture level, this unit is composed of a constant multiplier by $\log_2 e$, a specific bus arrangement to implement $1 + v_i$ and a shift unit to compute the result (see Figure 3.61b).

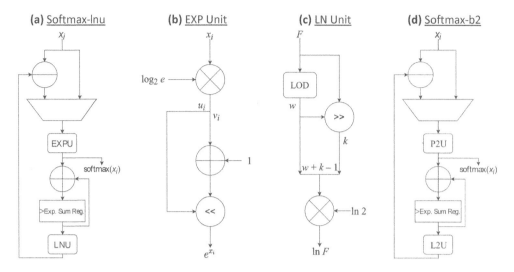

Figure 3.61: Architectures of the approximate Softmax-lnu and Softmax-b2 designs. **(a)** Overview of the Softmax-lnu architecture. **(b)** Softmax-lnu exponent unit. **(c)** Softmax-lnu natural logarithm unit. **(d)** Overview of the Softmax-b2 design.

$$e^{x_i} = 2^{x_i \cdot \log_2 e} = 2^{u_i + v_i} = 2^{u_i} \cdot 2^{v_i} \approx 2^{u_i} \cdot (1 + v_i) \tag{3.21}$$

The natural logarithm is computed using Equation (3.22), where $F = \sum_{j=1}^{n} e^{x_j}$ is expressed as $2^w \cdot k$, with $w \in \mathbb{Z}$ and $k \in [1, 2)$ and the base-2 logarithm of k is approximated with the linear fitting function $k - 1$. The natural log unit consists of 4 main subunits: a leading one detector that determines w, a shift unit that computes k, a specific bus arrangement to get the base-2 logarithm of F, and a constant multiplier by $\ln 2$ (see Figure 3.61c).

$$\ln F = \ln 2 \cdot \log_2 F = \ln 2 \cdot (w + \log_2 k) \approx \ln 2 \cdot (w + k - 1) \tag{3.22}$$

The architecture includes other hardware units that compute the maximum input value, scale the inputs, perform the division in the logarithmic domain, and allow for processing a variable number of softmax inputs.

3.7.3.3 Softmax-b2 Design

The **softmax-b2** design implements the approach of computing a softmax-like function with powers of 2 instead of natural exponentials, and it exploits a domain transformation with base-2 logarithm and power-2 operations (see Equation (3.23)).

$$\text{pow2}\left(\log_2\left(2^{x_i} / \sum_{j=1}^{n} 2^{x_j}\right)\right) = \text{pow2}\left(x_i - \log_2\left(\sum_{j=1}^{n} 2^{x_j}\right)\right) \tag{3.23}$$

The proposed approximation reduces the complexity of the hardware implementation of the *softmax-lnu* design, thanks to the removal of two constant multipliers.

Compared to the *softmax-lnu* design, the *softmax-b2* architecture (see Figure 3.61d) avoids the preliminary multiplication by $\log_2 e$ in the exponential unit and the final multiplication by $\ln 2$ in the logarithmic unit, by implementing the power-2 and base-2 logarithm units, respectively.

3.7.4 Approximate Squash Designs

The proposed approximate squash designs are called *squash-norm*, *squash-exp* and *squash-pow2*.

The squash function requires the computation of the norm of the input vector and the squashing coefficient multiplied by the input vector to produce the output vector, as shown in Equation (3.24).

$$ \mathbf{y} = \frac{\|\mathbf{x}\|^2}{1 + \|\mathbf{x}\|^2} \frac{\mathbf{x}}{\|\mathbf{x}\|} \tag{3.24} $$

The first design uses a specific norm approximation [25], while the remaining two techniques introduce novel solutions for approximating the squashing coefficient.

3.7.4.1 *Squash-norm Design*

The *squash-norm* design is inspired by the specific Euclidean norm approximation proposed by Chaudhuri *et al.* [25], which is shown in Equation (3.25).

$$ \|\mathbf{x}\| \approx D_\lambda(\mathbf{x}) = |x_{i_{max}}| + \lambda \sum_{\substack{i=1 \\ i \neq i_{max}}}^{n} |x_i| \tag{3.25} $$

This architecture does not need the square root operator and the multiplications needed to square the vector components. Still, it involves the computation of the absolute values and the maximum absolute value components. The parameter λ depends on the number of vector components, and it is selected accordingly [228].

The designed architecture is mainly composed of two units. The norm unit computes the approximate norm, and the squashing unit produces the squash outputs (see Figure 3.62a).

The norm unit implements the Chaudhuri approximation [25] in Equation (3.25). It consists of multiple arithmetic modules. A specialized component computes the absolute value of the inputs, the accumulator sums up the absolute values, a unit computes the maximum absolute value, a subtractor gets the second term of the formula, a multiplier scales the sum by λ, and an adder adds the maximum value to the sum (see Figure 3.62b).

The squashing unit is composed of two look-up tables that implement the squashing coefficient and a multiplier that computes the squash outputs as the product between the inputs and the squashing coefficient (see Figure 3.62c).

To comply with the two CapsNet models employed in our experiments, the squash architecture can process 4, 8, 16, or 32 inputs.

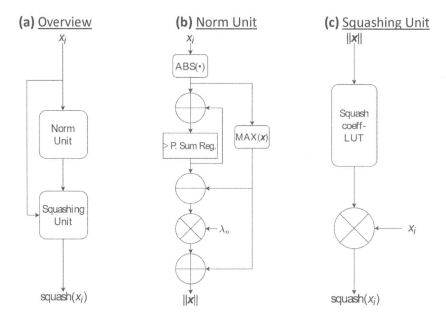

Figure 3.62: Architectures of the approximate Squash-norm design. (**a**) Overview of the Squash-norm architecture. (**b**) Squash-norm norm unit. (**c**) Squash-norm squashing unit.

3.7.4.2 Squash-exp Design

The **squash-exp** design exploits a piecewise approximation of the squashing coefficient $\|\mathbf{x}\|/(1 + \|\mathbf{x}\|^2)$ in two ranges of norm values. The coefficient is approximated with the nonlinear function $1 - e^{-\|\mathbf{x}\|}$ in the first range and with direct mapping in the second range. Such a range of norm values is derived experimentally from executing the inference steps with two CapsNet models on two datasets.

At the architecture level, this design mainly consists of two computational units: the norm and squashing units.

The norm unit performs the Euclidean norm of the input vector. It consists of a multiplier that squares the input components, an accumulator that sums up the squared inputs, and two look-up tables that implement the square root function over two specific ranges of squared norm values (see Figure 3.63a).

The squashing unit performs the piecewise approximation of the squashing coefficient to compute the outputs. In the first range, the nonlinear function is implemented with a component composed of a 2's complement of the norm value, a natural exponent unit, and a subtractor. The second-range approximation is implemented with a look-up table. The final multiplier computes the squash outputs (see Figure 3.63b).

3.7.4.3 Squash-pow2 Design

The **squash-pow2** design builds on the piecewise approximation of the squashing coefficient used in the *squash-exp* architecture, but the approximating nonlinear function used in the first range of norm values is $1 - 2^{-\|\mathbf{x}\|}$.

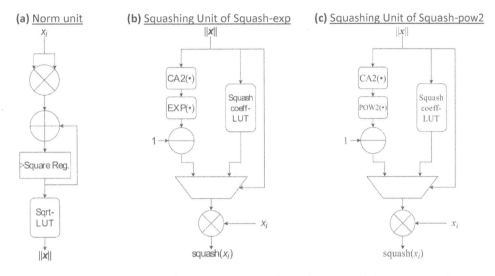

Figure 3.63: Architectures of the approximate Squash-exp and Squash-pow2 designs. (a) Norm unit of the Squash-exp and Squash-pow2 architectures. (b) Squash-exp squashing unit. (c) Squash-pow2 squashing unit.

At the architecture level, the exponential unit does not have the constant multiplication by $\log_2 e$, which is replaced to implement the power-2 unit (see Figure 3.63c). The hardware efficiency is obtained at the cost of a larger worst-case approximation error due to the squashing coefficient in the low norm value range.

3.7.5 Evaluation of the Approximate Softmax and Squash Designs

In the following, we evaluate the approximate softmax and squash designs in terms of inference accuracy loss and hardware implementation metrics.

First, we explore the inference accuracy loss induced by the proposed softmax and squash approximations in 4 case studies, with two CapsNet models on two image classification datasets. Then, we synthesize the complete architectures and analyze our designs' power consumption, area usage, and timing performance.

The goal of the evaluation is to explore possible *tradeoffs* between the hardware implementation cost of the approximate designs and the classification accuracy loss of a CapsNet using the approximations.

3.7.5.1 Experimental Setup

We describe the approximate softmax and squash algorithms in Python and execute extensive software simulations to evaluate the quality of each approximation compared to the respective exact function. The experiments are conducted for over 1 000 input vectors in a specific range. We analyze the *Mean Error Distance* between the maximum and average component errors in absolute and relative terms, respectively.

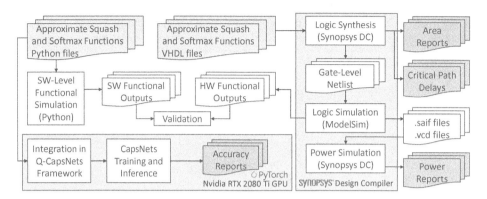

Figure 3.64: Setup and tool-flow for conducting our experiments.

To evaluate how the softmax and squash approximations affect the inference accuracy of the complete CapsNets, we implement the approximate functions in a Python-based CapsNet model provided by the Q-CapsNets framework. We execute an image classification task with two CapsNet models, the ShallowCaps [236] and the DeepCaps [220], on two image datasets, the MNIST [118] and the Fashion-MNIST [284].

As shown in Figure 3.64, our experimental setup consists of software and hardware components. We use a Python-based environment with PyTorch library and Nvidia CUDA Toolkit to execute the inference on an Nvidia GeForce RTX 2080 Ti GPU. We conduct the quantization of the approximate softmax and squash data to comply with the hardware implementation and we test the quantized approximate functions in quantized CapsNet models (see Table 3.16). Using the Q-CapsNets framework, we quantize activations and weights of the CapsNet models and input data of the softmax and squash functions.

We implement the designed architectures in VHDL and perform functional simulations using ModelSim to check the results against the Python model outputs. We synthesize the architectures in a 45nm academic technology library using the

TABLE 3.16: Percentage of *quantized* inference accuracy.

	MNIST		Fashion-MNIST	
	ShallowCaps	DeepCaps	ShallowCaps	DeepCaps
exact functions	99.44	99.35	92.42	94.69
softmax-lnu	99.46	**99.42**	92.37	**94.71**
softmax-b2 (ours)	**99.49**	99.33	92.33	94.64
softmax-taylor	99.42	99.41	**92.47**	94.69
squash-exp (ours)	99.18	98.79	91.32	**94.76**
squash-pow2 (ours)	99.00	98.58	89.05	94.62
squash-norm	**99.26**	**99.23**	**92.51**	94.70

TABLE 3.17: Hardware characteristics with clock frequency 100 MHz.

	Area usage (μm^2)	Power consumption (μW)	Critical path delay (ns)
softmax-lnu	12,511	2,572	6.46
softmax-b2 (ours)	**11,169**	**2,244**	**4.22**
softmax-taylor	14,944	2,430	5.24
squash-exp (ours)	7,937	1,414	5.64
squash-pow2 (ours)	7,543	**1,340**	**4.17**
squash-norm	**6,806**	1,431	6.53

ASIC design flow with the Synopsys Design Compiler tool and obtain power consumption, area usage, and maximum path delay for each design (see Table 3.17). Finally, we conduct post-synthesis functional simulations and timing validation of the gate-level netlist.

3.7.5.2 Evaluating the Softmax

From the experimental evaluations, we derive the following key observations about the approximate softmax designs.

The **softmax-b2** design is the best solution in terms of hardware metrics. However, it exhibits the highest CapsNet accuracy loss in all the case studies except for the ShallowCaps on MNIST. Actually, the *b2* design consumes less area (-11% and -25%) and power (-13% and -8%) than the *lnu* and *taylor* designs. Moreover, it achieves the lowest critical path delay (-35% and -19% w.r.t. *lnu* and *taylor*).

The **softmax-taylor** design is the best choice regarding inference accuracy loss since it outperforms the other designs of the ShallowCaps for Fashion-MNIST. However, it has the worst area usage ($+20\%$ and $+35\%$ w.r.t. *lnu* and *b2*) and intermediate power consumption and critical path delay.

The **softmax-lnu** design shows the highest power consumption ($+15\%$ and $+5\%$ w.r.t. *b2* and *taylor*) and maximum path delay ($+53\%$ and $+23\%$) but intermediate area usage. Its performance in terms of inference accuracy loss is similar to the *taylor* design in all case studies, except for the ShallowCaps for Fashion-MNIST, where the *lnu* performs worse ($+0.1\%$ loss).

3.7.5.3 Evaluating the Squash

The **squash-norm** design is the best approximate squash solution regarding the CapsNet accuracy loss. It is also characterized by having the best area usage (-13% and -8% w.r.t. *exp* and *pow2*), but as a drawback, it shows the worst power ($+1\%$ and $+7\%$) and delay metrics ($+15\%$ and $+56\%$).

The **squash-pow2** design is the best option in terms of power consumption (-5% and -6% w.r.t. *exp* and *norm*) and critical path delay (-25% and -36%), and intermediate area usage. However, it implies the lowest CapsNet accuracy among all case studies.

The **squash-exp** design is characterized by an accuracy loss similar to the *norm* design in two case studies and significantly lower accuracy in the other two cases. In exchange for the reduced accuracy, it has intermediate power and delay metrics, but as a downside, it shows the worst area usage (+5% and +17% w.r.t. *pow2* and *norm*).

3.7.6 Summary

To enable efficient CapsNets inference on edge devices, diverse approximate designs for the most compute-intensive CapsNets operations (the softmax and squash) are designed and integrated into the CapsNets computing engine. The proposed softmax design approximating the natural exponential with powers of 2 significantly reduces the hardware complexity, with limited accuracy drop. The proposed squash designs based on piecewise approximations show interesting tradeoffs between accuracy, area, power consumption, and critical path delay. These findings contribute toward deploying CapsNets and other complex DNN models on resource-constrained devices.

3.8 SUMMARY OF HARDWARE AND SOFTWARE OPTIMIZATIONS FOR CAPSULE NETWORKS

This chapter has discussed a flow of optimizations for CapsNets, including a fast training framework, hardware designs of the computation unit and memory organizations, and other energy-efficient optimizations involving quantization and approximate computing. The design space of the solutions has been explored through heuristic algorithms that leverage the tradeoff between multiple design objectives, such as energy, latency, area, and memory. Such an end-to-end flow of designs and set of optimizations enable the deployment of CapsNets on edge devices with limited hardware resources. Nowadays, besides energy efficiency, a crucial aspect to consider when designing systems based on advanced ML models such as CapsNets and DNNs is their robustness against the vulnerability threats that undermine their correct functionality. Toward this, Chapter 4 discusses the security vulnerabilities, and Chapter 5 combines the energy efficiency and robustness objectives into an integrated design flow.

CHAPTER 4

Adversarial Security Threats for DNNs and CapsNets

This chapter systematically analyzes the vulnerabilities of advanced DNN models like CNNs and CapsNets against security threats. In particular, the robustness against affine transformations and adversarial attacks is analyzed. The design and evaluation flow is shown in Figure 4.1. Section 4.1 provides systematic analyses by comparing the robustness of two CapsNet models with two CNN models. In Section 4.1.4, the robustness against affine transformations is discussed. This section also includes the pre-processing methodology for generating affine-transformed versions of the datasets. Section 4.1.5 presents the robustness analysis against existing adversarial attacks, such as the PGD and Carlini-Wagner algorithms. Section 4.1.6 further discusses the impact of the CapsNets' routing algorithm on the robustness. In Section 4.2, a novel methodology for generating imperceptible and robust adversarial attacks is proposed and evaluated on various CNN and CapsNet models. Section 4.3 presents novel attack algorithms that generate adversarial examples that fake the effect of atmospheric conditions on the camera lens. They are evaluated on CNN and CapsNet models as well.

Major Contributions of the Chapter:

- **RobCaps methodology design:** It is a systematic methodology for analyzing the robustness of CapsNets against affine transformations and adversarial attacks and comparing it with traditional DNNs. It also investigates the robustness under the adversarial training defense and evaluates the impact of the dynamic routing on the CapsNets' robustness.

- **CapsAttacks methodology design:** It is an attack technique for generating targeted imperceptible and robust adversarial examples. The attack is evaluated on different CapsNets and DNNs for various benchmarks.

- **fakeWeather attacks design:** Based on the observations of how the natural weather events affect the images captured by the cameras, specialized masks have been designed to emulate the effect of atmospheric conditions such as snow, rain, and hail on the camera.

DOI: 10.1201/9781003530459-4

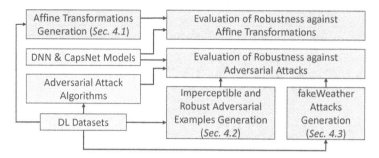

Figure 4.1: Overview of the design and evaluation flow of this chapter.

4.1 ROBCAPS: EVALUATING THE ROBUSTNESS OF CAPSNETS AGAINST AFFINE TRANSFORMATIONS AND ADVERSARIAL ATTACKS

CapsNets can hierarchically preserve the pose relationships between multiple objects for image classification tasks. Other than achieving high accuracy, another relevant factor in deploying CapsNets in safety-critical applications is the robustness against input transformations and malicious adversarial attacks.

In this section, we systematically analyze and evaluate different factors affecting the robustness of CapsNets, compared to traditional CNNs. Toward a comprehensive comparison, we test two CapsNet models and two CNN models on the MNIST, GTSRB, and CIFAR10 datasets, as well as the affine-transformed versions of such datasets. A thorough analysis shows which properties of these architectures better contribute to increasing the robustness and their limitations. CapsNets achieve better robustness against adversarial examples and affine transformations than a traditional CNN with a similar number of parameters. Similar conclusions have been derived for deeper versions of CapsNets and CNNs. Moreover, our results reveal that dynamic routing operations do not significantly improve the CapsNets robustness. Indeed, the main generalization contribution is due to the hierarchical feature learning through capsules.

4.1.1 System Overview

Our objective is to investigate the following research questions:

1. *Are CapsNets more robust than CNNs against adversarial attacks and affine transformations?*

2. *If yes, how can these phenomena be analyzed systematically?*

3. *Which CapsNet functions contribute more to the robustness improvement?*

Answering these questions is a challenging task. Firstly, we evaluate a good metric of comparison between CapsNets and CNNs, i.e., which network models give a fair and significant robustness comparison, which types of adversarial attacks are applied, etc. Then, it should be interesting to analyze the transferability of the adversarial attacks, i.e., white-box attacks. *If an adversarial example has been generated to fool network A, does it also fool network B?*

In a nutshell, our Novel Contributions are:

- We generate an affined-transformed version of the CIFAR10 and GTSRB datasets, called **affCIFAR** and **affGTSRB**, respectively.

- We compare the **robustness against affine trans-formations** for different datasets and networks.

- We compare the robustness **against adversarial attacks** for different datasets and networks. Further analyses have been carried on in the presence of a defense such as **adversarial training**.

- We evaluate the role of the **dynamic routing** toward the CapsNets robustness.

In summary, our key results show that the DeepCaps [220] is more robust than a deeper ResNet20 [84] against affine transformation and different types of adversarial attacks, increasing the complexity of the input data. As we will demonstrate, such robustness improvements also hold when the adversarial examples are transferred from one network to the other and vice-versa.

After showing the power of the capsules, we focus our analysis on the dynamic routing, which increases the confidence of the prediction, with a consequent accuracy improvement. By knowing that, our challenging question is: *Is the dynamic routing also helpful in guaranteeing the CapsNets robustness?* Our results and analyses provide great insights when relating CNNs and CapsNets against different adversarial attacks and affine transformations, as well as how CapsNets behavior changes when modifying model features.

4.1.2 RobCaps Methodology

The introduction of the CapsNets suggests that these architectures might be more robust toward adversarial attacks than other CNNs. To demonstrate this intuition, we present a detailed analysis to answer our main research questions and to show (1) if and why the CapsNet under attack provides a better response than traditional CNNs, and (2) which model quality plays an important role and their limits. Knowing the main differences between CapsNets and traditional CNNs, we explore the impact of these networks on affine transformations and adversarial attacks. Moreover, we study the role of different functions of a CapsNet on the robustness against these attacks. Toward a fair and comprehensive evaluation, the ShallowCaps results have been compared to three different architectures (chosen according to their properties, their number of parameters, and their depth) for three datasets, i.e., MNIST [118], GTSRB [92], and CIFAR10 [112].

- The *ResNet20* [84] is one of the best performing CNN architectures for the CIFAR10 dataset, used in various applications. It would be interesting to

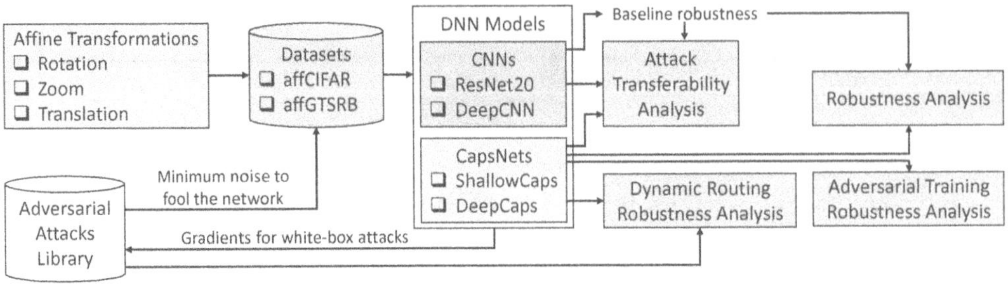

Figure 4.2: Overview of our RobCaps methodology.

compare the capabilities of the CapsNet with a widely used CNN, which is deeper and employs Residual Blocks with Conv and average pooling layers.

- A deeper CapsNet architecture, like the *DeepCaps* model [220]. Despite being deeper than the ShallowCaps, it has fewer parameters. The *DeepCaps* employs 4 groups of 2D Conv capsule layers with a 3D convolution layer in the last group and an FC capsule layer of 10 32D capsules.

- A traditional *deep CNN* with the same depth as the DeepCaps, but without multidimensional entities such as capsules. The dimensions of the layers are reshaped in a 2D fashion, using traditional Conv layers with batch normalization instead of capsules with squash compression and a conventional FC layer instead of the ClassCaps layer with dynamic routing. Its comparison w.r.t. the DeepCaps highlights the contribution to the robustness of 3D convolutions and capsules.

Our methodology, shown in Figure 4.2, is composed of the following steps:

1) **Evaluation of robustness on affine transformations:**

    i) Train our networks with the standard datasets using the same hyperparameters and data augmentation.

    ii) Generate the affine-transformed version of each dataset for a given set of affine transformations. For the CIFAR10 and the GTSRB datasets, we design two novel datasets generated using transformations such as random translations, rotations, and zooms (which we call *affCIFAR* and *affGTSRB*.

    iii) Use such affCIFAR and affGTSRB datasets for inference, as the case for the already existing affNIST [266], to evaluate the network's response to affine transformations.

2) **Evaluation of robustness on adversarial attacks:**

    We use the saved parameters of the trained models to evaluate the gradient with respect to the input for the two implemented white-box attacks. The key steps of our methodology are:

    i) Apply the projected gradient descent (PGD) attack for each architecture and each dataset to generate adversarial examples.

    ii) Test the networks with the generated adversarial inputs, evaluating the accuracy behavior when increasing the perturbation level.

    iii) Apply the Carlini Wagner attack (CW) for each dataset.

    iv) Evaluate the mean distortion required for the algorithm to misclassify 500 images of the test datasets and its fooling rate.

    v) Apply at the input to a network the adversarial image generated with another one to test the transferability of the attack.

    vi) Test the robustness when the adversarial training defense is applied.

3) **Analyzing the contribution of the dynamic routing to the CapsNet's robustness:**

    i) Modify the dynamic routing of the ClassCaps layer of the DeepCaps and then generate three versions of it with different routing algorithms.

    ii) Analyze the robustness against affine transformations.

    iii) Analyze the robustness against PGD and CW attacks.

4.1.3 Experimental Setup

These architectures have been trained with the 40×40 sized version of the MNIST dataset and tested on the affNIST for evaluating the robustness against affine transformations. For all the architectures tested on CIFAR10, input data have been resized before training, from 32×32 to 64×64, following the pre-processing steps in [220]. For the GTSRB, the input image size is kept to 32×32. The data augmentation and hyperparameters used for the training are kept the same for all the networks. As a regularization term, the CapsNets have the reconstruction loss provided by the decoder. For the evaluation of the loss function, we use the same as in [236] for CapsNets and the Cross-Entropy for CNNs.

    We implemented the attack algorithms using the Cleverhans library [65], adapted for the Keras framework with Tensorflow backend [1]. The networks have been trained on the Nvidia GeForce RTX 2080 Ti GPU with CUDA 10. To have a good comparison metric, we train different versions of the DeepCaps architecture, modifying or removing the dynamic routing.

4.1.4 Robustness Against Affine Trasformations

4.1.4.1 Affine-CIFAR10 (affCIFAR) and Affine-GTSRB (affGTSRB) Datasets Generation

While a dataset with affine transformed images of the MNIST dataset (affNIST) is already available, we create an affine version of the CIFAR10 and GTSRB datasets, which we call *affCIFAR* and *affGTSRB*, to compare the response of the networks. The test data was created by modifying the 10 000 test images from the original dataset with random affine transformations. Every image is transformed following these criteria:

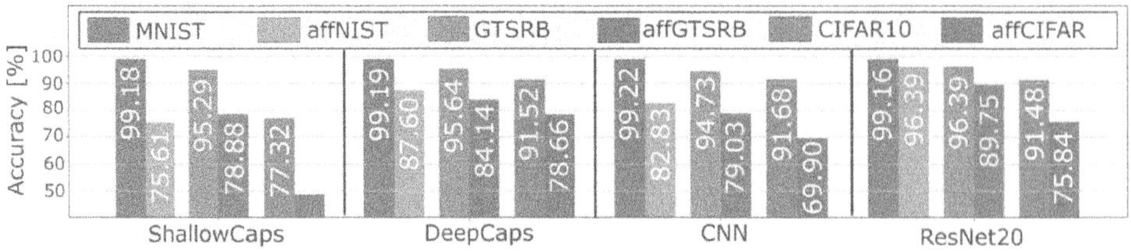

Figure 4.3: Robustness against affine transformations.

- *Translations:* random pixels translations in one or two dimensions by a factor between 10% and 25% of the input image size, with a fixed interval.

- *Rotations:* random rotations between +20 and −20 degrees with a fixed step.

- *Zooms:* the vertical and horizontal expansions are uniformly chosen between 0.8 (i.e., shrinking the image by 20%) and 1.2 (i.e., enlarging the image by 20%).

4.1.4.2 Affine Trasformations Results

For each model defined in Section 4.1.2, we evaluate the accuracy of all the datasets and their respective affine-transformed versions. The results are shown in Figure 4.3.

ShallowCaps vs. DeepCaps: As shown in Figure 4.3, the ShallowCaps on the CIFAR10 dataset achieve lower accuracy than the state-of-the-art (77.32%). Such limitation is solved by the DeepCaps, which reaches better results even when using the affine version of this dataset (78.66%). Thus, using a deeper architecture while keeping the same capsule structure, the DeepCaps model has fewer parameters and better generalization. Its accuracy for the CIFAR10 dataset (91.52%) and the affine-transformed datasets is much higher than the ShallowCaps. In fact, despite the shallower model reaching a good accuracy on the normal MNIST and GTSRB datasets, it is still unable to generalize as the DeepCaps against affine transformations. The improvement could also be explained by the presence of the 3D Conv layer. The effect of having 3D convolutions, compared to a stack of FC capsules, is similar to when we reach the generalization level offered by the Multi-Layer Perceptrons (MLP) and the CNNs. In the ClassCaps layer, each element of the transformation matrix learns if a capsule is correlated with each capsule of the following layer. On the contrary, with the 3D convolution, sliding a 3D kernel, the same weights are used among all the layer capsules. This characteristic also allows learning the presence of a particular feature if the input image is spatially transformed (e.g., translated, rotated, or zoomed), preserving the capsule structure.

DeepCaps vs. CNN and ResNet20: Another significant result is provided by comparing the response of the DeepCaps with a traditional CNN, having a similar base architecture. While the accuracy of the CNN on the MNIST, GTSRB, and CIFAR10 datasets is similar to the DeepCaps, the CNN's robustness against the affNIST, affGTSRB, and affCIFAR is much lower. These results confirm the benefits of capsules against affine transformations. Compared to the DeepCaps, the ResNet20 is deeper but has fewer parameters. It can generalize better for the affMNIST and affGTSRB but worse for the affCIFAR dataset. This apparently contradictory result is due to the difference in complexity between the datasets. While for simple datasets, a deep CNN, like the ResNet20, can generalize very well, for more complex tasks like the affCIFAR, it is outperformed by the DeepCaps. This observation highlights the capability of the capsule architectures to preserve spatial correlations between the features detected, and this difference w.r.t. deeper traditional CNNs is even more evident when the input dataset is composed of complex elements like the CIFAR10.

4.1.5 Robustness Against Adversarial Attacks

4.1.5.1 Projected Gradient Descent (PGD) Attack

We analyze the network response by increasing the perturbation level ε generated by the algorithm. Figure 4.4a,b, and c show the results for the MNIST, GTSRB, and CIFAR10 datasets.

ShallowCaps vs. ResNet20: Applying the PDG attack for the MNIST dataset, the ResNet20 is less vulnerable than other networks for low levels of ε. The ShallowCaps robustness behavior, not so far from the one of the ResNet20, outperforms the ResNet20 when $\varepsilon \approx 0.065$. Hence, despite the low number of layers, the ShallowCaps has a similar response under the PGD attack compared to a deeper CNN.

DeepCaps vs. ShallowCaps: According to the results, the ShallowCaps are more robust than the DeepCaps, in contrast to what happens for affine transformations. Increasing the depth of a CapsNet does not provide more robustness against perturbed images. Note, the ShallowCaps response for the CIFAR10 dataset has not been examined because of its very low baseline accuracy, which is not comparable with other networks.

DeepCaps vs. ResNet20 vs. CNN: For this kind of algorithm and the MNIST dataset, Figure 4.4a shows that the DeepCaps behaves worse than the ResNet20. On the contrary, for more complex datasets like CIFAR10 or GTSRB, the results in Figure 4.4 show that the ResNet20 is not as robust as for the MNIST dataset. Note that by increasing the size of the perturbation, the success rate of the attacks grows faster than on DeepCaps. Such an outcome is in line with the takeaway from Figure 4.3, which showed the DeepCaps be more robust than the ResNet20 against the transformations in affCIFAR.

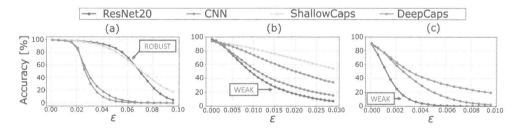

Figure 4.4: Robustness against the PGD attack for (a) the MNIST, (b) the GTSRB, and (c) the CIFAR10 datasets.

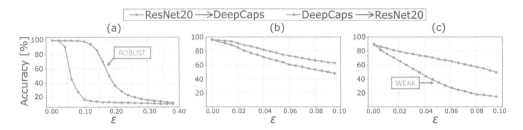

Figure 4.5: Transferability for the PGD attack: comparison of the network response for **(a)** MNIST, **(b)** GTSRB, and **(c)** CIFAR10 datasets.

The behavior of the CNN curves for GTSRB and CIFAR10 always stays below the curve of the DeepCaps. It means that the capsule architecture plays a fundamental role in improving the robustness against the PGD attacks when the dataset becomes more complex than the MNIST.

Transferability ResNet20 ⟺ DeepCaps: Toward a more comprehensive study of the robustness against the PGD, we analyze the transferability of the attacks, between the ResNet20 and the DeepCaps, presenting the two opposite behaviors. We provide the input of the DeepCaps the adversarial examples generated with the gradient of the ResNet20 and vice-versa. Figure 4.5 shows the transferability between these two networks for different datasets.

For the MNIST dataset, the attacks generated for the ResNet20, tested on DeepCaps, have a more significant effect than the other way round. This outcome confirms, like in Figure 4.5a, that the ResNet20 appears good for the generalization of the MNIST. The opposite results can be derived for the GTSRB and CIFAR10 dataset, where the DeepCaps shows greater robustness than the ResNet20 due to a better generalization ability for a more complex dataset.

4.1.5.2 Carlini Wagner (CW) attack

For a more solid comparison, the CapsNets and CNNs have also been tested against the CW attack, a different algorithm that does not define a threshold for the perturbation magnitude (like the ε in the PGD attack). It is an iterative targeted algorithm that tries to reduce the gap between the target and the predicted class (success rate) with the minimum perturbation (mean distortion), estimated as the l_2 distance. For a more robust network, the algorithm necessitates more iterations to obtain that the probability of the target class overcomes the probability of the correct class. Consequently, more iterations imply a higher l_2 distance between the original image and the adversarial example. For our estimations, we set a maximum of 10 iterations for the MNIST and 5 iterations for the CIFAR10 dataset. In addition, for the attacks on CIFAR10, the algorithm has been forced to set the confidence of the targeted class as 0.5 higher than the confidence of the correct label. Table 4.1 reports the fooling rate, i.e., the percentage of successful attacks, and the mean distortion for both the datasets.

TABLE 4.1: Robustness results against the CW attack.

Network	MNIST		GTSRB		CIFAR10	
	Mean Distortion	Fooling Rate	Mean Distortion	Fooling Rate	Mean Distortion	Fooling Rate
ShallowCaps	1.59	98.6%	1.31	100%	-	-
Deepcaps	1.24	86.8%	1.16	98.8%	0.34	100%
CNN	0.95	100%	0.59	100%	0.23	100%
ResNet20	0.94	100%	0.34	100%	0.12	100%

CapsNets vs. CNNs: The CW attack is very effective for traditional CNNs. It reaches 100% fooling rate for all three datasets. Similar findings were also made in [24]. On the other hand, both CapsNets show greater robustness (i.e., lower fooling rate) than CNNs, for the MNIST dataset (and also for GTSRB, even if the fooling rate of the DeepCaps is slightly lower than 100%). The CapsNets also require a higher mean distortion than the CNNs. Hence, the resulting adversarial example would be more perceptible. For the CIFAR10 dataset, the CW attack shows its effectiveness because, for all the networks, the fooling rate is 100%. However, we notice that CapsNets are more robust due to higher mean distortion.

DeepCaps vs. ShallowCaps: The DeepCaps appear more robust than the ShallowCaps, because of a lower fooling rate, despite having slightly lower mean distortion. Therefore, the depth and the 3D convolutions help to generalize better against the CW attack.

Transferability ResNet20 $\Longleftrightarrow$ DeepCaps: Table 4.2 shows the transferability of the attacks between ResNet20 and DeepCaps for the CW attack. The values report the accuracies of the two models that receive as input a sample of 500 targeted adversarial examples generated by the CW algorithm applied to the other network. The high accuracy values demonstrate the low level of transferability of the targeted CW attack. Despite this, the ResNet20 still achieves lower accuracy than the DeepCaps, thereby performing less robustly.

4.1.5.3 *DeepCaps defended with the PGD Adversarial Training*

We also evaluate the robustness of DeepCaps when the PGD adversarial training is applied compared to the normally trained DeepCaps. We chose an input perturbation equal to $\epsilon = 0.03$, with step size 0.005 in each algorithm iteration. From Figure 4.6, we can derive that the adversarial training increases the robustness of the DeepCaps against the PGD attack, both for the CIFAR10 and GTSRB datasets, because its classification accuracy is higher than the baseline DeepCaps.

The adversarial training with PGD defense helps the networks also against the CW attack. For both the datasets, from Table 4.3, comparing both the mean

TABLE 4.2: Transferability of the CW attack between the DeepCaps and the ResNet20.

Network	MNIST	GTSRB	CIFAR10
DeepCaps → ResNet20	97.4%	94.0%	86.8%
ResNet20 → DeepCaps	**97.8%**	**95.4%**	**89.2%**

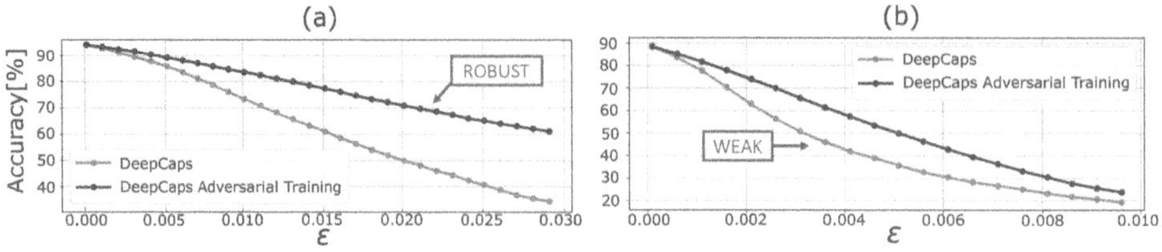

Figure 4.6: Adversarially vs. normally trained DeepCaps with **(a)** the GTSRB and **(b)** the CIFAR10 datasets.

distortion and the fooling rate, the defended DeepCaps appears more robust. Hence, adversarial training improves the model interpretability and reduces the learning of brittle features when the attack algorithm used for the defense differs from the one used for the actual attack.

4.1.6 Analyzing the Contribution of Dynamic Routing to the Robustness of the DeepCaps

As a further analysis, we investigate the contribution of the dynamic routing toward the CapsNets generalization and, as a consequence, toward their robustness. We train two versions of the DeepCaps architecture. (i) The original dynamic routing with 3 iterations has been replaced by a simple connection (i.e., one iteration of dynamic routing) in both the 3D Conv and the ClassCaps layer. (ii) The dynamic routing has been replaced by the self-routing algorithm in the last FC layer. Then, we run the experiments on such networks and compare them with the original DeepCaps.

4.1.6.1 *Affine Trasformations*

The results in Table 4.4 compare the accuracy achieved by the DeepCaps with and without dynamic routing, and with self-routing, for the MNIST, GTSRB, and CIFAR10 datasets. While the difference is minimal, the response of the DeepCaps without dynamic routing against affine transformations appears to be slightly better. For the CIFAR10 dataset, even if the accuracy with the standard dataset is higher with the dynamic routing compared to the case without it, the latter works better for the affCIFAR dataset. The self-routing shows some limits increasing the complexity of the datasets.

We can derive that the dynamic routing in CapsNets does not contribute significantly to the robustness against affine transformations. Indeed, it makes the DeepCaps much computationally heavier. The functionality of dynamic routing is to

TABLE 4.3: Adversarially and normally trained DeepCaps against the CW attack.

Network	GTSRB		CIFAR10	
	Mean Distortion	Fooling Rate	Mean Distortion	Fooling Rate
Normally trained DeepCaps	1.16	98.8%	0.34	100%
Adversarially trained DeepCaps	**1.44**	**98.6%**	**0.84**	**96.6%**

TABLE 4.4: Robustness results against affine transformations.

Network	MNIST40	GTSRB	CIFAR10	AffNIST	AffGTSRB	AffCIFAR
DeepCaps without dynamic routing	**99.27%**	**96.27%**	91.47%	87.72%	**84.54%**	**79.86%**
DeepCaps with dynamic routing	99.19%	95.29%	**91.52%**	87.60%	84.14%	78.66%
DeepCaps with self routing	99.25%	95.60%	90.5%	**88.15%**	83.17%	77.37%

inhibit the propagation of the activation vectors with lower contribution by lowering the values of the coupling coefficients in such connections. Instead, the transformation matrix learns the relationship between objects during the training. It could wrongly recognize some relationships between the inputs and a wrong output label, which the dynamic routing amplifies, together with the correct agreements. As a consequence, it increases the prediction confidence of the incorrect label.

4.1.6.2 Adversarial Attacks

The comparison analysis for the PGD attack applied to the MNIST, GTSRB, and CIFAR10 datasets are shown in Figure 4.7a, b, and c, respectively.

For the MNIST dataset, the DeepCaps with dynamic routing is slightly more robust than the version without it. On the contrary, for the CIFAR10, the accuracy of the DeepCaps without dynamic routing decreases faster when increasing the perturbation ε. We can conclude that increasing the complexity of the dataset, from MNIST toward the CIFAR10, the dynamic routing does not improve the classification capability when the input starts to be perturbed.

Table 4.5 shows the results of the CW attack. The self-routing seems to confer robustness with such an attack, even if the architecture with dynamic routing is outperformed by the one without it. Since the fooling rate is lower and the mean distortion is higher without dynamic routing, we can derive that the dynamic routing does not improve the robustness against such an attack. It confirms that dynamic routing does not contribute much to the generalization.

4.1.7 Summary

The proposed RobCaps methodology systematically studies the robustness of advanced DNN models, such as CNNs and CapsNets, against adversarial attacks and

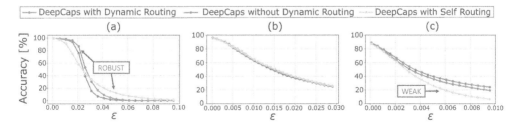

Figure 4.7: PGD results: comparison of the DeepCaps response for **(a)** MNIST, **(b)** GTSRB, and **(c)** CIFAR10 datasets.

TABLE 4.5: Robustness results against the CW attack.

	MNIST		GTSRB		CIFAR10	
Network	Mean Distortion	Fooling Rate	Mean Distortion	Fooling Rate	Mean Distortion	Fooling Rate
DeepCaps with dynamic routing	1.24	86.8%	1.16	98.8%	0.34	100%
DeepCaps without dynamic routing	1.62	74.0%	1.27	84.11%	0.46	100%
DeepCaps with self routing	2.28	48.6%	1.02	54.4%	0.52	99.2%

affine transformations. To evaluate the robustness against affine transformations, a methodology to generate the image transformation is proposed. The evaluations indicate that the DeepCaps model exhibits higher robustness than a similar-size CNN and the ResNet20 model. This observation is noticed since the DeepCaps shows higher accuracy than other DNN models in the presence of affine transformations and adversarial attacks. Such higher robustness is also obtained when adversarial training is employed. In this section, the robustness against existing adversarial attack algorithms has been studied, while the following Section 4.2 and Section 4.3 investigate the robustness against new adversarial attack methodologies.

4.2 CAPSATTACKS: A STUDY ON THE SECURITY VULNERABILITIES OF CAPSNETS AGAINST ADVERSARIAL ATTACKS

A large body of work has investigated adversarial examples for CNNs, but their effectiveness on CapsNets has not yet been investigated systematically. In our work, we study the vulnerabilities in CapsNets to adversarial attacks. These perturbations, added to the inputs, are small and imperceptible to humans but can fool the network into mispredicting. We propose a greedy algorithm to generate imperceptible adversarial examples in a black-box attack scenario automatically. We show that this attack applied to the GTSRB and CIFAR10 datasets misleads CapsNets in making a correct classification. This outcome can be catastrophic for smart CPS, like autonomous vehicles. Moreover, we apply the same adversarial attacks to a 5-layer CNN (LeNet), a 9-layer CNN (VGGNet), and a 20-layer CNN (ResNet). We analyze the outcome compared to the CapsNets, to study their different behaviors under adversarial attacks.

4.2.1 System Overview

In this section, we aim to address the following **key research questions:**

1. Is a CapsNet vulnerable to adversarial examples? If yes, how, why, and to what extent?

2. How does the CapsNets' vulnerability to adversarial attacks differ from that of the traditional CNNs?

Studying the vulnerability of the CapsNet to such adversarial attacks for the GTSRB dataset is crucial for autonomous vehicle use cases. Moreover, to our knowledge, we are the first to automatically generate an attack image for such

CapsNet in a black-box scenario. We compare the CapsNet robustness with the CNNs with 5 and 9 layers, and the DeepCaps robustness with a 20-layer ResNet.

In a nutshell, our Novel Contributions are:

1. We develop a **novel algorithm to generate targeted imperceptible and robust adversarial examples automatically**.

2. We **analyze the robustness** behavior of the CapsNet, the DeepCaps, a 5-layer CNN (LeNet), a 9-layer CNN (VGGNet), and a 20-layer CNN (ResNet), under **adversarial attacks** applied to the input images of the CIFAR10 and GTSRB datasets, and study their differences.

3. We **compare the robustness** of the CapsNets with traditional CNNs, under the **adversarial examples** generated by our algorithm.

In summary, our results show that the CapsNet has comparable robustness to a much deeper CNN like the VGGNet, while the LeNet is much more vulnerable to adversarial attacks, while the DeepCaps is more robust than the ResNet. Therefore, a fundamental step forward for the security of safety-critical applications can be done by employing deep and complex networks such as the DeepCaps.

4.2.2 Generation of Targeted Imperceptible and Robust Adversarial Examples

An efficient adversarial attack can generate *imperceptible* and *robust* examples to fool the network. Before discussing the details of our algorithm, we describe the importance of these two aspects.

4.2.2.1 Imperceptibility and Robustness

An adversarial example is typically considered *imperceptible* if the modifications of the original sample are so small that humans cannot notice them or they are hardly recognized. To create imperceptible adversarial examples, we need to add the perturbations in the pixels of the image with the highest standard deviation. The perturbations added in high-variance regions are less evident and more difficult to detect than the ones applied in low-variance pixels. Considering an area of $M \cdot N$ pixels x, the standard deviation (SD, Equation (4.1)) of the pixel $x_{i,j}$ can be computed as the square root of the variance, where μ is the average of the $M \cdot N$ pixels:

$$SD(x_{i,j}) = \sqrt{\frac{\sum\limits_{k=1}^{M}\sum\limits_{l=1}^{N}(x_{k,l} - \mu)^2 - (x_{i,j} - \mu)^2}{M \cdot N}} \tag{4.1}$$

Hence, if the pixel is in a high variance region, its standard deviation is high, and the probability of detecting a modification of the pixel is low. To quantify the imperceptibility, we define the distance (D, Equation (4.2)) between the original sample X and the adversarial sample X*, where $\delta_{i,j}$ is the perturbation added to the pixel $x_{i,j}$:

$$D(X^*, X) = \sum_{i=1}^{M} \sum_{j=1}^{N} \frac{\delta_{i,j}}{SD(x_{i,j})} \tag{4.2}$$

This value indicates the total amount of perturbation added to all the pixels under consideration. We define D_{MAX} as the maximum total perturbation tolerated by the human eye. The value of D_{MAX} can vary among different datasets or images because it depends on the resolution and the contrast between neighboring pixels.

An adversarial example is typically called *robust* if the gap function, i.e., the gap between the target class probability and the maximum class probability, is maximized (see Equation (4.3)).

$$GAP = P(target\ class) - max\{P(other\ classes)\} \tag{4.3}$$

For higher gap function values, the adversarial example becomes more robust since the changes in the probabilities due to the image transformations (e.g., resizing or compression) tend to be less effective. Indeed, if the gap is high, a variation of the probabilities could not be sufficient to misclassify.

4.2.2.2 Generation of the Adversarial Examples

Obtaining, at the same time, imperceptibility and robustness is complicated. Typically, a robust attack would require perceptible input changes, while an imperceptible attack does not change the classification much. We propose an iterative methodology deploying a heuristic algorithm to generate targeted imperceptible and robust adversarial examples automatically in a black-box scenario, i.e., we assume that the attacker has access to the input image and the output probabilities vector, but *not* to the network model. Our attack generation methodology is shown in Figure 4.8. Details are provided in Algorithm 13. The goal of our methodology is to modify the input image to maximize the gap function (i.e., *imperceptibility*) until the distance between the original and the adversarial example is under D_{MAX} (i.e., *robustness*).

4.2.2.3 Attack Methodology Discussion

The algorithm considers that every pixel has three different values since the images are based on three channels (red, green, and blue: RGB). Compared to the algorithm proposed in [145], our attack is applied to a set of pixels with the highest standard deviation at every iteration to create imperceptible perturbations. Moreover, *our algorithm automatically decides whether it is more effective to add or subtract the noise to maximize the gap*, according to the values of two parameters, $GAP(+)$ and $GAP(-)$. These changes increase the imperceptibility and robustness of the attack. For clarity, we have expressed the formula used to compute the standard deviation in a more comprehensive form.

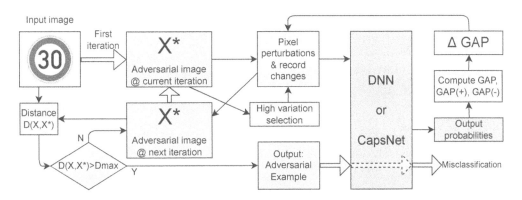

Figure 4.8: Our methodology to generate adversarial examples.

Algorithm 13: Adversarial Attack Generation.

---

1 **Given:** original sample X, maximum human perceptual distance D_{MAX}, noise magnitude δ, $M \cdot N$ pixels, target class, P, V;

2 **while** $D(X^*, X) < D_{MAX}$ **do**

3   Compute *Standard Deviation SD* for every pixel;

4   Select a subset P of pixels included in the region of $M \cdot N$ pixels with the highest *SD* for every channel;

5   Compute GAP, $GAP(-)$, $GAP(+)$;

6   **if** $GAP(-) > GAP(+)$ **then**

7          $VariationPriority(x_{i,j}) = [GAP(-) - GAP] \cdot SD(x_{i,j})$;

8   **else**

9          $VariationPriority(x_{i,j}) = [GAP(+) - GAP] \cdot SD(x_{i,j})$;

10   Sort in descending order *VariationPriority* for every channel;

11   Select V pixels with the highest *VariationPriority* between the three channels;

12   **if** $GAP(-) > GAP(+)$ **then**

13   Subtract noise with magnitude δ from the pixel in the respective channel;

14   **else**

15   Add noise with magnitude δ to the pixel in the respective channel;

16   Compute $D(X^*, X)$ as the sum of the $D(X^*, X)$ of every channel;

17   Update the original example with the adversarial one;

Our algorithm operates in the following steps:

1. Select a subset P of pixels, included in the area $M \cdot N$, with the highest SD for every RGB channel, making their possible modification difficult to be detected.

2. Compute the gap function as the difference between the probability of the target class and the maximum output probability.

3. For each pixel in P, compute $GAP(+)$ and $GAP(-)$: these values correspond to the gap function, estimated by adding and subtracting a perturbation unit to each pixel, respectively. These gaps help decide whether adding or subtracting the noise is more effective. For each pixel in P, we consider the highest value between $GAP(+)$ and $GAP(-)$ to maximize the distance between the two probabilities.

4. For each pixel in P, calculate the Variation Priority by multiplying the gap difference with the SD of the pixel. This value indicates the efficacy of the pixel perturbation.

5. For every channel, the P values of Variation Priority are ordered, and the highest V values are perturbed.

6. Only V values of the total $3 \cdot P$ are perturbed. The noise is added or subtracted according to the highest value of the previously computed $GAP(+)$ and $GAP(-)$.

7. Once the original input image is replaced by the adversarial example, the next iteration starts. The iterations stop when the distance D overcomes D_{MAX}.

4.2.3   Evaluation of the CapsAttack Methodology

4.2.3.1   Experimental Setup

For the analysis of the GTSRB dataset, we consider the CapsNet [236]. We implement it in TensorFlow to perform image classification on the GTSRB dataset [92] with an accuracy of 97.6%. This dataset has images of size 32×32 divided into 34 799 training examples and 12 630 testing examples. Each pixel intensity value spans from 0 to 1. The number of classes is 43. For evaluation purposes, we compare the CapsNet with a 5-layer CNN (LeNet) [118], trained for 30 epochs, and a 9-layer CNN (VGGNet) [276], trained for 120 epochs. Their accuracy for clean test images is 91.3% and 97.7%, respectively.

For the analysis of the CIFAR10 dataset, we consider the DeepCaps architecture [220], which is composed of 18 layers. We implement it in TensorFlow, and its classification accuracy on the CIFAR10 dataset [112] is 91.52%. The CIFAR10 dataset contains 50 000 training images and 10 000 testing images of size 32×32, divided into 10 classes. We compare it with a 20-layer ResNet [84], which has an accuracy with clean test images of 91.48%.

We apply our methodology, discussed in Algorithm 13, to the previously described CapsNet, DeepCaps, LeNet, VGGNet, and ResNet. We test it on two different examples to verify how our algorithm works. We consider $M = N = 32$, because the GTRSB and CIFAR10 datasets are composed of 32×32 images, $P = 100$, and $V = 20$. The value of δ equals 10% of the maximum value between all the pixels. The parameter D_{MAX} depends on the SD of the pixels of the input image: its value changes according to the examples because $D(X^*, X)$ does not increase in the same way for each example.

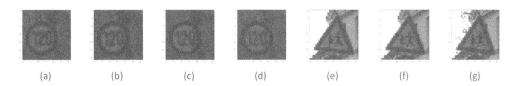

(a)   (b)   (c)   (d)   (e)   (f)   (g)

Figure 4.9: Images for the attack applied to the CapsNet: **(a)** Original input image of Example 1. **(b)** Image misclassified by the CapsNet at iteration 13 for Case I. **(c)** Image misclassified by the CapsNet at iteration 16 for Case I. **(d)** Image at iteration 12 for Case II. **(e)** Original input image for Example 2. **(f)** Image at iteration 5, applied to the CapsNet. **(g)** Image misclassified by the CapsNet at iteration 21.

4.2.3.2 Our Methodology Applied to the CapsNet

We test the CapsNet on two different examples of the GTSRB dataset, shown in Figure 4.9a (Example 1) and Figure 4.9e (Example 2). To test whether our methodology works independently from the choice of the target class, we distinguish two cases:

Case I: the target class is the class relative to the second highest initial output probability.

Case II: the target class is the class relative to the fifth highest probability between all the initial output probabilities.

By analyzing Case I and Case II, we can make the following key observations:

1. The CapsNet classifies the input image shown in Figure 4.9a as "120 km/h speed limit" (S8) with a probability equal to 0.0370. For Case I, the target class is "Double curve" (S21) with a probability equal to 0.0297. After 13 iterations of our algorithm, the image (Figure 4.9b) is classified as "Double curve" with a probability equal to 0.0339. Hence, *the probability of the target class has overcome the initial one*, as shown in Figure 4.10a. At this step, the distance $D(X^*, X)$ is equal to 434.20. By increasing the number of iterations, the robustness of the attack increases because the gap between the two probabilities increases, but also, the perceptibility of the noise becomes more evident. After the iteration 16, the distance grows above $D_{MAX} = 520$. The sample is represented in Figure 4.9c. This analysis shows that there is a tradeoff between robustness and imperceptibility.

   For Case II, the probability relative to the target class "Beware of ice/snow" (S30) is equal to 0.0249, as shown in Figure 4.10b. The gap between the maximum probability and the probability of the target class is higher than the gap in Case I. After 12 iterations, the network has not misclassified the image yet (Figure 4.9d). In Figure 4.10b, we can observe that the gap between the two classes has decreased, but not enough for a misclassification. However, at this iteration, the value of the distance overcomes $D_{MAX} = 520$. In this case, we show that our algorithm would need more iterations to misclassify at the cost of slightly perceivable perturbations.

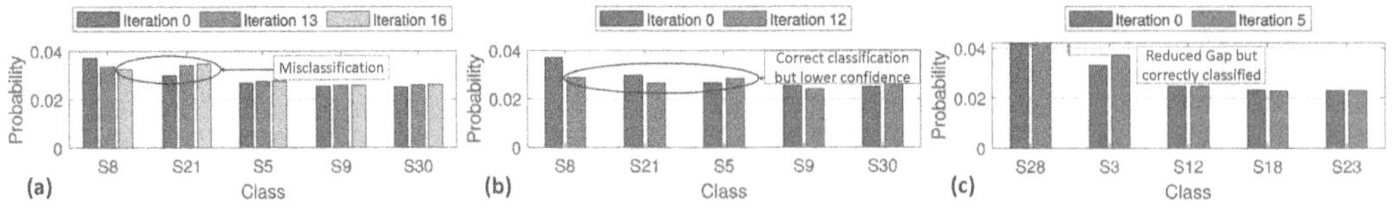

Figure 4.10: CapsNet results for the GTSRB dataset: **(a)** Output probabilities of Example 1—Case I: blue bars represent the starting probabilities, orange bars the probabilities at the point of misclassification, and yellow bars at the D_{MAX}. **(b)** Output probabilities of Example 1—Case II: blue bars represent the starting probabilities, and orange bars are the probabilities at the D_{MAX}. **(c)** Output probabilities of Example 2: blue bars represent the starting probabilities, and orange bars the probabilities at the D_{MAX}.

2. The CapsNet classifies the input image shown in Figure 4.9e as "Children crossing" (S28) with a probability equal to 0.042. The target class is "60 km/h speed limit" (S3) with a probability equal to 0.0331. After 5 iterations, the distance overcomes $D_{MAX} = 250$, while the network has not misclassified the image yet (Figure 4.9f) because the probability of the target class does not overcome the initial maximum probability, as shown in Figure 4.10c. The misclassification appears at the iteration 21 (Figure 4.9g). However, the perturbation is highly perceivable. Therefore, if this noise perception is not acceptable, such a solution would be discarded by our methodology, and a new solution would be searched, for which an adaptation of the constraints may be required, or a different input image is captured in a real-world system (e.g., a new image at a different distance from the camera).

4.2.3.3   Our Methodology Applied to the VGGNet and the LeNet

To compare the robustness of the CapsNet and the 9-layer VGGNet, we choose to evaluate the previous two examples, which have been applied to the CapsNet. For Example 1, we consider only Case I as the benchmark because Case II shows a similar behavior. The VGGNet classifies the input images with different output probabilities compared to the ones obtained by the CapsNet. Therefore, our metric to evaluate the resistance of the VGGNet against our attack is based on the value of the gap at the same distance.

To compare the robustness of the CapsNet and the 5-layer LeNet, we consider only Example 1 (Figure 4.11a) because Example 2 (Figure 4.11d) is already classified incorrectly by the LeNet. Note that the image of Example 2 belongs to the subset of images that are correctly classified by the CapsNet and the VGGNet, but incorrectly by the LeNet. Applying our algorithm to the LeNet, we observe that it is more vulnerable than the CapsNet and the VGGNet.

From our experiments, we make these key observations:

1. The VGGNet classifies the input image (Figure 4.11a) as "120 km/h speed limit" (S8) with a probability equal to 0.976. The target class is "100 km/h

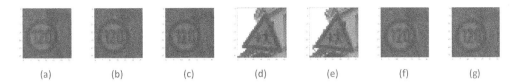

(a)	(b)	(c)	(d)	(e)	(f)	(g)

Figure 4.11: Images for the attack applied to the CNNs: **(a)** Original input image for Example 1. **(b)** Image at the iteration 3, applied to the VGGNet. **(c)** Image at the iteration 9, misclassified by the VGGNet. **(d)** Original input image for Example 2. **(e)** Image at the iteration 2, applied to the VGGNet. **(f)** Image at the iteration 6, misclassified by the LeNet. **(g)** Image at the iteration 13, misclassified by the LeNet.

speed limit" (S7) with a probability equal to 0.021. After 3 iterations, the distance overcomes $D_{MAX} = 520$, while the VGGNet has not misclassified the image yet (Figure 4.11b). Hence, our algorithm would need to perform more iterations before fooling the VGGNet, since the two initial probabilities were very distant, as shown in Figure 4.12a. Such scenario appears after 9 iterations (Figure 4.11c), where the probability of the target class is 0.483.

2. The VGGNet classifies the input image (Figure 4.11d) as "Children crossing" (S28) with a probability equal to 0.96. The target class is "Beware of ice/snow" (S30) with a probability of 0.023. After 2 iterations, the distance overcomes $D_{MAX} = 250$, while the VGGNet has not misclassified the image yet (Figure 4.11e). As in the previous case, this scenario is due to the high gap between the initial probabilities, as shown in Figure 4.12b. We can also notice that the VGGNet reaches D_{MAX} in a lower number of iterations than the CapsNet.

3. The LeNet classifies the input image (Figure 4.11d) as "120 km/h speed limit" (S8) with a probability equal to 0.672. The target class is "30 km/h speed limit" (S1) with a probability equal to 0.178. After 6 iterations, the perturbations fool the LeNet, because the image (Figure 4.11f) is classified as the target class with a probability equal to 0.339. The perturbations become perceptible after 13 iterations (Figure 4.11g), where the distance overcomes $D_{MAX} = 520$.

4.2.3.4 Our Methodology Applied to the DeepCaps and ResNet20 on the CIFAR10 Dataset

We test the DeepCaps and ResNet on two different images of the CIFAR10 dataset, shown in Figure 4.13a (Example 3) and in Figure 4.13d (Example 4). Both analyses have been conducted by choosing the target class as the second highest probability between the initial output probabilities.

The following key observations can be derived from our experiments:

1. For Example 3, both the DeepCaps and the ResNet correctly classify the input image (Figure 4.13a) as "truck" (S9), and for both networks, the target

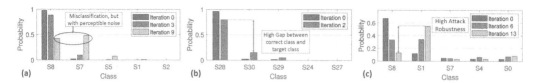

Figure 4.12: CNNs results for the GTSRB dataset: (a) Output probabilities of Example 1 on the VGGNet: blue bars represent the starting probabilities, orange bars the probabilities at the point of misclassification, and yellow bars at the D_{MAX}. (b) Output probabilities of Example 2 on the VGGNet: blue bars represent the starting probabilities and orange bars the probabilities at the D_{MAX}. (c) Output probabilities of Example 1 on the LeNet: blue bars represent the starting probabilities, orange bars the probabilities at the point of misclassification, and yellow bars at the D_{MAX}.

class is "ship" (S8). As shown in Figure 4.14a, *the DeepCaps is fooled by the attack*. After 6 iterations of the attack, the image is classified as "ship" with a probability of 0.421. Increasing the number of iterations increases the gap between the probabilities, thus making the attack more robust. After 11 iterations, the distance has overcome $D_{MAX} = 520$, and the adversarial example generated at this point is shown in Figure 4.13b. Similarly, *the attack also fools the ResNet*. After 5 iterations, it is classified as "ship" with a probability of 0.376. At the iteration 8 (see Figure 4.13c), the probability associated to the class "ship" is 0.433, while the distance has overcome $D_{MAX} = 520$.

2. Example 4 (Figure 4.13d) is correctly classified as a "bird" by the DeepCaps, with a probability equal to 0.847. The second highest probability, which will be the attack's target class, is associated with the class "horse" (S7). After 9 iterations, the distance overcomes $D_{MAX} = 450$, while the image shown in Figure 4.13e is still correctly classified as a "bird" by the DeepCaps with a probability equal to 0.524. The yellow bars in Figure 4.14c show that the image in Figure 4.13f is classified as a "horse" with a probability equal to 0.365, but

Figure 4.13: Images for the attack applied to the DeepCaps and ResNet20: (a) Original input image for Example 3. (b) Image at the iteration 11, misclassified by the DeepCaps. (c) Image at the iteration 8, misclassified by the ResNet20. (d) Original input image for Example 4. (e) Image at the iteration 9, applied to the DeepCaps. (f) Image at the iteration 14, misclassified by the DeepCaps. (g) Image at the iteration 9, misclassified by the ResNet20.

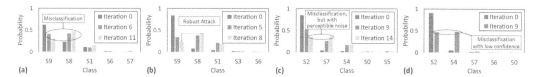

Figure 4.14: CIFAR10 results: **(a)** Output probabilities of Example 3 on the DeepCaps: blue bars represent the starting probabilities, orange bars represent the probabilities at the point of misclassification, and yellow bars denote probabilities at the D_{MAX}. **(b)** Output probabilities of Example 3 on the ResNet20: blue bars represent the starting probabilities, orange bars represent the probabilities at the point of misclassification, and yellow bars denote probabilities at the D_{MAX}. **(c)** Output probabilities of Example 4 on the DeepCaps: blue bars represent the starting probabilities, orange bars denote the probabilities at the D_{MAX}, and yellow bars represent the point of misclassification with $D(X^*, X) > D_{MAX}$. **(d)** Output probabilities of Example 4 on the ResNet20: blue bars represent the starting probabilities, orange bars denote the probabilities at the point of misclassification, which coincides with the D_{MAX}.

the distance is way beyond D_{MAX}. Hence, *only a perceptible noise can mislead the DeepCaps.*

3. The Example 4 (Figure 4.13d) is correctly classified as a "bird" by the ResNet, with a probability equal to 0.910. The target class is "deer" (S4). After 9 iterations, *the probability of the target class has overcome the initial one.* As shown in Figure 4.14d, the ResNet classifies the image in Figure 4.13g as a "deer" with a probability equal to 0.483. At this point, the distance has also reached $D_{MAX} = 450$.

4.2.3.5   Attack Vulnerability Comparison between the CapsNet and the CNNs

From our analyses, we can observe that the vulnerability of the 9-layer VGGNet to our adversarial attack is slightly lower than the vulnerability of the CapsNet, since the former requires more perceivable perturbations to be fooled. Our observation is corroborated by the results in Figure 4.15, where the value of $D(X^*, X)$ increases more sharply for the VGGNet than for the CapsNet. Hence, the noise perception in the image can be measured as the value of $D(X^*, X)$ divided by the number of iterations. Note that the noise in the VGGNet becomes perceivable after a few iterations. Moreover, we can observe that the choice of the target class plays a key role in the attack's success.

We also notice other features that lead to the differences between the VGGNet and the CapsNet. The VGGNet is deeper and contains a larger number of weights, while the CapsNet can achieve a similar accuracy with a smaller footprint. This effect causes a disparity in the prediction confidence between the two networks. It is clear that the CapsNet has a much higher learning capability than the VGGNet, but this phenomenon does not reflect in the prediction confidence. Indeed, comparing

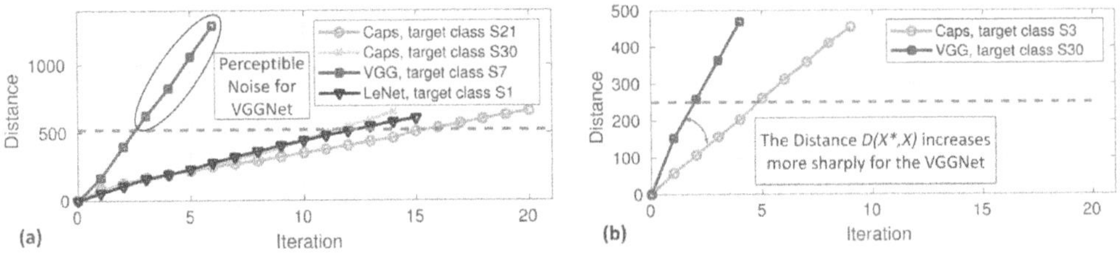

Figure 4.15: $D(X^*, X)$ behavior for **(a)** Example 1, and **(b)** Example 2.

Figure 4.10 and Figure 4.12, we can notice that the output probabilities predicted by the CapsNet are close to each other, even more than the LeNet. However, the perturbations do not affect the CapsNet's output probabilities as much as for the CNNs. The LeNet, even though it has a similar depth and a similar number of parameters, is more vulnerable than the CapsNet.

By comparing the DeepCaps with the ResNet20, we can notice that, despite the prediction confidence being slightly higher for the ResNet, the DeepCaps is less vulnerable to these perturbations. For instance, as noticed in Figure 4.14, after 9 iterations of the attack running on Example 4, the ResNet is fooled, while the DeepCaps still correctly classifies.

4.2.4 Summary

This section presents the proposed CapsAttacks methodology for generating targeted imperceptible and robust adversarial examples. It is an iterative procedure that introduces image perturbations in a black-box scenario. The evaluations are conducted on various CNN and CapsNet models, and the output probability variations across different attack iterations are analyzed in detail. Aligned with the observations noticed in the previous Section 4.1, the CapsNets exhibit higher adversarial robustness than CNNs. In particular, the DeepCaps shows higher robustness than the ResNet20. Further robustness analyses comparing CNNs and CapsNets will be discussed in the following Section 4.3.

4.3 FAKEWEATHER: ADVERSARIAL ATTACKS FOR DNNS EMULATING WEATHER CONDITIONS ON THE CAMERA LENS OF AUTONOMOUS SYSTEMS

Recently, DNNs have achieved remarkable performances in many applications, while several studies have enhanced their vulnerabilities to malicious attacks. In this section, we emulate the effects of natural weather conditions for introducing plausible perturbations that mislead the DNNs. Observing the effects of such weather perturbations on the camera, we model these patterns to create different masks that fake the effects of atmospheric conditions such as rain, snow, and hail. Even though the perturbations injected by our attacks are visible, their presence is unnoticed due to their association with natural events. We test our proposed *fakeWeather* attacks on multiple CNN and CapsNet models and report significant accuracy drops when such adversarial perturbations are applied. This work introduces a new security threat for DNNs, which is especially severe for safety-critical applications and autonomous systems.

4.3.1 System Overview

The key goal for an adversarial attack and its applicability in practical use cases consists of not being detected as adversarial but rather as plausible/common. The most straightforward approach is to inject a minimal amount of perturbations, to make the differences between the clean and adversarial images imperceptible to the human eye. However, the attacker needs to access a set of information, including DNN model architecture and parameters, inputs, and outputs (i.e., in *white-box* settings), or only inputs and outputs (i.e., in *black-box* settings). Even the most advanced decision-based black-box attacks still have access to the DNN predicted output class for each image. However, in practice, it may be difficult to obtain such information due to the protection mechanisms applied by the DNN-based system developers. Moreover, another critical limitation resides in the fact that even the most query-efficient algorithms [279] need to perform a certain amount of queries (i.e., inference passes) to generate the adversarial perturbation, which might not be practical in case of stringent real-time constraints, due to the latency overhead caused by the queries.

Considering these limitations of the adversarial attacks that aim at injecting imperceptible perturbations to the original images, our approach follows a different strategy. *Our novel idea is to introduce perturbations to the input image so that it is not considered adversarial since it resembles a natural scene captured by the camera.* Even though the differences between the clean image and the adversarial image may be noticed, the adversarial image is hardly categorized as "adversarial" since it simply captures a plausible natural condition. The reason is due to the fact that traditional adversarial ML evaluates the comparison between the adversarial image and the original image. However, in real-world practice, it is impossible to evaluate it since we can only access image recorded by the camera. Noticeably, our methodology is advantageous compared to previous works since it is conducted in what we call a *true black-box setting*, i.e., a scenario where the attacker has no information about the DNN architecture and parameters nor its outputs. The only information needed is the size of the input image for generating adversarial masks of that size. Moreover, our attack algorithm does not require any query. Hence, it can easily be applied at run time.

Toward this, we observe how the camera perceives natural weather conditions, such as rain, snow, and hail. We exploit this observation by designing *fakeWeather* attack algorithms that fake these effects on the camera. An overview of its functionality is illustrated in Figure 4.16. Our approach can be used not only as an adversarial attack algorithm to mislead the DNN but also as a data augmentation technique for reinforcing the DNN training under these conditions. Our contributions can be summarized as follows:

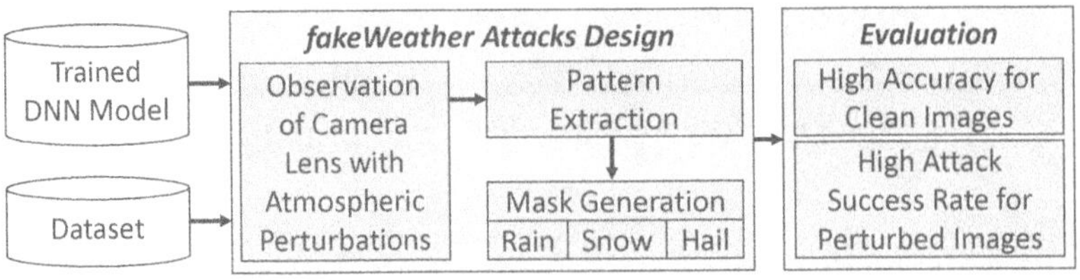

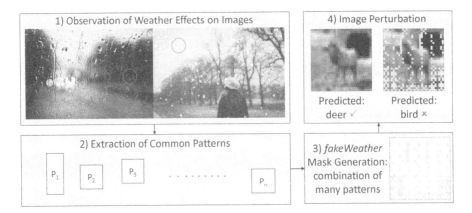

Figure 4.16: Overview of the fakeWeather attacks functionality.

- We observe several images of natural weather events that affect the camera and identify the patterns that are more common in such images.

- By only knowing the image size, we design three *fakeWeather* masks that emulate the effect of such atmospheric conditions on the camera.

- We evaluate the *fakeWeather* attacks on multiple DNN models (LeNet-5, ResNet-32, CapsNet) for the CIFAR10 dataset, and obtain a success rate of the attacks varying between 30% and 82.5%.

4.3.2 fakeWeather Attacks Design

4.3.2.1 *Problem Formulation and Assumptions*

Considering the previous discussions, we propose the **fakeWeather** methodology. An in-depth view of its key steps is shown in Figure 4.17. The final goal is to produce a finite set of perturbations with certain patterns that resemble the effect of natural weather events. Therefore, such patterns are crafted by faking that the camera lens is dirty due to atmospheric perturbations (such as rain, snow, and hail). After observing their effects on several real-world examples, the common patterns are extracted and reproduced for generating the perturbation masks. The attacks are conducted in what we call a *true black-box setting*, i.e., assuming that:

Figure 4.17: Overview of the *fakeWeather* attack methodology, highlighting the key steps.

- the adversary has no information about the DNN model architecture, its parameters, and its output;

- the only information available for the attacker is the size of the input images.

4.3.2.2 Observation of Weather Conditions

The *fakeWeather* attacks are performed by introducing drops of water and snowflakes. A common water drop has a spherical shape, while a snowflake has a hexagonal shape. However, in practical use cases, these weather conditions do not represent the camera's primary focus. A camera captures scenes of rain and snow differently, resulting in a set of blurry dots that overlap with the image. For instance, considering vision for smart mobility, the camera can be placed either outside the vehicle (and therefore exposed to the weather conditions) or inside the vehicle but close to the window. Without loss of generality, we model a drop or a snowflake as a single pixel w.r.t. the image of $h \times l$ pixels, where h and l represent the height and length, respectively.

4.3.2.3 Pattern Extraction and Mask Generation

According to the previous considerations, the *fakeWeather* methodology extends the formulation of the One Pixel Attack [260], in which the perturbation of a *single pixel* is defined as an array of 5 elements (x, y, r, g, b) where:

- (x, y) represent the coordinates of the pixel to be modified;

- (r, g, b) indicate the pixel's color in RGB format.

Hence, an adversarial pattern combines multiple pixel attacks where the perturbation introduced on the pixel i can be written as in Equation (4.4). An example of how to generate the adversarial pattern is shown in Figure 4.18.

$$pixel_i = (x_i, y_i, r_i, g_i, b_i) \tag{4.4}$$

The colors, i.e., the values of (r_i, g_i, b_i), are determined according to the weather condition:

- **rain**: $(r_r, g_r, b_r) = (208, 209, 214)$;

- **snow** and **hail**: $(r_s, g_s, b_s) = (249, 242, 242)$.

Specific patterns are generated for each type of *fakeWeather* attack (i.e., rain, snow, and hail). Common patterns are extracted from natural images and reproduced to form the set of pixel coordinates (x_i, y_i) that belongs to the attack mask. Once designed, the same mask is applied to all the images under attack.

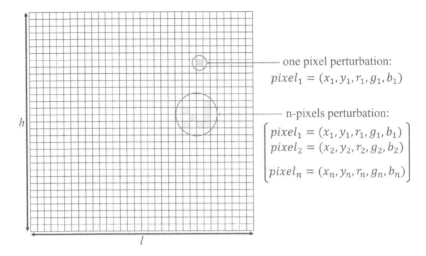

Figure 4.18: Encoding of pixel perturbations that form the adversarial pattern.

4.3.2.4 *fakeRain Attack*

The mask employed in the *fakeRain* attack is designed based on the combination of several water drops. The camera lens can be naturally soiled due to the rain, where the water drops make up different patterns. We can recognize three real-case scenarios, categorized as an agglomerate of drops, drop patches, and drop lines. As shown in Figure 4.19, the next step consists of modeling these patterns in terms of perturbed pixel coordinates.

The *Agglomerate Pattern* can be modeled by combining together 5 pixels to form a cross sign, according to the sketch in Figure 4.20a and Algorithm 14. The *Patch*

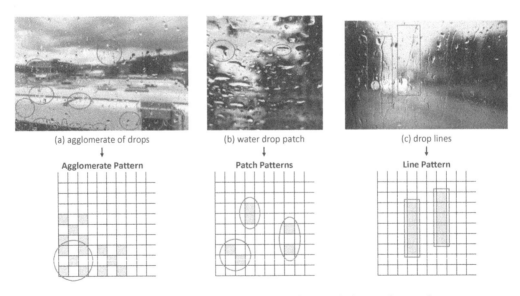

Figure 4.19: Several patterns of water drops observed from the real environment. (**a**) agglomerate of drops, (**b**) water drop patch, (**c**) drop lines.

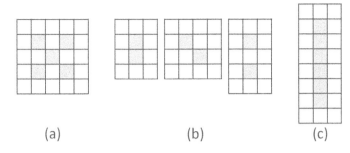

(a)   (b)   (c)

Figure 4.20: A graphical representation of
(a) Agglomerate Pattern, (b) Patch Patterns,
and (c) Line Pattern.

Figure 4.21: V-shaped fakeRain attack.

Pattern (see Figure 4.20b) can have three different shapes, namely the *vertical patch*, which can be modeled as two consecutive pixels that share the same x coordinate (lines 4-6 of Algorithm 15), the *diagonal patch*, modeled as two pixels forming a diagonal (lines 10-17 of Algorithm 15, and the *two dots patch*, in which two pixels are separated by a blank space (lines 20-22 of Algorithm 15). The *Line Pattern*, shown in Figure 4.20c, is modeled as a vertical line of n pixels (see Algorithm 16).

Algorithm 14: Agglomerate Pattern

Input: Coordinate (x_0, y_0)
Output: Agglomerate Pattern P_a
1 $P_a = \varnothing$;
2 $k = 0$;
3 **for** $i \leftarrow 0$ **to** 2 **do**
4   **for** $j \leftarrow 0$ **to** 2 **do**
5   **if** $(i + j = 0 \lor i + j = 2 \lor i + j = 4)$ **then**
6           $P_a \leftarrow pixel_k = (x_0 + i, y_0 + j, r_r, g_r, b_r)$;
7           $k \leftarrow k + 1$;

Moreover, in rainy conditions, we can observe that the water drops tend to concentrate in the bottom corners of the image. Hence, to emulate this effect, in the *fakeRain* attack, a *V-shape* is created to divide the image into two areas (see the example in Figure 4.21). Below the *V*, several agglomerate patterns are densely concentrated. Above the *V*, path and line patterns are more sparsely distributed. Algorithm 17 describes the procedure for generating the *fakeRain* mask. Note that it is a three-step process where (i) several agglomerate patterns are added (see line 2 of Algorithm 17), (ii) other agglomerate patterns are added if the coordinate is below the *V* (line 5 of Algorithm 17), and (iii) different types of patch patterns and line patterns are added above the *V* (line 7 of Algorithm 17).

Algorithm 15: Patch Pattern

Input: Coordinate (x_0, y_0), Type t
Output: Patch Pattern P_p

1   $P_p = \varnothing$;
2   **switch** t **do**
3   **case** 0 **do** // Vertical Patch
4   **for** $j \leftarrow 0$ **to** 1 **do**
5         $P_p \leftarrow pixel_j = (x_0, y_0 + j, r_r, g_r, b_r)$;

6   **case** 1 **do** // Diagonal Patch
7       $k = 0$;
8   **for** $i \leftarrow 0$ **to** 1 **do**
9   **for** $j \leftarrow 0$ **to** 1 **do**
10   **if** $(i + j = 1)$ **then**
11             $P_p \leftarrow pixel_k = (x_0 + i, y_0 + j, r_r, g_r, b_r)$;
12             $k \leftarrow k + 1$;

13   **case** 2 **do** // Two Dots Patch
14   **for** $j \leftarrow 0$ **to** 1 **do**
15         $P_p \leftarrow pixel_j = (x_0, y_0 + 2 \cdot j, r_r, g_r, b_r)$;

Algorithm 16: Line Pattern

Input: Coordinate (x_0, y_0), Length n
Output: Line Pattern P_l

1   $P_l = \varnothing$;
2   **for** $j \leftarrow 0$ **to** $n - 1$ **do**
3     $P_l \leftarrow pixel_j = (x_0, y_0 + j, r_r, g_r, b_r)$;

4.3.2.5 fakeSnow Attack

The *fakeSnow* attack is designed based on the assumption that a snowflake can be modeled as a single pixel because the dimension of each snowflake is relatively small, as observed in Figure 4.22. According to these considerations, the snow pattern P_s consists of a single pixel, which can be modeled as in Equation (4.5), where (x_0, y_0) represents the coordinate where the snow pattern is constructed.

$$P_s \leftarrow pixel_0(x_0, y_0, r_s, g_s, b_s) \tag{4.5}$$

Another key feature observed from real images is that the snowflakes are more densely concentrated close to the horizon line. In practice, this behavior can be modeled by cutting the image into three parts through two horizontal lines, as shown in Figure 4.23, and placing more dense snow patterns in the middle region while keeping the top and the bottom of the image relatively less populated by

---

Algorithm 17: fakeRain Mask Generation

Input: Image size: length l and hight h
Output: fakeRain Mask M_r

1   $M_r = \varnothing$;
2   $M_r \leftarrow P_a(\{0, ..., l-3\}, 0)$;
    `// use many agglomerate patterns in the first line`
3   **for** $(i, j) \in (\{0, ..., l-3\}, \{0, ..., h-3\})$ **do**
4   **if** $(i + j < \frac{h+l}{4}) \vee (l - i + j < \frac{h+l}{4})$ **then**
5        $M_r \leftarrow P_a(i, j) \vee \{\}$;
       `// sparsely add agglomerate patterns below the V`
6   **else**
7        $M_r \leftarrow P_p(i, j, t) \vee P_l(i, j, n) \vee \{\}$;
       `// sparsely add patch patterns or line patterns above the`
       `V`

Figure 4.22: Several snowflakes observed, which can be modeled as single dots.

snow patterns. The generation of the mask for the *fakeSnow* attack is described in Algorithm 18. It proceeds in different manners based on the vertical coordinate j. In the middle region of the image, equally-spaced dense snow patterns are added to the *fakeSnow* mask (line 9 of Algorithm 18). In the upper and lower parts of the image, rows of dense and sparse (i.e., largely spaced) snow patterns are alternatively added (lines 4-7 of Algorithm 18).

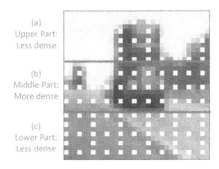

Figure 4.23: Mask for the fakeSnow attack, divided into three parts.

Algorithm 18: fakeSnow Mask Generation

Input: Image size: length l and hight h
Output: fakeSnow Mask M_s

1   $M_s = \varnothing$;
2   **for** $j, \in \{0, 2, 4, ..., h - 2\})$ **do**
3   **if** $(j < \frac{h}{3} - 1) \vee j > \frac{2h}{3} - 1)$ **then**
         `// upper and lower parts`
4   **if** $j \equiv 0 \mod 4$ **then**
5            $M_s \leftarrow P_s(\{0, 3, 6, 9, ..., l - 2\}, j + 1)$;
6   **else** `// skip some snow patterns`
7            $M_s \leftarrow P_s(\{0, 6, 12, ..., l - 2\}, j + 1)$;
8   **else** `// middle part`
9         $M_s \leftarrow P_s(\{0, 3, 6, 9, ..., l - 2\}, j + 1)$;
         `// add dense snow patterns`

4.3.2.6   fakeHail Attack

Compared to the snow, a hail scene produce relatively larger ice balls perceived by the camera, as shown in Figure 4.24. Therefore, the hail pattern is not modeled as a single pixel but as an agglomerate of 8 pixels, as described in Algorithm 19.

Since the hail patterns appear irregularly, the *fakeHail* mask can be generated through a collection of hail patterns, as described in Algorithm 20. Note that the hail patterns are sparsely injected because, for each coordinate, the hail pattern can be injected into the mask or not (line 3 of Algorithm 20).

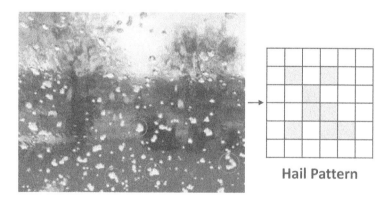

Hail Pattern

Figure 4.24: Observation of hail conditions, which lead to the design of the hail pattern.

Algorithm 19: Hail Pattern

Input: Coordinate (x_0, y_0)
Output: Hail Pattern P_h
1   $P_h = \varnothing$;
2   $k = 0$;
3   **for** $i \leftarrow 0$ **to** 3 **do**
4   **for** $j \leftarrow 0$ **to** 3 **do**
5   **if** $(i = j \wedge i < 2) \vee (i + j = 3) \vee (i = 2 \wedge j \neq 2)$ **then**
6           $P_h \leftarrow pixel_k = (x_0 + i, y_0 + j, r_s, g_s, b_s)$;
7           $k \leftarrow k + 1$;

Algorithm 20: fakeHail Mask Generation

Input: Image size: length l and hight h
Output: fakeHail Mask M_h
1   $M_h = \varnothing$;
2   **for** $(i, j) \in (\{0, ..., l - 4\}, \{0, ..., h - 4\})$ **do**
3      $M_h \leftarrow P_h(i, j) \vee \{\}$;

4.3.3   Evaluation of the fakeWeather Attacks

4.3.3.1   *Experimental Setup*

We conducted the experiments on three DNN models, which are the LeNet-5 [118], the ResNet-32 [84], and the CapsNet [236], trained for the CIFAR10 dataset [112]. It is a collection of $50\,000$ training images and $10\,000$ testing images of size $32 \times 32 \times 3$, divided into 10 classes.

The LeNet has been trained for 200 epochs, using a batch size of 128, weight decay 0.0001, and a learning rate scheduler that reduces its value from 0.05 to 0.0004. The 32-layer ResNet has been trained for 200 epochs, using a batch size of 128, weight decay of 0.0001, and a learning rate that decreases from 0.1 to 0.001. The CapsNet has been trained for 200 epochs with a batch size of 64 and a learning rate of 0.001. For clean test images, we measure an accuracy of 74.88%, 92.31%, and 79.82% for the LeNet, ResNet, and CapsNet, respectively.

Afterward, the *fakeWeather* masks have been applied to 200 testing samples and the adversarial success rate has been evaluated for each attack type (i.e., *fakeRain*, *fakeSnow* and *fakeHail*) and each DNN model. The training, the implementation of the *fakeWeather* attacks, and their evaluation have been conducted using the Keras framework with the TensorFlow [1] back-end and executed on an ML-workstation equipped with two Nvidia GeForce RTX 2080 Ti GPUs.

TABLE 4.6: Evaluation of the Adversarial Success Rate (ASR) for the LeNet, the ResNet, and the CapsNet on the CIFAR10 dataset. Our proposed *fakeWeather* attacks have been compared to the 1-pixel, 3-pixel, and 5-pixel attacks [260].

ASR on Attack	LeNet	ResNet	CapsNet
1-pixel	63%	34%	19%
3-pixel	92%	79%	39%
5-pixel	93%	79%	36%
fakeRain (ours)	72%	67%	36%
fakeSnow (ours)	75.5%	79.5%	30%
fakeHail (ours)	82.5%	78.5%	63%

4.3.3.2 *fakeWeather Attacks Evaluation*

Table 4.6 reports the results in terms of Adversarial Success Rate (ASR) for the *fakeRain*, *fakeSnow* and *fakeHail* attacks. This metrics indicate the ratio between the misclassified examples and all the tested examples. The results are compared with the state-of-the-art 1-pixel, 3-pixel, and 5-pixel attacks proposed by Su et al. [260]. Moreover, Figure 4.25 shows a collection of adversarial examples generated with the *fakeWeather* attacks.

fakeRain Evaluation

The *fakeRain* attack is successful for the LeNet and the ResNet, since their ASRs are 72% and 67%, respectively. The ResNet is slightly more robust than the LeNet,

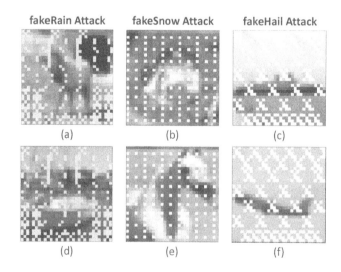

Figure 4.25: Examples of a few images of the CIFAR10 dataset on which the *fakeWeather* attacks are applied. (**a**) and (**d**): *fakeRain* adversarial examples. (**b**) and (**e**): *fakeSnow* adversarial examples. (**c**) and (**f**): *fakeHail* adversarial examples.

because of its deeper structure. The ASR decreases to 36% for the CapsNet since its model architecture that groups neurons into capsules, along with the dynamic routing, helps in better encoding the spatial relations between image features. The example in Figure 4.25a shows the image of a deer on which the *fakeRain* mask is applied. All three DNN models erroneously classify it as a "bird", while its clean version is correctly classified as a "deer". Similarly, the image in Figure 4.25d is incorrectly classified as a "truck" by both the LeNet and the ResNet, while its clean version is correctly predicted as a "ship". However, the CapsNet still classifies its adversarial example as a "ship".

fakeSnow Evaluation

For the *fakeSnow* attack, the relations between the ASRs of the three DNN models are similar to the observations made for the *fakeRain* attack, where the CapsNet is more robust than the other CNNs. However, the ASR values are higher for the ResNet than the LeNet. The example in Figure 4.25b showing a frog with the *fakeSnow* mask is correctly classified by the CapsNet. However, it is incorrectly predicted as a "cat" by the ResNet and as a "truck" by the LeNet. Its clean image is correctly classified as a "frog" by all the DNNs. The horse in Figure 4.25e is correctly classified by the CapsNet and the ResNet, while the LeNet classifies it as a "deer".

fakeHail Evaluation

The ASR relative to the *fakeHail* attack is significantly higher than the previous attacks, particularly for the CapsNet. Due to the relatively large perturbations introduced by the hail patterns (i.e., 8-pixel perturbations), the *fakeHail* mask can break the spatial relations learned by the CapsNet and lead to many misclassified samples. The example in Figure 4.25c represents a ship with the *fakeHail* mask, which is incorrectly classified as an "airplane" by the CapsNet and the LeNet, and as a "truck" by the ResNet. The image in Figure 4.25f is incorrectly classified as a "deer" by the ResNet, as a "cat" by the LeNet, and as a "frog" by the CapsNet, despite showing an airplane.

4.3.3.3 Case Studies: Output Probability Variations under fakeWeather Attacks

For a more comprehensive evaluation, we analyze the output probability variations when different types of *fakeWeather* attacks are applied to the ResNet, LeNet, and CapsNet models. For reference, the 10 classes of the CIFAR10 dataset are associated with a digit $0 - 9$ according to the convention in Table 4.7.

Figure 4.26 shows, as an example, the image of a "truck" of the CIFAR10 dataset and the corresponding adversarial examples obtained with the *fakeWeather* attacks. Figure 4.27 shows how such images are classified by different DNN models. The clean image is correctly predicted as the class 9, i.e., "truck" by the LeNet, despite having relatively low confidence (see Figure 4.27a). When each of the *fakeWeather* masks is applied, the LeNet predicts the image as a "frog" with quite high confidence. The probability variations for the ResNet have a different behavior. The clean image is correctly classified by the ResNet with high confidence (see Figure 4.27b), while the *fakeWeather* attacks produce different outcomes. With the *fakeRain* mask the image is classified as an "automobile" by the ResNet, with the *fakeSnow* mask the highest

TABLE 4.7: Class labels for the CIFAR10 dataset.

#	Class
0	airplane
1	automobile
2	bird
3	cat
4	deer
5	dog
6	frog
7	horse
8	ship
9	truck

probability belongs to the class "bird", and the ResNet classifies the adversarial *fakeHail* image as an "airplane". The CapsNet's output probabilities, while they are more concentrated toward the middle values, i.e., 1/10, report that the clean image is correctly classified (see Figure 4.27c), while for all the *fakeWeather* attacks, the highest probability belongs to the class "horse".

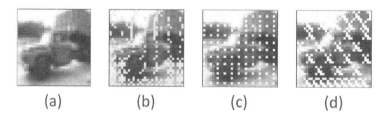

Figure 4.26: Example showing a "truck" to which the *fakeWeather* attacks are applied. (**a**) Clean image, (**b**) *fakeRain* image, (**c**) *fakeSnow* image, and (**d**) *fakeHail* image.

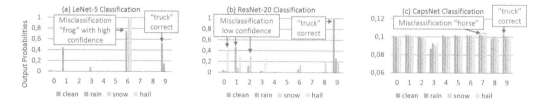

Figure 4.27: Analysis of the output probability variation for a "truck" to which the *fakeWeather* attacks are applied. (**a**) Output probabilities for the LeNet. (**b**) Output probabilities for the ResNet. (**c**) Output probabilities for the CapsNet.

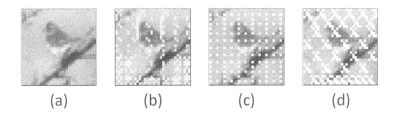

Figure 4.28: Example showing a "bird" to which the *fakeWeather* attacks are applied. (a) Clean image, (b) *fakeRain* image, (c) *fakeSnow* image, and (d) *fakeHail* image.

Figure 4.28 shows the image of a "bird" of the CIFAR10 dataset and the corresponding adversarial examples obtained with the *fakeWeather* attacks. Figure 4.29 shows how such images are classified by different DNN models. The clean image is already misclassified as an "airplane" by the LeNet (see Figure 4.29a). With the *fakeRain* or the *fakeHail* mask, the LeNet classifies the adversarial image as a "frog", while the adversarial *fakeSnow* image is classified as a "truck". The clean image is correctly classified by the ResNet as a "bird" with high confidence (see Figure 4.29b). The *fakeRain* and *fakeHail* adversarial images are classified as a "cat", while the *fakeSnow* is unsuccessful because the image is still correctly classified by the ResNet, even though with lower confidence than the clean image. The CapsNet correctly classifies the clean image by a narrow margin compared to the other classes (see Figure 4.29c). The *fakeRain* and *fakeSnow* attacks produce adversarial images that are classified as a "frog" by the CapsNet, while the image with the *fakeHail* mask is correctly classified by the CapsNet.

4.3.3.4 Results Discussion and Comparison

Following the above-discussed results, we can make the following observations:

- All the *fakeWeather* attacks produce a high ASR for the LeNet and ResNet ($ASR > 65\%$).

- The *fakeHail* attack is the strongest because it achieves an ASR of 63% for the CapsNet and higher ASR for the other DNNs.

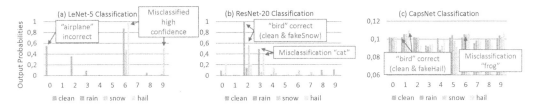

Figure 4.29: Analysis of the output probability variation for a "bird" to which the *fakeWeather* attacks are applied. (a) Output probabilities for the LeNet. (b) Output probabilities for the ResNet. (c) Output probabilities for the CapsNet.

Compared to the methods of [260], our *fakeWeather* methods have higher ASR than the 1-pixel attack for every DNN (see Table 4.6). However, the 3-pixel and 5-pixel attacks have higher ASR than our attacks. Note that, while the approach used in [260] is based on an evolutionary algorithm that requires several queries, our methodology does not need any query. Yet, the ASR of the CapsNet for the *fakeHail* attack is 27% higher than the 5-pixel attack.

4.3.3.5 *Future Outlooks and Applicability*

From another point of view, our contributions, other than a methodology for generating adversarial attacks in real-time without queries, can be viewed as a data augmentation technique for generating synthetic samples of weather scenes. We envision the possibility of expanding the dataset with images that contain *fakeWeather* masks and training DNN-based classifiers more robustly to such atmospheric phenomena, in a similar way as the adversarial training functionality [148]. Since the only information needed is the image size, its high scalability makes our *fakeWeather* attack methodology suitable for any vision-based outdoor application.

4.3.4 Summary

The proposed fakeWeather attacks are methodologies to generate adversarial examples by emulating the effects of atmospheric phenomena on the camera lens. Observing a set of images under weather conditions, the patterns captured by the camera lens are modeled to create dedicated fakeRain, fakeSnow, and fakeHail masks. The proposed attacks are operated in a so-called true black-box setting, where the adversary has no access to the DNN model parameters and its output. One of the key advantages of this procedure is that the attack algorithm does not need any query at runtime. Therefore, the adversary can apply the attack in real-time with very little latency. The evaluations on various CNN and CapsNet models show high adversarial success rates of the attacks.

4.4 SUMMARY OF ADVERSARIAL SECURITY THREATS FOR DNNS AND CAPSNETS

This chapter has discussed several robustness analyses, comparing the CNNs with the CapsNets. Among the vulnerability threats, the affine transformations and adversarial attacks for image classification applications have been studied. Moreover, novel methodologies for generating adversarial attacks have been proposed. Extensive evaluations have demonstrated that CapsNets show superior robustness than CNNs with similar sizes, while also, in some cases, they have higher robustness than deeper CNN models like the ResNet. The following Chapter 5 will discuss the challenges and methodologies to combine various optimization objectives, such as robustness and efficiency, into an integrated design flow.

Integration of Multiple Design Objectives into NAS Frameworks for CapsNets and DNNs

This chapter discusses methodologies for designing frameworks that integrate multiple design objectives into the design flow. Integrating multiple optimization objectives is challenging since it typically leads to a search space explosion. Therefore, several optimizations for exploring the search space quickly and accurately are proposed. First, Section 5.1 discusses the flow employed for conducting multi-objective optimizations. Afterward, as case studies, two multi-objective NAS frameworks are discussed. Section 5.2 presents an HW-aware NAS framework that jointly optimizes for accuracy and hardware efficiency, expressed in the form of memory, latency, and energy consumption. Section 5.3 discusses a framework for conducting robust HW-aware NAS, in which the adversarial robustness is also included in the optimization objectives.

5.1 FLOW FOR DESIGNING INTEGRATED FRAMEWORKS WITH MULTIPLE DESIGN OBJECTIVES

Figure 5.1 shows the flow of our integrated HW-aware NAS framework. The core of the methodology consists of finding the set of optimization objectives that need to be optimized during the search. The multi-objective optimization tool searches for Pareto-optimal DNN model candidates w.r.t. the objectives. Due to the large design space and the enormous amount of time required for exact evaluations of all the metrics, several optimizations need to be employed to reduce the exploration time. The DNN execution in hardware, including all the design-time optimizations (e.g., quantization and data reuse), is modeled to estimate the efficiency with analytical computations. The accuracy and robustness of the DNNs are modeled and evaluated

DOI: 10.1201/9781003530459-5

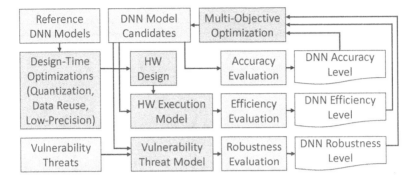

Figure 5.1: Overview of the design flow for integrating multiple optimization objectives, as shown in this chapter.

conjointly. The following Sections 5.2 and 5.3 will discuss all the optimization steps for designing the framework in more detail.

Major Contributions of the Chapter:

- **HW execution model**: it analytically models the hardware execution of different DNN and CapsNet layers on a given specialized accelerator. It computes latency, memory usage, and energy consumption for computing each operation.

- **NASCaps framework design:** it searches the DNN model architecture configurations based on convolutional and capsule layers to be executed on a given hardware accelerator. To explore the design space, a specialized multi-objective genetic algorithm has been deployed to define the Pareto-frontier between accuracy and energy efficiency.

- **RoHNAS framework design:** it conducts a multi-objective hardware-aware NAS for convolutional and capsule networks, where the robustness against adversarial attacks is one of the optimization objectives, together with energy, memory, and latency. Different adversarial perturbation values are selected based on their respective impact on the DNNs' robustness.

5.2 NASCAPS: A FRAMEWORK FOR NEURAL ARCHITECTURE SEARCH FOR OPTIMIZING ACCURACY AND HARDWARE EFFICIENCY OF CONVOLUTIONAL CAPSNETS

Among DNN models, CapsNets encode and learn spatial correlations between different input features, thereby obtaining superior learning capabilities than traditional (i.e., non-capsule-based) DNNs. However, designing CapsNets using conventional methods is tedious and incurs significant training effort. Recent studies have demonstrated that powerful methods to automatically select the optimal DNN configuration for a given set of applications and training datasets are based on the NAS algorithms. Moreover, due to their extreme memory and computational requirements, DNNs are employed using the specialized hardware accelerators in IoT-Edge/CPS devices.

In this section, we propose **NASCaps**, an automated framework for the hardware-aware NAS of different DNN models, covering both traditional convolutional DNNs and CapsNets. We investigate the efficacy of deploying a multi-objective Genetic Algorithm (e.g., based on the NSGA-II evolutionary algorithm). The proposed framework can jointly optimize the DNN accuracy and the corresponding hardware efficiency, expressed in terms of memory, energy, and latency of a given hardware accelerator executing DNN inference. Besides supporting the traditional layers of a DNN (such as Conv and FC), our framework is the first to model and support the specialized capsule layers and dynamic routing in the NAS flow. We evaluate our framework generating different DNN configurations on different datasets, and demonstrate the tradeoffs between the different output metrics.

5.2.1 System Overview

In the early stage of deep learning, the DNN architectures were manually designed. However, their structures became very complex. Therefore, NAS methodologies emerged as an attractive procedure for selecting the optimal DNN model for a given set of applications and training datasets. Most automatic tools based on a NAS algorithm only focus on optimizing the DNN accuracy. Only a few of them have recently considered the hardware metrics in the optimization problem, for instance, evaluating the hardware resources (e.g., #FLOPs, memory requirements) available for performing the DNN inference. To our knowledge, none of them include the possibility of employing capsule layers and dynamic routing in the design space, which are inevitable for automatically designing the CapsNets.

Toward this, we propose **NASCaps**, a framework for the NAS of DNNs, which not only incorporates the most common DNN layer types (such as Conv, FC) but also, *for the first time, the capsule layers.* Our framework supports multi-objective hardware-aware optimizations since it investigates the network accuracy and accounts for different hardware efficiency parameters (such as latency, memory usage, and energy consumption) that are crucial for embedded DNN inference accelerators.

However, the wide variety of possible configurations that should be explored to obtain an exhaustive set of Pareto-optimal solutions might dramatically explode. In addition, despite adopting the most advanced learning policies and employing high-end GPU clusters, complex CapsNets and CNNs typically require a long training time. Complete detailed post-synthesis hardware measurements are not practical for this search due to their long simulation times. These limitations challenge the applicability of such an exploration in real-case HW/SW co-design searches with stringent time-to-market constraints.

To address the above challenges, we employ different optimizations and integrate them into our *NASCaps* framework (Figure 5.2). The steps are summarized in the following **novel contributions**:

- We present a framework, called *NASCaps*, to automatically search the DNN model architecture configurations based on Conv layers and capsule layers.

- We analytically model the operations involved in the CapsNet architectures, including the different types of capsule layers and the dynamic routing.

- We model the functional behavior of a given specialized CapsNet and CNN hardware accelerator at a high level to quickly estimate the latency, memory usage, and energy consumption when different DNN architectural models are executed.

- Based on the NSGA-II method, we developed a specialized multi-objective genetic algorithm to solve a multi-objective Pareto-frontier selection of DNN architectures while optimizing the neural network's accuracy, energy consumption, memory usage, and latency.

- To reduce the training time for exploring different solutions, we devise a methodology to evaluate the accuracy of partially-trained DNNs. The number of training epochs is selected based on the tradeoff between training time and Pearson correlation coefficient w.r.t. fully-trained DNNs.

- During the exploration phase, we trained and evaluated more than 600 candidate DNN solutions running on the GPU-HPC computing nodes equipped with four high-end Nvidia V100-SMX2 GPUs. The Pareto-optimal solutions generated by our *NASCaps* framework are competitive w.r.t. the previous state-of-the-art accuracy values for CapsNets, i.e., the DeepCaps, while improving the corresponding hardware efficiency, thereby opening new avenues toward the deployment of high-accurate DNNs at the edge.

5.2.2 NASCaps Framework

5.2.2.1 Framework Overview

Our multi-objective *NASCaps* framework generates and evaluates convolutional- and capsule-based DNNs, by performing a multi-objective NAS, to find a set of accurate

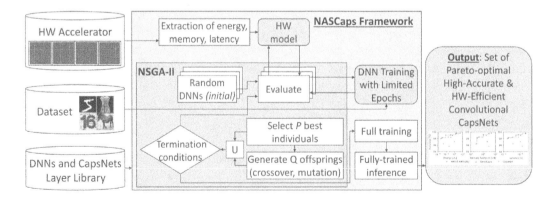

Figure 5.2: Overview of our *NASCaps* framework, showing different components and their interconnections defining the workflow.

yet resource-efficient DNN models, i.e., jointly considering the DNN validation accuracy, energy consumption, latency, and memory footprint. The search is based on our specialization of the genetic NSGA-II algorithm [42], to enable a search with multi-objective comparison and selection among the generated candidate DNNs.

An overview of the structure and workflow of the *NASCaps* framework is shown in Figure 5.2. As input, it receives the configuration of the underlying hardware accelerator (that would execute the generated DNN in the real-world scenario) and a given dataset used for DNN training, as well as a collection of the possible types of layers that can be used to form different candidate DNNs. First, we create a layer library that includes Conv layers, capsule layers (as defined in [236]), and the CapsCell and FlatCaps layers defined in [220]. We envision that, due to the modular structure of our framework, other types of layers can easily be integrated into its future versions to extend the search space further, also thanks to the use of a simple modular representation of the candidate networks relying on the combination of single-layer descriptors.

The automated search is initialized with N randomly-generated DNNs used as input to start the evolutionary search process. Each candidate DNN is evaluated in terms of its validation accuracy after training for a limited number of epochs. This optimization is designed to curtail the computational cost and reduce the required search time while keeping a good correlation w.r.t. the full-training accuracy, measured with the Pearson correlation coefficient. Moreover, each DNN under test is also characterized for its energy consumption, latency, and memory footprint, by modeling its inference processing considering the final real-world use case of executing the generated DNN on a specialized DNN hardware accelerator. At this evaluation point, the genetic algorithm proceeds to the next step, finding a new Pareto-frontier that contains the best candidate DNN solutions at each iteration. At the end of this selective procedure, the Pareto-optimal DNN solutions are fully-trained for 100 epochs for the MNIST, Fashion-MNIST, and SVHN datasets and for 300 epochs for the CIFAR10 dataset to make an exact accuracy evaluation. In the following subsections, we discuss the key components of our framework in detail.

5.2.2.2 *Parametric Modeling of CapsNet Layers and Architectures*

The proposed genetic-based *NASCaps* framework relies on an explicit position-based representation for each layer of the candidate DNNs. This representation allows defining the key parameters of each layer uniquely.

The DNN layers have been constructed using a *layer descriptor*, which encodes the information needed to build and model a given candidate network in a very compact form. Each layer descriptor is a 9-element position-based structure, thus guaranteeing the modularity for constructing any given DNN architecture. **The elements of the layer descriptor are listed as follows:**

1. type of layer,

2. size of the input feature maps n_{in},

3. number of input channels ch_{in},

4. number of input capsules $caps_{in}$,

5. kernel size $kernel_{size}$,

6. stride size $stride_{size}$,

7. size of the output feature maps n_{out},

8. number of output channels ch_{out},

9. number of output capsules $caps_{out}$.

Such a representation allows describing even more complex structures by simply defining a new layer *type*. For instance, a layer descriptor can define a more complex repeating structure composed of multiple elements, like a CapsCell in the DeepCaps architecture. This way, the DeepCaps architecture has been described with six layer descriptors. The first one is for the single Conv layer, followed by four CapsCell blocks and a final Class Capsule layer.

The complete DNN architecture description is then completed by two non-layer terms that allow encoding the position of a skip connection and an indicator, called *resize flag*, to explicitly indicate if the input resizing is required. Figure 5.3 shows the proposed format to describe a candidate DNN architecture, referred to as the *genotype*.

5.2.2.3 Modeling the Execution of CapsNets in Hardware Accelerators

The *NASCaps* framework can receive any given hardware accelerator executing DNN inference as an input. For illustration, we showcase the modeling of the CapsAcc accelerator. This choice is related to the fact that it supports the execution of all the capsule layers. Starting from the RTL-level description of the CapsAcc architecture, we extract and model the different micro-architectural configurations at a higher abstraction level, which constitutes the inputs for our model. First, the description of the operation-specific parameters of the layers is presented. Afterward, the global parameters strictly related to the CapsAcc accelerator are discussed.

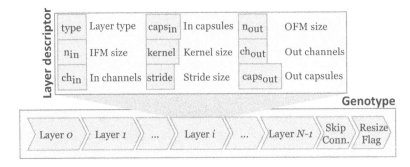

Figure 5.3: Proposed structure of the genotype.

TABLE 5.1: Equations for the operation-specific modeling of CapsNets.

Operation	weights	sums_per_out	data_per_weight
ConvCaps layer	$(ch_{in} \cdot kernel_{size}^2 + 1) \cdot ch_{out} \cdot caps_{out} \cdot caps_{in}$	$(kernel_{size}^2 + 1) \cdot ch_{in} \cdot caps_{in}$	$(n_{out})^2 \cdot ch_{in} \cdot caps_{in}$
ConvCaps3D layer	$(ch_{in} \cdot kernel_{size}^3 + 1) \cdot ch_{out} \cdot caps_{out} \cdot caps_{in}$	$(kernel_{size}^3 + 1) \cdot ch_{in} \cdot caps_{in}$	$(n_{out})^2 \cdot ch_{in} \cdot caps_{in}$
ClassCaps layer	$(ch_{in} \cdot n_{in}^2 + 1) \cdot ch_{out} \cdot caps_{out} \cdot caps_{in}$	$(n_{in}^2 + 1) \cdot ch_{in} \cdot caps_{in}$	1
Dynamic Routing	$ch_{in} \cdot kernel_{size}^2 \cdot ch_{out}$	$caps_{in}$	1

Operation-Specific Modeling for different Layers

The operation-specific parameters that can be extracted from the execution of different operations in the hardware are the following:

- *weights*: number of weights in the layer,

- *sums_per_out*: number of terms to be added for an output value,

- *data_per_weight*: number of feature maps multiplied by the same weight.

For each operation, these parameters are computed by different equations due to the different nature of the respective types of computations (see Table 5.1). Note that, by setting $caps_{in}$ and $caps_{out}$ to 1, the *ConvCaps* and *ClassCaps* layers become a traditional Conv layer and FC layer, respectively.

Global Parameter Modeling

Our models estimate the latency and the energy consumption of the inference of one input, for a given *CapsNet*, while the memory footprint is computed as the sum of the number of weights for each layer. They are modeled for each operation in a modular way (i.e., bottom-up). First, the weights must be loaded onto the PE array, then reused as long as they need to be multiplied by other inputs. Afterward, the next group of weights is loaded until all the computations of the layers are done (see Equations 5.1-5.3). The model has been validated by comparing the results with the hardware implementation of the CapsAcc accelerator. The adopted model parameters are the following:

- *w_load_cycles*: number of clock cycles required to load the weight onto the PE array,

- *w_loads*: number of groups of weights loaded onto the PE array,

- *cycles(l)*: number of cycles required to execute the layer *l*,

- *ma*: number of memory accesses,

- en_{mem}: energy consumption of a single memory accesses,

- pwr_{PEA}: power consumption of the PE array.

$$w\_load\_cycles = 16 \tag{5.1}$$

$$w\_loads = \left\lceil \frac{weights}{16 \cdot \min(16, sums\_per\_out)} \right\rceil \tag{5.2}$$

$$cycles(l) = w\_load\_cycles \cdot w\_loads + data\_per\_weight \qquad (5.3)$$

The overall latency is then computed as the sum of the contributions of the layers (see Equation (5.4)).

$$latency = \sum_{l \in L} cycles(l) \cdot T \qquad (5.4)$$

In Equation (5.5), the number of memory accesses is computed by distinguishing whether the operation is a Conv layer. Such a distinction has been implemented by analyzing the value of $data\_per\_weight$, which is greater than 1 for Conv layers and 1 otherwise.

$$ma = \begin{cases} 256, & \text{if } data\_per\_weight = 1 \\ 16 \cdot \max(sums\_per\_out - 15, 1), & \text{otherwise} \end{cases} \qquad (5.5)$$

The energy of the accelerator (see Equation (5.6)) is estimated as the sum of the energy of memory accesses and the sum of the power consumption of each layer processed in the PE array, multiplied by its latency (period T and the number of cycles). Note that the average power consumption of the PE array is used in our model.

$$energy = \left\lceil \frac{ma \cdot 8}{128} \right\rceil \cdot en_{mem} + \sum_{l \in L} cycles(l) \cdot T \cdot pwr_{PEA} \qquad (5.6)$$

5.2.2.4 The Multi-Objective NSGA-II Algorithm

The selection of the Pareto-optimal solutions for the *NASCaps* framework is based on the NSGA-II evolutionary algorithm [42]. It has a main loop (lines 2-11 of Algorithm 21) whose iterations represent a single generation of the overall evolution process of an initial population. The initial population (sized n) is randomly generated and can be referred to as P_1 (line 1 of Algorithm 21). This set of solutions represents the initial parent generation of the algorithm. The crossover among the solutions belonging to P_t (line 3) allows the generation of a new set of offspring individuals Q_t. At this point, the population $P_t \cup Q_t$ is sorted according to a non-domination criterion. For each iteration of the inner loop (lines 6-11), the candidate solutions are grouped into different fronts F_i. The ones included in the first front F_1 represent the best-found solutions for the overall population. Each subsequent front ($F_2, F_3, \dots$) is constructed by removing all the preceding fronts from the population and finding a new Pareto-front. Since the first front may be composed of less than n individuals, the solutions from subsequent fronts will also be selected to be part of the following parent generation.

To have precisely n parents in the output set, the solutions that are part of the last front are ranked using the crowded distance comparison approach (line 11), which consists of sorting the population of that front according to each objective function value in ascending order. These steps are shown in Figure 5.4. Only half of

---

Algorithm 21: The genetic NSGA-II algorithm used in our *NASCaps* framework.

Require: search space S, sizes of population $|P|, |Q|$, number of generations g

Ensure: Pareto set $F \subseteq P_1 \times P_2 \times \cdots \times P_k$

1   $P_1 \leftarrow RandomConfigurations(|P|)$;

2   **for** $g = 1 \ldots G$ **do**

3      $Q_i \leftarrow CrossoverAndMutate(P_i, |Q|)$;

4      $T \leftarrow EstimateParameters(P_i \cup Q_i)$;

5      $P_{i+1} \leftarrow \emptyset$;

6   **while** $|P_{i+1}| < |P|$ **do**

7         $F = PickPareto(T)$;

8   **if** $|P_{i+1}| + |F| \leq |P|$ **then**

9           $P_{i+1} \leftarrow P_{i+1} \cup F$;

10   **else**

11           $P_{i+1} \leftarrow P_{i+1} \cup DistanceCrowding(F, |P| - |P_{i+1}|)$;

12 **Return:** $PickPareto(P_g)$;

---

the population becomes part of the following parent generation, while the other half is discarded.

These steps repeat for a certain number g of generations. The complete pseudocode is reported in Algorithm 21, where the following procedures are used:

- *RandomConfigurations(n)* randomly generates n configurations belonging to the search space.

- *CrossoverAndMutate(X, n)* generates n new offsprings from parents P by crossover and mutation.

- *EstimateParameters(X)* evaluates the new candidate solutions from a set X.

- *PickPareto(X)* selects the Pareto-optimal solutions from a set X, and these solutions are removed from the set.

- *DistanceCrowding(X, n)* returns n solutions from a set X.

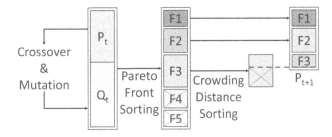

Figure 5.4: Sorting of the population.

The advantage of a multi-objective algorithm lies in the fact that it re-constructs the Pareto-front at each generation, aiming to cover all the possible solutions. The algorithm's output is a set of non-dominated solutions.

Crossover and mutation operations

The two key operators in the progression of a genetic algorithm are crossover and mutation. The standard single-point **crossover** operation allows the generation of the offspring solutions, given two parent solutions P_a and P_b that have been previously randomly picked among the current population candidates. The genotypes of the two parent individuals are split into two parts each. The splitting point is pseudo-randomly selected. Initially, a cut point is randomly chosen. Then, a series of checks are performed to verify the validity of the output genotypes. The following criteria have been applied to choose the splitting point correctly:

- the cut-points are chosen to ensure that the generated DNN is made up of at least one initial Conv layer and a minimum of 2 capsule layers,

- no Conv layer is placed between two capsule layers.

Note, the reason behind the second constraint is that capsules aim to derive higher-level information w.r.t. Conv layers. At this point, the actual crossover operation is performed. As shown in Figure 5.5, the last parts of the parent genes P_a and P_b are switched.

The second fundamental operation performed by the algorithm is **mutation**. As it has been implemented for our *NASCaps* framework, the operator performs a mutation by randomly choosing one of the layer descriptors from the genotype of the input candidate network, and by randomly modifying one of the main parameters of the selected layer with a probability p_m. In particular, the parameters that can be affected by a mutation are the kernel size, the strides, the number of output capsules, and the position of the skip connection.

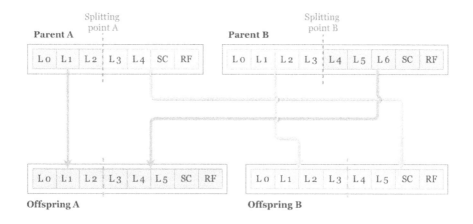

Figure 5.5: Example of crossover between two genotypes.

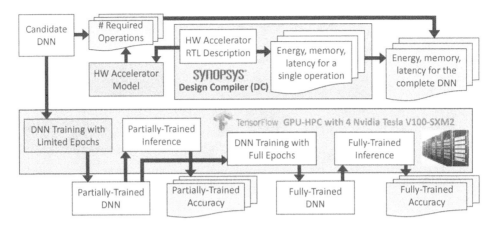

Figure 5.6: Setup and tool-flow for conducting our experiments.

After these two operations, a further step is performed to ensure the validity of the output genotypes that, in many cases, will represent an invalid DNN. This correction step allows properly adjusting the input and output tensor dimensions for every layer for genotypes derived from a mutation or a crossover operation, which can randomly modify or join different parent genotypes.

5.2.3 Evaluation of the NASCaps Framework

5.2.3.1 Experimental Setup

The overview of our experimental setup and tool flow is shown in Figure 5.6. The training and testing for accuracy of the candidate DNNs have been conducted with the TensorFlow library [1], while extensive experiments are performed using the GPU-HPC computing nodes equipped with four NVIDIA Tesla V100-SXM2 GPUs. Our proposed *NASCaps* framework has been evaluated for the MNIST [118], Fashion MNIST (FMNIST) [284], SVHN [186] and CIFAR10 [112] datasets. The implementation of the HW model is based on the CapsAcc architecture. The core PEs were synthesized using the Synopsys Design Compiler with a 45nm CMOS technology node and a clock period T of 3ns.

The experiments were divided into three steps.

1. In the first step, a basic random search has been performed to investigate how many training epochs are necessary to train the candidate DNNs and evaluate their accuracy in the loop of the genetic NSGA-II algorithm.

2. During the second step, the search algorithm for finding Pareto-optimal DNN architectures for the energy, memory, latency, and accuracy objectives is executed.

3. Finally, the selected Pareto-optimal DNNs have been fully-trained.

To evaluate the transferability of the selected DNNs w.r.t. different datasets, the selected DNNs have been fully-trained also for the other datasets. Moreover, the following settings have been used to conduct the experiments:

- Initial parent population size $|P| = 10$.

- Offspring population size: $|Q| = 10$.

- Maximum number of generations for the genetic loop: $g = 20$.

- Mutation probability: $p_m = 10\%$.

- $kernel_{size} \in \{3 \times 3, 5 \times 5, 9 \times 9\}$.

- $stride_{size} \in \{1, 2\}$.

- $ch_{out} \in \{1, 2, \ldots, 64\}$.

- $caps_{out} \in \{1, 2, \ldots, 64\}$.

These values and the training hyper-parameters (e.g., batch sizes, number of epochs and learning rate) have been selected by conducting a set of preliminary experiments and considering reasonable run times.

5.2.3.2 Results for Reduced Training Epochs for Full-Training Accuracy Estimation

One of the most crucial aspects of the NAS lies in its high computational exploration cost due to the *large number of candidate DNNs* that constitute the population and the *time-consuming training steps needed to evaluate the accuracy*. To limit the time needed to perform the complete search and its computational cost, we propose a two-stage evaluation approach.

1. The first step consists of training the population of candidate networks with a limited number of epochs, producing a set of partially-trained DNNs. The validation accuracy obtained by the partially-trained DNNs has been used to evaluate the Pareto-fronts in the NSGA-II algorithm. The choice of the number of epochs has been determined carefully by analyzing the impact of different epoch sizes over the achieved accuracy for different datasets.

2. Afterward, the candidate networks that show their accuracy and hardware efficiency in a Pareto-front are fully-trained to evaluate their actual validation accuracy.

Hence, this approach allowed using only a reduced number of training epochs to predict the full-training accuracy of the DNNs. *This approach has been tested using 66 randomly generated DNNs (in addition to CapsNet and DeepCaps architectures) and performing a full training on them* while recording the obtained validation accuracy at each training epoch. The Pearson correlation coefficient (PCC) [208] has been

TABLE 5.2: Pearson correlation coefficient (PCC) and median cumulative training time expressed in seconds (MCTT) for the MNIST, Fashion-MNIST (FMNIST), SVHN, and CIFAR10 datasets.

Epoch n.		1	3	5	10	15	20
MNIST	PCC	0.8407	0.9998	0.9999	1.0000	1.0000	1.0000
	MCTT	55.4	166.2	277.0	554.0	831.0	1108.0
FMNIST	PCC	0.8306	0.8963	0.9013	0.9935	0.9989	0.9998
	MCTT	86.2	258.7	431.1	862.3	1293.4	1724.6
SVHN	PCC	0.6812	0.8733	0.9518	0.9531	0.9667	0.9876
	MCTT	128.3	385.0	641.6	1283.3	1924.9	2666.6
CIFAR10	PCC	0.2969	0.4259	0.7279	0.9334	0.9518	0.9879
	MCTT	61.6	184.7	307.9	615.8	923.6	1231.5

computed to analyze the correlation between the accuracy of the fully-trained DNNs and the accuracy of the same DNNs at the intermediate steps.

Table 5.2 shows the values of the PCC, computed between the accuracy of the DNNs after n training epochs and their accuracy after full training. The median cumulative training time needed to perform an n epoch training is also reported. As expected, this study allowed us to determine that more complex datasets require a larger number of training epochs to distinguish the most promising networks from the rest correctly. For the case of the MNIST dataset, 5 epochs are sufficient to reach a PPC equal to 0.9999. Instead, for the CIFAR10 dataset, such a high confidence value is never reached within the first few epochs. In this case, 10 training epochs are selected, which ensure a PCC equal to 0.9334. This choice leveraged the tradeoff between the correlation coefficient and the required training time. Of course, a larger number of training epochs can also be selected, but it would drastically increase the exploration time due to the DNN training, which is a crucial parameter to consider when large populations or several generations are explored by the $NASCaps$ framework. On the other hand, the selection performed after 10 epochs of training allowed to discard more Pareto-dominated candidate networks than what would have been discarded after 5 epochs. For the Fashion-MNIST and SVHN datasets, the selection stage has also been performed after 5 training epochs.

Note that a specific set of networks can be discarded relatively early, i.e., after a few training epochs, since they do not improve their accuracy much. The candidate networks that pass the selection stage can then complete their training. A second selection stage is beneficial for performing a more fine-grained selection of the candidate networks and avoiding the tedious and computational-hungry full-training of Pareto-dominated DNNs.

5.2.3.3 NASCaps Results for the Partially-Trained DNNs

Our $NASCaps$ framework is first applied to the MNIST dataset to evaluate its efficiency and correct behavior. The number of generations is set to 20, but a

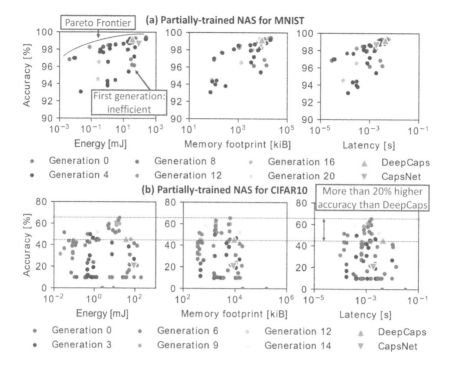

Figure 5.7: Partially-Trained DNN NAS for **(a)** the MNIST dataset, and **(b)** the CIFAR10 dataset. The color shows in which generation the solution occurs first.

maximum time-out of 12 hours has been imposed for MNIST and Fashion-MNIST, while a 24-hour maximum search time has been used for CIFAR10 and SVHN.

The search for the *MNIST-NAS* lasted for 20 complete generations, and the single candidate networks were trained for 5 epochs. This setup led to train and evaluate a total of 210 DNNs. The resulting individual solutions are compared to the two reference state-of-the-art solutions, which are the CapsNet and DeepCaps architectures. In Figure 5.7a, each DNN architecture is represented w.r.t. the four objectives of the search.

The Fashion-MNIST search ended at its 19th generation (in 12 hours) and evaluated a total of 200 candidate architectures. The search for the SVHN dataset lasted for 12 generations, allowing us to evaluate 130 architectures. For the CIFAR10 dataset, the search reached its 14th generation, with a total of 150 tested architectures.

Figure 5.7 shows how the evolutionary search algorithm progressed for the MNIST and CIFAR10 datasets. Note that the red dots, i.e., the initial population at generation 0, represent *randomly generated* DNNs. The objectives significantly improve during the following iterations when our evolutionary algorithm finds better candidate DNN architectures using crossover and mutation operations iteratively. The reduced epoch training allowed us to evaluate many candidate networks (a total of nearly 700 architectures) based on convolutional and capsule layers. This method led to finding multiple candidate architectures that have reached an accuracy up to 30.86% higher than the best among the partially-trained state-of-the-art solutions, i.e., within the limits of a strongly reduced training time. For instance, the NAS for the CIFAR10 dataset produced a network with an accuracy of 76.46% after 10 epochs, while the DeepCaps architecture reached only 45.60% accuracy within the same training interval. This corroborates that our *NASCaps* can generate networks with higher accuracy than DeepCaps-like structures when constrained to short training time.

5.2.3.4 NASCaps Results for the Selected Fully-Trained DNNs

After the first selection stage, the candidate DNNs belonging to the Pareto-optimal subsets have been fully trained to evaluate their final accuracy. Figure 5.8 shows the Pareto-optimal solutions at the end of the full-training process.

NASCaps for the MNIST Dataset

The highest-accuracy architecture found during the MNIST search reached an accuracy of 99.65% in 93 epochs of training. However, that particular solution requires $2.8\times$ more energy, $2.5\times$ more time, and $2.4\times$ more memory w.r.t. the CapsNet architecture. The red front in Figure 5.8a also highlights other interesting solutions belonging to the derived Pareto-optimal front, with a slightly lower accuracy, but *up to a couple of orders of magnitude lower energy, memory, and latency* achieved by our identified solutions.

NASCaps for the Fashion-MNIST Dataset

One of the Pareto-optimal solutions in Figure 5.8b achieves an accuracy of 92.15% in 51 epochs. This solution improved the latency (-79.38%), energy (-88.43%), and memory footprint (-63.05%) compared to both the CapsNet and DeepCaps architectures, with almost the same accuracy as the last one, which is 93.94%.

NASCaps for the SVHN Dataset

The set of experiments for the SVHN dataset in Figure 5.8c produced a solution that reached an accuracy of 93.17%, i.e., 3.52% lower than the DeepCaps, in 56 epochs of training. This solution also significantly reduced the energy by 97.05% and latency by 29.56%, compared to the DeepCaps, but it requires $1.6\times$ more memory. On the other hand, another interesting solution reached an accuracy of 92.53% while requiring 30.59% lower energy, 59.63% lower latency, and 62.70% lower memory, compared to the DeepCaps.

NASCaps for the CIFAR10 Dataset

A solution found by the CIFAR10-NAS in Figure 5.8d achieved an accuracy of 85.99% after 300 epochs of training while significantly improving all the other objectives compared to the DeepCaps architecture. This particular solution (*NASCaps-C10-best* in Table 5.3) reduced the energy consumption by 52.12%, the latency by 64.34%, and the memory footprint by 30.19% compared to the DeepCaps executed on the CapsAcc accelerator. However, it encountered a slight accuracy drop of about 1% when using the same training settings. Table 5.3 reports also other Pareto-optimal DNN architectures found by our *NASCaps* framework for the CIFAR10 dataset.

Transferability of the Selected DNNs Across Different Datasets

To test the transferability of the DNN solutions found by our *NASCaps* framework, the dataset-specific DNNs have also been trained and tested on the rest

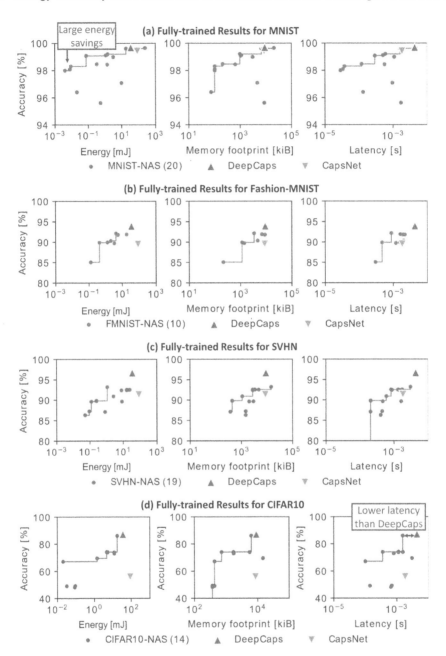

Figure 5.8: Fully-trained DNN results for (a) the MNIST, (b) the Fashion-MNIST, (c) the SVHN, and (d) CIFAR10 datasets.

of the considered datasets. Table Table 5.4 reports the matrix of highest-accuracy solutions obtained by this transferability analysis.

The *NASCaps-C10-best* architecture of Table 5.3 resulted also particularly accurate for the other datasets. For the MNIST dataset, it achieved an accuracy of 99.72% in 37 epochs of training, which is also higher than the solutions found by the MNIST-NAS. For the Fashion-MNIST dataset, it reached an accuracy of 93.87%

TABLE 5.3: Selected CIFAR10 architectures after 300-epoch training.

Architecture	Accuracy	Energy	Latency	Memory
DeepCaps	87.10%	36.30 mJ	4.29 ms	9 052 kiB
NASCaps-C10-best	85.99%	17.38 mJ	1.53 ms	6 319 kiB
NASCaps-C10-a0d	74.11%	4.53 mJ	1.12 ms	1 718 kiB
NASCaps-C10-9fd	74.00%	5.11 mJ	0.36 ms	713 kiB
NASCaps-C10-658	73.91%	5.06 mJ	1.54 ms	5 573 kiB
CapsNet	55.85%	88.80 mJ	1.82 ms	8 573 kiB

in 32 epochs of training, which is even higher than the DeepCaps after 100 epochs of training. When tested on the SVHN dataset, it reached an accuracy of 96.59%, thus outperforming the highest-accuracy DNN found during the SVNH-NAS. The *NASCaps-C10-best* architecture is similar to the DeepCaps, but it has two initial Conv layers and three CapsCell blocks without skip connection. The highest-accuracy architecture found by the MNIST-NAS also performed well with the Fashion-NMIST dataset, reaching an accuracy of 93.34% after 91 epochs of training.

The results reported in Table 5.4 show how the solution *NASCaps-C10* is the best overall architecture found during the four searches performed. The evolutionary process was based on a random initial parent population newly generated at each search. Moreover, the small size of the initial parent population may have contributed to a non-convergence of the four dataset-specific searches that have been performed. Also, not all four searches reached the same generation at the end of the experiments.

5.2.3.5 Summary of Key Results

The above results show how our *NASCaps* framework has been able to explore multiple solutions with diverse tradeoffs, thanks to the usage of an evolutionary algorithm for a multi-objective search. It has been possible to generate and test 690 candidate networks for the four dataset-specific searches. Using four high-end NVIDIA Tesla V100-SXM2, our *NASCaps* framework required 90 GPU-hours to test the partially-trained candidate networks. The new 64 Pareto-optimal architectures have been fully-trained, requiring in total additional 682 GPU-hours (i.e., 28 days). Our approach allowed us to outperform many objectives of the state-of-the-art

TABLE 5.4: Highest-Accuracy DNNs found by the dataset-specific NAS, which are then trained for the other datasets for 100 epochs.

Architecture	MNIST	FMNIST	SVHN	CIFAR10
NASCaps-MNIST-best	99.65%	93.34%	96.36%	71.44%
NASCaps-FMNIST-best	99.49%	92.15%	93.12%	68.34%
NASCaps-SVHN-best	99.51%	91.43%	93.17%	63.72%
NASCaps-C10-best	99.72%	93.87%	96.59%	76.46%

solutions when performing the full training, despite the strict time constraints applied to the single searches. In summary, our framework allowed us to:

- Derive some efficient architectures, such as the above-discussed *NASCaps-C10-best* that reached an almost similar accuracy as of the state-of-the-art while significantly improving all other objectives of the search, i.e., energy, memory, and latency.

- Perform early candidate selection while achieving high accuracy after the full training.

- Achieve good transferability between different datasets, as demonstrated by the fact that the *NASCaps-C10-best* DNN, which is found for the CIFAR10-specific search, outperforms other dataset-specific searches also on other datasets.

5.2.4 Summary

The NASCaps framework is proposed to conduct HW-aware NAS. The optimization objectives of the framework are classification accuracy and hardware efficiency, expressed in terms of latency, energy consumption, and memory footprint when executed on the specialized hardware accelerators. It not only models and incorporates the most common types of DNN layers (such as Conv, FC) but also the different types of capsule layers and dynamic routing. To speed up the evaluation time, the functional behavior of the convolutional and capsule layer execution in specialized hardware accelerators are modeled to quickly estimate memory, energy, and latency, for different DNN model inferences. A genetic algorithm based on the principles of the NSGA-II algorithm is proposed to solve the multi-objective optimization problem and select Pareto-frontiers of DNN models.

Moreover, to further reduce the training time, the accuracy of the DNN candidates is evaluated after a limited number of training epochs (i.e., partial training), while the Pareto-optimal DNNs are fully trained. Integrating accuracy and hardware efficiency into a NAS framework is challenging and requires a significant design effort. Adding the robustness property as an optimization objective in the flow would further increase the design space and require dedicated optimizations. The challenges and the proposed solutions for integrating the robustness objective into the framework will be discussed in Section 5.3.

5.3 ROHNAS: A NAS FRAMEWORK WITH CONJOINT OPTIMIZATION FOR HARDWARE EFFICIENCY AND ADVERSARIAL ROBUSTNESS OF CONVOLUTIONAL AND CAPSNETS

DNNs are computationally-complex and vulnerable to adversarial attacks. To address multiple design objectives, we propose *RoHNAS*, a novel NAS framework that jointly optimizes for adversarial robustness and hardware efficiency of DNNs executed on specialized hardware accelerators. Besides the traditional convolutional DNNs,

RoHNAS additionally accounts for complex types of DNNs such as CapsNets. To reduce the exploration time, *RoHNAS* analyzes and selects appropriate values of adversarial perturbation for each dataset to employ in the NAS flow. Extensive evaluations on multi-GPU-HPC nodes provide a set of Pareto-optimal solutions, leveraging the tradeoff between the above-discussed design objectives. For example, a Pareto-optimal DNN for the CIFAR10 dataset exhibits 86.07% accuracy while having a latency of 4.47 ms, an energy of 38.63 mJ, and a memory footprint of 11.85 MiB.

5.3.1 System Overview

Traditionally, the adversarial robustness of a given DNN is investigated a posteriori, i.e., once the DNN is already designed. Another metric typically analyzed a posteriori is the hardware efficiency of a DNN implemented on a given hardware accelerator. Hence, such a lack of awareness challenges the feasibility of its implementation on resource-constrained devices. *The goal of this work is to integrate these diverse yet important objectives into a NAS framework to obtain Pareto-optimal solutions that explore the potential tradeoffs between different design objectives like computational complexity, memory, energy, latency, and security.* Including the DNN robustness into the optimization goals of the NAS is challenging because, besides the challenges in its representation in the design framework, it might lead to a massive search space explosion due to several additional factors and extremely time-consuming training and evaluations of numerous candidate solutions.

Our work performs joint optimizations for the hardware efficiency and adversarial robustness, thereby leading to the increased complexity of the optimization problem, as well as considerable training time to evaluate the DNN robustness. Moreover, it is quite challenging to model, implement and evaluate the hardware execution of different DNNs and CapsNets (including Conv layers, FC layers, and dynamic routing) in the NAS design flow.

To address the above-discussed challenges, we propose the novel *RoHNAS* framework that integrates multiple optimization objectives (like hardware efficiency and adversarial robustness) for diverse types of DNNs, like CNNs and CapsNets. *RoHNAS* employs the following key mechanisms:

1. For architectural model flexibility and fast hardware estimation, we employ analytical models of the layers and operations of DNNs and CapsNets, and their mapping and execution on specialized accelerators.

2. To speed up the robustness evaluation, we analyze and choose the values of the adversarial perturbations, which provide valuable differences when performing the NAS with DNNs subjected to such adversarial perturbations.

3. We develop a specialized evolutionary algorithm, following the principles of the NSGA-II method, to conduct a multi-objective Pareto-frontier selection, with conjoint optimization for energy, memory, latency, and adversarial robustness of DNNs.

4. To reduce the overall training time, we evaluate the DNNs trained for a limited number of epochs, while the Pareto-optimal DNNs are evaluated after full training to obtain the exact results.

We have implemented our *RoHNAS* using the TensorFlow library and evaluated more than 900 DNNs for the MNIST, Fashion-MNIST, and CIFAR10 datasets. Extensive validations are performed on Nvidia's multi-V100 GPU-HPC nodes requiring weeks to months of experimentation time.

5.3.2   RoHNAS Framework

Our evolutionary algorithm-based NAS methodology performs a multi-objective search. It automatically searches for inherently robust yet hardware-efficient DNN models by selecting Pareto-optimal candidates in terms of energy, latency, memory footprint, and robustness. The search space comprises both CapsNets and traditional CNNs. The workflow of our *RoHNAS* framework is shown in Figure 5.9, and is explained in detail in the following subsections.

The framework's inputs are the hardware accelerator, the algorithm for generating the adversarial attack, and the dataset. After modeling the hardware accelerator analytically, the appropriate values of the adversarial perturbation to employ in the search are selected. This process consists of analyzing the accuracy vs. adversarial perturbation curve and focusing on the high variation region that corresponds to the highest slope of the curve. After selecting the values of the adversarial perturbation to employ in the search, the evolutionary search algorithm (based upon the principles of the NGSA-II genetic algorithm [42]) performs an iterative exploration using crossover, mutation, and best DNN candidate selection based on the objectives. To speed up the process during the evolutionary algorithm, the adversarial robustness is evaluated

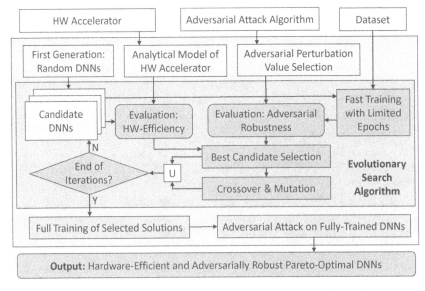

Figure 5.9: Overview of our *RoHNAS* framework and its key functionalities.

after a fast training, i.e., for DNNs trained with a limited number of epochs, where its number is determined based on the Pearson Correlation Coefficient [208]. Toward generating exact robustness results, the set of Pareto-optimal DNN models are fully-trained, and the robustness against the adversarial attack on fully-trained DNNs is evaluated.

5.3.2.1 Design Space Reduction by Selecting an Appropriate Adversarial Perturbation Value

By considering several topologies and strengths of adversarial perturbations, the design space can potentially explode. Hence, the *RoHNAS* framework restricts the design space by automatically selecting the values of adversarial perturbations to be used in the NAS for a given dataset. Algorithm 22 summarizes the proposed procedure. For each element of the test dataset, the adversarial example is generated through the PGD algorithm [148] (line 4). Here we use PGD for illustrative reasons, and other adversarial attack algorithms can be integrated into our *RoHNAS* framework. The parameter ε determines the amount of adversarial perturbation. When considering the accuracy variation w.r.t. ε, the region in which the slope is highest is in the middle of the graph, which corresponds to half of the clean accuracy, i.e., $\frac{Acc_0}{2}$ when considering that Acc_0 is the clean accuracy. By exploiting this intuition, our algorithm selects ε_{NAS}, which is the adversarial perturbation amount that provides the closest accuracy to the desired value of $\frac{Acc_0}{2}$. The selected value of ε_{NAS} is employed in the *One EPS* search, which optimizes for the robustness against one perturbation value. Moreover, aiming at covering a broader spectrum of adversarial perturbation range, the *Two EPS* search is devised. ε_{low} and ε_{high} are selected (lines 10-11), and the NAS is conducted by optimizing for the adversarial accuracy with both values.

5.3.3 Evaluation of the RoHNAS Framework

5.3.3.1 Experimental Setup

The PGD adversarial attack algorithm [148] has been implemented with the CleverHans library [65]. The hardware model has been implemented using the NASCaps library, which is based on the CapsAcc architecture synthesized using the Synopsys Design Compiler tool, with a 45nm technology node and a clock period of 3 ns. The training and testing of the DNNs, implemented in TensorFlow [1] have been running on the GPU-HPC computing nodes equipped with four NVIDIA Tesla V100-SXM2 GPUs. Note that our experiments were running for 2 000 GPU hours with our fast evaluation method and 8 000 GPU hours for the complete training and PGD attack evaluation. Without these exploration time reductions, or by considering more complex optimization problems (e.g., deeper DNN models or larger datasets), the exploration time would have lasted several GPU months.

The search algorithm is initialized with a random population of 10 elements, running for a maximum of 20 iterations of the genetic loop. The offspring population size is 10, and the mutation probability is 10%. Each Conv layer can be composed of

---

Algorithm 22: Adversarial Perturbation Selection.

Input: Deep Neural Network: N;

Test Dataset: $\mathcal{D} = \bigcup_j X_j$;

Adversarial Perturbation Budget: $\varepsilon_i \in \mathcal{E} = [\varepsilon_{MIN}, \varepsilon_{MAX}]$;

Output: Perturbation to apply for the NAS: ε_{NAS};

1   $Acc_0 = Accuracy(N(D))$;

2   **for** $i \in < \mathcal{E} >$ **do**

3   **for** $j \in < \mathcal{D} >$ **do**

4      $X'_{ij} = PGD(N, \varepsilon_i, X_j)$;

5   **end**

6     $\mathcal{D}'_i = \bigcup_j X'_{ij}$;

7     $Acc_i = Accuracy(N(\mathcal{D}'_i))$;

8   **end**

9   $\varepsilon_{NAS} = \varepsilon_i \;:\; Acc_i \approx \frac{Acc_0}{2}$;

10   $\varepsilon_{low} \approx \frac{\varepsilon_{NAS}}{10}$;

11   $\varepsilon_{high} \approx 3 \cdot \varepsilon_{NAS}$;

---

a 3×3, 5×5, or 9×9 kernel, with a stride of either 1 or 2. The channels and capsule dimensions span between 1 and 64.

5.3.3.2   Selection of Adversarial Perturbation for the NAS

The amount of adversarial perturbation is a crucial parameter to be selected for performing the NAS. Following the above-discussed procedure, the Pareto-optimal DNNs of the NASCaps library have been tested under the PGD attack, with different values of the adversarial perturbation ε. The results reported in Figure 5.10 show that, as expected, the higher ε is, the lower the DNN accuracy drops. The selected values for the NAS are detailed in Table 5.5. The selection process follows the procedure described in Algorithm 22. The *One EPS* column refers to the search using a single value of ε, while the *Two EPS* column refers to a search conducted with two different values of ε, which are called ε_{low} and ε_{high}. Note that a simple dataset like the MNIST requires a relatively high adversarial perturbation to impact the DNN robustness. On the other hand, on a more complex dataset like the CIFAR10, a smaller perturbation is already sufficient to misclassify a specific set of inputs.

5.3.3.3   RoHNAS Results with Fast DNN Robustness Evaluation

To reduce the exploration time, our algorithm trains the DNNs only for a limited number of epochs, which results in a fast robustness evaluation. The similarity w.r.t. the full-training robustness has been measured through the Pearson Correlation Coefficient [208], using the procedure described in Section 5.2. The choice of 10 training epochs for the CIFAR10 dataset and 5 epochs for the Fashion-MNIST and

Figure 5.10: Analysis of the DNN robustness under the PGD attack, with different adversarial perturbation values, for **(a)** MNIST, **(b)** Fashion-MNIST, and **(c)** CIFAR10.

MNIST datasets leverages the tradeoff between a high correlation and low training time.

The results of the *RoHNAS - One EPS* with fast robustness evaluation are reported in Figure 5.11. The earliest generation of the algorithm produces sub-optimal DNN solutions, while most Pareto-optimal solutions are found in the latest generation. Note that, for the *RoHNAS* evaluated on the CIFAR10 dataset, the latest generations produce DNNs that are less robust against the PGD attack but still belong to the Pareto-frontier due to the low energy consumption. Note that several candidate DNNs found in the earliest generations are highly vulnerable to the PGD attack and are automatically discarded by the Pareto-frontier selection.

5.3.3.4   RoHNAS Exact Results for Pareto-Optimal DNNs

The Pareto-optimal DNNs selected at the previous stage have been *fully-trained* to obtain an exact robustness evaluation. The DNNs for MNIST and Fashion-MNIST have been trained for 100 epochs, while 300 training epochs have been used for CIFAR10. The results reported in Figure 5.12 show tradeoffs between the design objectives. In Figure 5.12a, a Pareto-optimal solution found by the *RoHNAS* framework for the CIFAR10 dataset achieves an accuracy of 86.07% while having a memory footprint of 11.85 MiB, an energy consumption of 38.63 mJ, and a latency of 4.47 ms. Similarly, a solution for the Fashion-MNIST dataset in Figure 5.12b reaches an accuracy of 93.40% while having 6.40 ms latency, 61.19 mJ energy, and 16.82 MiB memory. Note that, while the *Two EPS* search finds Pareto-optimal solutions in the

TABLE 5.5: Selected values of the adversarial perturbation ε for the NAS, for MNIST, Fashion-MNIST, and CIFAR10 datasets. There are also reported values of ε_{low} and ε_{high} for the *Two EPS* search.

	Two EPS ε_{low}	One EPS ε	Two EPS ε_{high}
MNIST	3e-3	3e-2	1e-1
F-MNIST	1e-3	1e-2	3e-2
CIFAR10	3e-5	3e-4	1e-3

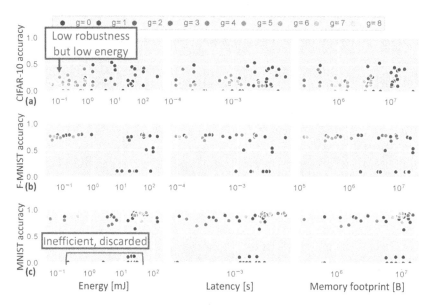

Figure 5.11: *RoHNAS'* fast evaluation of DNN robustness under PGD attack, showing tradeoffs w.r.t. energy, latency, and memory footprint. (a) Results for CIFAR10. (b) Results for Fashion-MNIST. (c) Results for MNIST.

middle range of energy, other interesting low-energy solutions are found by the *One EPS* search. The Pareto-optimal DNN search for the MNIST dataset covers a more heterogeneous range of values, leveraging the tradeoffs between different objectives.

The *RoHNAS* framework has been compared with other state-of-the-art DNN and CapsNet architectures and NAS methodologies that include capsule layers in the search space. Figure 5.13 shows the comparison between our *RoHNAS* framework (*One EPS* setting), NASCaps, CapsNet [236] and DeepCaps [220]. For the MNIST dataset, the Pareto-optimal solutions generated with the *RoHNAS* framework are particularly robust for a large range of perturbation ε. Indeed, the accuracy starts decreasing at around one order of magnitude higher ε than NASCaps. For the Fashion-MNIST, the robustness behavior of the Pareto-optimal DNNs selected with the *RoHNAS* framework is closely related to the CapsNet. Instead, for the CIFAR10 dataset, the *RoHNAS* DNNs' behavior is comparable to the DeepCaps for low values of ε, while a Pareto-optimal *RoHNAS* solution offers good robustness also with higher adversarial perturbation.

The evaluation of the *RoHNAS* framework with the *Two EPS* setting is shown in Figure 5.14. Compared to the *One EPS* setting, the NAS produces different levels of robustness w.t.r. ε for the MNIST and Fashion-MNIST datasets. However, for the CIFAR10 dataset, the *Two EPS* search leads to less robust results than the *One EPS* counterpart.

5.3.4 Summary

The proposed RoHNAS is a NAS framework jointly optimizing hardware efficiency (latency, energy, and memory footprint) and robustness against adversarial attacks.

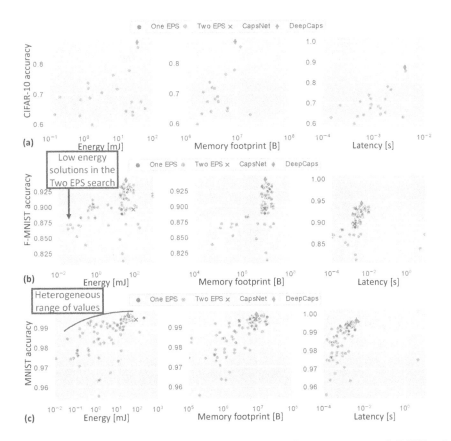

Figure 5.12: *RoHNAS'* exact robustness evaluation of Pareto-optimal DNN solutions under the PGD attack, showing tradeoffs w.r.t. hardware-efficiency. (**a**) Results for CIFAR10. (**b**) Results for Fashion-MNIST. (**c**) Results for MNIST.

Building upon the NASCaps framework discussed in Section 5.2, adversarial robustness is integrated into the framework as another optimization objective. To speed up the robustness evaluation, the values of the adversarial perturbations that provide valuable differences when performing the NAS with DNNs subjected to such adversarial perturbations are selected. Afterward, the adversarial examples with the chosen perturbation values are generated to evaluate the DNN robustness. A specialized multi-objective optimization algorithm is devised by employing analytical models of the hardware execution of the CNN and CapsNet operations and conducting training for a limited number of epochs. It is based on the genetic NSGA-II algorithm, and it performs a multi-objective Pareto-frontier selection with conjoint optimization for energy, memory, latency, and adversarial robustness of DNNs.

5.4 SUMMARY OF INTEGRATION OF MULTIPLE DESIGN OBJECTIVES INTO NAS FRAMEWORKS FOR CAPSNETS AND DNNS

This chapter has proposed methodologies to integrate several design objectives into a single framework. The emerging trends of neural architecture search techniques have

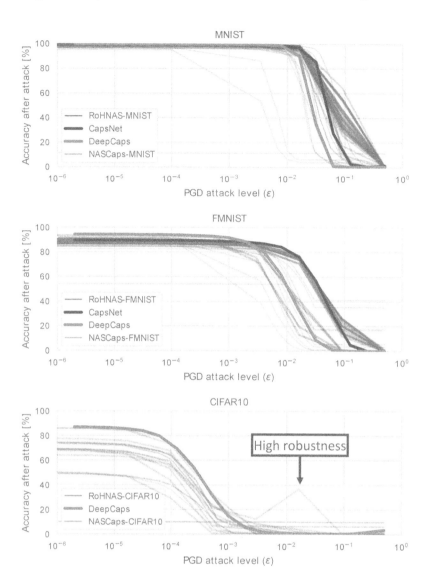

Figure 5.13: Evaluation of the *RoHNAS* framework with the *One EPS* settings, compared to other state-of-the-art architectures and NAS algorithms.

driven the way to design high-accurate DNN models. However, the high accuracy alone does not automatically guarantee high energy efficiency and robustness. Toward this, the proposed flow also integrates hardware efficiency and robustness as optimization objectives of the NAS algorithm. Therefore, the DNN architectural and model parameters are shaped to leverage the tradeoffs between accuracy, robustness, and hardware efficiency when executed on specialized hardware accelerators. While such specialized accelerators significantly reduce DL inference's power and energy consumption, shifting the computation into the event-based domain is another promising way. In fact, it is possible to reduce the power consumption of complex DL

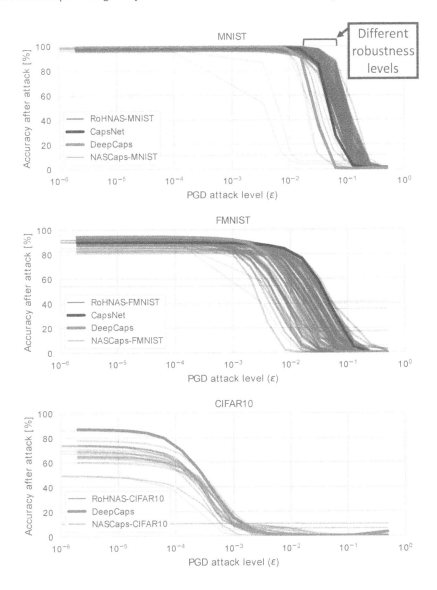

Figure 5.14: Evaluation of the *RoHNAS* framework with the *Two EPS* settings, compared to other state-of-the-art architectures and NAS algorithms.

tasks by several orders of magnitude by executing event-based SNNs on neuromorphic hardware platforms, compared to using conventional computing infrastructures. Toward this, Chapter 6 discusses efficient implementations and optimizations for executing complex SNN tasks on the Loihi processor, which is one of the most advanced neuromorphic architectures. Moreover, Chapter 7 discusses several security threats for SNNs and the potential defensive countermeasures.

Efficient Optimizations for Spiking Neural Networks on Neuromorphic Hardware

This chapter presents methodologies and optimization techniques for deploying SNNs on neuromorphic hardware. The Intel Loihi processor is used as a target computing platform to deploy energy-efficient SNNs. An overview of the Loihi chip is discussed in Section 6.1. Afterward, different applications were treated and deployed. Section 6.2 presents a methodology for implementing efficient SNNs for gesture recognition. First, the analysis to optimize the DNN-to-SNN conversion is discussed in Section 6.2.2. Then, the pre-processing method for enabling the training of event data in the DNN domain is presented in Section 6.2.3. Toward applications more oriented to autonomous cars, Section 6.3 presents efficient implementations of event-based SNNs for car recognition, while Section 6.4 presents SNNs for lane detection implemented on the Loihi neuromorphic processor.

Major Contributions of the Chapter:

- **DNN-to-SNN conversion analysis:** A systematic analysis has been conducted to optimize the tunable parameters involved in the DNN-to-SNN conversion process.

- **Pre-processing methodology for event-based training in the DNN domain:** It accumulates events into a compatible format for traditional DNN training, properly selecting the accumulation parameters. Experiments are conducted on event-based gesture recognition applications.

- **CarSNN design:** It is a methodology for designing SNNs for event-based car detection and deploying them on the Loihi neuromorphic processor. The design decisions have been made toward leveraging the tradeoffs between accuracy and energy efficiency while fitting on a limited Loihi neurocores budget and providing low-latency responses.

DOI: 10.1201/9781003530459-6

- **LaneSNNs design:** It is a methodology for designing SNNs for event-based lane detection, following the semantic segmentation approach, and deploying them on the Loihi neuromorphic chip. A pre-processing method reduces the computational complexity by reducing the resolution of input and output images. A novel loss function combines the Weighted Binary Cross Entropy and the Mean Squared Error measured to improve the accuracy.

6.1 OVERVIEW OF THE LOIHI NEUROMORPHIC PROCESSOR

The Intel Loihi chip [40], based on a neuromorphic mesh of 128 neurocores, executes the neuron computations in a highly parallel and power-efficient asynchronous manner. The neurocore management is guaranteed by 3 embedded x86 processors, and an asynchronous network-on-chip (NoC) allows communication between neurons.

6.1.1 Neuron Model

The Loihi architecture implements the well-known *CUrrent BAsed Leaky-Integrate-and-Fire (CUBA-LIF)* neuron. Each neuron is modeled as a charge reservoir. A current spike on the output axons is generated when such a charge overcomes the voltage threshold. The two internal state variables of the model are the synaptic response current $u_i(t)$ and the membrane potential $V_i(t)$. A postsynaptic neuron i receives in input a train of spikes that are sent by a presynaptic neuron j. The spikes can be represented as a train of Dirac delta functions at time t_k, as in Equation (6.1).

$$\sigma_j(t) = \sum_k \delta(t - t_k) \tag{6.1}$$

The train of spikes is then processed by a synaptic filter input response $\alpha_u(t)$, which is defined as in Equation (6.2), where $H(t)$ is the step function, and τ_u a time constant.

$$\alpha_u(t) = \frac{e^{-\frac{t}{\tau_u}}}{\tau_u} H(t) \tag{6.2}$$

Each filtered spike train is multiplied by the synaptic weight w_{ij} associated with the synapse that connects neurons i and j, and added with an additional bias current b_i to compute the synaptic response current in the Equation (6.3).

$$u_i(t) = \sum_j w_{ij}(\alpha_u * \sigma_j)(t) + b_i \tag{6.3}$$

The membrane potential then integrates the synaptic current as in Equation (6.4). Every time the membrane potential overcomes the voltage threshold θ_i, the neuron i emits an output spike and its membrane potential is reset to the v_{rest} value.

$$\dot{v}_i(t) = -\frac{1}{\tau_v} v_i(t) + u_i(t) - \theta_i \sigma_i(t) \tag{6.4}$$

Note that the time constant τ_v is responsible for the *leaky* behavior of the model [40].

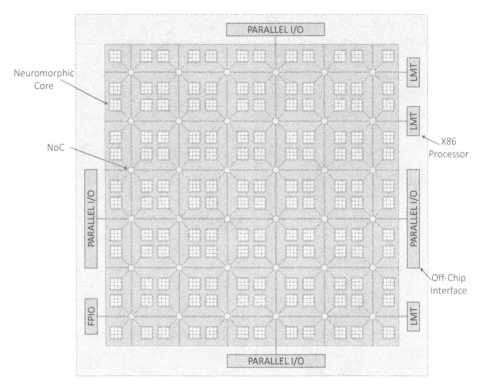

Figure 6.1: Architectural view of the Loihi chip.

6.1.2 Chip Architecture

As shown in Figure 6.1, a Loihi chip is composed of 128 neuromorphic cores (*neurocores*), and each neurocore can implement up to 1024 primitive spiking neural units (*compartments*), which emulate trees of spiking neurons. The spikes generated by each neuron are delivered to all the compartments belonging to its synaptic fan-out through the asynchronous NoC in the form of packetized messages, following a *mesh operation* executed over a series of algorithmic timesteps. This process uses a *barrier synchronization mechanism* to ensure that all neurons are ready to proceed coherently to the next timestep. To implement wider and deeper SNNs that do not fit on a single 128-neurocore chip, multiple chips can be combined together without any latency increase due to the message exchange. The off-chip communication interface extends the mesh up to 4 096 on-chip cores and up to 16 384 hierarchically connected cores. The 3 embedded ×86 processors, called *Lakemounts*, guarantee the correct functioning of the entire system. They can also be used to probe the performance of the chips and transfer information to the user.

The mesh operation is composed of the following sub-operations:

1. Each neurocore independently iterates over its compartments, and if a compartment neuron is in a spike-firing state, the spike message is generated.

2. All the messages are distributed to all the neurocores containing synaptic fan-outs through the NoC.

3. When a neurocore ends the internal distribution of spikes to its neurons, it sends a barrier synchronization message received by the neighbor neurocores. This message has the effect of flushing all the traveling spikes. After that, another barrier message notification is generated by the same neurocore.

4. When all the neurocores receive the second signal, the timestep is incremented.

The microarchitecture of a single neurocore is composed of four units:

1. The **Synapse** unit is responsible for routing the input spikes to the appropriate compartments and retrieving the corresponding synaptic weights from memory.

2. The **Dendrite** unit manages the synaptic current and membrane voltage for each compartment. It is also responsible for verifying whether a neuron is firing and delivering this information to the Axon.

3. The **Axon** unit generates the output spikes, in which each message is associated with the specific address of postsynaptic neurons.

4. The **Learning** unit, using the spike traces at the output of the neurocore and other local information, updates the synaptic weights according to the learning rule.

6.1.3 Tools to Support Loihi Developers

A solid tool flow is essential for enabling large-scale usage of the hardware architecture and conducting cutting-edge research. The software stacks abstract away the users from the low-level hardware details, allowing them to focus on high-level modeling of algorithms, network architectures, and learning rules.

Shortly after the Loihi was made available for researchers, the *NxSDK* [129] API was released. Through this API, a programmer can define the SNN model architecture and its parameters, such as decay time constants, spike impulse values, synaptic weights, refractory delays, spiking thresholds, and custom learning rules. Moreover, external stimulus spikes can be injected into designated connections at specified timesteps. The network state and power/energy consumption can be monitored at runtime. After checking that the specifications comply with the hardware support, the compiler [130] greedily assigns network entities (compartments, synapses, learning rules) to the available resources to minimize the occupied neurocores.

To ease the development of complex and deep SNNs, *NxTF* [233] provides a programming interface derived from Keras and a compiler optimized for mapping deep convolutional SNNs to the multi-core Intel Loihi architecture. It supports both SNNs trained directly on spikes and models converted from traditional DNNs through *SNN-ToolBox* [234], processing both sparse event-based and dense frame-based datasets.

Recently, other SNN simulators like *PyNN* [41], *Nengo* [12, 222], and *Brian* [171, 258] has been extended with the support to map the model onto the Loihi neuromorphic hardware.

6.2 EFFICIENT SNN FOR RECOGNIZING GESTURES ON LOIHI

SNNs can be implemented with high energy efficiency on neuromorphic processors like the Intel Loihi and fed by event-based cameras. However, non-spiking DNNs with many layers can achieve relatively high accuracy on image classification and recognition tasks, while the research on SNN learning rules for real-world applications is not mature yet. The accuracy results for SNNs are typically achieved either by converting the trained DNNs into SNNs or by directly deploying and training SNNs in the spiking domain. To enable the conversion from a DNN to an SNN, we perform a comprehensive analysis of this process, specifically designed for Intel Loihi, showing our methodology for designing an SNN that achieves nearly the same accuracy as its corresponding DNN. Toward the event-based sensors, we design a pre-processing technique evaluated for the DvsGesture dataset, which allows it to be used in the DNN domain. Therefore, based on the outcome of the first analyses, we train a DNN for the pre-processed DvsGesture dataset and convert it into its equivalent SNN for its deployment on the Intel Loihi chip, which enables real-time gesture recognition. The results report that our SNN achieves 89.64% classification accuracy and occupies only 37 Loihi cores.

6.2.1 System Overview

A promising approach to training SNNs in a supervised learning environment is to train a DNN with state-of-the-art backpropagation techniques and then assign the trained parameters (weights and biases) to an equivalent SNN representation by applying a conversion process. This approach has shown promising results, primarily because it allows us to get the best from the two worlds. The converted SNN behaves like a normal SNN, with its benefits in terms of latency and efficiency. At the same time, we can train the network using efficient methodologies that ensure high-accuracy results in classification tasks. However, such a conversion mechanism may not always provide the expected results. Many aspects must be considered, like the original DNN structure, the training process, and the parameters that control the DNN-to-SNN conversion. This behavior is accentuated when the converted SNN is deployed on limited-precision hardware like the Intel Loihi chip, which restricts the degree of freedom of the conversion process.

This section presents a complete DNN-to-SNN design process, systematically discussing the effects of the key parameters used in the conversion. We evaluate their effects and extract important general rules that can be successfully applied to deploy an SNN for the Intel Loihi or similar neuromorphic platforms. Once we have an SNN that achieves high accuracy on both the MNIST and the CIFAR10 datasets, we also evaluate it on the DvsGesture dataset, which comprises 11 gestures recorded with a DVS event-based camera. The main challenge when implementing the DNN-to-SNN conversion mechanism to get a trained SNN is that we cannot train a DNN on the event series generated by the DVS camera. Hence, we first need to collect the events into frames and then train the DNN on such a converted dataset. We discuss different pre-processing techniques and report the accuracy results achieved by the DNN on the converted dataset. Then, after performing the conversion, the SNN is tested on the DvsGesture dataset, and afterward, it can be deployed for real-time classification on the Intel Loihi.

In a nutshell, our Novel Contributions are:

- We perform a comprehensive parameter analysis of the process of converting a DNN into an SNN.

- We design a pre-processing method for the DvsGesture dataset through frame-based accumulation to make such a dataset compatible with the DNN domain.

- We train a given DNN for the pre-processed DvsGesture dataset and convert it to an SNN that can then be deployed on the Intel Loihi.

6.2.2 DNN-to-SNN Conversion

The DNN-to-SNN conversion mechanism has shown promising results in terms of accuracy consistency among the original DNN and the converted SNN [234]. To reach these results, the trained parameters of the DNN must be efficiently converted into the corresponding parameters of the SNN. This process also requires considering the intrinsic differences between the two models, and some adjustments are consequently required to obtain a correct conversion. During training, for each connection among two neurons of the consecutive layers i and $i+1$, the weight $w_{i,i+1}$ is learned. Moreover, for each neuron of the layer $i+1$, also the bias b_{i+1} is derived. In the equivalent SNN model, these parameters must be translated into their equivalent values for the spiking neural model. Specifically referring to the Intel Loihi model, the conversion works as follows:

- the bias b_{i+1} is associated to the bias current u_{bias} of the neuron n_{i+1}.

- $w_{i,i+1}$ is directly set as the weight of the synapse connecting neurons n_i and n_{i+1}.

Besides the learned parameters, each DNN layer has to be converted to an equivalent spiking version. It means that each layer is composed of equivalent spiking neurons that adopt the neuron model of the Loihi architecture. To implement the DNN-to-SNN conversion, we use the *SNNToolBox* (SNN-TB) [234], an open-source conversion tool compatible with the Loihi's Python NxSDK-0.9.5.

The results obtained with the conversion mechanism may not be always optimal due to specific constraints of the Loihi neurocores and several limitations of the NxSDK API. Therefore, we present a case study for the DNN-to-SNN conversion, specifying a set of general guidelines for achieving a converted SNN that reaches similar accuracy levels as the corresponding DNN.

6.2.2.1 *Evaluation Metrics for the Conversion Process Quality*

The conversion mechanism requires a series of preliminary considerations for a successful conversion. First, the Loihi architecture adopts limited precision synaptic

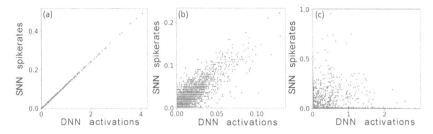

Figure 6.2: Examples of correlation plots between the DNN activations and their converted SNN spikerates.

weights, defined in the interval $[-256, 255]$. On the other hand, the trained DNN adopts full-precision weights. Therefore, preliminary quantizing the DNN-trained weights are key to get a precise converted SNN. In this quantization phase, the distribution of the input weights has a significant role in the outcome of the conversion. The input weights must be clipped into the Loihi quantized range. Hence, a tight weight distribution can be mapped to the quantized interval without relevant errors. On the other hand, outliers in the distribution of the original weights can be the primary source of an imprecise conversion since very high weights are clipped to fit into the quantized interval. It leads to possible inconsistencies between the pre- and post-quantization weight distributions. To decrease the strong outliers in the final trained weights, the L2 regularization, applied both on activations and kernels during training, helps to keep weights in a limited range.

A good practice to evaluate the conversion quality is to look at the **correlation plots** between the DNN activations and the corresponding SNN output spikerates. Figure 6.2 shows three typical correlation plots that can be obtained with good and bad conversion processes.

The plot in Figure 6.2a is an example of a good correlation plot, where the DNN activations are appropriately converted into SNN spikerates, being all the points distributed along the main diagonal. On the contrary, the plot in Figure 6.2b shows a relatively worse conversion, in which the DNN activations and the SNN spikerates are distributed along the diagonal, but the collection of points is not confined to the desired range. The plot in Figure 6.2c is another example of a bad conversion, but in this case, the activations and the spikerates are not correlated.

6.2.2.2 Tunable Conversion Parameters

Many structural parameters can be tuned during the DNN-to-SNN conversion, and a detailed analysis of their effects on the converted SNN is needed. These parameters affect the spiking neuron model, the network's characteristics, and the experiment duration.

- **Reset mode**: The reset mode defines the neuron's behavior after a spike. As previously said, the neuron spikes whenever its membrane potential exceeds the threshold V_{th}. After the spike occurs, the membrane potential is reset to a certain value that depends on the chosen reset mode:

- *Hard Reset*: The membrane potential is reset to a value equal to 0 after the neuron spikes. This solution is less computationally expensive but also relatively less accurate.

- *Soft Reset*: The membrane potential is reset to a value corresponding to the difference between the membrane threshold and the highest value reached by the membrane potential. This solution is more expensive but relatively more accurate than the hard reset since the number of compartments required to simulate each neuron is doubled.

- **Desired Threshold to Input Ratio (DThIR)**: The weights of the input DNN model have to be converted to synaptic weights of the SNN. Due to the limited dynamic range of spiking neurons, the outputs may saturate due to an excessively high input provided by some out-of-scale synaptic weights. Therefore, it is necessary to normalize the network and set a constant ratio between the incoming neuron inputs and its membrane threshold [45].

- **Experiment duration**: This parameter defines the number of timesteps for which the network receives the same input image, i.e., the inference time. A longer duration provides the network more time to output its prediction, but it increases the latency of the system.

The development of the DNN architecture is realized using the python Keras API, which is one of the APIs supported by Intel NxSDK. Loihi's Python NxSDK currently does not support all Keras layers. The only supported layers are reported in Table 6.1. This limitation must be considered during the development of a DNN architecture.

6.2.2.3 DNN Training

To study the behavior of the conversion mechanism, a small network has been used to evaluate the process. Such a network, denoted *cNet*, is a CNN that contains only Conv layers and a final dense layer. Its structure is reported in Table 6.2.

To achieve a better conversion, both activation and weight *L2 Reguralization* are applied to the network layers. In both cases, its value is set to $1 \cdot 10^{-4}$. Using regularization during training is preferable to prevent from the divergence of the parameter distribution and avoiding information loss due to the quantization process of the parameters.

The datasets for which the analyses have been performed are the MNIST [118] and CIFAR10 [112]. The intensity levels are normalized between 0 and 1 for each input image. Both networks are implemented in Keras, using TensorFlow [1] backend. The training is conducted with the following policies:

TABLE 6.1: Layers supported by NxSDK.

Dense	Flatten	Reshape	Padding
AvgPooling2D	DepthwiseConv2D	Conv1D	Conv2D

TABLE 6.2: *cNet* architecture for the MNIST dataset.

Layer	features	Kernel	stride	Output Shape	Activation
Input	1			$28 \times 28 \times 1$	ReLU
Conv2D	16	4×4	2	$13 \times 13 \times 16$	ReLU
Conv2D	32	3×3	1	$11 \times 11 \times 32$	ReLU
Conv2D	64	3×3	2	$5 \times 5 \times 64$	ReLU
Conv2D	10	4×4	1	$2 \times 2 \times 10$	ReLU
Flatten				40	
Dense				10	Softmax

- *learning rate decay:* after initializing it to 0.001, it is halved after 15 consecutive epochs without validation accuracy increases until it reaches a final value of $5 \cdot 10^{-7}$.

- *Adam optimizer* [110].

- *Small data augmentations*, with width and height shifts of 0.1, and $10°$ rotations.

After training, the test accuracy values achieved by the networks are reported in Table 6.3.

6.2.2.4 Conversion Process

The trained DNN model is converted into its equivalent SNN model via the SNN-TB tool. The conversion mechanism requires four main steps:

- **Parsing**: The toolbox extracts the relevant information from the original model, discarding layers that are not used in the inference phase (Dropout, BatchNormalization, etc.) and converting the MaxPooling-2D layers that may be present into the supported AveragePooling-2D. The parsed model is used as a reference for the following conversion.

- **Conversion**: An NxSDK-compatible spiking model is obtained by applying a normalization process that adjusts the weights and biases to the constrained dynamic range of the spiking neurons, to satisfy the selected value of *DThIR*.

TABLE 6.3: Accuracy results of the DNN models.

Nework	Dataset	Accuracy
cNet	MNIST	98.79%
cNet	CIFAR10	78.92%

TABLE 6.4: Constraints of the Loihi neurocores.

Neurocore constraints	
max compartments	1024
max fan-in axons	4096
max fan-out axons	4096

- **Partition**: The conversion process needs to find a valid partition of the neural network on the Loihi chip. Some constraints have to be respected to have a valid partition. These constraints, reported in Table 6.4, are related to the synaptic fan-in and fan-out of every neurocore and the maximum number of neurons that can be mapped onto a single neurocore.

- **Mapping**: The partition is mapped onto the Loihi, and the model is now ready to be used in the SNN deployment.

6.2.2.5 Experimental Setup

All the experiments are conducted on the Intel Neuromorphic Research Cloud (NRC) server, using one of the available Loihi partitions. The experiments are executed on the Nahuku32 board, which is composed of 32 Loihi chips. The three main tunable conversion parameters that have been analyzed for fine-tuning conversion are the *reset mode*, *DThIR*, and *experiment duration*. Several experiments have been conducted to evaluate the effects of these parameters on the final SNN accuracy.

6.2.2.6 Results Varying the DThIR

In this stage, we evaluate the conversion results varying the DThIR. The experiment duration is set to 256 timesteps, which is a reasonable choice for both the soft and hard resets, as we will discuss later. The tested DThIR levels are $2^1, 2^3$, and 2^5. Selecting higher levels is usually not an optimal solution because the membrane potential threshold may get too large. The results are reported in Figure 6.3.

Analysis for MNIST: In both soft reset and hard reset cases, the SNN accuracy is equivalent to the DNN accuracy value for DThIR $= 2^1$ and 2^3. However, when the parameter is increased to 2^5, the accuracy drops in both soft and hard reset cases.

Analysis for CIFAR10: Also, in this case, the highest accuracy is reached for DThIR $= 2^1$, for both hard and soft resets. However, the accuracy starts decreasing when the DThIR is set to 2^3 and reaches a minimum when the DThIR is increased to 2^5.

As a consequence, a value of DThIR $= 2^1$ is chosen for the following further analysis.

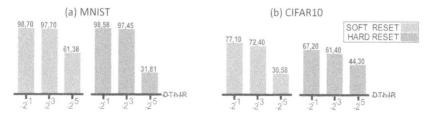

Figure 6.3: *cNet*, results varying the DThIR on **(a)** MNIST and **(b)** CIFAR10.

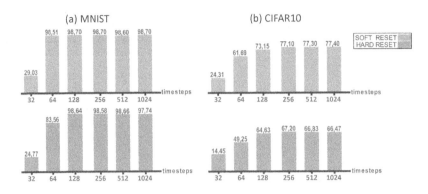

Figure 6.4: *cNet*, results varying the experiment duration on **(a)** MNIST and **(b)** CIFAR10.

6.2.2.7 *Results Varying the Experiment Duration and Reset Mode*

These analysis aim at finding a good compromise between experiment duration and reset mode. We expect to get more precise results in terms of output latency by choosing a longer duration. Moreover, the soft reset should provide higher accuracy values. The results are reported in Figure 6.4.

Analysis for MNIST: Looking at the results for the MNIST dataset, a test accuracy equal to 98.70% (i.e., only 0.09% lower than the DNN accuracy) is reached with the soft reset for an experiment duration longer than 64 timesteps. On the other hand, at least 128 timesteps for the hard reset are needed to reach the same level of accuracy. Moreover, the accuracy reached by both the hard and the soft reset remains stable also for a more extended experiment duration.

Analysis for CIFAR10: The results for the CIFAR10 dataset clearly show that the DNN accuracy of 78.92% is never reached for the hard reset case. The maximum accuracy of 67.20% is reached when the experiment duration is longer than 256 timesteps. On the other hand, despite not achieving the same results as the corresponding DNN, the soft reset achieves better performance than the hard reset. An accuracy equal to 77.10% is reached with 256 timesteps, slowly growing to 77.40% with a longer experiment of 1024 timesteps.

For an experiment duration of 256 timesteps, the average time to execute a single inference step of image classification and the Intel Loihi chip usage are reported in Table 6.5. Looking at the occupied neurocores for both the MNIST and CIFAR10 cases, the soft reset uses more cores.

TABLE 6.5: Accuracy results of the DNN models.

Reset Mode	Dataset	Classification time	Neurocores
soft	MNIST	8.312 ms	27
hard	MNIST	6.464 ms	20
soft	CIFAR10	21.371 ms	37
hard	CIFAR10	26.159 ms	29

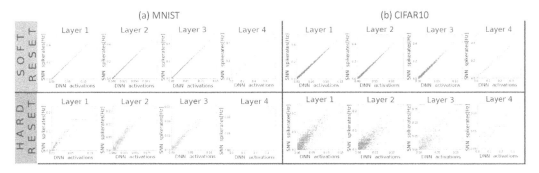

Figure 6.5: Correlation plots for the first 4 layers of *cNet* after its conversion to the corresponding SNN model, for (a) MNIST and (b) CIFAR10.

To better understand why the soft reset achieves better results than the hard reset, we compare the correlation plots of the converted layers. Figure 6.5 shows the correlation plots of the first 4 layers, both for the soft reset and hard reset versions and on both datasets. For each case, we apply an experiment duration of 256 timesteps and a DThIR equal to 2^1.

At first glance, it is immediately noticed that the correlation plots of the soft reset conversion are more compliant with the expected behavior when compared to the hard reset conversion, both for the MNIST and CIFAR10 datasets. Looking at the experiment for MNIST using soft reset, the correlation plot of the first layer shows a perfect conglomeration of activations (x-axis) vs. spikerates (y-axis) along the main diagonal. This means that the conversion of this layer is working as desired, having all the SNN neurons spiking at a rate equivalent to their corresponding DNN activations. Similar principles are adopted for the following layers.

Looking at the experiment for MNIST using hard reset, the correlation plots show a relatively worse conversion behavior. The points in the first layer are distributed with an overlapped-staircase behavior. The same observation is noted in the second layer, where a dilatation of the agglomerate of points is also present along the x-axis. However, both in the 3rd and 4th layers correlation plots, the points are sufficiently compacted along the diagonal, and the final accuracy achieved by this SNN is similar to the DNN accuracy.

For the CIFAR10 analysis, the soft reset provides good correlation plots, despite the points form a thicker agglomerate compared to the MNIST case. On the other hand, the hard reset provides worse results. The correlation between the activations and the spikerates is relatively less evident, with a general behavior more emphasized than the MNIST case. The analyses reported in these results justify the 10% accuracy drop encountered using the hard reset conversion, as seen in Figure 6.3 and Figure 6.4.

Overall, the use of the *soft reset* mode provides higher accuracy results due to the lower information loss during the conversion, as clearly illustrated by the correlation plots in Figure 6.5. A good choice for the value of the experiment duration seems to be ≥ 256 timesteps. A shorter duration may lead to an accuracy loss, as shown for the CIFAR10 dataset. On the other hand, having more than 512 timesteps does not lead to a higher accuracy, as shown in the MNIST and CIFAR10 results. Finally, a DThIR value equal to 2^1 seems to be the best way to reduce the conversion loss. f

6.2.3 Pre-Processing Method for the DvsGesture Dataset

Event-based data are ideal when used at the input of the SNNs due to their intrinsic asynchronous and spiking behavior. However, in this context, we are training a network in the DNN domain, and only in the second stage, we convert it into an equivalent SNN. This approach forces us to find an alternative representation of the input data, as the DNN is not trainable on pure sequences of events. A valid solution would be to train the DNN with a frame series obtained by collecting the incoming events. However, the following choices have to be made to achieve a good conversion into frames:

- Choose the number of events to collect into a single frame.

- Select the size of the frame and its number of channels.

- Set a policy for positive and negative events accumulation.

6.2.3.1 Events Accumulation

As reported in [232], there are two accumulation approaches:

1. *Time-based accumulation:* all events that occur in a fixed time window are accumulated in a single frame.

2. *Quantitative-based accumulation:* a fixed number of consecutive events are accumulated in a single frame.

The first solution ensures that the timing information within frames is preserved. On the other hand, the second solution guarantees that every frame will have the same amount of information. However, it may not be a good choice regarding gesture recordings since the number of events generated by a gesture within a fixed time window also depends on the type of the gesture itself. Not all gestures produce the same amount of events per second. Hence, using a quantitative approach, the number of the generated frames depends on the number of events produced by the gesture. The same gestures with the same time length may lead to a different amount of frames, having different event rates.

Consequently, the final dataset will result in an imbalance, having a diverse number of frames per class, both in the train and test sets. To balance the dataset, we may reduce the number of frames per gesture to a value equal for all classes, but this would result in a drastic reduction of the used information from the original event-based recordings. Therefore, based on these considerations, the time-based accumulation is preferable because it guarantees a balanced dataset. Hence, the results relative to the quantitative-based accumulation are not discussed in the following section.

6.2.3.2   Time Window Size

The number of events per second varies from gesture to gesture and between different trials of the same gesture. A mean value of 98 events/ms is computed by evaluating the original dataset over all the available gestures of the different trials. This information gives a relevant starting point in choosing the time window size each frame has to cover. In this research, the time windows of 60ms, 150ms, 235ms and 300ms are explored. Choosing a time window of less than 60ms would bring an insufficient amount of events collected per frame, thus preventing a proper classification. On the other hand, an accumulation time longer than 300ms would lead to a total of less than 3 frames per second, which we consider the minimum for a real-world application.

A single frame might also have more than one channel, each of them covering a subset of the whole time window. For instance, a frame covering a window of 300ms can have 3 channels, where each channel covers a sub-windows of 100ms. This solution generates frames where the temporal information is preserved because the channels cover consecutive time sections.

Moreover, another solution consists of using overlapped frames, i.e., when the time windows covered by two consecutive frames are partially overlapped. For instance, using an overlap factor of 2 with frames of 300ms, the frames would cover partially overlapped ranges. The first frame would be $[0ms; 300ms]$, and the next would cover the range $[150ms; 450ms]$. *There are several advantages in choosing this solution:*

- The number of frames generated from the original dataset is multiplied by the overlap factor, leading to a bigger dataset that provides better training results.

- The frames can cover different time windows, augmenting the temporal information in the dataset.

- The system's throughput is multiplied by the overlap factor.

In our experiments, we select an overlap factor of 2. Using an overlap factor $n > 2$ would generate redundant overlapped frames. On the contrary, a value $n < 2$ would reduce the benefits of having overlapped frames.

6.2.3.3   Events Polarity

Each event carries the x and y coordinates of the detected event and the polarity of the event, which can be either positive or negative.

- The first possibility is to accumulate the positive and negative events in two different channels of the frame, c_+ and c_-. Both the channel pixels are initialized to 0, and when a positive event is detected, the pixel (x, y, c_+) is increased by 1. On the other hand, a negative event increments the pixel (x, y, c_-) by 1. Finally, the pixel intensities are normalized to the range $[0; 255]$. Since the accumulation of oppositely signed events forms a trace of the gesture motion over time, this solution prevents information loss because the polarity information becomes relevant when the gestures differ only w.r.t. their sense of rotation.

- The second solution (inspired by the work of [232]) is to accumulate all positive and negative events on the same channel, keeping the polarity information. All pixels are initialized to a mean value of 128 and incremented or decremented by 1 depending on the event polarity.

- The third possibility (as inspired by the work of [232]) is to discard the polarity and collect all the events into a single channel by simply incrementing the pixel (x, y) every time a positive or a negative event occurs.

The above-described solutions have been tested on the DNN, and based on the accuracy achieved, the following considerations can be observed. Overall, the best solution is the third, where the polarity is discarded. The 2-channel accumulation solution has not shown particular improvements in the final accuracy compared to the case of the discarded polarity. At the same time, having two channels for separately storing the polarity comes with a set of drawbacks, such as an increased dimension of the DNN and increased size of the dataset. Moreover, the number of occupied neurocores for the converted SNN is higher than using a single channel, which also impacts the system's latency. For this reason, the 2-channel policy can be discarded. Considering the 1-channel polarity accumulation, the obtained results have shown an accuracy drop ($\simeq -4\%$) w.r.t. the discarded polarity case. This approach leads to having frames with generally a high pixel intensity level, all initialized to a non-zero value, thus leading to lower classification results. For these reasons, in Table 6.6, only the results achieved without signed polarity accumulation are reported.

6.2.3.4 Frame Size

Lastly, the dimension of the frame is chosen. The original recordings have a dimension of 128×128. However, such a dimension may be too high when used as an input to our converted SNN, leading to a large number of neurocores required to deploy the SNN on Loihi and increasing the prediction latency. Hence, we resized the image to a dimension of 32×32 by applying a preliminary Average Pooling step. This process is also helpful in removing the noisy events from the original recordings, thereby producing input frames that only contain the relevant gesture information. Also, a 64×64 size has been evaluated, but the DNN accuracy results did not show any improvement over the 32×32 size. On the other hand, a 16×16 size would be too small for achieving good recognition by the DNN.

Another solution, proposed by [102] for the same dataset, is to collect only the events inside a 64×64 attention window that moves and keeps track of the incoming gestures. Afterward, the Average Pooling is applied to the 64×64 frame, reducing its size to 32×32.

This solution has been implemented and evaluated, but the accuracy was ($\simeq -5\%$) lower than the one achieved with the whole image frame. Such an accuracy drop may be due to the removal of the gesture itself from its contest by shrinking the input window to the area where the actual gesture takes place. In this way, the DNN may not distinguish between equivalent gestures executed with opposite arms.

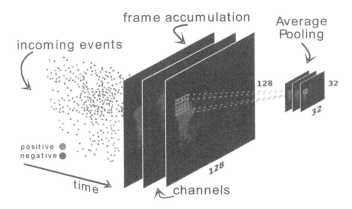

Figure 6.6: DvsGesture pre-processing: the number of frame channels may depend on the chosen polarity policy or, in a time-based accumulation, on the time length of each channel.

6.2.3.5 Dataset Structure

In the above-discussed pre-processing approaches, the frames are associated with their corresponding labels and accumulated into a **train set** and a **test set**. The dataset dimension depends on the chosen pre-processing approaches. Fewer frames are generated with longer time windows, whereas the amount of frames increases as the time window covered by each frame gets shorter. The pre-processing stages are summarized in Figure 6.6.

6.2.4 Evaluation of the Accuracy Results

All the generated pre-processed datasets have been tested with the *cNet* network, along with the same training parameters for MNIST and CIFAR10. This procedure has been followed to ensure that the accuracy differences between the DNN and SNN depend on the data pre-processing step and are not related to the network architecture or the training policies.

The conversion process has been conducted by applying the soft reset mode, and an experiment duration of 256 timesteps, with DThIR=2^1, since these are the settings showing the best results for both the MNIST and the CIFAR10 analyses. Using the previously-discussed pre-processing analysis, a set of different frame-converted datasets has been realized. In all these datasets, the frame size is set to 32×32, and the event polarity is discarded. The converted datasets differ in the possible use of the temporal overlapping between frames, the frame accumulation time duration, and the number of channels per frame. Table 6.6 shows the accuracy results for the DNN on the different post-processed datasets.

Dataset D1 indicates that choosing a time window of only 60ms gives relatively low accuracy results, similar to the case of dataset D2, where the time range covered by each channel is doubled. This behavior can be attributed to a few events accumulated for each channel.

TABLE 6.6: Pre-processing techniques applied to the original gesture DVS dataset and relative DNN accuracy. For all the datasets, the frame size equals 32×32, and the polarity information is discarded. Each generated dataset has been tested with the *cNet* DNN.

Dataset	duration(ms)	overlap	channels	DNN accuracy
D1	60 (10 per ch.)	✗	6	85.23%
D2	60 (20 per ch.)	✗	3	85.44%
D3	150 (50 per ch.)	✗	3	87.89%
D4	235 (78 per ch.)	✗	3	88.63%
D5	300 (100 per ch.)	✗	3	88.33%
D6	100	✗	1	74.14%
D7	235 (78 per ch.)	2	3	88.87%
D8	300 (100 per ch.)	2	3	**90.46%**

When observing the datasets D3-5, the time window is progressively incremented until a maximum duration of 300ms is covered. The results show that a high level of accuracy is reached with a 3-channel frame covering a period of 235ms.

Dataset D6 has been realized to investigate whether using a single channel frame could be a reasonable solution. In this case, the accuracy drop can be attributed to the fact that the single frame does not contain temporal information since all the events are accumulated in a single channel.

When observing the datasets D7 and D8, an overlap factor of 2 is introduced. The accuracy increases to reach a value of 90.46% in dataset D8, which is the best-obtained value.

The *cNet* DNN model trained on dataset D8 is then converted to its equivalent SNN and deployed on the Loihi platform. The converted SNN reaches a test accuracy of 89.64%, which is only 0.82% lower than the original DNN representation. Moreover, the average time needed for classifying an input frame is 11.43ms. These results must be compared with the state-of-the-art test accuracies achieved in [8] and in [248]. The work in [8] reaches a test accuracy of 94.59% with a 64×64 frame size, whereas the accuracy achieved on a 32×32 frame drops down to 90.78%. This last value is only 1.14% higher than the one obtained in this research using frames with the same dimension of 32×32, but it is obtained with a much bigger DNN (having 16 Conv layers with many more feature maps per layer) than the one used in this work (see Table 6.2 for our network configuration). However, we did not consider employing such large and deep networks to maintain low resource utilization and low latency for real-time embedded implementations.

In [248], the test accuracy reached on a smaller portion of the original dataset (1.5 seconds per gesture) is 93.64%, which is 4% higher w.r.t. the one obtained with our methodology. However, since their SNN is designed and trained from scratch (i.e., not using a conversion mechanism), they have directly used the original event-based dataset, avoiding an inevitable information loss related to the pre-processing step.

Regarding latency, with our best solution (D8), the total time needed for a frame classification is $150ms + 11.42ms = 161.42ms$. Since the overlap factor is 2, the next frame starts after 150ms. Therefore, we considered 150ms per frame. This configuration provides a throughput of 6.24 frames-per-second, a feasible solution for a real-time system.

6.2.5 Summary

The proposed methodology demonstrates an end-to-end application for event-based SNNs on the Loihi neuromorphic processor. First, the DNN-to-SNN conversion process is analyzed, and different optimizations are applied to reduce the accuracy loss due to the conversion. Then, toward the usage of the event-based sensors, a pre-processing method is designed to use event datasets, such as the DvsGesture, in the DNN domain. Gesture recognition is one of the most common benchmarks in the neuromorphic community, while this is not the only application that can be executed on Loihi. For example, other tasks more related to autonomous vehicles can be performed, such as car detection and lane detection, as will be discussed in the following Section 6.3 and Section 6.4, respectively.

6.3 CARSNN: AN EFFICIENT SNN FOR EVENT-BASED AUTONOMOUS CARS ON THE LOIHI NEUROMORPHIC PROCESSOR

Autonomous Driving (AD) related features enable new forms of mobility that are also beneficial for intelligent and autonomous systems like robots, smart industries, and smart transportation. The decisions must be made quickly and in real time for these applications. Moreover, in the quest for electric mobility, these operations must follow the low power policy without affecting the autonomy of the means of transport or the robot much. These two challenges can be tackled using SNNs. SNNs achieve high performance with low latency and power consumption when deployed on specialized neuromorphic hardware. In this section, we use an SNN connected to an event-based camera to face one of the fundamental AD problems, i.e., the classification between cars and other objects. To consume lower power than traditional frame-based cameras, we use a Dynamic Vision Sensor. The experiments are conducted following an offline supervised learning rule and mapping the learned SNN model on the Intel Loihi Neuromorphic Research Chip. Our best experiment achieves an accuracy of 86% for the offline implementation, which drops to 83% when ported onto the Loihi Chip. The Neuromorphic Hardware implementation has a maximum of 0.72 ms of latency for every sample and consumes only 310 mW. To our knowledge, this work is the first implementation of an event-based car classifier on a Neuromorphic Chip.

6.3.1 System Overview

Since each task represents a real-time problem, we want the entire decision-making system to have good reactivity with very low latency, to minimize the chance of catastrophic car accidents due to late decisions. Another challenge is related to the system's robustness, which must operate in all conditions, particularly for different illumination and weather conditions. Moreover, the system should be optimized for low power consumption, an important design criterion for automotive, especially in the context of battery-driven electric mobility.

In our research, we focus on the *"cars vs. background"* classification problem. To overcome these limitations, we identify three main research objectives:

1. the system should use the major robust vision engine, i.e., an event-based camera;

2. the network should be a low-complexity event-based SNN for energy-constrained systems;

3. the developed SNN should fulfill the system constraints to be implemented onto a neuromorphic hardware chip.

Following these research goals, we design, optimize, and implement the SNN on the Intel Loihi Chip [40], and evaluate it on the N-CARS dataset [252]. It is based on the Asynchronous Time-based Image Sensor (ATIS) [211], which is an event-based camera.

6.3.2 Problem Analysis and General Design Decisions

For the classification problem that we face, we use a supervised learning method and train the network based on the desired behavior. Each sample is composed of a stream of events, where a stream represents the same object to classify. Within the same sample, the present spikes are correlated in time and space with the past and future spikes [252]. To achieve good performance, we have to consider this temporal correlation and use a learning method capable of exploiting this property. As claimed in [283], the STBP is one of the best offline learning methods since it achieves very high classification accuracy in tasks that involve event-based camera streams. It also uses TD and SD to compute the gradients and train the SNN. Hence, we employ this learning method in our experiments.

As it is also a real-time problem, the system should be very reactive and generate the correct prediction in a few milliseconds. Since we need a very reactive prediction, we can use only a subset of input information to implement the **Attention Window** strategy. To find the area that focuses the attention on input data, we analyze and evaluate the event occurrences in the train and test sets of the N-CARS dataset [252]. Due to the relatively large dataset dimension, such a study resembles a good approximation of the real problem and does not impact the generalization property of our system.

The event occurrences in different attention windows are evaluated in Figure 6.7. Most of the events are contained in the region of size 50×50 in the bottom-left corner, both in the train and test sets. Hence, as reported in Table 6.7, we can denote this as the *first attention window*. The *second attention window* also starts from the bottom-left corner and has a doubled size (i.e., 100×100).

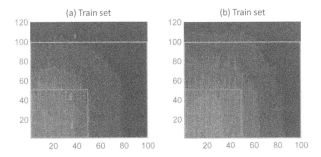

Figure 6.7: Event occurrences on **(a)** train and **(b)** test sets of the N-CARS dataset.

Considering its practical implementation on an existing **Neuromorphic Hardware**, the **Intel Loihi Chip**, the network is designed following all its constraints, summarized in Table 6.8.

A summary of the general design decisions taken after analyzing the problem is shown in Table 6.9.

6.3.3 CarSNN Methodology

Our methodology for designing the SNN model for the *"cars vs. background"* classification, which we call **CarSNN**, is composed of a three-step process, as shown in Figure 6.8. After defining the SNN model architectures considering different attention windows, we discuss the methods to find the parameters for SNN training and feeding the input data.

6.3.3.1 CarSNN Model Design

To achieve good classification results, our *CarSNN* receives the input events from two distinct polarity channels, one for positive and the other for negative events. Toward the problem generalization, we consider this as a multi-classification problem (i.e., not as a simple binary classification problem). Therefore, the output layer of

TABLE 6.7: Delimited points for *Attention windows.*

Attention window	P. 0 (x,y)	P. 1 (x,y)	P. 2 (x,y)	P. 3 (x,y)
First attention window	(0,0)	(0,50)	(50,50)	(50,0)
Second attention window	(0,0)	(0,100)	(100,100)	(100,0)

TABLE 6.8: Main constraints for developing the SNN implemented on the *Intel Loihi Neuromorphic Research chip.*

Property	Constrain
Maximum Compartments per Core	1024 Compartments
Maximum fan-in of a Core	4096 Pre-Synapses
Maximum fan-out of a Core	4096 Post-Synapses
Synaptic fan-in state size	128 KB

TABLE 6.9: General decisions taken after analyzing the problem.

Properties of the problem	Decision
Knowledge of the correct output	Use of supervised learning rule
Time and space correlation	Consider TD and SD
Real-time	Use simple SNN
High-performance vision sensor	Use event-based camera
Accurate profiling of real problem	Use N-CARS dataset
Many events in limited area	Use attention windows
Low power consumption	Use Neuromorphic Chip

the *CarSNN* consists of two neurons corresponding to the two possible classes, one for cars and one for background objects.

Since the architecture proposed in [257] achieved high classification accuracy and low latency on the DvsGesture dataset [8], we modify this model to correctly function for the N-CARS dataset. Compared to the model of [257], our *CarSNN* has different kernel sizes, padding, and output channels on the first Conv layer, and different sizes of the last two dense layers.

Based on the attention window analysis, we design three different SNNs for the three different sizes of input images:

1. Size 128×128 (Table 6.10): the model is very similar to the SNN proposed in [257]. Since this size is larger than the N-CARS dataset image size, which is 120×100, the exceeding pixels do not produce spikes and are padded by zeros (i.e., no event). Such an image size is equal to the resolution of the ATIS DVS camera [211]. Hence, this network can be easily implemented with it.

2. Size 50×50 (Table 6.11): this uses the first attention window.

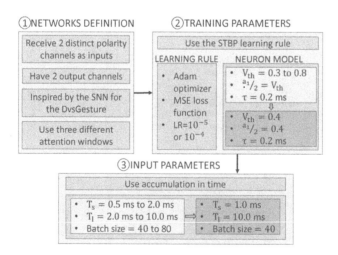

Figure 6.8: Three-step process was followed to design our *CarSNN* with the training and feeding input parameters.

3. Size 100×100 (Table 6.12): this uses the second attention window.

TABLE 6.10: SNN model for full-size images (input size 128×128).

Layer type	In ch.	Out ch.	Kernel size	Padding	Stride
Av. pooling	2	2	4	–	–
Convolution	2	32	3	1	1
Av. pooling	32	32	2	–	–
Convolution	32	32	3	1	1
Av. pooling	32	32	2	–	–
Dense	2048	1024	–	–	–
Dense	1024	2	–	–	–

TABLE 6.11: SNN model for first attention window (input size 50×50).

Layer type	In ch.	Out ch.	Kernel size	Padding	Stride
Av. pooling	2	2	4	–	–
Convolution	2	32	3	1	1
Av. pooling	32	32	2	–	–
Convolution	32	32	3	1	1
Av. pooling	32	32	2	–	–
Dense	512	144	–	–	–
Dense	144	2	–	–	–

TABLE 6.12: SNN model for second attention window (input size 100×100).

Layer type	In ch.	Out ch.	Kernel size	Padding	Stride
Av. pooling	2	2	4	–	–
Convolution	2	32	3	1	1
Av. pooling	32	32	2	–	–
Convolution	32	32	3	1	1
Av. pooling	32	32	2	–	–
Dense	1568	512	–	–	–
Dense	512	2	–	–	–

6.3.3.2 Parameters for Training

Using a backpropagation-based supervised learning rule, such as the STBP, it is possible to tune several hyper-parameters. We focus our attention on:

- **loss function**: we adopt the **Mean Squared Error** (**MSE**) loss criterion, since it achieves the highest performance in [283];

- **optimizer**: we use **Adam** [110], because it seems the best for the STBP;

- **learning rate (lr)**: after some preliminary tests, we find the best value is around $1e^{-5}$ and $1e^{-4}$. The training is faster with the latter value since the SNN achieves good accuracy results in fewer epochs.

Since the adopted SNN learning rule is directly implemented on the LIF neurons, other specific parameters can be adjusted. We mainly focus on the formalization of the membrane potential update ($u_i^{t+1,n}$) and highlight the membrane potential decay factor τ (Equation (6.5)).

$$u_i^{t+1,n} = u_i^{t,n}\tau(1 - o_i^{t,n}) + \sum_{j=1}^{l(n-1)} w_{ij}^n o_j^{t+1,n-1} + b_i^n \qquad (6.5)$$

Another key parameter of a LIF neuron is its **threshold** (V_{th}). If the membrane potential overcomes this level, an output spike is generated, and the potential is reset to a specific value. For every experiment, all the neurons have the same V_{th} and 0 as the reset value.

The third parameter to set ($\frac{a_1}{2}$) is related to the approximation of the derivative of the spiking nonlinearity. We model it as a rectangular pulse function defined in Equation (6.6):

$$h_1(u) = \frac{1}{a_1} \operatorname{sign}\left(|u - V_{th}| < \frac{a_1}{2}\right) \qquad (6.6)$$

In the following, we conduct some experiments to set the previously discussed parameters, focusing on V_{th}. We made these decisions:

- V_{th}: we change this value from 0.3 to 0.8 and evaluate which curve achieves the best accuracy;

- $\frac{a_1}{2}$: it assumes the same value of the threshold, as this assumption is made in [283];

- τ: this value must be small to have a good approximation of the neuron model and in particular of $f(o_i^{t,n})$. We set it to 0.2 ms.

To speed up this process and achieve good performance, we introduce an accumulation mechanism. We accumulate the spikes at a constant time rate called sample time (T_{sample}); for these first experiments, such a value is set to 10 ms. Every T_{sample} time, we construct a new input image for the SNN. The events that compose the image are summed by the following simple rule, based on which each pixel can have a maximum of one spike per channel. Each derived image is maintained stable to the input of the proposed SNN by a time window of 15 time steps. Therefore, this accumulation mode can compress the input information. The accuracy that we evaluate refers to every sample (i.e., accumulated image) trained for 300 epochs. Table 6.13 and Figure 6.9 report the results of these experiments, in which we use the SNN with the full size image (Table 6.10).

TABLE 6.13: Experiments to find the best value of V_{th}.

input size	V_{th}	$\frac{a_1}{2}$	τ	T_{sample}	batch size	lr	accuracy
			ms	ms			%
128×128	0.3	0.3	0.2	10	20	$1e^{-5}$	83.0
128×128	**0.4**	0.4	0.2	10	20	$1e^{-5}$	**84.0**
128×128	0.5	0.5	0.2	10	20	$1e^{-5}$	82.4
128×128	0.6	0.6	0.2	10	20	$1e^{-5}$	81.9
128×128	0.8	0.8	0.2	10	20	$1e^{-5}$	82.6

From Table 6.13, we notice that the best accuracy is achieved when V_{th} is equal to 0.4. Moreover, from Figure 6.9, we can notice that, while a V_{th} of 0.3 leads to a relatively high accuracy after a few epochs, the training curve with V_{th} equal to 0.4 have less instability than for the other experiments. These two reasons lead us to select 0.4 for the V_{th} parameter.

6.3.3.3 Parameters for Feeding the Input Data

The input spikes are fed to the SNN with an accumulation strategy to speed up the training. Despite this limitation, we notice from the experiments conducted in Table 6.13 that the accuracy is relatively high. Hence, we keep this property that gives us some advantages:

- decrease power consumption;

- increase the reactivity of the system because input data are compressed.

Moreover, We also define an upper bound to the system's latency of 10 ms. Therefore, for the train, we take only 10 ms from the sample stream with a random initial point. It is defined as the maximum acceptable sample length (T_l). With this constraint, two different procedures can be followed:

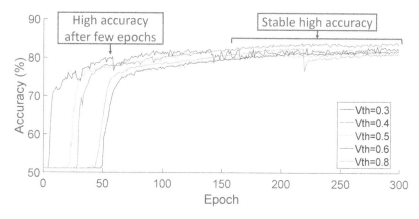

Figure 6.9: Percentage of accuracy for the experiment made to evaluate the best value for V_{th}.

1. accumulate the spikes every T_l time ($T_{sample} = T_l$) and predict a unique input image for the whole input stream, as we did in the previous experiments;

2. accumulate the spikes to have more than one input image for every input stream ($T_{sample} < T_l$), then see what the class with majority prediction is.

We conduct analyses to find the best sample time and the accuracy variation with two different batch sizes (BS on Table 6.14). In these experiments we use the second procedure for the image accumulation and we set the parameters as follows: $V_{th} = 0.4$, $\frac{a_1}{2} = 0.4$, $\tau = 0.2\ ms$.

The training lasts for 200 epochs. To speed up this process, we use a learning rate equal to $1e^{-4}$ and a minimum batch size equal to 40. We also use three metrics to evaluate the accuracy:

- one-shot accuracy on test data ($acc._s$): it is the accuracy found on all the samples were taken at T_s of the test dataset;

- accuracy on test data ($acc._{test}$): it is the accuracy for all the sample streams of the test dataset, calculated based on the majority prediction of the part of the stream with sample length equal to T_l;

- accuracy on train data ($acc._{train}$): it is the counterpart of the accuracy on test data but computed on train streams of the dataset.

The results in Table 6.14 provide us with the necessary feedback for setting the value of T_s. If it is small (like 0.5 ms), there are more points for the same stream

TABLE 6.14: Experiments to find the best value for T_s, T_l and batch size.

Input size	T_s	T_l	BS	lr	$acc._s$	$acc._{test}$	$acc._{train}$
	ms	ms			%	%	%
128×128	1.0	2.0	80	$1e^{-4}$	80	79	83
128×128	1.0	4.0	80	$1e^{-4}$	80	80	86
128×128	1.0	6.0	80	$1e^{-4}$	51	51	51
128×128	1.0	8.0	80	$1e^{-4}$	80	79	89
128×128	1.0	2.0	40	$1e^{-4}$	80	77	86
128×128	1.0	4.0	40	$1e^{-4}$	80	83	88
128×128	1.0	6.0	40	$1e^{-4}$	72	70	90
128×128	**1.0**	**8.0**	40	$1e^{-4}$	**81**	**86**	91
128×128	1.0	10.0	40	$1e^{-4}$	80	86	**94**
128×128	2.0	10.0	40	$1e^{-4}$	51	51	51
100×100	0.5	10.0	40	$1e^{-4}$	75	80	84
100×100	**1.0**	**10.0**	40	$1e^{-4}$	**81**	**85**	**92**
100×100	2.0	10.0	40	$1e^{-4}$	51	51	51
50×50	0.5	10.0	40	$1e^{-4}$	67	71	79
50×50	1.0	10.0	40	$1e^{-4}$	71	75	81
50×50	**2.0**	10.0	40	$1e^{-4}$	**74**	**77**	**83**

sample. However, it is challenging to train the SNNs, because the accumulation has not effect, and the temporal correlation is lost. On the other hand, the accuracy decreases when we use high T_s (i.e., 2 ms). The best trade-off is obtained when T_s equals 1 ms.

Moreover, the batch size affects the training process. To have high accuracy, its value should be limited to 40.

In the first experiments of Table 6.14, we consider only the variation of T_l and BS. As expected, with constant BS and same value of $acc._s$, the $acc._{test}$ increases or remains stable with the increase of the T_l. This behavior is due to having more sub-predictions to compute the final result when T_l is large. The non-deterministic training process justifies the changes in the $acc._s$.

6.3.4 Evaluation of our CarSNN Methodology

The STBP learning method is based on backpropagation without using local information. Moreover, the gradients are computed with differential equations that are not directly implementable into the on-chip learning engine of the Intel Loihi Neuromorphic hardware. For these reasons, our *CarSNN* is trained offline, and the resulting parameters are mapped onto the neuromorphic chip.

6.3.4.1 *Experimental Setup*

Coherently with the analysis in previous sections, to train and validate the prediction system, we use the N-CARS dataset [252]. We also consider this dataset for the two fundamental reasons that it collects event-based camera streams and is the largest labeled event-based dataset acquired in real-world conditions.

We describe and implement the SNNs using the PyTorch library [204]. We model the SNNs' functional behavior using the formula of Equation (6.5) that contains the mechanism to update the membrane potential.

We ran the experiments on a workstation equipped with the CentOS Linux release 7.9.2009 operating system, an Intel Core i9-9900X CPU, and Nvidia GeForce RTX 2080 Ti GPUs.

The setting of the hyper-parameters is summarized in Table 6.15.

We randomly shuffle the dataset streams, and take the sample of T_l starting from a random initial point. We set the BS to 40, which gives the best accuracy in the previous experiments (according to Table 6.14) and maintains a reasonable training time duration. We set the same values of $T_s = 1$ ms and $T_l = 10$ ms for these three experiments to have a fair comparison. These two values leverage the tradeoff found from the results in Table 6.14. The learning rate (lr) is reduced by 0.5 every

TABLE 6.15: Parameters of the experiments.

Epochs	T_s	T_l	BS	lr	V_{th}	$\frac{a_1}{2}$	τ
	ms	ms					ms
200	1.0	10.0	40	$1e^{-3}$ to $1e^{-6}$	0.4	0.4	0.2

TABLE 6.16: Results of the offline training experiments.

Input size	$acc._s$	$acc._{test}$	$acc._{train}$
	%	%	%
128×128	80.1	85.7	93.6
100×100	80.5	86.3	95.0
50×50	72.6	78.7	85.3

20 epochs, starting from $1e^{-3}$. With this mechanism, the accuracy slightly increases compared to having a fixed lr.

Only the weights are updated during training to ease the model mapping onto the Loihi Neuromorphic Chip, while the bias is forced to 0. The training process lasts for 200 epochs, and every sample taken at T_s time is evaluated for 20 time steps. With these software and hardware settings, the training for a single epoch on all the dataset samples are measured to be about 300 seconds. For the inference, the mean latency for all samples, given at the time T_s, is about 0.8 ms.

6.3.4.2 Accuracy Results for CarSNN Offline Training

Table 6.16 shows the results in terms of accuracy for the offline implementation.

The accuracy results for the attention window of size of 100×100 are comparable to the values for the full image size (128×128), and indeed exhibit slightly higher $acc._{test}$ and $acc._{train}$. This effect can be explained because the cropped part of the sample is not relevant for the correct classification and may lead to an SNN misbehavior. On the other hand, the input streams consisting of a small part of the original image (50×50) lead to a significant accuracy decrease.

Moreover, from the results in Table 6.16, we can notice overfitting due to the gap between $acc._{train}$ and $acc._{test}$. It can be considered to be the upper bound of the accuracy for our developed *CarSNN* models.

6.3.4.3 CarSNN Implemented on Loihi

To implement our network on the Loihi Neuromorphic Chip, we have to exploit some similarities between its model and our offline model used in the previous experiments. Equation (6.7) reports how the Compartment Voltage (*CompV*), which represents the membrane voltage of a neuron is evaluated in the Loihi chip.

$$CompV_{t+1} = CompV_t \frac{2^{12} - \delta_v}{2^{12}} + CompI_{t+1} + bias \qquad (6.7)$$

The Compartment Current (*CompI*) is formulated by Equation (6.8), where the sum expression accumulates the weighted incoming spikes from j^{th} pre-synaptic neuron.

$$CompI_{t+1} = CompI_t \frac{2^{12} - \delta_i}{2^{12}} + 2^{6+wgtExp} \sum_j w_j s_{j_{t+1}} \qquad (6.8)$$

In Equations 6.7 and 6.8, we can set the following parameters:

- δ_i: Compartment Current Decay;

- δ_v: Compartment Voltage Decay;

- $bias$: bias component on $CompV$;

- $wgtExp$: value used to implement very different weights between different SNN layers.

Comparing between the formulation of our offline model (i.e., Equation (6.5)) and the Equation (6.7), we notice its similarity to Equations 6.9 to 6.12.

$$CompV_t = u_t \tag{6.9}$$

$$CompI_t = \sum_j w_j o_{j_{t+1}} \quad if \ \delta_i = 2^{12} \tag{6.10}$$

$$\frac{2^{12} - \delta_v}{2^{12}} = \tau \tag{6.11}$$

$$bias = b \tag{6.12}$$

We implement only the *CarSNN* described in Table 6.10, which achieves good offline accuracy results (as indicated in Table 6.16) and it represents the most complex developed network, based on power consumption, latency, and number of neurons.

The Intel Loihi Neuromorphic Hardware uses only 8 bits to store weights. The maximum weight range is $(-7, 6)$. Since these values are different between layers and the $wgtExp$ is limited we:

1. multiply weights and V_{th} by 25 (this value does not consider the default multiplication for 2^6 weights and V_{th} made on the Loihi);

2. use all the 8 bits to store our values.

According to Equations 6.9-6.12, the other neuromorphic hardware parameters can be adjusted.

All the setup parameters are summarized in Table 6.17.

We define our *CarSNN* through the Intel Nx SDK API version 0.9.5 and run it onto the Nahuku32 partition. In particular, we use the NxTF-supported Layers, such as NxConv2D, NxAveragePooling2D, and NxDense utilities. This kind of implementation is helpful to automatically improve the performance of the SNN in a simple manner. The *CarSNN* is tested on the N-CARS dataset. Every sample at T_s is replicated for 10 timestep, and we insert a blank time of 7 timestep between samples. The number of timesteps per inference is equal to 17. This decision is made to follow the real-time constraint of a maximum inference latency of 1 ms.

TABLE 6.17: Translation of parameters to the Loihi Chip.

Offline implementation			Loihi implementation		
Parameter	Value	Precision	Parameter	Value	Precision
V_{th}	0.4	Floating point 64 bits	$V_{th\ mant}$	10	Fixed point 12 bits
$weight$	×1	Floating point 64 bits	$weight$	×25	Fixed point 8 bits
τ	0.2	Floating point 64 bits	δ_v	3276	Fixed point 12 bits
b	0	Floating point 64 bits	$bias$	0	Fixed point 8 bits
–	–	Floating point 64 bits	δ_i	0	Fixed point 12 bits

In the results reported in Table 6.18, the mean latency, referred to as the time used to evaluate every sample at T_s, is calculated by multiplying the mean total execution time (in timesteps) for the number of timesteps per inference.

The maximum latency is referred to as the maximum "spiking time" for every timestep, considering the time when the Loihi Chip is used and makes the classification decision. This value can be used to evaluate whether the latency constraint is met. It does not include the time overhead used to exchange results between the chip and the host system, which can be suppressed by directly using output ports.

From Table 6.18, the following observations can be made:

- The $acc._{test}$ for the implementation onto the Loihi chip is 2.6% lower than the offline application.

- The maximum latency does not exceed T_s (1 ms).

Table 6.19 describes the power and energy consumption of the application implemented on the Neuromorphic Chip. In particular:

- *LakeMounts Power*: it is the consumption of the embedded processors [40] used to manage neurons and exchange messages with the host system.

- *Neuro-cores Power*: it represents the consumption of the neurons.

- *System Power*: it is the consumption of the entire system, where a large portion is represented by the static power consumed by the inactive cores of the used partition. It uses only 2 neurocores out of 32.

- *Energy per inference*: it is the mean energy consumed to classify one sample.

Hence, Table 6.19 reports the energy and power consumption of the application implemented on the Loihi Chip, which is several orders of magnitude lower than the same measure on GPUs.

TABLE 6.18: Results of the *CarSNN* implemented onto the Loihi Chip.

$acc._s$	$acc._{test}$	Neurons	Synapses	Neurocores	Mean latency	Max latency
%	%	number	number	number	μs	μs
72.16	82.99	54,274	5,122,048	151	899.6	≈ 700

TABLE 6.19: Power and energy consumption of the *CarSNN* implemented onto the Loihi Chip.

LakeMounts Power	Neurocores Power	System Power	Energy per Inference
mW	mW	mW	μJ
40.8	314.5	1375.4	319.7

6.3.4.4 Comparison with the State-of-the-Art

To our knowledge, *CarSNN* is the first Spiking CNN designed to perform event-based *"cars vs. background"* classification on neuromorphic hardware. It is also the first method that uses statistical analysis of events occurrences to indicate different attention windows on it. In this work, we use a simple yet efficient technique for event accumulation in time to maintain the correlation between spikes. Among the related works, to achieve good performance, the time correlation is supported with different methods:

- Histograms of Averaged Time Surfaces (HATS) [252]: it uses local memory to calculate the average of Time Surfaces, which represents the recent temporal activity within a local spatial neighborhood.

- Hierarchy Of Time Surfaces (HOTS) [117]: it uses a hierarchical computation of Time Surfaces between the layers.

- Gabor-filter [17]: it considers the spatial correlation between events and assigns them to the channels based on this information.

In HATS [252], all approaches are evaluated with a simple linear Support Vector Machine (SVM) on the N-CARS dataset. The results of such a simple classifier method are compared with our *CarSNN* in Table 6.20. The Gabor-filter method adopts a two-layer SNN before the SVM. Since the upper bound of T_l is 10 *ms* for the real-time constraint, the comparison is made considering this limitation.

As highlighted in Table 6.20, our *CarSNN* achieves better accuracy with a limited T_l than the Linear SVMs implemented after the use of different and more complicated accumulation approaches.

TABLE 6.20: Comparison of results for $T_l = 10$ *ms*.

Classifier (Accumulation approach)	$acc._{test}$
Linear SVM (HOTS)	≈ 0.54
Linear SVM (Gabor-SNN)	≈ 0.66
Linear SVM (HATS)	≈ 0.81
CarSNN (128×128 attention window)	0.86
CarSNN (100×100 attention window)	0.86
CarSNN (50×50 attention window)	0.79

6.3.5 Summary

The proposed CarSNN models are efficient SNN classifiers for event-based "car vs. background" classification. The training parameters, input parameters, and network model are determined with the proposed methodology. Moreover, an attention window mechanism is used to accumulate the events in the region where most events occur. Two versions of the proposed CarSNN models outperform the related works by 5% accuracy at the same latency while also achieving low power consumption on the Loihi chip. It represents a prominent method for resource-constrained event-based autonomous systems on neuromorphic hardware, as will be demonstrated in Section 6.4 for a lane detection application.

6.4 LANESNNS: SPIKING NEURAL NETWORKS FOR LANE DETECTION ON THE LOIHI NEUROMORPHIC PROCESSOR

AD-related features represent essential elements for the next generation of mobile robots and autonomous vehicles focused on increasingly intelligent, autonomous, and interconnected systems. The applications using these features must provide, by definition, real-time decisions, and this property is critical to avoid catastrophic accidents. Moreover, all the decision processes require low power consumption to increase the lifetime and autonomy of battery-driven systems. These challenges can be addressed by efficiently implementing SNNs on Neuromorphic Chips and using event-based cameras instead of traditional frame-based cameras.

In this work, we present a new SNN-based approach, called *LaneSNN*, to detect the lanes marked on the streets using event-based camera streams. We develop four novel SNNs characterized by fast response and low complexity, and train them using an offline supervised learning rule. Then, we implement and map the learned SNNs models onto the Intel Loihi Neuromorphic Research Chip. We develop a novel method for the loss function based on the linear composition of Mean Squared Error (MSE) and Weighted binary Cross Entropy (WCE) metrics. Our experimental results report a maximum Intersection over Union (IoU) measure of 0.62 and a very low power consumption of 1 W. The best IoU is obtained with an SNN implementation that occupies only 36 neurocores on the Loihi chip while providing a low latency of less than 8 ms for recognizing an image, thereby enabling real-time performance. The IoU values provided by our networks are comparable with the state-of-the-art but at a much lower power consumption of 1 W.

6.4.1 System Overview

To be able to drive safely, autonomous vehicles and mobile robots must continuously analyze the surrounding environment and consider any slightest variation to make the best decision and prevent catastrophic accidents. Hence, the *decision process* must occur in real-time. Moreover, the developed AD system should maintain low energy consumption.

Following these research objectives, we design, optimize, and implement SNNs on the Intel Loihi Neuromorphic Research Chip [40], and evaluate them on the DET dataset [33]. Moreover, the vision system is based on an event-based DVS camera [28].

We introduce **LaneSNNs** to detect pixels that represent the lanes on general images collected by an event-based camera. Our key contributions are:

- we follow the *Semantic Segmentation* approach to implement the algorithms;

- we adopt a *dataset pre-processing unit* to reduce the resolution of input and output images and to guarantee low complexity;

- we introduce a *novel loss function* that provides a trade-off between the *Weighted Binary Cross Entropy* and the *Mean Squared Error* measures;

- we implement the SNNs on the *Intel Loihi Neuromorphic Research Chip*;

- as evaluation, we analyze results in the form of different *Pareto Curves*, and we compare our results with the state-of-the-art.

6.4.2 Problem Analysis and General Design Decisions

6.4.2.1 Lane Detection Techniques

The lane detection is one of the fundamental tasks in the AD field. We aim to design and develop a device for automatically recognizing which parts of an image collected by a camera corresponding to the lanes marked on the street. Among the literature, there exist three general classes of methods used to detect and recognize sub-parts of an image [264]:

1. **Object detection**: the device recognizes the coordinates of some points which constitute the lanes [35]. After that, to obtain an output image, these results must be post-processed to get the labeled image, thus increasing latency and power consumption.

2. **Semantic segmentation**: the device distinguishes only two classes and determines the class of each pixel coming from the input image by individually looking at it. At the output, we can generate an image where the pixel intensities define its class [197] [119].

3. **Instance segmentation**: it is based on the similar principles as the semantic segmentation, but the lanes can be grouped into different classes [197] [119].

A real-time response from the detection device is required to leave more time for the decision-making part of the AD vehicle. Moreover, we are mainly focused on the position of the detected lanes. Therefore, we choose to use the semantic segmentation approach, which can achieve good performance with reduced latency and power consumption.

6.4.2.2 Dataset Pre-Processing

Coding of Input Information into Spikes: The DET dataset comprises labeled grey-scale raw images captured by the DVS camera. To extract the spiking information and directly feed the SNNs with them, we use the *rate coding* technique. Hence, we compare pixel intensities to random values for converting them into spike trains with the Poisson distribution.

Reducing the Spatial Resolution: The DET Dataset is recorded by the *CeleX V* DVS camera [28], and it is composed of input and label images with high resolution in space (1280×800 pixels per image for both the inputs and the labels). This property can be beneficial during the training of AI networks. In fact, it contains sufficient input information for better understanding how to generalize the task. On the other hand, the labels with very high resolution lead to a considerable imbalance between lane and background classes, thus decreasing the accuracy when using a semantic segmentation approach [35].

Moreover, we design SNN models that can be directly deployed on the Loihi Neuromorphic Chip [40]. The used Neuromorphic device has some limitations for collecting output spike counters related to the output neurons. Our preliminary analyses indicate that a maximum of 400 spike counters can be implemented. Hence, we reduce the label images' size to only 400 pixels. We also reduce the resolution of the input image size to 1600 pixels to be coherent with the resized output image dimension.

To prevent the SNNs from a possible *overfitting problem*, before reducing the image size, we perform *data augmentation*. In this specific case, we use 271 random training images and related labels and perform random *vertical translation* (between -100 and 100 pixels) and *rotation* (between $-30°$ and $30°$).

To reduce the dimension of the dataset images, we use two subsequent steps:

1. *Vertical cropping*: for each image, we crop the top 300 pixels rows and the bottom 200 pixels rows that do not contain relevant information.

2. *Average resizing*: we resize the images from size 1280×300 to 80×20 for the inputs and 40×10 for the labels. This operation is made by the area interpolation mechanism implemented through the *OpenCV Python library*.

For the label images, before the *average resizing* step, we give the intensity value of 400 to all the lane pixels (*denormalization step*). Then, after resizing, each pixel with an intensity greater than 0 is labeled as a lane, and its value is normalized to 1. This mechanism is required because we operate resizing on a large scale, and without the *denormalization/normalization* step, we may lose the thinnest lanes.

The steps for reducing the size of the dataset images are summarized in Figure 6.10.

6.4.2.3 Learning Rule

The DET dataset comprises three labeled parts: training, validation, and testing. Hence, it is convenient to implement a supervised learning rule for the SNNs to obtain

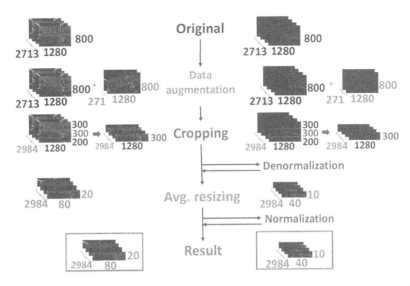

Figure 6.10: Steps followed to resize the images of the training set of the DET dataset. The input images are on the right, while the label images are on the left. For the testing set, we do not perform *data augmentation*, while all the other steps remain unchanged.

higher performance with limited training time rather than using an unsupervised learning rule. More specifically, we decided to use a *direct supervised learning rule* to reduce the system's latency. To obtain the input spike trains through the *rate coding* strategy, the spikes are correlated in time and space because they are based on the same image. Hence, to achieve high performance, we use the *Spatio-Temporal Back-Propagation (STBP)* [283] learning rule that considers both spatial and temporal domains. The core of this learning rule is described through Equations 6.13 and 6.14. More details are discussed in [283].

$$\frac{\partial L}{\partial \boldsymbol{b}^n} = \sum_{t=1}^{T} \frac{\partial L}{\partial \boldsymbol{u}^{t,n}} \cdot \frac{\partial \boldsymbol{u}^{t,n}}{\partial L \boldsymbol{b}^n} = \sum_{t=1}^{T} \frac{\partial L}{\partial \boldsymbol{u}^{t,n}} \tag{6.13}$$

$$\frac{\partial L}{\partial \boldsymbol{W}^n} = \sum_{t=1}^{T} \frac{\partial L}{\partial \boldsymbol{u}^{t,n}} \cdot \frac{\partial \boldsymbol{u}^{t,n}}{\partial x^{t,n}} \cdot \frac{\partial x^{t,n}}{\partial W^n} = \sum_{t=1}^{T} \frac{\partial L}{\partial \boldsymbol{u}^{t,n}} \cdot \boldsymbol{o}^{t,n-1} \tag{6.14}$$

They are used to perform the **Gradient Descendent Optimization Algorithm**. Using the implementation of the STBP learning rule, the derivative of a smooth function replaces the derivative of the spiking nonlinearity, following the **Surrogate Gradient** [185] strategy.

6.4.2.4 Loss Function

The lane and background classes in the DET dataset are also imbalanced after the dataset pre-processing step. Therefore, we employ the *Weighted Binary Cross-Entropy* (WCE) loss function [88] that is a variant of the more common *Binary*

Cross-Entropy (BCE) loss function. It is described in Equation (6.15), where $\hat{y}$ is the predicted probability of having a lane in a determined pixel, and y represents the class value, which can be positive ($y = 1$) or negative ($y = 0$).

$$L_{WCE}(y, \hat{y}) = -(\beta \cdot y \cdot \log(\hat{y}) + (1 - y) \cdot \log(1 - \hat{y})) \tag{6.15}$$

The WCE function introduces a slight improvement for the unbalanced labels because the positive class (i.e., the presence of the lane) is weighted by the coefficient β that balances the positive and negative prediction.

However, the STBP learning rule [283] is always studied with the implementation of the *Mean Squared Error* (MSE) loss function (Equation (6.16)), which is not widely used for segmentation problems [97].

$$L_{MSE} = \frac{\sum_{i=1}^{n}(y_i - \hat{y}_i)^2}{n} \tag{6.16}$$

Therefore, for the lane detection task, we introduce a novel loss function that combines the benefits of both MSE and WCE. This joint weighted loss function can be formalized by the eq. (6.17).

$$L_{MSE \ \& \ WCE} = (1 - p) \cdot L_{MSE} + p \cdot L_{WCE}, \tag{6.17}$$

where p denotes the parameter related to the WCE contribution and $(1 - p)$ denotes the MSE contribution, such that $0 \geq p \geq 1$.

6.4.3 LaneSNNs Design

6.4.3.1 *LaneSNNs Methodology Overview*

Based on the above discussion, we discuss the design of our LaneSNN networks, along with specific design decisions. To summarize the most important steps of our design, we present our *design methodology* in Figure 6.11.

6.4.3.2 *Input and Output*

To be coherent with the choices made on the DET dataset discussed in Section 6.4.2, since we generate only one spike train per pixel from each raw gray-scale image, we implement our networks with only one input channel.

The output size needs to be consistent with the dimension of the label images of the modified DET dataset. Hence, the last layer should have 400 output neurons, one for each pixel. Their firing rates represent the probability of the corresponding pixel being a lane in the resulting image.

6.4.3.3 *Network Architectures*

In literature, there are many algorithms based on NNs for facing general semantic segmentation tasks. They can be classified into two classes according to their implementation:

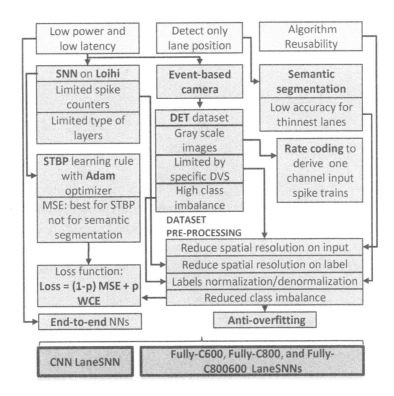

Figure 6.11: Design methodology of *LaneSNNs* models. On the top, there are the three main desired properties (grey boxes). In the middle, the different *design steps* and *decisions* (blue boxes) are made to follow the properties and overcome the *research challenges* (red boxes). The outcome is the design of four LaneSNN models at the bottom.

- *End-to-End*: these algorithms use only the NN without any pre and post-processing steps to tackle the lane detection problem. Usually, in these cases the network is split into two subsequent parts, i.e., reducing (*downsampling*) and increasing (*upsampling*) the image size during the elaboration [181].

- *More than one step*: the NN represents only a part of the whole detection algorithm, and it is useful for other more complex conventional algorithms [143] when these standalone NNs achieve low performance [106].

For reducing the latency and power consumption of the complete system, we choose to implement *End-to-End* algorithms. For the Loihi implementation, we design the networks through the NxTF library [233]. It can describe only basic layers such as Conv, FC, and average pooling.

We develop a spiking CNN inspired by the analysis made by the works in [106] [140]. In the first work [106], a small FC network is deployed at the end of the NN as the *upsampling* part. The second work [140] emphasizes the importance of Conv layers over others types for the *downsampling* structure.

TABLE 6.21: Structure of *CNN LaneSNN*.

Layer type	In ch.	Out ch.	Kernel size	Padding	Stride	% Dropout
Convolution	1	4	3	1	1	–
Convolution	4	4	3	1	1	–
Convolution	4	8	3	1	2	–
Convolution	8	8	3	1	1	–
Convolution	8	16	3	1	2	–
Dropout	16	16	–	–	–	10
Dense	1600	400	–	–	–	–

Therefore, we design our first network, called **CNN LaneSNN** (see Table 6.21), with five Conv layers by which the input sample image size (80×20) is reduced to 20×5 pixels for each of the 16 channels. Afterward, the image enters into the upsampling region made of 400 output neurons connected to the following Conv layer. Moreover, we adopt a *dropout layer*.

To decrease the power consumption further, we develop simpler structures that use only one or two FC hidden layers. Moreover, low-complexity FC SNNs are likely to consume low power and are easily implementable onto a Neuromorphic Chip.

Therefore, we develop two FC networks with 800 and 600 neurons for the *hidden layer* (**Fully-C800 LaneSNN**, Table 6.22, and **Fully-C600 LaneSNN**, Table 6.23, respectively), and a structure with two FC *hidden layers* called **Fully-C800600 LaneSNN**. (Table 6.24).

6.4.3.4 Anti-Overfitting Techniques

Due to the label imbalance of the DET dataset [33], the networks hardly generalize the task due to overfitting issues. This problem is primarily noticed in the layers of the networks that present many connections. For this reason, in the *CNN LaneSNN*, we insert a dropout layer between the last Conv layer and the FC layer. Since the

TABLE 6.22: Structure of *Fully-C800 LaneSNN*.

Layer	Number of neurons
Input	1600 (image of size 80×20)
Hidden	800
Output	400 (image of size 40×10)

TABLE 6.23: Structure of *Fully-C600 LaneSNN*.

Layer	Number of neurons
Input	1600 (image of size 80×20)
Hidden	600
Output	400 (image of size 40×10)

TABLE 6.24: Structure of *Fully-C800600 LaneSNN*.

Layer	Number of neurons
Input	1600 (image of size 80×20)
Hidden	800
Hidden	600
Output	400 (image of size 40×10)

dropout percentage is not so high, it does not hamper the network training. Its value of 10% is selected after some preliminary experiments.

For the other developed networks, we do not apply dropout strategies because, due to the small complexity of the networks, this operation can drastically reduce the achieved results.

We use the *Gaussian noise insertion* technique before all four networks' layers. We define its entity with the *relative standard deviation* σ_r. All the inserted Gaussian noise have σ_r equal to 0.1 for each layer of each developed network.

Finally, we apply the *decoupled weight decay regularization* on every layer of every network (Equation (6.18) [142]), where:

- w_{t+1} and w_t are respectively the new and the old synaptic weights on which we apply the optimizer;

- λ defines the rate of the weight decay per step;

- $\nabla f_t(w_t)$ is the tth batch gradient;

- lr is the learning rate.

$$w_{t+1} = (1 - \lambda) \cdot w_t - lr \cdot \nabla f_t(w_t), \qquad (6.18)$$

Table 6.25 summarizes all the implemented strategies.

6.4.4 Evaluation of LaneSNNs

As discussed in section 6.4.2, we perform the training of the network with the STBP learning rule. It uses Equations 6.13 and 6.14 [283] to evaluate the gradients. These computations are too elaborated to be executed onto the on-chip learning engine of the Intel Loihi Neuromorphic Chip. Therefore, our *LaneSNNs* are trained offline,

TABLE 6.25: Implemented anti-overfitting strategies.

Anti-overfitting strategy	Networks	Where/when	Entity
Data augmentation	All	Train dataset	+271 images
Dropout	CNN	Before output layer	10%
Gaussian noise	All	Input of all layers	$\sigma_r = 0.1$
Weight decay	All	Optimization steps	different values of λ

and then we implement the networks achieving the best results on the neuromorphic hardware.

6.4.4.1 Accuracy Definition

The outputs of our LaneSNNs represent the probabilities for each pixel to be classified as a lane. Compared to a direct prediction of the class, the probability prediction is a more flexible method, which allows us to tune and even calibrate the threshold for interpreting the predicted probabilities.

To derive the best threshold level for the predicted probabilities, we study the graphs that correlate the *Precision* and *Recall* values (**PR curves** [39]) evaluated in Equation (6.19).

$$\text{Precision} = \frac{TP}{TP + FP}, \quad \text{Recall} = \frac{TP}{TP + FN} \tag{6.19}$$

- *Precision* is the number of lane pixel predictions matched with the label (*True Positive* or *TP*), divided by the number of pixels predicted as lane (*True Positive* and *False Positive* or *FP*).

- *Recall* is the number of lane pixel predictions matched with the label (*TP*), divided by the number of lane pixels in the label (*TP* and *False Negative* or *FN*).

Then we define the **F-measure** (see Equation (6.20)) to find the best threshold to balance the two parameters.

$$\text{F-measure} = 2 \cdot \frac{\text{Precision} \cdot \text{Recall}}{\text{Precision} + \text{Recall}} \tag{6.20}$$

To distinguish between lanes and background classes, the F-measure is computed for all the possible thresholds applied to the output probabilities, and its maximum value, which corresponds to the best threshold, is selected. Moreover, to fairly compare the performance of our networks, we use the **Intersection over Union** (**IoU**) value (Equation (6.21) [225]).

$$IoU = \frac{|\text{Predicted lanes} \cap \text{True lanes}|}{|\text{Predicted lanes} \cup \text{True lanes}|} \tag{6.21}$$

We compute the best thresholds for every N predicted image, and we define the overall best threshold as their numerical mean (Equation (6.22)).

$$\overline{best\ th} = \frac{\sum\limits_{i=1}^{N} best\ th_i}{N} \tag{6.22}$$

Afterward, we apply the $\overline{best\ th}$ on the results and compute the IoU value distinctly for each image (Equation (6.23)).

$$IoU = \frac{\sum\limits_{i=1}^{N} IoU_i(\overline{best\ th})}{N} \tag{6.23}$$

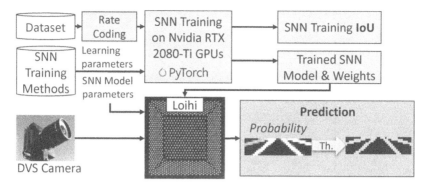

Figure 6.12: Setup and tool flow for conducting our experiments.

6.4.4.2 Experimental Setup

Our *LaneSNNs*, described using the PyTorch library [204], are trained on the DET dataset [33], after performing the pre-processing operations discussed in Section 6.4.2. We ran the experiments on a workstation equipped with an Intel Core i9-9900X CPU and multiple Nvidia GeForce RTX 2080 Ti GPUs. An overview of the tool flow used for conducting the experiments is shown in Figure 6.12.

We use the STBP learning rule [283] and the loss function described in Equation (6.17) for computing the distance between prediction and labels during training. Through these modifications, the complete training set has $241\,837$ and $951\,763$ pixels representing the lane and the background classes, respectively. It corresponds to a negative (background) over a positive (lanes) ratio of 3.93. Hence, to contrast the imbalance, we set the coefficient β of Equation (6.17) to 4.0 for every experiments. On the other hand, the value p used to set the percentage of loss derived by the WCE over the MSE functions varies from 0.0 to 0.5 for each experiment. We observe that the insertion of the MSE contribution leads to a faster SNN convergence. Focusing on other specific learning hyper-parameters, we set:

- **Optimizer**: we use *Adam* [110], since it is efficient when coupled with the STBP. On that, we apply the *decoupled weight decay* strategy [142]. We vary λ of Equation (6.18) from 0.0 to $5e^{-4}$ with steps of $1e^{-4}$.

- **Learning rate** (**lr**): we use the fixed learning rate approach varying in the range from $1e^{-5}$ to 1^e-3. These values are selected after preliminary analyses and guarantee the convergence of the method in a few epochs.

The adopted learning rule is based on LIF neurons. The formalization of the membrane potential update ($u_i^t + 1, n$) is defined in Equation (6.24), where:

- $u_i^{t,n}$ is the membrane potential before the update;

- $o_i^{t,n}$ represents the presence (1) or the absence (0) of a spike generated on the output axon;

- $\sum_{j=1}^{l(n-1)} w_{ij}^n o_j^{t+1,n-1}$ represents the incoming synaptic weighted spikes;

- b_i^n is a bias term.

$$u_i^{t+1,n} = u_i^{t,n} \tau (1 - o_i^{t,n}) + \sum_{j=1}^{l(n-1)} w_{ij}^n o_j^{t+1,n-1} + b_i^n \qquad (6.24)$$

The tunable parameters of a LIF neuron are:

- **membrane threshold** (V_{th}): it is the same for all neurons, and its value changes from 0.2 to 1.0;

- **membrane reset potential** (V_{reset}): for all the experiments, its value is the same for every neuron, and it is always set to 0 V;

- **membrane time constant** (τ): for all the experiments, it is set to 0.2 ms.

Moreover, the STBP learning rule uses the *surrogate gradient* mechanism to approximate the derivative of the spiking nonlinearity with simpler functions. For this purpose, the rectangular pulse function is adopted (Equation (6.25)).

$$h_1(u) = \frac{1}{a_1} \text{sign} \left(|u - V_{th}| < \frac{a_1}{2} \right) \qquad (6.25)$$

This assumption is coherent with the work of [283] since different types of approximations do not involve a significant accuracy variation, and the rectangular pulse function represents an efficient formula developed for this purpose.

Therefore, according to Equation (6.25), we can adjust the parameter $\frac{a_1}{2}$ that represent the pulse width. It has the same value as V_{th}, as made in [283].

All the experiments run for 200 training epochs with a batch size of 4. The batch size value, set based on a preliminary analysis, represents a trade-off between the achieved accuracy and the training time.

We create a single spike train for each gray-scale input image pixel. Moreover, since every spike train is made of 36 time steps, it can collect up to 30 spikes. The spike trains per image are not computed offline before training but are generated at run-time. Therefore, they are different for each training epoch to increase the training process robustness. Since this information is provided as input without applying any accumulation mechanism, the *LaneSNNs* analyze each input image for 30 time steps.

6.4.4.3 *LaneSNNs Implemented on Loihi*

For implementing our trained LaneSNNs onto the Intel Loihi Neuromorphic Chip, we have to set its model parameters such as *Compartment Voltage threshold* ($V_{th\ mant}$), *Compartment Current Decay* (δ_i), *Compartment Voltage Decay* (δ_v), *Compartment Bias* (*bias*), *Synaptic Weights* (*weight*) and *Weight Exponent* (*wgtExp*).

We multiply weights and V_{th} by a factor (k) calculated from the weight magnitudes of all the SNN synapses as in Equation (6.26):

$$k = \frac{2^4 - 1}{\max_{all\ synapses}(|weight_i|)} \qquad (6.26)$$

TABLE 6.26: Translation of parameters to the Loihi Chip for the *LaneSNNs* (For the Loihi the *weight* bits also include the *wgtExp* bits).

Offline implementation			Loihi implementation		
Parameter	Value	Precision	Parameter	Value	Precision
V_{th}	$\times 1$	Float 64 bits	$V_{th\ mant}$	$\times k$	Fixed 12 bits
weight	$\times 1$	Float 64 bits	*weight*	$\times k$	Fixed 8 bits
τ	0.2	Float 64 bits	δ_v	3276	Fixed 12 bits
b	0	Float 64 bits	*bias*	0	Fixed 8 bits
–	–	Float 64 bits	δ_i	0	Fixed 12 bits

In the multiplication of the weights by k, we use the whole dynamic range for the maximum value, thus minimizing *wgtExp*. All the setup parameters are summarized in Table 6.26.

We implement all the trained LaneSNNs onto the Loihi Neuromorphic Chip, considering all the possible values of V_{th}, λ and lr, characterized by the best parameter p. This implementation is conducted using the Intel Nx SDK API version 1.0.0 running onto the Nahuku32 partition. This code is developed using the *NxTF* Layers and in particular *NxConv2D* and *NxDense* utilities [233]. The *LaneSNNs* are tested on the testing set of the DET dataset [33]. We use the same method for feeding the input images for the offline training. Hence, we create a spike train for every pixel of each input image on-the-fly. Every spike train lasts for 30 time steps. We insert a blank time equal to 10 time steps between two consecutive samples.

To compute of the *IoU* measure, we find the best threshold directly from the reconstructed images at the output of the Loihi chip.

6.4.4.4 *Pareto Optimal Solutions*

We can analyze multiple Pareto-optimal models to efficiently evaluate the *LaneSNNs* implemented onto the Intel Loihi. Therefore, we use the **Pareto Optimal frontier curve** to find the best trade-off solutions between the achieved **IoU** and:

1. **latency**, i.e., the mean time duration required for the classification of all the pixels of a single image (Figure 6.13a);

2. **power consumption** of the entire Intel Loihi chip (Figure 6.13b);

3. **network complexity**, number of neurocores occupied (Figure 6.13c).

From the first graph (Figure 6.13a), we can see that within the Pareto-optimal front, the maximum time to detect the lanes on a stream of 30 time steps is limited to **7.27 ms** and it is achieved by the *Fully-C800* network. It can be decreased to 6.02 *ms* with a reduction on *IoU* of about 6%. In the second graph (Figure 6.13b), we can observe that the lowest Pareto-optimal power consumption is measured by the simplest *Fully-C600* network, but the highest *IoU* is reached by the *Fully-C800* network. Overall, the power consumption of the Loihi chip does not vary much around $1W$.

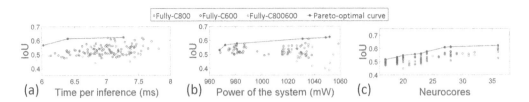

Figure 6.13: *The legend is common for all figures.* Pareto-optimal solutions for Fully-C800, Fully-C600, and Fully-C800600 *LaneSNNs.* **(a)** IoU vs. Time per inference. **(b)** IoU vs. Power. **(c)** IoU vs. Neurocores.

Figure 6.13c shows that, among the Pareto-optimal solutions, the *Fully-C600* network is the simplest because of the lower number of occupied neurocores. Moreover, the best *IoU* is measured by the *Fully-C800* network, but its complexity is significantly greater than the minimum value.

6.4.4.5 Best Results for Each LaneSNN

The best results obtained in terms of *IoU* for each type of *LaneSNN* for both offline and online implementations are summarized in Table 6.27.

The *CNN LaneSNN* has the lowest *IoU* results for both online and offline implementations. Its GPU implementation achieves an acceptable level of *IoU*, but this value decreases for the online implementation due to the weight approximation errors propagating layer by layer during the offline-to-online translation.

The highest offline result is measured by the *Fully-C800600* network that has two FC hidden layers. However, it has a lower *IoU* for the online implementation than the value achieved by the simpler FC networks *Fully-C600* and *Fully-C800*. The best online *IoU* result is achieved by the *Fully-C600* network, which is the simplest SNN. Moreover, despite being slightly greater, its online and offline *IoU* measures are comparable to the results obtained with the *Fully-C800* network.

6.4.4.6 Comparison with the State-of-the-Art

For this application, less complex SNNs can be effectively implemented into the Loihi Neuromorphic Chip and achieve competitive performances for real-time embedded systems with low power consumption and low latency. This is also favored by using event-based cameras as vision sensors of the AD system. On the other hand, in

TABLE 6.27: Best *IoU* measures achieved by the different *LaneSNNs* for offline (*GPU*) and online (*Loihi*) implementations.

IoU CNN		IoU Fully-C600		IoU Fully-C800		IoU Fully-C800600	
GPU	*Loihi*	*GPU*	*Loihi*	*GPU*	*Loihi*	*GPU*	*Loihi*
0.598	0.208	0.637	0.527	0.633	0.542	**0.652**	0.416
0.551	0.349	0.632	**0.623**	0.629	0.613	0.590	0.550

TABLE 6.28: Comparison of IoU achieved by different algorithms for lane detection problem faced by the semantic segmentation approach.

Classifier	$IoU_{offline}$	IoU_{online}	Number of parameters
FCN	0.585	–	132.27 M
DeepLabv3	0.585	–	39.05 M
RefineNet	0.614	–	99.02 M
LaneNet	0.647	–	0.53 M
SCNN	0.673	–	25.16 M
LDNet	0.767	–	5.71 M
CNN LaneSNN (**ours**)	0.598	0.349	1.39 M
Fully-C600 LaneSNN (**ours**)	0.637	0.623	1.20 M
Fully-C800 LaneSNN (**ours**)	0.633	0.613	1.60 M
Fully-C800600 LaneSNN (**ours**)	0.652	0.550	2.00 M

literature, many algorithms involve non-spiking NNs to tackle the lane detection problem.

For a fair comparison, we evaluate the results of state-of-the-art networks on the same dataset (DET dataset [33]). Therefore, all these NNs also use a DVS camera as the vision sensor for the system.

The results of the state-of-the-art techniques, which are FCN [140], DeepLabv3 [27], RefineNet [131], LaneNet [187], SCNN [198] and LDNet [181], are compared to our *LaneSNNs* in Table 6.28.

We can notice that our *CNN LaneSNN* achieves higher performance than the FCN and DeepLabv3 algorithms despite their use of more complex networks to make their predictions. The FCN uses AlexNet [113] made of five Conv layers, three pooling layers, and three FC layers. DeepLabv3 [27] is composed of Atrous Spatial Pyramid Pooling (ASPP) layers. It probes an incoming Conv layer with filters at multiple sampling rates. This method is not developed on the Loihi yet since NxTF facilities [233] do not implement the ASPP layers. Moreover, it achieves lower performance than RefineNet (based on long residual connections), LaneNet (based on upsampling layers), SCNN (based on slice-by-slice convolutions), and LDNet (based on ASPP, many convolution stacks, and upsampling layers). These structures cannot be implemented onto the Loihi with the NxTF facilities [233] that support pooling, FC, and traditional convolution layers.

All the other FC *LaneSNNs* have IoU comparable with LaneNet and overcome the performance of more complex algorithms. Moreover, the *Fully-C800600 LaneSNN* achieves a similar result as the one obtained by the SCNN algorithm while using less than $10\times$ parameters. On the other hand, the highest IoU result has been achieved by the LDNet, at the price of very high complexity, and it cannot be implemented onto a neuromorphic hardware device.

The above-discussed considerations do not take into account that all *LaneSNNs* are tested on the modified DET dataset and not on the original dataset, as it is for all the other discussed algorithms. However, the pre-processing step for the DET dataset allows all the *LaneSNNs* to be directly implementable on the Loihi Neuromorphic Chip, achieving competitive performance also online.

6.4.5 Summary

The proposed LaneSNN methodology consists of a set of optimizations for conducting event-based lane detection on the Loihi neuromorphic processor. The core of the methodology is based on the semantic segmentation approach. The SNN training is based on a novel loss function that combines the WCE and MSE metrics to take advantage of the supervised STDP rule. The SNNs deployed with the proposed LaneSNN methodology represents the first implementation of the event-based lane detectors on the Loihi chip and show high performance and power efficiency gains compared to the related works implemented on conventional computation platforms.

6.5 SUMMARY OF EFFICIENT OPTIMIZATIONS FOR SPIKING NEURAL NETWORKS ON NEUROMORPHIC HARDWARE

This chapter has discussed a set of optimizations and implementations of SNNs on the Loihi neuromorphic hardware chip. By knowing the specifications and resource constraints of the target hardware platform, several optimization techniques are applied to implement energy-efficient SNNs. The DNN-to-SNN conversion process requires a comprehensive analysis specifically designed to implement the converted SNN into the Intel Loihi. Even if conducted offline, the architectural models and training rules for the SNNs need to be tailored for the Loihi implementation to allow their feasibility and enhance their performance and energy efficiency. Compared to the non-spiking DNNs implemented on conventional architectures, the SNNs implemented on neuromorphic processors exhibit high-efficiency gains. However, their robustness against vulnerability threats remains an ongoing research challenge. Toward this, the following Chapter 7 will discuss the security threats for SNNs. The event-based nature of SNNs and their different computational principles compared to traditional DNNs require dedicated security analyses and offer unique possibilities to enhance their robustness.

Security Threats for SNNs on Discrete and Event-Based Data

This chapter investigates the vulnerabilities of SNNs against security threats. Novel attack methodologies and defensive countermeasures are proposed. The analyses are conducted both on discrete data, as well as on event-based data. The flow followed in this chapter is shown in Figure 7.1. Section 7.1 provides a comparative analysis of the security vulnerabilities of SNNs and DNNs with respect to the adversarial noise. Section 7.2 presents a cross-layer attack that threatens the SNNs' robustness. A carefully crafted adversarial input noise triggers a hardware Trojan that injects bit-flips in the most vulnerable weight locations. Section 7.3 studies the inherent robustness of SNNs and explores different values of the SNNs' structural parameters, which are the neuron's firing voltage threshold and time window boundary. Toward the SNNs' security for event-based data, Section 7.4 presents a methodology for improving the robustness against adversarial attacks by employing noise filters for DVS sensors. Moreover, Section 7.5 presents a set of stealthy yet efficient adversarial attack methodologies targeted to perturb the event sequences and test them in the presence of noise filters for DVS cameras.

Major Contributions of the Chapter:

- **Robustness analysis of SNNs:** An in-depth methodology is designed to evaluate the robustness of SNNs and compare it to non-spiking DNNs. It investigates their robustness against random noises added to the inputs and against crafted adversarial examples.

- **NeuroAttack methodology design:** It injects bit-flips in specific weight memory locations to fool SNNs and DNNs. The attack is triggered when a crafted adversarial pattern is provided in the input image.

- **Robust SNN designs by tuning their structural parameters:** A systematic methodology is designed for investigating the SNN robustness. It explores the impact of SNNs' structural parameters for designing robust SNNs.

DOI: 10.1201/9781003530459-7

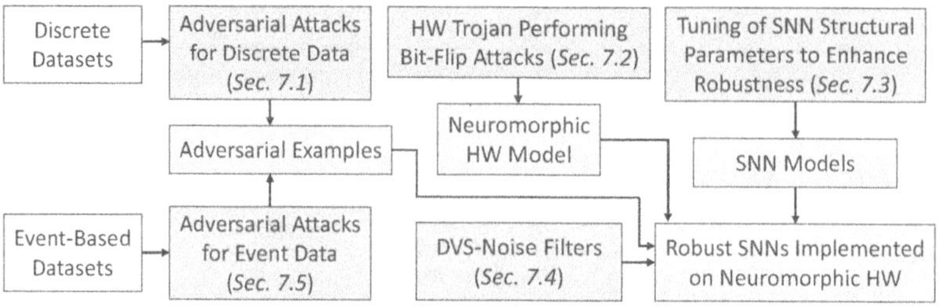

Figure 7.1: Overview of the flow for generating attacks and designing defensive countermeasures discussed in this chapter.

- **R-SNN methodology design:** It is an adversarial defense technique that employs noise filters for DVS to increase the SNNs' robustness.

- **DVS-Attacks design:** It is a set of adversarial attack methodologies that perturb DVS signals. It also contains specifically crafted attacks that fool SNNs in the presence of DVS noise filters.

7.1 SECURITY EVALUATION OF SNNS VS. DNNS

SNNs present many advantages in terms of energy efficiency and biological plausibility compared to standard non-spiking DNNs. Prior works have demonstrated that DNNs are susceptible to adversarial attacks, i.e., minimal perturbations added to the input can lead to targeted or random misclassifications. In this section, we aim to investigate the security of SNNs. Toward this, we comparatively study the security vulnerabilities in DNNs and SNNs with respect to the adversarial noise. Afterward, we propose a novel black-box attack methodology. Without knowing the internal structure of the SNN, it employs a greedy heuristic to generate imperceptible and robust adversarial examples for the given SNN. To obtain a fair comparison, we conduct an in-depth evaluation of our methodology for a Spiking Deep Belief Network (SDBN) and a DNN with the same number of layers and neurons, for understanding the differences between SNNs and DNNs when subjected to adversarial examples. Our work opens new avenues of research toward the SNNs' robustness, considering their similarities to the human brain's functionality.

7.1.1 System Overview

In this section, we aim to generate imperceptible and robust adversarial examples for SNNs under black-box settings. Prior works [10] studied the vulnerabilities of SNNs under white-box settings, while we consider a black-box assumption, which makes the attacker stronger in a wide range of real-world environments. For a fair comparison during the evaluation, we apply these attacks to an SDBN and a DNN with the same number of layers and neurons. First, we analyze the vulnerability of SDBNs to random and adversarial noise, for identifying the similarities/differences w.r.t. DNNs. Our experiments demonstrate that when a random noise is applied to a given SDBN, its classification accuracy decreases for higher noise magnitude. Moreover, when our attack is applied to SDBNs, we notice that the output probabilities exhibit a different behavior than for the case of DNNs. While the adversarial example remains imperceptible, misclassification is not always achieved in the SDBNs.

In short, we make the following *novel contributions*:

- We analyze the variation in the accuracy of an SDBN when random noise is added to the inputs.

- We evaluate the improved generalization capability of the SDBN when adding random noise to the training images.

- We develop an automated methodology to create imperceptible adversarial examples for DNNs and SNNs.

- We apply our methodology for generating adversarial examples to an SDBN *(the first attack of this kind applied to SDBNs)* and a DNN and evaluate their imperceptibility and robustness.

7.1.2 Analysis: Applying Random Noise to SDBNs

7.1.2.1 *Spiking Deep Belief Networks*

Deep Belief Networks (DBNs) [15] are widely used multi-layer networks for classification tasks and have been implemented in many domains such as audio processing, visual processing, images and text recognition [15]. DBNs are constructed by stacking pre-trained Restricted Boltzmann Machines (RBMs), which are energy-based models consisting of two layers of FC neurons. RBMs are typically trained with unsupervised learning algorithms to extract the information stored in the hidden neurons, and then a supervised approach is conducted to train an ML classifier based on these features [85].

Spiking DBNs (SDBNs) improve the energy efficiency and computation speed compared to DBNs. Such behavior has already been observed in the work of [192], which proposed a DBN model composed of 4 RBMs of $784 - 500 - 500 - 10$ neurons, respectively. After its offline training, it is transformed into the event-based domain to increase the processing efficiency and computational power. The RBMs are trained with Persistent Contrastive Divergence (CD), an unsupervised learning rule that employs Gibbs sampling, a Markov-Chain Monte-Carlo algorithm that optimizes for fast parameter convergence, selectivity, and sparsity [229]. Once every RBM is trained, their feature information is saved in the hidden neurons to use as input for the following layer. Afterward, a supervised learning algorithm [87], based on the features coming from the unsupervised training, is implemented. The RBMs of this model use the *Siegert* function [250] in their neurons. It allows having a good approximation of the firing rate of LIF neurons used for CD training. Hence, the neurons of an SDBN generate Poisson spike trains, according to the *Siegert* formula.

This represents a significant advantage in terms of speed and power consumption compared to the classical DBNs based on a discrete-time model [192]. *Since there has been no prior work on studying the security vulnerabilities of such SDBNs, we aim at investigating these aspects in a black-box setting, which is important for their real-world applications in safety-critical systems.*

7.1.2.2 Experimental Setup

As a case study, we consider an SDBN [192] composed of 4 FC layers of $784 - 500 - 500 - 10$ neurons, respectively. We implement this SDBN in Matlab for analyzing the MNIST database. Each pixel intensity is encoded as a value in the range between 0 and 255. The input data are scaled to the range $[0, 0.2]$ to directly convert intensities into spikes. In our experiments, the pixel intensities are represented as the probability that a spike occurs.

7.1.2.3 Understanding the Impact of Input Random Noise on the Accuracy of an SDBN

We evaluate the accuracy of the SDBN for different noise magnitudes applied to three different sets of images:

- to all the training images.

- to all the test images.

- to both the training and test images.

To test the SDBN's vulnerability, we apply two different types of noises: *normally distributed* and *uniformly-distributed* random noise.

Table 7.1 and Figure 7.2 report the results of our experiments. The initial accuracy obtained for the clean image without applying noise is 96.2%. When applying the noise to the test images, the SDBN accuracy decreases accordingly with a noise magnitude increase, more evidently in the case of the normally distributed random noise. The reason for this behavior is that the standard normal distribution contains a broader range of values than the uniform distribution. For both noise distributions, the accuracy significantly decreases when the noise magnitude is around 0.15 (see the values highlighted in red in Table 7.1).

When the noise is applied only to the training images, the SDBN accuracy does not decrease much like in the previous case, for the noise magnitude (δ) lower than

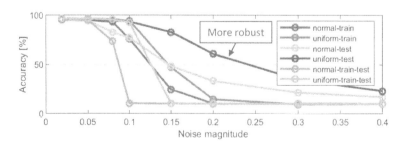

Figure 7.2: Normal and uniform random noise added to all the pixels of the MNIST dataset.

TABLE 7.1: Evaluation of the SDBN accuracy for two different types of random noise with different noise magnitude values. The red and blue values help the reader identify the accuracy results discussed in the text. (ACC stands for Accuracy, and TR&TST indicates noise applied to both Training and Test Datasets)

ACC	TRAIN	TEST	TR&TST	TRAIN	TEST	TR&TST
δ	NORMALLY			UNIFORMLY		
0.02	96.65	94.73	96.54	96.8	96.02	96.81
0.05	95.19	94.42	94.99	96.7	95.64	96.72
0.08	92.99	82.73	73.64	95.89	94.64	95.56
0.1	76.01	77.07	10.39	94.34	93.36	92.8
0.15	24.61	48.23	10.32	47.03	82.76	10.51
0.2	10.26	33.34	10.05	14.64	60.79	10.16
0.3	10.31	21.52	9.88	9.59	34.9	10.16
0.4	10.27	17.05	10.34	9.98	23.16	10.03

0.1. On the contrary, for $\delta = 0.02$, the accuracy increases (see the blue-colored values in Table 7.1) w.r.t. the baseline (i.e., without noise). Indeed, adding noise to training samples improves the generalization capability of the network. Therefore, its capability to correctly classify new unseen samples also increases. This observation, as was analyzed in other scenarios for DNNs with back-propagation training [91], is also valid for our SDBN model. However, the accuracy drops significantly if the noise is equal to or greater than 0.1. This behavior indicates that the SDBN cannot learn input features due to the inserted noise. Thus it is unable to classify the inputs correctly.

When the noise is added to both the training and test samples, we observe that the behavior noticed for the noise added to only the training images is accentuated. The accuracy is similar to or higher than the baseline for low noise magnitudes (mainly in the uniform noise case). For noise magnitudes larger than 0.1 (more precisely, 0.08 for normal noise), the accuracy decreases more sharply than for the case of noise added only to the training images. This value of noise magnitude represents a threshold of tolerable noise for the SDBN. Hence, the network cannot classify well when the noise is too high.

7.1.2.4 *Applying Noise to a Restricted Window of Pixels*

In this study, we add a random noise with normal distribution to a restricted area of pixels of the test images. Considering a rectangle of 4×5 pixels, we analyze two scenarios:

- The noise is applied to 20 pixels on the top-left corner of the image. The accuracy variation is represented by the blue-colored line in Figure 7.3. As expected, the accuracy remains almost constant since the noise affects irrelevant pixels. The resulting image for a noise of 0.3 is shown in Figure 7.4b.

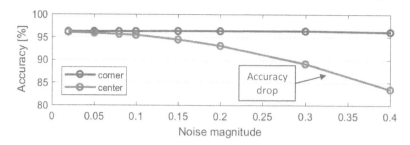

Figure 7.3: Normal random noise applied to some pixels of the MNIST test images.

- The noise is applied to 20 pixels in the middle region of the image, with coordinates $(x, y) = ([14\ 17], [10\ 14])$. Compared to the previous case, the accuracy decreases more significantly (orange-colored line of Figure 7.3) since some white pixels that represent the handwritten digits (and therefore the important ones for the classification) are modified by the noise. The resulting image for a noise of 0.3 is shown in Figure 7.4c. This analysis shows that the location of noise insertion impacts the accuracy, thereby unleashing a potential vulnerability of SNNs that adversarial attacks can exploit.

7.1.2.5 Key Observations from our Analyses

From the above analyses, we derive the following key observations that an adversarial example generation methodology can exploit.

- The normally-distributed noise has a higher impact than the uniform counterpart because the accuracy decreases more sharply.

- For a low noise magnitude added to the training images, we observe a small accuracy improvement due to the improved generalization capabilities of SDBNs.

- When the noise is applied to a restricted window of pixels, the effect of the perturbation is more evident if the window is located in the center of the image

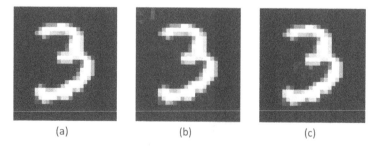

Figure 7.4: Comparison between images with normally distributed random noise with a magnitude of 0.3 applied to the corner and the center of the image. (**a**) Without noise. (**b**) Noise applied to the top-left corner. (**c**) Noise applied to the center.

(or generally speaking, in the input regions belonging to the features that are key for the correct classification), as compared to the corner. This behavior is due to the noise applied to the pixels, which play an important role in accurate feature learning and, consequently, in the correct classification.

7.1.3 Our Novel Methodology to Generate Imperceptible and Robust Adversarial Examples

Similar to the case of DNNs, the objective of a good attack on SNNs is also to generate adversarial images that are difficult to be detected by a human eye (i.e., imperceptible) and resistant to physical transformations (i.e., robust). Therefore, for better understanding, we first discuss these two aspects.

7.1.3.1 *Imperceptibility of Adversarial Examples*

Creating an imperceptible example means adding perturbations to the pixels while ensuring that humans do not notice them. We consider an area $A = N \cdot N$ of pixels x, and we calculate the standard deviation of a pixel ($SD(x_{i,j})$ as in Equation (7.1).

$$SD(x_{i,j}) = \sqrt{\frac{\sum\limits_{k=1}^{N}\sum\limits_{l=1}^{N}(x_{k,l} - \mu)^2 - (x_{i,j} - \mu)^2}{N \cdot N}} \tag{7.1}$$

Here, μ is the average value of the pixels belonging to the $N \cdot N$ area. If a pixel has a large standard deviation, a perturbation added to it is more hardly recognized by the human eye than a pixel with a low standard deviation. The sum of all perturbations δ added to the pixels of the area A allows us to compute the distance ($D(X^*, X)$) between the adversarial sample X^* and the original one X. Its formula is shown in Equation (7.2).

$$D(X^*, X) = \sum_{i=1}^{N}\sum_{j=1}^{N}\frac{\delta_{i,j}}{SD(x_{i,j})} \tag{7.2}$$

Such a value can be used to monitor imperceptibility. In fact, the distance $D(X^*, X)$ indicates how much perturbation is added to the pixels of the area A. Therefore, the maximum perturbation tolerated by the human eye can be associated with a specific value of the distance, D_{MAX}. The value of D_{MAX} can vary among different images or datasets since it depends on the resolution and the contrast between neighboring pixels.

7.1.3.2 *Robustness of adversarial examples*

Many adversarial attack methods are used to maximize the probability of the target class to ease the classifier misclassification of the image [67][148]. The main problem of these methods is that they do not account for the relative difference between the class probabilities, i.e., the gap, defined in Equation (7.3).

$$Gap(X^*) = P(target\ class) - max\{P(other\ classes)\} \tag{7.3}$$

Therefore, a minimal modification of the probabilities can make the attack ineffective after an image transformation. To improve the robustness, it is desirable to increase the difference between the target class probability and the highest probability among the other classes, i.e., to maximize the gap function.

7.1.3.3 How to Automatically Generate Attacks for SNNs?

Obtaining both imperceptibility and robustness at the same time is complicated. Typically, a robust attack would require perceptible changes in the input, while an imperceptible attack does not change the classification much. We designed a heuristic algorithm to generate imperceptible yet robust adversarial examples for SNNs automatically. Note that our technique also applies to DNNs. Leveraging the same methodology for generating adversarial examples for both SNNs and DNNs enables a fair comparison. Our algorithm is based on the black-box model assumption, i.e., the attacks are performed on some pixels of the image without knowing the network architecture. Given the maximum allowed distance D_{MAX} such that human eyes cannot detect perturbations, the problem can be expressed as in Equation (7.4).

$$\arg\max_{X^*} Gap(X^*) \ s.t. \ D(X^*, X) \leq D_{MAX} \tag{7.4}$$

In summary, *the purpose of our iterative algorithm is to perturb a set of pixels for maximizing the gap function, thus making the attack robust while keeping the distance between the samples below the desired threshold for the perturbation to remain imperceptible.*

Based on the key observations of our previous analyses, our iterative methodology (see Algorithm 23) perturbs only a window of pixels of the image. We choose a certain value N that defines an area of $N \cdot N$ pixels and perform the attack on a subset of M pixels within the $N \cdot N$ region.

After computing the standard deviation for the selected $N \cdot N$ pixels, we calculate the gap function, i.e., the difference between the probability of the target class and the highest probability between the other classes. Then, the algorithm decides whether to add a positive or a negative noise to the pixels. Therefore, we compute two parameters for each pixel, $Gap^+(X^*)$ and $Gap^-(X^*)$. $Gap^+(X^*)$ is the value of the gap function computed by adding a perturbation unit to a single pixel, while $Gap^-(X^*)$ is its counterpart, computed by subtracting a perturbation unit. According to the difference between these values and the gap function and considering the standard deviation, we compute the variation priority, a function that indicates the effectiveness of the pixel perturbation. For example, if $Gap^-(X^*)$ is greater than $Gap^+(X^*)$, subtracting the noise will be more effective than adding it to the pixel because the difference between $P(target\ class)$ and $max[P(other\ classes)]$ will increase more. Once the *VariationPriority* vector is computed, its values are sorted, and the highest M values of the $N \cdot N$ window are perturbed. The noise is added to or subtracted from the selected M pixels depending upon the highest value between $Gap^+(X^*)$ and $Gap^-(X^*)$. Then, the algorithm starts the next iteration by replacing the original input image with the created adversarial one. The iterations terminate

---

Algorithm 23: Methodology for Generating Adversarial Examples for SNNs and DNNs

---

1 **Given:** network (SNN or DNN), original sample X, maximum human perceptual distance D_{max}, noise magnitude δ, area A of $N \cdot N$ pixels, number of pixels to perturb M

2 **while** $D(X^*, X) < D_{MAX}$ **do**

3   Compute *Standard Deviation SD* for every pixel of A;

4   Compute $Gap(X^*)$, $Gap^-(X^*)$, $Gap^+(X^*)$;

5   **if** $Gap(X^*)^- > Gap(X^*)^+$ **then**

6         $VariationPriority(x_{i,j}) =$

7         $[Gap^-(X^*) - Gap(X^*)] \cdot SD(x_{i,j})$;

8   **else**

9         $VariationPriority(x_{i,j}) =$

10         $[Gap^+(X^*) - Gap(X^*)] \cdot SD(x_{i,j})$;

11   Sort $VariationPriority$ in descending order;

12   Select M pixels with highest $VariationPriority$;

13   **if** $Gap(X^*)^- > Gap(X^*)^+$ **then**

14   Subtract noise with magnitude δ from the pixel;

15   **else**

16   Add noise with magnitude δ to the pixel;

17   Compute $D(X^*, X)$;

18   Update the original example with the adversarial one;

---

when the distance between original and adversarial examples overcomes the maximum perceptual distance.

7.1.4 Evaluation of our Attack Methodology

7.1.4.1 *Experimental Setup*

Using the methodology of Algorithm 23, we attack the same SDBN as the one analyzed in Section 7.1.2 and a DNN. To achieve a fair comparison, we design the DNN for our experiments having the same set of parameters as the SDBN, i.e., composed of four FC layers of $784 - 500 - 500 - 10$ neurons, respectively. The DNN is trained with the scaled conjugate gradient backpropagation algorithm [174], and after training, its achieved classification accuracy on the MNIST dataset is 97.13%.

For discussion, we start with a test image labeled as "five" (see Figure 7.5). It is classified correctly by both networks but with different output probabilities. We use a value of δ equal to 10% of the pixel intensity scale range and a D_{MAX} of 22 to compare the attacks. We distinguish two cases having different search window sizes:

(I) Figure 7.5a: $N = 5$ and $M = 10$. Based on the analysis in Section 7.1.2, we define the search window in a central area of the image that is affected by high variation, as shown by the red square.

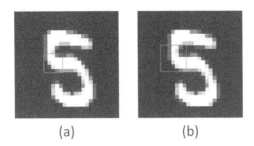

(a)   (b)

Figure 7.5: Selected area of pixels to attack. (a) 5×5 area. (b) 7×7 area.

(II) Figure 7.5b: $N = 7$ and $M = 10$. It can be interesting to observe the difference w.r.t. in case I: in this situation, we perturb the same amount M of pixels, chosen from a search window containing 24 more pixels.

7.1.4.2 DNN Under Attack

The baseline DNN classifies our test sample as a "five" with its associated probability equal to 98.79%, as shown in the blue-colored bars of Figure 7.6. The target class is "three" for both cases. The classification results of their respective adversarial images are shown in Figure 7.6 for both cases. From the results in Table 7.2, we observe that having a small search window leads to a more robust attack than having larger search windows. The generated adversarial examples are shown in Figure 7.7.

7.1.4.3 SDBN Under Attack

Our baseline SDBN, without attack, classifies our test sample as a "five" with a probability equal to 82.69%. The complete set of initial "clean-case" output probabilities is shown in Figure 7.8. We select "three" as the target class.

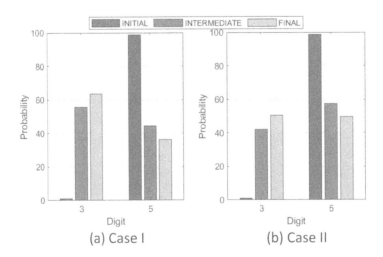

Figure 7.6: Output probabilities of the DNN. (a) Attack using the search window of case I. (b) Attack using the search window of case II.

TABLE 7.2: Results of our simulations for the DNN.

(**Case I**) After 14 iterations, the target class probability has exceeded the correct class. Figure 7.7a shows the sample at this stage (denoted as an *intermediate* in Figure 7.6a). In the following iteration (see Figure 7.7b), the gap between the two classes increases, thus increasing the robustness but also the distance. The sample at this point (denoted as *final* in Figure 7.6b) corresponds to the attack output since at iteration 15, the distance falls above the threshold.

(**Case II**) After 11 iterations (denoted as *final* in Figure 7.6b), the sample (in Figure 7.7d) is classified as a "three". Since at iteration 12 the distance is already higher than D_{MAX}, Figure 7.7c shows the sample at the 10th iteration, whose output probabilities are denoted as an*intermediate* in Figure 7.6b.

CASE	ITER	P MAX CLASS	P TARGET CLASS	DISTANCE
I	0	**98.79**	**0.89**	0
I	14	**44.16**	**55.74**	20.18
I	15	**36.25**	**63.67**	21.77
II	0	**98.79**	**0.89**	0
II	10	**57.53**	**42.01**	16.29
II	11	**49.45**	**50.32**	21.19

The results in Table 7.3 show that, in contrast to the attack applied to the DNN, for case I:

- The SDBN output probabilities do not change monotonically when increasing the iterations of our algorithm.

- At the 20th iteration, the SDBN classifies the target class with a probability of 31.08%, while $D(X^*, X) = 7.79$.

- At the other iterations, before and after iteration 20, the output probability of correctly classifying the image as the original class still dominates.

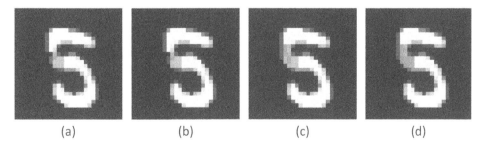

(a) (b) (c) (d)

Figure 7.7: Adversarial samples were applied to the DNN. (**a**) 14th iteration of case I. (**b**) 15th iteration of case I. (**c**) 10th iteration of case II. (**d**) 11th iteration of case II.

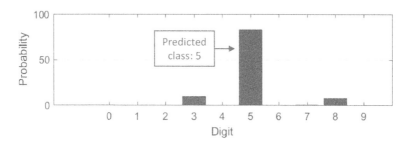

Figure 7.8: Output probabilities of the SDBN for the original sample.

Meanwhile, for case II, we observe that:

- At the 9th iteration, the SDBN misclassifies the image. The probability of classifying it as a "three" is 50.60%, with a distance $D(X^*, X) = 10.91$. As a side note, the probability of classifying it as an "eight" is 49.40%.

- At the other iterations, before and after the 9th, the output probability of classifying the image as a "five" is higher than 50%.

7.1.4.4 Comparative Discussion between the SDBN and the DNN

We can notice how the DNN is vulnerable to the attacks generated by our algorithm, while the SDBN exhibits a very different response to the attack. The output probabilities of the SDBN do not follow the expected trend but may sporadically lead to misclassification. Each image pixel is converted to a spike train. Thus, a slight modification of the pixel intensity can have unexpected consequences, like incorrect feature detection. The SNN sensitivity of the targeted attack is clearly different from the DNN sensitivity for a similar case.

7.1.5 Summary

In this section, the security vulnerabilities of SNNs have been studied and compared to DNNs. After analyzing the robustness against random noise, a methodology for generating imperceptible and robust adversarial examples is proposed. The robustness

TABLE 7.3: Results of our simulations for the SDBN.

CASE	ITER	P MAX CLASS	P TARGET CLASS	DISTANCE
I	0	**82.69**	**7.64**	0
I	20	**60.29**	**31.08**	7.79
I	21	**66.21**	**11.80**	8.15
II	0	**82.69**	**7.64**	0
II	9	**0**	**50.60**	10.91
II	10	**64.94**	**12.03**	11.76

of SNNs and DNNs against this attack has been analyzed. This study highlights the different responses against adversarial attacks between SNNs and DNNs. The following sections further investigate the vulnerabilities of SNNs.

7.2 NEUROATTACK: EXTERNALLY TRIGGERED BIT-FLIPS FOR SNNS

Due to their proven efficiency, ML systems are deployed in a wide range of domains. More specifically, SNNs emerged as a promising solution to the energy efficiency, accuracy, and resource-utilization challenges in ML systems. While their deployments are going mainstream, they suffer from inherent security and reliability issues. In this section, we propose NeuroAttack, a cross-layer attack methodology that threatens the SNNs' robustness by exploiting low-level reliability issues through a high-level attack. Notably, we trigger a fault-injection-based sneaky hardware backdoor through a carefully crafted adversarial input noise. Our results on DNNs and SNNs show a critical integrity threat to state-of-the-art ML techniques.

7.2.1 System Overview

The focus of this work is to show a new attack methodology threatening the integrity of both the DNNs and SNNs. We design a cross-layer attack that transforms a circuit-level vulnerability into a system-level security flaw. We exploit memory bit-flips in neural synaptic weights through a hardware Trojan triggered by a surgical adversarial attack.

To the best of our knowledge, this is the first end-to-end attack against SNNs that exploits circuit-level backdoors through a high-level input pattern.

In summary, the contributions in this section are as follows:

- We analyze the resilience of SNNs to errors.

- We propose a methodology to trigger a bit-flip attack remotely using an adversarial input pattern.

- We introduce **NeuroAttack**, a hardware Trojan triggered by an input noise. We design and evaluate different versions of the noise pattern triggering the Trojan.

- We show the practicality of our NeuroAttack methodology on DNNs and SNNs, by converting pre-trained DNNs into the spiking domain.

7.2.2 Bit-Flip Resilience Analysis of SNNs

7.2.2.1 Statistical Analysis of Random Bit-Flips

In this section, we investigate the resilience of SNNs to random bit-flips in their parameters. Two different networks, whose architectures are reported in Table 7.4 and Table 7.5, have been implemented. The first network is the so-called *Multilayer Perceptron* (MLP), while the second newtork is the LeNet-5.

TABLE 7.4: Structure of the Multilayer Perceptron network.

Layer	Output shape
Input	784
Dense	1200
Dense	1200
Dense	10

The two networks have been trained for 30 epochs. They reach a test accuracy on the MNIST dataset of 95.54% for the MLP and 99.05% for the LeNet. Weights and biases are quantized to 8 bits. The first study is a statistical analysis of both networks. The *bit-flip probability*, which represents the probability for which the weights are subjected to bit-flips, is set between 0% and 95% to have 20 distinct points. The results are averaged over 5 independent runs. The results of accuracy against the *bit-flip probability* for the MLP and the LeNet are shown in Figure 7.9a and Figure 7.9b, respectively.

These results show that the accuracy is significantly reduced in the MLP also for a low *bit-flip probability*. However, for networks with many parameters, a high number of parameters undergo bit-flips even for low values of *bit-flip probability*. The situation is clear looking at Figure 7.9a and Figure 7.9b, which depict the average accuracy (right axis, red line) compared to the average number of flipped bits (left axis, blue line), for the MLP and the LeNet, respectively. The number of flipped bits with the same bit-flip probability appears to be more than one order of magnitude lower in the LeNet than in the MLP. This analysis shows the high resiliency of a neural network whose performance is only degraded for large errors in the network parameters. However, as demonstrated in the following section, these networks are only resilient to probabilistic attacks while showing a very different behavior in the case of targeted errors that an adversary can apply.

TABLE 7.5: Structure of the LeNet network [118].

Layer	Output shape	Output maps	Kernel size	Strides
Input	(28, 28, 1)	-	-	-
Conv2D	(28, 28, 32)	32	(5,5)	(1,1)
MaxPool2D	(14, 14, 32)	-	-	(2,2)
Conv2D	(10, 10, 48)	48	(5,5)	(1,1)
MaxPool2D	(5, 5, 48)	-	-	(2,2)
Dense	256	-	-	-
Dense	84	-	-	-
Dense	10	-	-	-

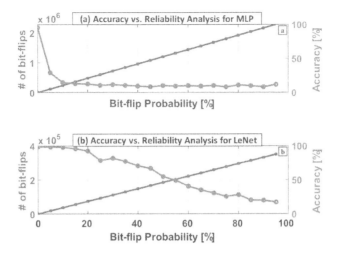

Figure 7.9: Accuracy and number of bit-flips vs bit-flip probability for **(a)** the MLP, and **(b)** the LeNet network.

7.2.2.2 *Bit-Flip with Gradient Search Algorithm*

Analysis for the MNIST Dataset: In this section, we discuss a way to reduce the accuracy of a given network by applying errors to the lowest possible number of bits. The gradients of the loss function with respect to the network's parameters are analyzed similarly to what is done during the learning phase while taking inspiration from the work of [221]. The gradients computation returns a list of n-dimensional arrays with the same shape of the parameters. The highest gradient in absolute value is selected and its corresponding parameter is reconsidered the target parameter. To obtain the maximum reduction of accuracy, one bit of the target parameter is flipped. Then, the target parameter is masked to avoid that it is considered at the next iteration. The results demonstrate that the accuracy is highly reduced for a small number of bit-flips of the MLP (see the blue line in Figure 7.10) and for the LeNet (see the red line in Figure 7.10), considering a global analysis of the parameters. Note that only 30 bit-flips are sufficient to crush the accuracy of the two networks completely.

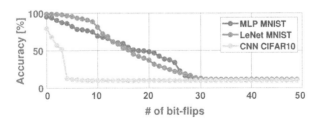

Figure 7.10: Accuracy vs. number of bit-flips for MLP@MNIST, LeNet@MNIST, and CNN@CIFAR10.

TABLE 7.6: CNN structure used in the experiments on CIFAR10.

Layer	Output shape	Output maps	Kernel size	Strides
Input	(32, 32, 3)	-	-	-
Conv2D	(32, 32, 32)	32	(3,3)	(1,1)
Conv2D	(30, 30, 32)	32	(3,3)	(1,1)
MaxPool2D	(15, 15, 32)	-	-	(2,2)
Dropout 0.25	(15, 15, 32)	-	-	-
Conv2D	(15, 15, 64)	64	(3,3)	(1,1)
Conv2D	(13, 13, 64)	64	(3,3)	(1,1)
MaxPool2D	(6, 6, 64)	-	-	(2,2)
Dropout 0.25	(6, 6, 64)	-	-	-
Dense	512	-	-	-
Dropout 0.25	512	-	-	-
Dense	10	-	-	-

Analysis for the CIFAR10 Dataset: Similar experiments have been also performed for the CIFAR10 dataset [112], which is composed of 60 000 training and 10 000 test RGB 32×32 images. The CNN used in our experiments, whose architecture is reported in Table 7.6, reaches an accuracy of 79% after 50 epochs of training.

The *gradient search algorithm* is applied to all the parameters of the network. Similar results compared to the previous cases are achieved. However, the orange line in Figure 7.10 shows that the accuracy drop is more emphatic. The accuracy reaches a plateau at around 10% for only 4 bit-flips, a more critical result than for the LeNet and the MLP on the MNIST dataset.

7.2.3 NeuroAttack Methodology

7.2.3.1 Threat Model

The attack phase is supposed to be applied within the supply chain where a malicious agent can insert hardware Trojans. Indeed, modern integrated circuit design often involves several design houses, fabrication houses, third-party IPs, and electronic design automation tools that are supplied by different vendors. Such a horizontal production model makes security extremely difficult to preserve during the supply chain [3]. Moreover, the attack is in a *grey-box* setting, i.e., the attacker has complete knowledge of the systems' architecture and internal parameters but is unaware of the training dataset and training hyperparameters.

7.2.3.2 Hardware Trojan Design

The hardware Trojan is designed to perform fault injection (i.e., bit-flips) in the network parameters to degrade its accuracy and undermine its integrity. The malicious behavior is triggered through a specifically crafted input noise. The idea is to trigger fewer hidden hardware Trojans built into the circuit during the supply

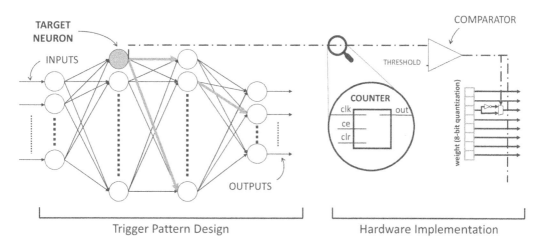

Figure 7.11: Scheme of the Trojan attack for the MLP with the counter added present only in SNN implementation.

chain. Taking advantage of the previous analyses, hardware stealthy Trojans are inserted at appropriate locations. Each Trojan consists of a 2-way multiplexer where one input is the original bit, and the other input is the complemented bit derived through an inverter. The multiplexer's selection signal is at the logic value high only if a trigger is added to the input image. Therefore, the network will behave correctly when a new input is supplied, providing high accuracy for the clean dataset. However, if a trigger is inserted in the input image in the form of hidden noise, the fault injections will be activated, and the accuracy will be degraded significantly. The setting is explained in Figure 7.11, in which the grey neuron is the target neuron and the orange arrows represent the synapses with bit-flip applied. To generate the selection signal of the multiplexers, the output of the target neuron is compared against a threshold chosen according to the results of our experiments. Note that the goal of the trigger is that neuron's output exceeds the threshold when the perturbation is added to the image, and not when the clean input is given. The first step of the methodology is to select a particular neuron that satisfies the desired behavior. To transfer the approach from the DNN to the SNN domain, a counter accumulates the number of spikes at the input of the comparator. Moreover, the threshold must be converted from its analog value to the corresponding spike rate. The counter is reset at the end of the processing of every input.

7.2.3.3 *Trigger Pattern Design*

Since there is a direct relationship between the analog output value of a neuron and its corresponding spike rate, the knowledge learned through the DNN analysis can be transferred to the SNN implementation. Moreover, a good correlation between analog values and spike rates is necessary when using the SNN toolbox for the DNN-to-SNN conversion. We aim to embed the trigger into one neuron of the network, called the *target neuron.* In other words, the objective of our proposed technique is that such a target neuron fires in the presence of a carefully designed mask in the input image. The design is composed of several steps:

- **Selecting the target layer**: the choice of the target neuron strongly depends on the target layer selection. In the case of a CNN, the layer choice is directly related to the choice of the size of the trigger mask. The reason is that neurons belonging to deeper Conv layers are connected to a larger input image area. The higher the order of the layer, the larger the image area that will account for the trigger. In the first Conv layer, the position, shape, and value of the gradients are quite clear and correspond to the *feature map* of the neurons. The gradients cover the entire image for neural networks with only dense layers (e.g., MLPs). In this case, if a smaller trigger pattern is desired, a mask that does not comprehend the entire area covered by the gradients can be crafted.

- **Choosing the target neuron**: The target neuron is selected as the one with the highest value among the sum of absolute values of weights connected to the neurons of the previous layer. This is modeled by Equation (7.5).

$$argmax_t(\sum_{i=1}^{N} ABS(W_{layer_{i,t}})) \qquad (7.5)$$

- **Choosing the triggering mask**: A *random initial image* is generated, and the network is inferred with that image, leading to a value $initial_{OUTPUT_k}$ at the output of the target neuron. The parameter $target_{OUTPUT_k}$ is chosen to be much higher than $initial_{OUTPUT_k}$. A cost function is then defined in Equation (7.6), where $\delta_i = target_{OUTPUT_i} - initial_{OUTPUT_i}$, i is the index of each neuron in the target layer.

$$cost = \frac{\sum_{i=1}^{N} \delta_i^2}{N} \qquad (7.6)$$

Let k be the index of the target neuron. We redefine the above expression as in Equation (7.7).

$$cost = \frac{\delta_1^2 + \delta_2^2 + ... + \delta_k^2 + ... + \delta_N^2}{N} \qquad (7.7)$$

For each δ_i it is imposed that $target_{OUTPUT_i} = initial_{OUTPUT_i}$ except for δ_k, where $target_{OUTPUT_k} \neq initial_{OUTPUT_k}$. To understand which part of the image influences the target neuron, the derivative of the cost function is computed w.r.t. the pixels of the random input image. Based on this, a mask M is created, and a *random initial trigger* is generated through the dot product between the mask and the *random initial image*. The mask may also be chosen differently, but it must overlap with the gradient matrix.

- **Generating the trigger**: The trigger generation algorithm (see Algorithm 24) is inspired by the work of Liu et al. [139]. In the first line, the initialization parameters are set. val_{min} and val_{max} help manage the trigger imperceptibility but should always lie in the range $(0, 1)$. The loop iterates until the cost reaches a specific threshold or until a maximum number of iterations. The gradients Δ are first computed and then limited by a mask suited for the gradients. Compared to the algorithm in [139], line 6 is added to limit the minimum and maximum values for the pixels in the trigger.

Algorithm 24: Trigger generation loop.

---

1 **Initialize:** val_{min}, val_{max}, lr, epc, $epochs$, th, $cost$;
2 **while** $cost < th$ and $epc < epochs$ **do**
3 $\quad \Delta = \dfrac{\partial cost}{\partial x}$;
4 $\quad \Delta = \Delta \cdot M$;
5 $\quad x = x - lr \cdot \Delta$;
6 $\quad x = clip(x, val_{min}, val_{max})$;
7 $\quad epc = epc + 1$;
8 **return** x;

At the end of the loop, the trigger is generated with pixels' values optimized to induce the saturation of the target neuron. If the parameter $target_{OUTPUT_k}$ is too high, the target neuron will reach a lower value, which we call $final_{value_k}$. A *threshold* is chosen such that, if the neuron's output value exceeds the threshold, the output of the comparator is set to logic high, and the multiplexers are switched. Consequently, for each targeted weight, the selected bit is complemented. The *threshold* is calculated through Equation (7.8), where ξ is a parameter that depends on the network architecture and the attack method.

$$threshold = final_{value_k} - \xi, \qquad (7.8)$$

- **Trigger application**: The trigger can be applied to the image in two ways: (1) as a stamp applied to the image or (2) as a noise added to the image. In the first case, the pixel values in the trigger region are exactly the optimal ones generated by the loop described in lines 2-7 of Algorithm 24. However, this solution could be less imperceptible. In that case, a careful selection of the layer and trigger mask parameters (position, dimension, max_{val}) should be made. The second case could be of more general interest since it produced good imperceptibility results, as shown in the following Section 7.2.4. Moreover, knowing the pixel intensity distribution helps to choose the trigger parameters.

TABLE 7.7: Structure of the networks, parameters, and results for our experiments.

Net	Layer	val_{max}	ξ	$target_{OUTPUT_k}$	$initial_{\nabla AL_k}$	$final_{\nabla AL_k}$	$exceed_{ORIGINAL}$	$exceed_{MODIFIED}$
MNIST LeNet	1st Conv2D	0.3	0.1	100	0.04	0.21	0	10000
MNIST LeNet	2nd Conv2D	0.3	0.1	100	0.08	1.56	5	7585
MNIST MLP	1st Dense	0.1	0.1	100	0.05	1.21	15	9904
CIFAR10 CNN	1st Conv2D	0.3	0.1	100	0.02	0.23	4	10000

7.2.4 Evaluation of the NeuroAttack Methodology

7.2.4.1 Experimental Setup

Both the original and the modified dataset are used for inference, and the number of times both datasets make the target neuron exceed the threshold is recorded. Possibly, some images from the original dataset saturate the neuron, causing an undesired activation of the Trojans for an $exceed_{ORIGINAL}$ amount of times. However, to obtain a stealthy attack, a carefully crafted trigger should lead to keeping this value to almost zero. Hence, the accuracy is not noticeably reduced if the input trigger is not present. We call $dim_{DATASET}$ the number of images in the dataset, $exceed_{ORIGINAL}$ the number of images from the original dataset in which the threshold is exceeded, and $exceed_{MODIFIED}$ the number of images from the modified dataset in which the threshold is exceeded. Therefore, the attack aims at being both practical and stealthy, and thereby simultaneously satisfy the following conditions:

1. $exceed_{ORIGINAL} << exceed_{MODIFIED}$

2. $exceed_{ORIGINAL} << dim_{DATASET}$

3. $exceed_{MODIFIED} \simeq dim_{DATASET}$

The results obtained using the MNIST and CIFAR10 datasets on the MLP, LeNet and CNN networks are discussed in the following sections.

7.2.4.2 Results on the MNIST Dataset

Targeting the **first Conv layer** of the LeNet-5 with parameters reported in the first row of Table 7.7, the trigger shown in Figure 7.12d is produced.

Figures 7.12a, b, and c show the *random initial image*, the initial gradient values, and the mask M, respectively. The mask is crafted to reflect the shape of the gradients.

(a) (b) (c) (d) (e) (f)

Figure 7.12: Process of trigger generation in the first Conv layer of the LeNet. (a) Initial input trigger. (b) Gradients of the selected neuron. (c) Mask created through gradients. (d) Final trigger after loop. (e) and (f) are two images with the applied trigger.

(a) (b) (c) (d) (e) (f)

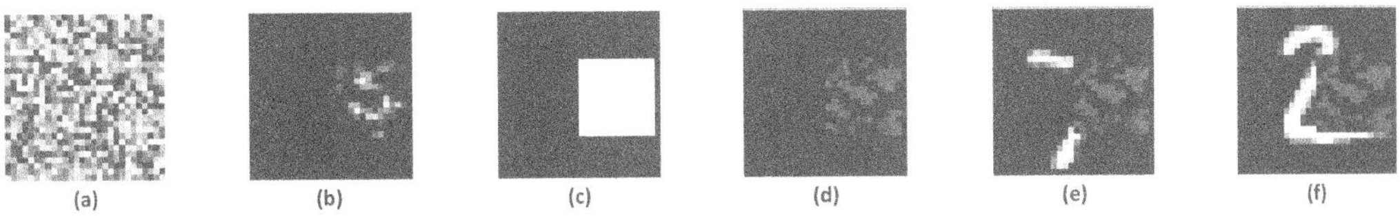

Figure 7.13: Process of trigger generation in the second Conv layer of the LeNet. **(a)** Initial input trigger. **(b)** Gradients of the selected neuron. **(c)** Mask created through gradients. **(d)** Final trigger after loop. **(e)** and **(f)** are two images with the applied trigger.

The images from both the original and modified test sets (two examples from the latter are shown in Figures 7.12e and f) are inferred. The results are reported in Table 7.7, where $exceed_{ORIGINAL} = 0$ and $exceed_{MODIFIED} = 10000$.

Targeting the **second Conv layer**, the obtained results are significantly different. The trigger is more perceptible and overlapped with a significant part of the images, as can be seen in Figure 7.13. In this case, with the same experimental settings, the obtained statistics are $exceed_{ORIGINAL} = 5$ and $exceed_{MODIFIED} = 7585$, as also reported in Table 7.7.

This demonstrates that targeting a neuron in the second Conv layer leads to a relatively worse result. In fact, we can observe that, on average, the gradients are higher than the gradients corresponding to a target neuron in the first Conv layer. We define the correlation between the target neuron and the masked area of the image S as in Equation (7.9), where $\gamma_{i,j}$ is the gradient corresponding to the pixel with indexes i,j in the trigger mask, and M is the size of the side trigger, in case of a square trigger.

$$S = \frac{\sum_{i,j}^{N} \gamma_{i,j}}{M^2} \tag{7.9}$$

It can be seen that in the first convolution layer $S = 2.21 \cdot 10^{-5}$, whereas in the second convolution layer $S = 1.4 \cdot 10^{-6}$. This clearly shows that for a neuron in the 2nd layer, the variation with the input pixel is much lower. If we call ρ the value in Equation (7.10), we can see that it is getting lower when choosing target neurons belonging to deeper layers.

$$\rho = exceed_{MODIFIED} - exceed_{ORIGINAL} \tag{7.10}$$

Considering the MLP, a square mask is created and put in the bottom-right corner. Its side is varied between 5 and 17 pixels, with steps of 2 pixels. Since, in the beginning, the area of the trigger is too small, there are not enough pixels to optimize the saturation of the target neuron. The difference between $initial_{value_k}$ and $final_{value_k}$ results in a small value. Moreover, a huge number of images from the original dataset make the target neuron exceed the threshold, leading to a small value of ρ. On the one hand, a larger area of the trigger increases ρ as can be seen in Figure 7.14 and, on the other hand, it leads to a less stealthy trigger.

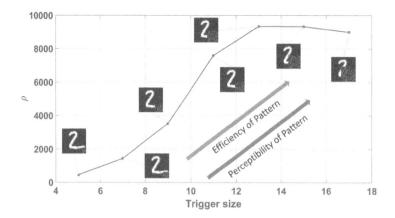

Figure 7.14: Plot of ρ with respect to the trigger size.

In the case of the MLP network, an interesting result is obtained with a lower value of $val_{max} = 0.1$. Even though we are targeting the first layer, the gradients are covering the complete image (Figure 7.15b) since it is an FC layer. Hence, we create a mask suited for the gradient, which spans across the whole image, as shown in Figure 7.15c. In this case, the trigger is applied as a noise in the image. Due to the low value of val_{max}, the trigger is imperceptible, as shown in Figures 7.15e and f. We obtained a very high ρ, shown in Table 7.7, and high imperceptibility at the expense of more challenging applicability.

7.2.4.3 Results on the CIFAR10 Dataset

In this case, targeting the first layer, with parameters set as shown in Table 7.7, the trigger shown in Figure 7.16d is produced. The superposition of the trigger on the original images (two examples) is shown in Figures 7.16f and h.

7.2.4.4 Hardware Overhead

Given the amount M of bit-flips applied, the hardware overhead is constituted as the following.

1. M inverters, constituted by 2 transistors each.

2. M 2-way multiplexer, constituted by 16 transistors each in a 4 NANDs implementation.

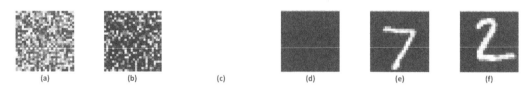

Figure 7.15: Process of trigger generation in the first layer of the MLP. (a) Initial input trigger. (b) Gradients of the selected neuron. (c) Mask created through gradients. (d) Final trigger after loop. (e) and (f) are two images with the applied trigger.

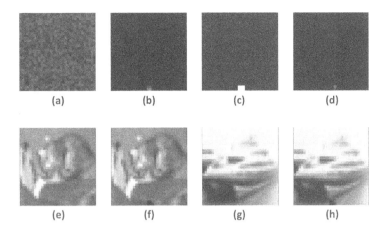

Figure 7.16: Process of trigger generation in the first layer of the CNN for the CIFAR10 dataset. (a) Initial input trigger. (b) Gradients of the selected neuron. (c) Mask created through gradients. (d) Final trigger after loop. (e) First image from the dataset. (f) First image with trigger applied. (g) Second image from the dataset. (h) Second image with trigger applied.

3. *In the case of a DNN*, a digital comparator, whose complexity depends on the neuron's fanout.

4. *In the case of an SNN*, a counter to count the spikes, and a comparator to check when the counter reaches a particular value.

The overhead of multiplexers and inverters can be estimated as $(2 + 16) \times M$. From the experiments reported in Section 7.2.2, it is clear that an amount of about just 30 bit-flips is enough to completely crash the performances of the DNN for the two networks operating on the MNIST dataset, or 4 bit-flips in the case of the CNN operating on the CIFAR10 dataset. The hardware overhead of inverters and multiplexers, calculated in terms of transistors, is about $(2 + 16) \times 30 = 540$ in the first case, whereas it is just $(2 + 16) \times 4 = 72$ in the second case. In the case of an SNN, a counter is added, whose module should be at least as large as the maximum spiking rate a neuron can have. The number of transistors needed for a module N counter is given by $\#_{transistors} = (N - 2) \times 6 + (N \times 4) \times 4$, where the first addend gives the contribution of the AND gates, whereas the second gives the contribution of the T-type flip-flops.

7.2.5 Summary

The proposed NeuroAttack methodology exploits the bit-flip resilience analysis to design a stealthy hardware Trojan that flips the most significant weight bits of an SNN or a DNN. The backdoor Trojan is triggered by a carefully-crafted adversarial pattern, which is, in practice, imperceptible elsewhere. The proposed attack represents a critical threat to the trustworthiness of both DNNs and SNNs. It is applicable in practice with little hardware overhead, while it does not affect the internal structure of SNNs. However, as will be demonstrated in the following Section 7.3, the SNNs have higher inherent robustness compared to DNNs. Moreover, it can be further enhanced by tuning its structural parameters, like the threshold voltage and the time window for sampling the spikes.

7.3 ROBUST SNN METHODOLOGY THROUGH INHERENT STRUCTURAL PARAMETERS

Recent works [114, 127] showed the inherent robustness of SNNs to security attacks without considering the variability in their structural spiking parameters. This section explores the security enhancement of SNNs through internal structural parameters. Specifically, we investigate the SNN robustness to adversarial attacks with different values of the neuron's firing voltage thresholds and time window boundaries. We thoroughly study the SNNs' security under different adversarial attacks in the strong white-box setting, with different noise budgets and under variable spiking parameters. Our results show a significant impact of the structural parameters on the SNNs'' security, and promising sweet spots can be reached to design trustworthy SNNs with 85% higher robustness than a traditional non-spiking DNN system. To the best of our knowledge, this is the first work that investigates the impact of structural parameters on the SNNs' robustness to adversarial attacks.

7.3.1 System Overview

While the reliability and security of traditional (i.e., non-spiking) DNNs against adversarial attacks have been thoroughly studied, the corresponding analysis of the SNNs' robustness is still under-explored. Due to their bio-inspired aspect, higher behavioral dimensions are present in SNNs compared to non-spiking DNNs. Therefore, a more comprehensive study is required to understand the inherent behavior of SNNs, especially under adversarial attacks. Toward this, the following key questions need to be investigated:

(Q1) *How do the spiking structural parameters (i.e., threshold voltage and time window) affect the SNNs' behavior under attack?*

(Q2) *Are SNNs inherently robust against adversarial attacks, regardless of the structural parameters?*

(Q3) *Does a combination of structural parameters that provide high accuracy also guarantee high robustness?*

To address these research questions, the following key contributions are proposed:

- We propose a systematic methodology for analyzing the SNN robustness. We are the first to explore the impact of neurons' structural parameters (i.e., spiking threshold voltage V_{th} and time window boundary T) on the SNNs' robustness against the strong white-box adversarial attacks.

- The SNN learnability and security studies show that the SNNs' inherent robustness is strongly conditioned by these structural parameters.

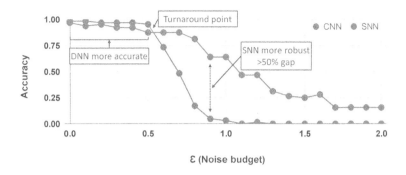

Figure 7.17: PGD adversarial attack applied to a CNN and an SNN that have the same number of layers with equal size and an equal number of neurons.

- We design trustworthy SNNs, by fine-tuning their structural parameters around the previously found sweet spots. For instance, a 5-layer SNN trained on the MNIST dataset achieves up to 84% accuracy improvement compared to a corresponding CNN when the PGD attack with $\varepsilon = 1.5$ noise budget is applied.

7.3.2 Case Study Analysis: Comparison DNNs vs. SNNs with the same Architectural Model

To highlight the importance of the problem, we conducted a motivational case study. We trained a 5-layer CNN, with 3 Conv layers and 2 FC layers on the MNIST dataset [118] using the PyTorch framework [204], and an SNN with the same number of layers and neurons per layer with the Norse framework [209]. We applied the white-box PGD attack [148] on both networks and monitored the accuracy variation w.r.t. the noise budget ε. The results reported in Figure 7.17 indicate that the CNN has higher accuracy for low noise magnitude. However, after the turnaround point of $\varepsilon = 0.5$, the SNN clearly shows a more robust response to the attack than its CNN counterpart, with an accuracy gap higher than 50%. For $\varepsilon > 0.5$, the accuracy of the CNN decreases sharply, while the slope for the accuracy drop in the SNN is lower. This outcome motivated us to investigate the inherent robustness of the SNNs further.

These experiments give a quick overview of the high potential of SNNs in terms of security compared to traditional DNNs. However, while these experiments are run using the default SNN structural parameters, one cannot generalize this observation until a deeper analysis is made.

7.3.3 Threat Model

7.3.3.1 Adversary Knowledge

In our experiments, we assume the strongest case where an attacker is attempting to design adversarial attacks to fool an SNN classifier in a white-box attack scenario. We assume a powerful attacker who has the full knowledge of the victim classifier's architecture and parameters (including the structural parameters V_{th} and T). The attacker uses this knowledge to create adversarial examples.

7.3.3.2 Attack Generation

We evaluate the SNNs' robustness using one of the most widely used attacks, the PGD [148]. It is one of the strongest iterative variants of the FGSM where the adversarial example is generated following Equation (7.11).

$$x^{t+1} = \mathcal{P}_{\mathcal{S}_x}(x^t + \alpha \cdot sign(\nabla_x \mathcal{L}_\theta(x^t, y))) \tag{7.11}$$

Where $\mathcal{P}_{\mathcal{S}_x}()$ is a projection operator projecting the input into the feasible region $\mathcal{S}_x$, and α is the additive noise at each iteration. The PGD attack tries to find the perturbation that maximizes the loss of a model on a given sample while keeping the perturbation magnitude lower than a given budget. It is an iterative gradient-based attack that is considered a high-success attack.

7.3.4 Robustness Exploration Methodology

Our study explores the SNNs' robustness under different adversarial noise budgets, and this, for different (V_{th}, T) parameters combinations. Figure 7.18 gives an overview of the different components of our methodology. It is composed of the following two main steps. **(1)** The first step of the exploration is meant to exclude combinations of structural parameters that are not propitious for efficient learning in SNNs. Indeed, there is no interest in studying the robustness of SNNs with low baseline performance. **(2)** In the second step, for all (V_{th}, T) settings that enable the SNN training to converge efficiently, we proceed with a robustness exploration.

Algorithm 25 details our robustness exploration methodology. Lines 1 and 2 browse the n threshold voltages and m time windows to explore. Once the training is launched (line 3), we proceed to the SNN learnability study for the given combination

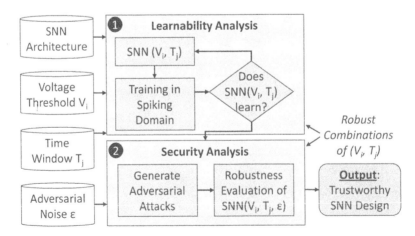

Figure 7.18: Methodology steps for exploring the SNN robustness, varying the threshold voltage V_{th}, the time window T, and the adversarial perturbation ε.

(V_{th}, T). As shown in line 4, the learnability is quantitatively verified by setting a minimum baseline accuracy level below which we consider the SNN learning inefficient. This value depends on the SNN architecture, learning method, dataset, and application. In our case study, we use this accuracy threshold equal to 70% as it is typically achieved by state-of-the-art SNNs [209].

The security analysis starts from line 5. It generates adversarial examples with different noise budgets to fool the SNN. The noise budget models the aggressiveness allowed within the attack generation; the higher the noise budget, the more aggressive the attack is. First, the counter of successful attack generation cases is initialized (line 6). Then, we browse the dataset $\mathcal{D}$ (line 7) to generate the adversarial attacks using PGD, as shown in line 8. Afterward, the algorithm verifies if the generated example can fool the SNN (lines 9-10), i.e., if the attack forced the output to a wrong label, and accordingly increment the adversarial success counter. Then the robustness is evaluated for every ε value as the rate of attacks for which the adversary failed to generate an adversarial example that fools the victim SNN (line 11). Hence, by tracking the accuracy slope w.r.t. ε, we can compare the robustness of each model to adversarial attacks.

Algorithm 25: Robustness Exploration Algorithm.

Inputs:
Membrane Voltage Thresholds: $Vth = V_i \ /i \in [1, n]$;
Spiking Time Windows: $T = T_j / j \in [1, m]$;
Adversarial Noise Budgets: $\varepsilon = \varepsilon_k \ /k \in [1, p]$;
SNN Architectures: $S_{ij} = SNN(V_i, T_j)$;
Labeled Test Set: $\mathcal{D} = (X_t, L_t)$;
Accuracy threshold: A_{th}
Output: Robustness Level

1 **for** $i \leftarrow 1$ **to** n **do**
2   **for** $j \leftarrow 1$ **to** m **do**
3   Train$(S_{ij} = SNN(V_i, T_j))$;
4   **if** $Accuracy(S_{ij}) \geq A_{th}$ **then**
       // S_{ij} learns
5   **for** $k \leftarrow 1$ **to** p **do**
6   Adv = 0;
7   **for** $X_t \leftarrow 1$ **to** $< \mathcal{D} >$ **do**
           // Adversarial Attack
8            $X_t^* = PGD(S_{ij}, \varepsilon_k, X_t)$;
9   **if** $S_{ij}(X_t^*) \neq L_t$ **then**
10   Adv++ ;
11   Robustness $(\varepsilon_k)= 1 - \frac{Adv}{<\mathcal{D}>}$;

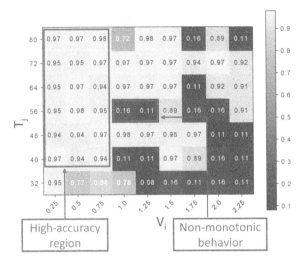

Figure 7.19: Heat map showing the accuracy of SNNs trained on the MNIST dataset under different combinations of V_{th} and T.

7.3.5 Evaluation of the SNNs' Robustness

7.3.5.1 Experimental Setup

Our experiments are performed using Norse [209], a library that expands PyTorch [204] with primitives for bio-inspired neural components, thereby allowing to train and run SNNs in the spiking domain. The adversarial attacks are implemented using Foolbox v3.1.1 [224]. The SNN architecture is a Lenet-5 adapted to the spiking domain using the LIF neuron model and trained on the MNIST database [118]. The experiments are run on an Nvidia GeForce RTX 2080 Ti GPU.

7.3.5.2 Learnability Study

Before studying the robustness when varying the structural parameters, we need to define our exploration space. The default values of the threshold voltage and time window parameters are $(V_{th}, T) = (1, 64)$. Therefore, we focus on having an overview of the learnability of SNNs in the neighborhood of these settings. Figure 7.19 shows the accuracy heat map for different (V_{th}, T) combinations. The horizontal and vertical axes denote V_{th} and T, respectively. Different colors denote the accuracy of the SNN. Note that the highest-accuracy combination tends to be toward the top-left corner, i.e., low V_{th} and high T. However, the heat map is not monotonic. For example, there are combinations with an accuracy lower than 16%, surrounded by combinations with an accuracy higher than 89%.

While it is evident that studying the robustness of non-learnable combinations is not useful, we use this map as a reference to track the behavior of SNNs under attack with different noise budgets.

7.3.5.3 Security Study

In this section, we investigate the robustness of SNNs while increasing the attacks' adversarial noise magnitude in a white-box scenario. We first proceed to a holistic exploration under all previous combinations of V_{th} and T. Figure 7.20 shows the accuracy degradation of SNNs under the PGD attack with noise magnitudes of 1 and 1.5.

The first fascinating insight we extract from Figure 7.20 is that high baseline learnability (without adversarial attacks) is not a guarantee of robustness. Moreover, we notice a different evolution of the SNNs w.r.t. adversarial attacks based on their respective structural parameters. More specifically, two SNNs with a starting comparable accuracy may have different behaviors under attack. For example, both combinations $(V_{th}, T) = (0.5, 80)$ and $(V_{th}, T) = (0.75, 72)$ start with 97% accuracy. However, while the accuracy of the first combination (as highlighted in Figure 7.20a) drops to 27% under $\varepsilon = 1$ attack budget, the second loses only 6% of its initial accuracy under the same attack noise magnitude.

Figure 7.20b shows a more accentuated behavior for large adversarial perturbations ($\varepsilon = 1.5$), where more than half of the heat map has SNN accuracies lower than 20%. It is interesting to note that the accuracy of the SNN with $(V_{th}, T) = (0.75, 48)$ has dropped to 2% when $\varepsilon = 1.5$, while it was relatively higher (86%) when $\varepsilon = 1$. On the other hand, the SNN with $(V_{th}, T) = (1, 80)$ shows relatively high robustness against the PGD attack since the SNN accuracy has not dropped much (from 72% when $\varepsilon = 0$ and $\varepsilon = 1$ to 66% when $\varepsilon = 1.5$).

7.3.5.4 CNNs' vs. SNNs' Robustness Comparison

In this section, we analyze a set of insightful (V_{th}, T) combinations and track their impact on the SNNs' robustness compared to the Lenet-5 CNN trained on

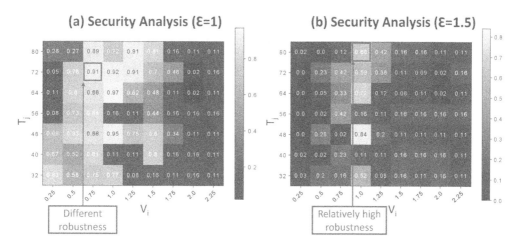

Figure 7.20: Heat maps showing the SNN accuracy for the MNIST dataset using different combinations of (V_i, T_j). (a) Security analysis for $\varepsilon = 1$. (b) Security analysis for $\varepsilon = 1.5$.

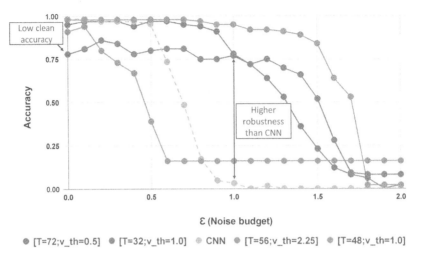

Figure 7.21: Robustness of SNNs tested on MNIST with different V_{th} and T parameters under the PGD attack and compared to the Lenet-5 CNN.

the same dataset. Figure 7.21 compares the robustness of SNNs with different structural parameters w.r.t. its correspondent CNN. This figure shows the impact of structural parameters on SNNs' security in a more detailed fashion. In fact, while the combination $(V_{th}, T) = (2.25, 56)$ achieves lower robustness than the CNN, up to 85% higher robustness is reached by the combination $(V_{th}, T) = (1, 48)$. Another interesting case is represented by the combination $(V_{th}, T) = (1, 32)$, whose clean accuracy is only 78% (as highlighted in Figure 7.21), while it has 75% higher accuracy than the CNN when a strong noise budget (i.e., $\varepsilon > 1$) is applied.

7.3.6 Summary

In this section, the robustness of DNNs and SNNs has been studied, and the reasons for the higher SNN robustness against adversarial attacks have been highlighted. Moreover, the proposed robustness exploration methodology enables fine-tuning of the structural parameters of the SNNs to increase their robustness. The evaluations show that these structural parameters have a strong impact on the SNN robustness, and a dedicated exploration is required before employing SNNs for safety-critical applications. These findings make SNNs attractive solutions for robust and efficient deep learning systems.

While the above-discussed analyses in this chapter focus on SNN security for discrete data, the SNNs have shown high-efficiency gains when they operate from event-based data, e.g., by receiving a stream of events captured by a DVS camera as input. Toward this, the security-related issues for event-based SNNs are discussed in the following Section 7.4 and Section 7.5.

7.4 R-SNN: A METHODOLOGY FOR ROBUSTIFYING SNNS THROUGH NOISE FILTERS FOR DVS

SNNs aim to provide energy-efficient learning capabilities when deployed on neuromorphic chips with event-based DVS cameras. This section studies the SNNs' robustness against adversarial attacks on such DVS-based systems and proposes *R-SNN*, a novel methodology for robustifying SNNs through DVS-noise filtering. We generate adversarial attacks on DVS signals and apply noise filters for DVS sensors to defend against adversarial attacks. Our results demonstrate that the noise filters successfully prevent the SNNs from being fooled. The SNNs in our experiments achieve more than 90% accuracy on the DvsGesture [8] and NMNIST [193] datasets under different adversarial threat models.

7.4.1 System Overview

Similar to the issue of traditional DNNs, the SNNs' trustworthiness is also threatened by adversarial attacks. Although some preliminary studies have been conducted, such a problem is unexplored for event-based SNN systems. As a starting point, the techniques for designing robust SNNs can be inspired by the recent advancements in defense mechanisms for DNNs, where adversarial learning algorithms, loss/regularization functions, and image preprocessing have emerged. The latter approach consists of suppressing the adversarial perturbation through dedicated input filtering. Noteworthy, for SNN-based systems fed by DVS cameras, the attacks and preprocessing-based defenses for frame-based sensors cannot be directly deployed due to differences in signal properties. Hence, specialized noise filters for DVS sensors [133] must be employed.

The impact of DVS signal filtering for secure neuromorphic computing is a new and open research problem. Toward this, we devise *R-SNN*, a novel methodology that employs attack-resistant noise filters on DVS signals as a defense strategy for robustifying SNNs against adversarial attacks. Since the DVS cameras also contain temporal information, the generation process of adversarial perturbation is technically different compared to traditional adversarial attacks on images, in which only the spatial information is considered. Therefore, the temporal information must be leveraged to develop a robust defense.

In short, our *key contributions* are the following:

- We analyze the impact of noise filtering for DVS under multiple adversary threat models, i.e., by placing the filter at different stages of the system or assuming different knowledge of the adversary.

- We generate adversarial perturbations for the DVS signal to attack SNNs.

- *R-SNN Design Methodology:* we propose a methodology to apply specialized DVS-noise filters for increasing the robustness of SNNs against adversarial attacks.

- Our experimental results exhibit high SNN robustness against adversarial attacks under different adversary threat models.

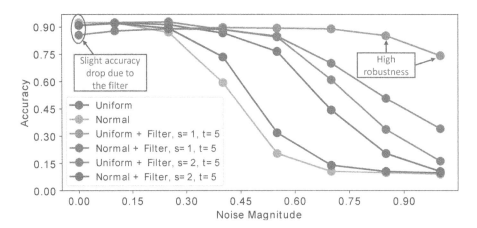

Figure 7.22: Analyzing the impact of applying normal and uniform noise to the DvsGesture dataset.

7.4.2 Case Study Analysis: SNN Robustness against Random Noise

As a preliminary analysis for motivating our study in the above-discussed research directions, we conduct the following experiments. We trained a 4-layer Spiking CNN, with 2 Conv layers and 2 FC layers, for the DvsGesture dataset [8] using the SLAYER method [248] on an ML-workstation with two Nvidia GeForce RTX 2080 Ti GPUs. For every frame of events, we inject uniform and normally-distributed random noise in the testing dataset, and we measure the classification accuracy. Moreover, to mitigate the effects of the perturbations, the filter of [133] is applied, with different spatio-temporal parameters (s and t). The obtained accuracy w.r.t. different noise magnitudes are shown in Figure 7.22. As highlighted in the figure, the filter slightly reduces the accuracy of the SNN when no noise is applied. However, the SNN becomes more robust when the filter is applied in the presence of noise. For instance, when considering normally distributed noise with a magnitude of 0.55, the filter with $s = 1$ and $t = 5$ improves the accuracy by 64%. Such a filter works even better when uniformly-distributed noise is applied. Indeed, the perturbations with a large magnitude of 0.85 and 1 are filtered out well as the SNN maintains a relatively high accuracy of 85% and 74%, respectively.

7.4.3 R-SNN Methodology

7.4.3.1 Noise Filters for Dynamic Vision Sensors

Event-based cameras [128] are bio-inspired sensors for acquiring visual information directly correlated to the light variations in the scene. The DVS cameras work asynchronously, not recording frames with precise timing. Instead, the sensors record negative and positive brightness variations in the scene. Thus, each pixel encodes a brightness change in the scene. Pixels are independent and can record both positive and negative light variations. The event-based sensors consume significantly less power than classical frame-based image sensors since the data is recorded only when a brightness variation is detected in the scene. Therefore, no information is recorded in the absence of light changes, leading to close to zero power consumption. Therefore, DVS sensors can be efficiently deployed on edge devices and directly coupled to neuromorphic hardware for SNN-based applications.

DVS sensors are mainly subjected to background activity noise caused by thermal activity and junction leakage current [191]. When the DVS is stimulated, a window of neighbor pixels activates simultaneously, generating events. Therefore, the actual events show a higher spatio-temporal correlation than the noisy events. This empirical observation is exploited for filtering out the noise [133]. The correlation between events in a spatio-temporal neigborhood is computed. If the correlation is lower than a specific threshold, the events are likely capturing noise and are filtered out. Otherwise, they are kept. The procedure is reported in Algorithm 26, where s and t are the only filter parameters used to determine the dimensions of the spatio-temporal neighborhood. For large values of s and t, only a few events are filtered out. The filter's decision is made by the comparison between $t_e - M[x_e][y_e]$ and t (lines 8-9 of Algorithm 26).

Algorithm 26: Noise filter in the spatio-temporal domain.

    Inputs:
    a list of events E in the form (x_e, y_e, p_e, t_e), which correspond to the x-coordinate, the y-coordinate, the polarity, and the timestamp of the event e, respectively
    a 128×128 matrix M
    the spatial and temporal filter parameters s and t
    Output: a filtered list of events E

1 Initialize $M = 0$;
2 Order the events E from the oldest to the newest;
3 **for** e *in* E **do**
4   **for** i *in* $(x_e - s, x_e + s)$ **do**
5   **for** j *in* $(y_e - s, y_e + s)$ **do**
6   **if** *not* $(i == x_e$ *and* $j == y_e)$ **then**
7                 $M[i][j] = t_e$;

8   **if** $t_e - M[x_e][y_e] > t$ **then**
9   Remove e from E;

7.4.3.2 Adversarial Attacks in the Spatio-Temporal Domain

Currently, adversarial attacks are deployed in many DL applications. They represent a serious threat to safety-critical applications. A successful attack aims to generate small perturbations to fool the network. Recently, some preliminary studies on adversarial attacks for SNNs have been conducted [10, 245]. *However, these previous works do not analyze the attacks on frames of events coming from DVS cameras.*

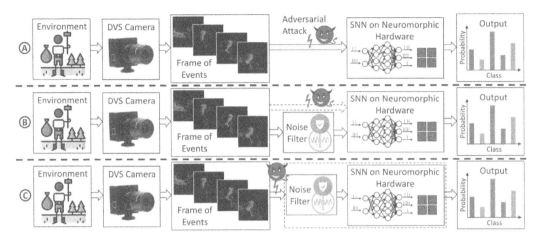

Figure 7.23: Adversarial threat models are considered in this work. (**a**) The adversary introduces adversarial perturbations to the frames of events at the input of the SNN. (**b**) The noise filter is inserted as a defense to secure the SNNs against adversarial perturbations while the adversary is unaware of the filter. (**c**) The adversary is aware of the presence of the noise filter and sees it as a preprocessing step of the SNN.

For the adversarial attacks on images, the perturbations are introduced in the spatial domain only. However, when considering adversarial attacks on videos, which are sequences of image frames, the attack algorithm can also perturb the temporal domain. While it is expected that the perturbations added to one frame propagate to other frames through temporal interaction, perturbing only a sparse subset of frames makes the attack stealthy. Indeed, state-of-the-art attacks on videos only add perturbations to a few frames, which propagate to other frames to misclassify the video.

7.4.3.3 *Adversary Threat Models*

In our experiments, we assume different threat models in the system setting, as shown in Figure 7.23. In all three scenarios, the given adversarial attack algorithm perturbs the frames of events generated from the DVS camera to fool the SNN. In the threat model Ⓐ, the attacker has access to the frames of events at the input of the SNN. In the threat model Ⓑ, the DVS noise filter is inserted in the system in parallel to the adversarial perturbation conducted by the attacker. It means that the attacker is unaware of the filter. Since, under these assumptions, the attack could be relatively weak, we also analyze the threat model Ⓒ, in which the attacker is aware of the presence of the DVS noise filter. In such a scenario, the filter is seen as a preprocessing step and embedded in the attack loop.

7.4.3.4 *Adversarial Attack Generation for Frames of Events*

The generation procedure for the adversarial attack for frames of events works as follows. Inspired by the algorithms of attacks for frame-based videos, we devise the specialized attack algorithm for the DVS signal. Algorithm 27 describes the step-by-step procedure of our methodology. It is an iterative algorithm that progressively computes the perturbation values based on the SNN's loss function (lines 2–17 of Algorithm 27) for every frame series of the dataset D. A mask M decides in which subset of event frames the perturbation should be added (line 3 of Algorithm 27). Then, the output probability and its respective loss, computed in the presence of the perturbation, are obtained in lines 5 and 6 of Algorithm 27. Finally, the perturbation values are calculated based on the input gradients w.r.t. the loss.

Algorithm 27: The SNN Adversarial Attack Methodology.

Inputs:

a mask M able to select only certain frames

a dataset D composed of DVS images

a perturbation P to be added to the images

the output probability *prob* of a certain class

Output: perturbed dataset

1 **for** *d in D* **do**

2   **for** *i in max_iteration* **do**

3   Add P to d only to the frames selected by M;

4   Calculate the prevision on the perturbed input;

5   Extract *prob* of the actual class of d;

6   Update the loss value: $loss = -log(1 - prob)$;

7   Calculate the gradients and update P;

7.4.3.5 *Our Proposed Defense Methodology*

Our methodology for defending SNNs is based on specialized DVS-noise filtering. The details for selecting efficient values of the spatial parameter s and temporal parameter t of the filter are reported in Algorithm 28. For different threat models, it automatically searches for the best combination of s and t by applying the attack in the presence of the filter with the given parameters. The accuracy of the SNN in such conditions is compared to the previously recorded highest accuracy (line 8 of Algorithm 28). At the output, the parameters s' and t', which provide the highest accuracy, are found.

7.4.4 Evaluation of the R-SNN Methodology

7.4.4.1 *Experimental Setup*

In our experiments, we used two event-based datasets, the DvsGesture [8] and the NMNIST [193]. The former is a collection of 1077 samples for training and 264 for testing, grouped into 11 classes. The latter is a spiking conversion of the original frame-based MNIST dataset [118]. It contains 60 000 training and 10 000 testing samples generated by an ATIS event-based sensor [211] that is moved while capturing

---

Algorithm 28: The R-SNN Defense Methodology.

Inputs:
the collection M of adversarial threat models
the adversarial attack A
a DVS noise filter $F(s,t)$ with spatial parameter s and temporal parameter t
the set $\mathcal{S}$ of possible values of s
the set $\mathcal{T}$ of possible values of t
the SNN network $N(F)$ that we want to robustify with F
Output: Values s' and t' for a robust defense in M

1 **for** m *in* M **do**
2 $\quad$ Set the relative positions of A and F, based on m;
3 $\quad$ $Acc' = 0$;
4 $\quad$ $s' = 0$;
5 $\quad$ $t' = 0$;
6 $\quad$ **for** s *in* $\mathcal{S}$ **do**
7 $\quad\quad$ **for** t *in* $\mathcal{T}$ **do**
8 $\quad\quad\quad$ **if** $Accuracy(N(F(s,t))) \geq Acc'$ **then**
9 $\quad\quad\quad\quad$ $Acc' =$ Accuracy$(N(F(s,t)))$;
10 $\quad\quad\quad\quad$ $s' = s$;
11 $\quad\quad\quad\quad$ $t' = t$;

---

the original MNIST images projected on an LCD screen. For the DvsGesture dataset, we considered the 4-layer SNN as described in [248], with two Conv layers and two FC layers. It has been trained for 625 epochs using the SLAYER backpropagation method [248], using a batch size of 4 and a learning rate of 0.01. For the NMNIST dataset, we employed a spiking multilayer perceptron with two FC layers [248], trained for 350 epochs with the SLAYER backpropagation method [248], using a batch size of 4 and learning rate of 0.01. We implemented the SNNs using the PyTorch framework [204] on an ML-workstation with two Nvidia GeForce RTX 2080 Ti GPUs. We also implemented the adversarial attack algorithm and the noise filter of [133] in PyTorch.

7.4.4.2 SNN Robustness under Attack Without the Noise Filter

For the threat model Ⓐ, the attacker introduces the adversarial perturbations directly to the input of the SNN. In this case, as shown in the black bar of Figure 7.24a, the SNN for the DvsGesture dataset is not protected by the filter and the accuracy drops to 15.15%. A similar behavior is noted on the SNN for the NMNIST dataset, where the attack reduces the accuracy to 4% (91% reduction, see the black bar in Figure 7.24b). We noticed that for both datasets, the largest accuracy drop is already obtained after the attack algorithm's first iteration. Further iterations of the algorithm do not appear to reduce the accuracy to a greater extent.

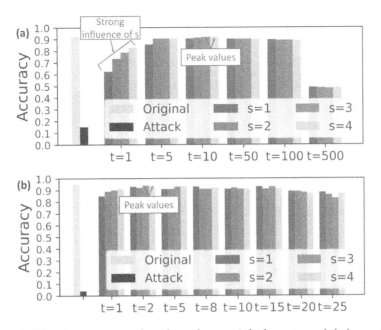

Figure 7.24: SNN robustness under the adversarial threat model A, and the threat model B with different parameters s and t of the filter. (a) Results for the DvsGesture dataset. (b) Results for the NMNIST dataset.

7.4.4.3 SNN Robustness under Attack by Noise Filter-Unaware Adversary

Afterward, we analyzed the SNN robustness for the threat model Ⓑ, that is the case in which the attacker can introduce a perturbation on the input but is not aware of the presence of the DVS filter. For this experiment set, the accuracy was much higher than for the threat model Ⓐ, proving the effectiveness of the filter as a defense method for guaranteeing high SNN robustness. The results obtained with our proposed *R-SNN* methodology, varying both the parameters s and t of the filters, are reported in Figure 7.24. On the SNN for the DvsGesture dataset, for a wide variety of values of s and t, the accuracy does not change much, settling around 90%, while with $t = 500$ it dropped to 48%. However, when $t = 1$, the influence of s is more evident. In fact, the accuracy scales from 62.5% when $s = 1$ to 83% when $s = 4$. In all the other cases, the difference is almost not noticeable. On the contrary, we can observe that the higher s is, the slower the filter processes all the data. Among the considered values, $t = 10$ produced the highest accuracy for every s, peaking at 91.67% with $s = 3$ and $s = 4$. On the SNN for the NMNIST dataset, a similar behavior is shown. For $t = 1$, the accuracy strongly depends on s. The peak of 94% accuracy is reached for $(s, t) = (3, 2)$ and $(s, t) = (4, 2)$. Note that this is only 1% lower than the original accuracy, i.e., with clean inputs. On the other hand, the accuracy drops below 90% for $t \geq 20$.

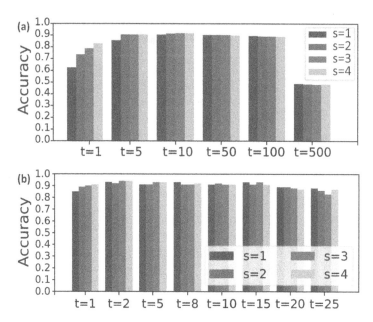

Figure 7.25: SNN robustness under adversarial threat model C. (**a**) Results for the DvsGesture dataset. (**b**) Results for the NMNIST dataset.

7.4.4.4 SNN Robustness under Attack by Noise Filter-Aware Adversary

We also evaluated the *R-SNN* methodology on the threat model Ⓒ, in which the attacker is aware of the presence of the filter. This time the filter is introduced as a part of the SNN, more specifically as a preprocessing stage. As expected, the filter is also effective as a defense mechanism in this scenario. The differences w.r.t. the threat model Ⓑ are not noticeable. Among the experiments for the DvsGesture dataset, the highest robustness is reached for $(s, t) = (3, 10)$ and $(s, t) = (4, 10)$, where the SNN exhibits an accuracy of 91.67% (see Figure 7.25a). For the NMNIST dataset, the highest robustness, i.e., with an accuracy of 94%, is measured for $(s, t) = (3, 2)$ and $(s, t) = (4, 2)$ (see Figure 7.25b). Such a result is a clear sign that this kind of attack cannot overcome the presence of the filter. Therefore, the attack algorithm cannot effectively learn the filter's functionality through a gradient-based approach, even though being aware of it.

7.4.4.5 Case Study: Output Probability Variation

To investigate the effect of the adversarial attack and the filter more in detail, we show a comprehensive case study on a test DvsGesture sample labeled as *left-hand wave*. Figure 7.26 reports the frames of events and output probabilities for each adversarial threat model presented in this section, as well as for the clean inputs and the filtered event series without attack. For the clean images, the SNN correctly classifies the events as class 2, which corresponds to the *left-hand wave* (see Figure 7.26a). By

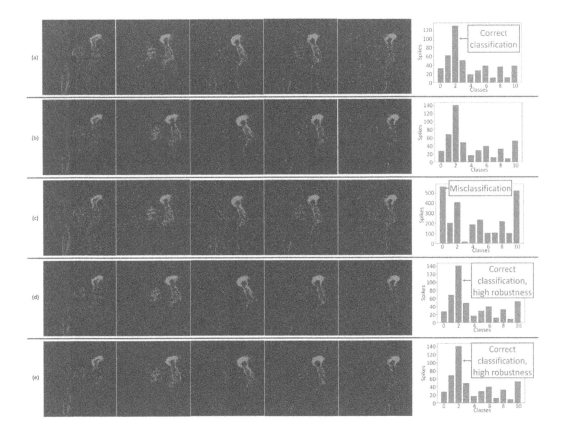

Figure 7.26: Detailed example of a sequence of events labeled as *left-hand wave*. On the left, the frames of events are shown. The histograms on the right-most column report the number of spikes emitted by the neurons of the last layer, which correspond to the output classes. **(a)** Clean event series. **(b)** Event series filtered with $s = 2$ and $t = 5$. **(c)** Event series under the adversarial threat model A, unfiltered. **(d)** Event series under the adversarial threat model B, filtered with $s = 2$ and $t = 5$. **(e)** Event series under the adversarial threat model C, filtered with $s = 2$ and $t = 5$.

filtering the input signal with $s = 2$ and $t = 5$, as shown in Figure 7.26b, the frames of events are visibly different from the previous case. However, the changes in the output probabilities are minimal, so the SNN correctly classifies the input. When the attack is applied, the output probability of the class 0, which corresponds to *hand clap*, exceeds the correct class. Note that, despite a great difference in the output probabilities, the modifications of the frames of events, compared to the clean event series, are barely noticeable (see Figure 7.26c). However, in the presence of the filter under the adversarial threat models Ⓑ and Ⓒ, the SNN correctly classifies the input. The high probability gap between the correct class and the other classes in Figure 7.26d and Figure 7.26e is an indicator of the high robustness of our defense method.

7.4.5 Summary

This section studied the robustness of SNNs against adversarial attacks on DVS-based systems. The proposed R-SNN methodology employs DVS-noise filtering to increase the robustness against the attacks. This work represents the first study of adversarial attacks on DVS signals and the first application of these filters as a defense mechanism against such attacks. It represents a proof-of-concept, which is extended by considering more advanced noise filters and specialized adversarial attack methodologies in the following Section 7.5.

7.5 DVS-ATTACKS: A SET OF ADVERSARIAL ATTACKS ON EVENT-BASED SNNS

Despite being energy-efficient when deployed on neuromorphic hardware and coupled with event-based DVS cameras, SNNs are vulnerable to security issues, such as adversarial attacks. Toward this, we propose *DVS-Attacks*, a set of efficient yet stealthy adversarial attack algorithms targeted to perturb the event sequences that form the input of the SNNs. Then, we demonstrate that noise filters for DVS can be employed as a defense technique against adversarial attacks. Afterward, we implement and test the attacks in the presence of two types of noise filters for DVS signals. The experimental results indicate that the filters can only partially protect the SNNs against our proposed *DVS-Attacks*. Even using the noise filter defenses, our proposed *Mask Filter-Aware Dash Attack* can reduce the SNN accuracy by more than 20% on the DvsGesture dataset and by more than 65% on the NMNIST dataset, compared to the original clean frames.

7.5.1 System Overview

Different security threats challenge the normal functionality of DNNs and SNNs. The DNN trustworthiness has been thoroughly investigated in recent years, highlighting that one of the most critical issues is represented by adversarial attacks. Although some initial studies have been conducted, SNNs' trustworthiness is a relatively unexplored problem. More precisely, DVS-based systems have not yet been systematically investigated for SNN security. The generation of adversarial attacks for DVS is an open research problem. Toward this, we propose *DVS-Attacks*, a set of adversarial attack algorithms for DVS signals, and test them in systems where noise filters are employed as a defensive mechanism against them. Since the DVS cameras also contain temporal information, the generation of adversarial examples is technically different than traditional adversarial attacks on images, in which only the spatial information is considered. Hence, the temporal information must be leveraged to develop the attack and defense mechanisms.

In a nutshell, we devise the following contributions:

- We propose *DVS-Attacks*, a set of adversarial attack methodologies injecting perturbations into DVS signals.

- In particular, the *MF-Aware Dash Attack* is specifically crafted to be resistant against the *Mask Filter* defense by adding perturbations only to a limited set of frames.

- The experimental results on the DvsGesture and NMNIST datasets show that the attacks fool the SNNs when no filter is employed. Moreover, the noise filters cannot fully protect against the *DVS-Attacks*, which represent a critical security threat for SNN-based neuromorphic systems.

7.5.2   Case Study Analysis: SNN Robustness against Random Noise

We perform the following experiments as a preliminary study to motivate our research in the above-discussed directions. We trained a 4-layer SNN with 2 Conv and 2 FC layers for the DvsGesture dataset [8] using the SLAYER method [248] in a DL-workstation having two Nvidia GeForce RTX 2080 Ti GPUs. For every frame of events, we perturb the testing dataset by adding normally-distributed random noise and measuring the classification accuracy. Moreover, to mitigate the effects of the perturbations, the *Background Activity Filter (BAF)* and the *Mask Filter (MF)* of [133] are applied, with various filter parameters. Figure 7.27 shows the accuracy results for different noise magnitudes. As highlighted in the figure, the filter may reduce the SNN's accuracy when no noise is applied. More than 20% accuracy drop is noticed on the *MF* with $T = 25$, and lower drops for the other filters. However, when subjected to noise, the SNN becomes more robust when the filter is applied. For instance, when considering normally distributed noise with a magnitude of 0.55, the *BAF* with $s = 1$ and $t = 5$ contributes for up to 64% accuracy improvement. On the other hand, *BAFs* with $s \geq 2$ do not increase the accuracy significantly compared to the unfiltered SNN. Moreover, *MFs* with $T \geq 100$ work even better than the BAFs when affected by large noise perturbations. Indeed, the perturbations with a magnitude of 1.0 are filtered out relatively well by the *MFs* with large T, while, for the same value of noise magnitude, both the *MFs* with $T \leq 50$ and the *BAF* with

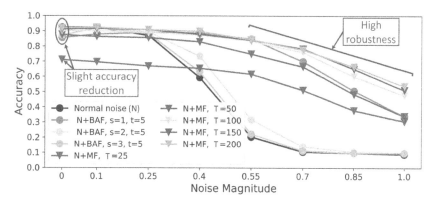

Figure 7.27: Analyzing the impact of applying the normally-distributed noise to the DvsGesture dataset, in the presence of *BAF* and *MF* noise filters.

$s = 1$ and $t = 5$ obtain an accuracy of only $\approx 33 - 34\%$. The key message learned from this study is that the noise filters for DVS signals can restore a large portion of SNN accuracy that would have been lost due to the perturbations. This motivates us to employ such filters as defense mechanisms against adversarial attacks.

7.5.3 Noise Filters for Dynamic Vision Sensors

7.5.3.1 Background Activity Filter

DVS sensors are typically affected by background activity noise generated by thermal noise and junction leakage current [191]. When the DVS sensor is stimulated, typically a neighborhood of pixels is simultaneously generating events. Therefore, the actual events have a higher spatio-temporal correlation compared to the noise-related events. This empirical intuition is exploited for generating the *Background Activity Filter (BAF)* [133]. If the correlation between events in a spatio-temporal neighborhood is lower than a certain threshold, the events are filtered out since they are likely due to noise. The procedure is reported in Algorithm 29, where the parameters S and T define the dimensions of the spatio-temporal neighborhood. For large S and T, several events are filtered out. The decision of the filter is made through the comparison between $t_e - M[x_e][y_e]$ and T (lines 8–9 of Algorithm 29).

Algorithm 29: *Background Activity Filter* for event-based sensors.

Inputs:
a list of events E in the form (x_e, y_e, p_e, t_e), which correspond to the x-coordinate, the y-coordinate, the polarity, and the timestamp of the event e, respectively
a 128×128 matrix M
the spatial and temporal filter parameters s and t
Output: a filtered list of events E

1 Initialize $M = 0$;
2 Order the events E from the oldest to the newest;
3 **for** *e in E* **do**
4   **for** *i in ($x_e - s, x_e + s$)* **do**
5   **for** *j in ($y_e - s, y_e + s$)* **do**
6   **if** *not ($i == x_e$ and $j == y_e$)* **then**
7                 $M[i][j] = t_e$;

8   **if** $t_e - M[x_e][y_e] > t$ **then**
9   Remove e from E;

7.5.3.2 Mask Filter

Another type of scenario of spontaneous noise activity is generated on the pixels with low temporal contrast. In this case, a *Mask Filter (MF)* is required to filter out such noise [133]. The procedure reported in Algorithm 30 shows that, compared to the *BAF*, the *MF* has only the temporal parameter T. The mask is activated if a pixel's activity exceeds T (lines 7-8 of Algorithm 30). After the mask is set, every event generated on a coordinate where the mask is active is removed (lines 10–11 of Algorithm 30). *Both the BAF and MF have been implemented and evaluated for intrinsic and parasitic noise added to DVS sensors, while their application as a defensive mechanism against adversarial attacks is still unexplored.*

Algorithm 30: *Mask Filter* for event-based sensors.

Inputs:
a list of events E in the form (x_e, y_e, p_e, t_e), which correspond to the x-coordinate, the y-coordinate, the polarity, and the timestamp of the event e, respectively

an $N \times N$ matrix M, where N is the size of the frames

an $N \times N$ *activity* matrix, representing the number of events produced by each pixel

the temporal threshold T

Output: a filtered list of events E

1 Initialize *activity* $= 0$;
2 **for** x *in range(N)* **do**
3   **for** y *in range(N)* **do**
4   **for** e *in E* **do**
5   **if** $(x, y) == (x_e, y_e)$ **then**
6                  $activity[x][y] += 1$;
7   **if** $activity[x][y] > T$ **then**
8              $M[x][y] = 1$;

9 **for** e *in E* **do**
10   **if** $M[x_e][y_e] == 1$ **then**
11   Remove e from E;

7.5.4 Threat Model

The system that we consider in our experiments is composed of a DVS camera for capturing the scenes of the environment as event sequences and a given SNN deployed on the neuromorphic device. As shown in Figure 7.28, the adversarial attacks and noise filters are located at the input of the SNN and can modify the sequences of events. We perform several experiments with different combinations of attacks and defenses. The noise filters described in Section 7.5.3 have been employed as a defense mechanisms. For the combinations where both attacks and defenses are applied to the system, the perturbations injected by the attack are applied before the filtering operation. In this way, it can filter out any events generated or modified by the attack,

Figure 7.28: Threat model considered in this work, where different types of adversarial attacks are deployed, and different types of DVS noise filters are applied as a defense.

thus aiming at making a strong defense in practical systems. The detailed discussion of the adversarial attack methodologies is conducted in the following Section 7.5.5.

7.5.5 DVS-Attacks Methodologies

7.5.5.1 Sparse Attack

The proposed *Sparse Attack* is an iterative algorithm that progressively updates the perturbation values according to the loss function (lines 2–7 of Algorithm 31) for every frame series of the dataset D. Its mask M determines in which subset of the event frames the perturbation should be added (line 3). Then, the output probability and its loss, obtained in the presence of the perturbation, are computed in lines 5 and 6, respectively. Finally, the perturbation values are updated according to the gradients of the inputs with respect to the loss (line 7).

Algorithm 31: *Sparse Attack* Methodology.

Inputs:
  a mask M able to select only certain frames
  a dataset D composed of DVS images
  a perturbation P to be added to the images
  the output probability *prob* of a certain class
  Output: perturbed dataset
1 **for** *d in D* **do**
2   **for** *i in max_iteration* **do**
3   Add P to d only to the frames selected by M;
4   Calculate the prevision on the perturbed input;
5   Extract *prob* for the actual class of d;
6   Update the loss value as $loss = -log(1 - prob)$;
7   Calculate the gradients and update P;

7.5.5.2 Frame Attack

The *Frame Attack* is a simple yet effective attack methodology that consists of adding a noise frame around the sample (see lines 4–5 of Algorithm 32). It does not require expensive calculations since the same perturbation (that forms the frame) is added to all the samples. Such a frame is not easy to spot in a dataset made of large images, like the DvsGesture (128×128), while its perturbations are more evident in the NMNIST dataset (34×34). One drawback is the overhead in terms of events added to the samples. In fact, the number of events dramatically increases for every frame since the attack targets each pixel of the boundary. Therefore, the sample size and the inference latency for processing the events with SNNs and filters increase as well.

Algorithm 32: *Frame Attack* Methodology.

   Inputs:
   an event-based dataset D
   a ($C \times N \times N \times T$) tensor $d \subset D$, where C represents the channels, N represents the frame dimensions, and T the sample duration
   Output: perturbed dataset
1 **for** d *in* D **do**
2   **for** x *in range(N)* **do**
3   **for** y *in range(N)* **do**
4   **if** $x == 0$ **or** $x == N-1$ **or** $y == 0$ **or** $y == N-1$ **then**
5             $d[:,x,y,:] = 1$;

7.5.5.3 Corner Attack

As the name suggests, the *Corner Attack* targets the corner of the images. It starts by targeting only two pixels on the top-left corner (lines 8–9 of Algorithm 33). Then, if the attack is not successfully fooling the SNN (line 11), the algorithm moves to the other corners. If some samples are still correctly classified after hitting all four corners, the perturbation size increases and the algorithm resumes back from the first corner. Before the updating phase, when the perturbation switches between corners or increases its size, the attack is applied to each sample in the dataset that was not corrupted yet. The number of samples reduces as the algorithm proceeds, and the process speeds up. The main characteristic of this attack is that the samples are affected by a different amount of perturbation. For example, while the SNN misinterprets the majority of the samples after a few iterations, other samples are perturbed for a longer time, thus making the attack easier to spot.

7.5.5.4 Dash Attack

The *Dash Attack* methodology is designed taking inspiration from the *Corner Attack*. Indeed, the two algorithms are pretty similar. The main difference is that in the *Dash Attack*, only two pixels are targeted at a time. The main structure of the algorithm is similar to the *Corner Attack*, as the *Dash Attack* starts targeting the top-left corner and modifying the first two pixels. Moreover, the x, y coordinates are updated to hit only two consecutive pixels within the same timestamp (see lines 14–22 of Algorithm 34). Hence, this attack is tough to spot, and the introduced perturbations

---

Algorithm 33: *Corner Attack* Methodology.

Input: an event-based dataset D made of $(C \times N \times N \times T)$ tensors, where C represents the number of channels, N the size, and T the duration of the sample; S is a list of the samples that compose D

Output: perturbed dataset

1 $x = 0$;
2 $y = 2$;
3 $left = True$;
4 **while** S *is not empty* **do**
5   **for** s *in S* **do**
6   **for** i *in range(N)* **do**
7   **for** j *in range(N)* **do**
8   **if** $i == x$ **and** ($left$ **and** $j < y$ **or** $\overline{left}$ **and** $j \geq N - y - 1$) **then**
9                       $s[:, i, j, :] = 1$;
10   The perturbed sample s is fed to the SNN, which produces a prediction P;
11   **if** P *is incorrect* **then**
12   Remove s from S;
13   **if** $x == 0$ **then**
14          $x = N - 1$;
15   **else**
16          $left = left$ **xor** 1;
17          $x = 0$;
18   **if** $\overline{left}$ **then**
19              $y = y + 1$;

---

do not cause a significant overhead of events on the samples. Moreover, all the samples under the *Dash Attack* are subjected to the same amount of perturbations.

7.5.5.5 MF-Aware Dash Attack

A critical issue of the above-discussed attacks, as will be discussed in Section 7.5.6, is their intrinsic weakness against the *MF*. They targeted both 'on' and 'off' channels of the same pixels for the whole sample duration. Hence, the distinction between the pixels modified by the attack and those not affected is evident since the number of events generated in the targeted pixel coordinates is significantly higher than those associated with the other coordinates that were not hit during the attack. In addition, we have to consider that the proposed attacks primarily focus on the boundaries of the images. Therefore, they do not typically overlap with useful information since, in the datasets that we used, the subject is centered. Therefore, by hitting the perimeter or

---

Algorithm 34: *Dash Attack* Methodology.

Input: an event-based dataset D made of $(C \times N \times N \times T)$ tensors, where C represents the number of channels, N the size, and T the duration of the sample; S is a list of the samples that compose D

Output: perturbed dataset

1 $x_{min} = 0$;
2 $x = 0$;
3 $y = 2$;
4 $left = True$;
5 **while** S *is not empty* **do**
6   **for** s *in* S **do**
7   **for** i *in range(N)* **do**
8   **for** j *in range(N)* **do**
9   **if** $i == x$ **and** $(left$ **and** $(j == y$ **or** $j == y - 1)$ **or** $\overline{left}$ **and** $(j == N - y$ **or** $j == N - y + 1))$ **then**
10                     $s[:, i, j, :] = 1$;
11   The perturbed sample s is fed to the SNN, which produces a prediction P;
12   **if** P *is incorrect* **then**
13   Remove s from S;
14   **if** $x == x_{min}$ **then**
15         $x = N - x_{min} - 1$;
16   **else**
17         $left = left$ **xor** 1;
18         $x = x_{min}$;
19   **if** $\overline{left}$ **then**
20             $y = y + 1$;
21   **if** $y > N/2$ **then**
22         $x_{min} = x_{min} + 1$;

---

the corners, there is a low risk of superimposing adversarial noise on the main subject. These considerations explain why the *MF* is successful in restoring the original SNN accuracy. The targeted pixel coordinates are easily identifiable given their large number of events, and the filter does not interfere with the useful information because modifications are mainly made at the edge of the image.

Based on these observations, we have designed an attack that aims to nullify the defense provided by the *MF*, which we call the *MF-Aware Dash Attack*. It receives as input the parameter *th*, which is related to the T parameter of the *MF* (recall from Algorithm 30), and limits the number of frames that can be modified for each pixel (line 11 of Algorithm 35). Therefore, the algorithm perturbs only a couple of pixels, as in the case of the *Dash Attack*. However, after perturbing *th* frames, it proceeds to the following frames (lines 13–14). The *MF-Aware Dash Attack* generates the visual effect of a dash advancing along a line. The larger the parameter th is, the slower the dash will seem to move along the image.

Algorithm 35: *MF-Aware Dash Attack* Methodology.

Input: an event-based dataset D made of $(C \times N \times N \times T)$ tensors, where C represents the number of channels, N the size, and T the duration of the sample; S is a list of the samples that compose D; th is a parameter associated with the activity threshold of the *MF*

Output: perturbed dataset

1 $x = 0$;
2 $y_0 = 2$;
3 $th_0 = 10$;
4 $left = True$;
5 **while** S *is not empty* **do**
6   **for** s *in* S **do**
7      $th = th_0, y = y_0$;
8   **for** t *in* T **do**
9   **for** i *in range(N)* **do**
10   **for** j *in range(N)* **do**
11   **if** $i == x$ **and** $t < th$ **and** (*left* **and** ($j == y$ **or** $j == y - 1$) **or** $\overline{left}$ **and** ($j == N - y$ **or** $j == N - y + 1$)) **then**
12              $s[0, i, j, t] = 1$;
13   **if** $t == th$ **then**
14          $th = th + th_0$, $y = y + 2$;
15   The perturbed sample s is fed to the SNN, which produces a prediction P;
16   **if** P *is incorrect* **then**
17   Remove s from S;
18   **if** $x == 0$ **then**
19      $x = N - 1$;
20   **else**
21      $left = left$ **xor** 1 , $x = 0$;
22   **if** $\overline{left}$ **then**
23        $y_0 = y_0 + 1$;

7.5.6 Evaluation of the DVS-Attacks

7.5.6.1 Experimental Setup

We conduct experiments on two datasets, the DvsGesture [8] and the NMNIST [193]. As classifier for the DvsGesture dataset, we employ the 4-layer SNN as described in [248], with two Conv layers and two FC layers, trained for 625 epochs using the SLAYER backpropagation method [248], with a batch size of 4 and a learning rate of 0.01. We measure a test accuracy of 92.04% on the clean dataset. As a classifier for the NMNIST dataset, we implement a multilayer perceptron with two FC layers [248], trained for 350 epochs using the SLAYER backpropagation method [248], with a batch size of 4 and a learning rate of 0.01. The test accuracy is 95% on the clean dataset. We implement the SNNs using the PyTorch framework [204] on a DL-workstation with two Nvidia GeForce RTX 2080 Ti GPUs. We also implement the adversarial attack algorithms and the noise filters using PyTorch.

7.5.6.2 Results for the Sparse Attack

The *Sparse Attack* on DVS frames successfully fools the SNNs on both benchmarks since the accuracy is significantly decreased to 15.15% for the DvsGesture dataset and 4% for the NMNIST dataset. By looking at the adversarial examples reported on the left side of Figure 7.29, no significant perturbations are visible, thus making the *Sparse Attack* stealthy. However, the accuracy may be easily restored using a noise filter. When the *BAF* filter is applied, for a wide range of values of the (s, t) parameters, the SNNs' accuracy exceeds 90% (as highlighted in Figure 7.29). The *Sparse Attack* can easily bypass the *MF* with low T. On the contrary, high robustness is achieved when $T \geq 50$ for the DvsGesture dataset and when $T \geq 25$ for the NMNIST dataset.

7.5.6.3 Results for the Frame Attack

The experimental results of the *Frame Attack* are reported in Figure 7.30. As expected, the perturbations are perceivable as a line added to the border of the scene.

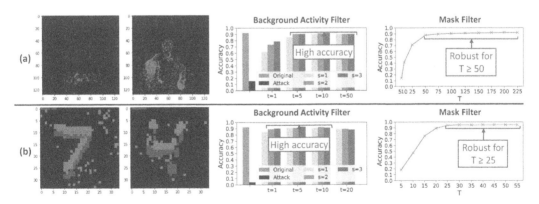

Figure 7.29: Evaluation of the *Sparse Attack*: frame samples and accuracy when the *BAF* and *MF* are applied, for **(a)** DvsGesture and **(b)** NMNIST.

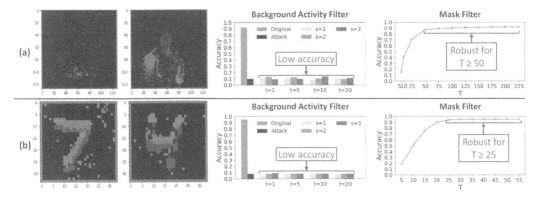

Figure 7.30: Evaluation of the *Frame Attack*: frame samples and accuracy when the *BAF* and *MF* are applied, for **(a)** DvsGesture and **(b)** NMNIST.

This feature is more accentuated on the NMNIST dataset, in which the resolution is 34×34 pixels. On the other hand, the perturbations are less perceivable on the 128×128 examples of the DvsGesture dataset. The accuracy drops to 9.85% and 8% under the *Frame Attack* for the two datasets, respectively. However, the *BAF* does not protect well as a defense against the *Frame Attack*. As highlighted in Figure 7.30, there exist no values of the (s, t) parameters of the *BAF* for which the SNNs' accuracy is almost restored. Indeed, the accuracy variation compared to the attack without the filter is relatively low. On the other hand, the *MF* stands out as a successful defense since the SNNs' accuracy values are high for large values of T.

7.5.6.4 *Results for the Corner Attack*

The *Corner Attack* is visibly stealthier than the *Frame Attack*. Indeed, the perturbations are only added to the corner of the images. For instance, the perturbation is noticeable at the top-left corner of the first example or the bottom-left corner of the second example of Figure 7.31b. Moreover, the SNNs are entirely fooled by the *Corner Attack*, since the accuracy without filter drops to 0%. The *BAF* works relatively better for the DvsGesture dataset than the MNIST dataset. However, the accuracy remains low in the presence of the *BAF* filter as a defense. The peak of only 15.15% accuracy for the SNN on the DvsGesture dataset is reached with $s = 1$ and $t = 5$, as highlighted in Figure 7.31a. Similarly to the *Frame Attack*, the *Corner Attack* can also be successfully mitigated when the *MF* with a large T is applied.

7.5.6.5 *Results for the Dash Attack*

The *Dash Attack* performs similar to the *Corner Attack*, but the perturbations are not strictly confined to a corner. In this way, the perturbations injected by the attack are very similar to the inherent background activity noise generated by the DVS camera capturing the events. For instance, the attack perturbations injected into the examples for the NMNIST dataset (see Figure 7.32b) might be confused with the background noise. Compared to the *Corner Attack*, while the SNNs' accuracy under

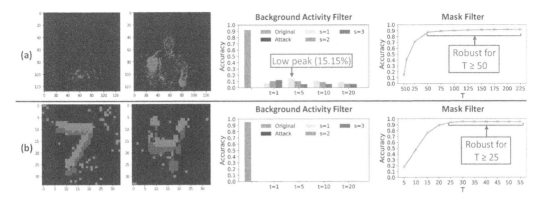

Figure 7.31: Evaluation of the *Corner Attack*: frame samples and accuracy when the *BAF* and *MF* are applied, for (**a**) DvsGesture and (**b**) NMNIST.

the *Dash Attack* without filter drops to 0%, the *BAF* defense produces a slightly higher accuracy for the DvsGesture dataset. However, the accuracy peak of 28.41% (highlighted in Figure 7.32a), obtained in the presence of the *BAF* with $s = 1$ and $t = 10$, is too low to consider the *BAF* as a suitable defense method against the *Dash Attack*. Once again, a robust defense for SNNs is guaranteed by the *MF* with large T.

7.5.6.6 *Results for the MF-Aware Dash Attack*

Figure 7.33 evaluates the experiments conducted on the *MF-Aware Dash Attack*, for different values of *th*. While the perceivability of the adversarial examples is similar to that of the *Corner* and *Dash Attacks*, the behavior of the *MF-Aware Dash Attack*, when noise filters are applied, is different. Moreover, the SNN's accuracy under attack without the filter reaches 7.95% for $th = 50$ on the DvsGesture dataset. The SNNs defended by the *BAF* show a moderate robustness level. When $s = 3$ and $t = 1$, the accuracy reaches 59.09% for the DvsGesture dataset when the *MF-Aware Dash Attack*

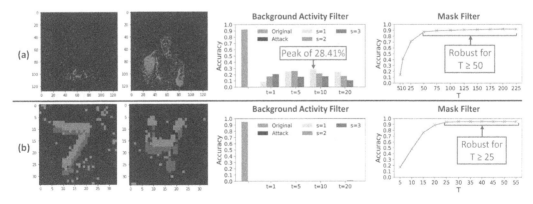

Figure 7.32: Evaluation of the *Dash Attack*: frame samples and accuracy when the *BAF* and *MF* are applied, for (**a**) DvsGesture and (**b**) NMNIST.

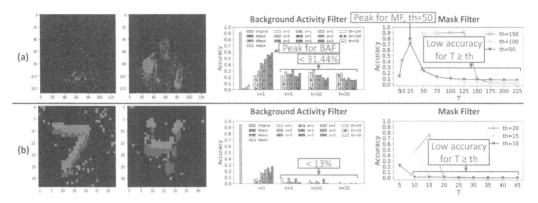

Figure 7.33: Evaluation of the *MF-Aware Dash Attack*: frame samples and accuracy when the *BAF* and *MF* are applied, for **(a)** DvsGesture and **(b)** NMNIST. The adversarial frame samples reported on the left side of the figure are generated with $th = 150$ for the DvsGesture dataset and $th = 20$ for the NMNIST dataset.

with $th = 50$ is applied. However, when $t \geq 5$, the accuracy is lower than 31.44% for the DvsGesture dataset and lower than 13% for the NMNIST dataset. The key advantage compared to the previous attacks resides in the behavior of the *MF-Aware Dash Attack* in the presence of the *MF*. If $T \geq th$, the SNN accuracy falls lower than 23.5% for the DvsGesture dataset and lower than 2% for the NMNIST dataset. On the contrary, the results when $T < th$ are similar to the behaviors obtained for the other attacks. For instance, the curve relative to the *MF-Aware Dash Attack* with $th = 50$ and $T = 25$ achieves an accuracy of 71.21% for the DvsGesture dataset, which is 20.83% lower than the clean SNN accuracy.

7.5.6.7 *Key Observations Derived from the Experiments*

By analyzing in more detail the results of the different attack methodologies, we can derive the following key observations:

- All the attack algorithms belonging to the *DVS-Attacks* set successfully fool the SNNs when no filter is applied as shown by the significant decrease in the SNNs' accuracy.

- The *Sparse Attack* is the stealthiest attack, while *Corner*, *Dash* and *MF-Aware Dash Attacks* are sthealtier than the *Frame Attack*.

- The *BAF* achieves good defense only for the *Sparse Attack*, while all the other attacks fool SNNs protected by the *BAF*. Some accuracy is recovered for the *MF-Aware Dash Attack*, but a significant accuracy loss is measured.

- Different (s, t) parameters of the *BAF* need to be evaluated to find the highest accuracy, and the combinations of these parameters leading to high accuracy may vary according to different attack algorithms.

- The *MF* with large *T* is a good defense against almost every attack, but it does not protect well against the *MF-Aware Dash Attack* since it is an adversarial attack designed explicitly to be successful in the presence of the *MF*.

- The best *MF-Aware Dash Attack*, with $th = 50$ for the DvsGesture dataset, and with $th = 10$ for the NMNIST dataset, lowers the accuracy of SNNs by more than 20% and 65% for the two datasets, respectively.

7.5.7 Summary

The proposed DVS-Attacks are a set of efficient yet stealthy adversarial attack methodologies for perturbing event sequences at the input of the SNNs. The noise filters for the DVS signals, such as the BAF and MF, can be used as defense mechanisms against adversarial attacks. The evaluations of the attacks in the presence of the filters show that the filters partially restore the SNN accuracy, but attacks specifically designed to be resistant to the filters, such as the MF-aware Dash Attack methodology, show a high attack success rate.

7.6 SUMMARY OF SECURITY THREATS FOR SNNS

This chapter has investigated several security analyses for SNNs and their comparison with DNNs. Different vulnerability threats have been investigated, including adversarial attack methodologies for discrete and event-based data and backdoor attacks that inject bit-flips. Moreover, a defense mechanism that tunes the SNNs' inherent structural parameters is leveraged to increase their robustness. Against attacks in the event-based domain, noise filters can be successfully applied. Nevertheless, specifically designed attacks show the potential to bypass such filters. This comprehensive set of analyses and studies enables advanced optimization strategies for deploying SNNs for safety-critical applications. Combining their high robustness with the low energy consumption of their implementation onto neuromorphic computing platforms, the SNNs represent promising solutions for robust and energy-efficient DL systems.

CHAPTER 8

Conclusion and Outlook

8.1 BOOK SUMMARY

DNNs have revolutionized the approach of generating high-accurate predictions for various tasks. However, they are computationally and memory intensive. Hence, their deployment on resource-constrained devices is challenging. Moreover, the current trends in the ML community demonstrated that, despite having high learning capabilities, advanced DL architectures pose even more stringent constraints due to their high complexity. In addition, DNNs suffer from various vulnerability threats that undermine their integrity and question their practical deployments in safety-critical applications.

This book tackles these challenges by exploiting the potential of energy reductions and security improvements of advanced DL systems. To enable this, *novel techniques are proposed at both the software and hardware levels*. Multi-objective techniques are employed to achieve cross-layer optimizations for energy efficiency and robustness. The high complexity of advanced DL models like CapsNets and SNNs requires dedicated designs and optimizations for energy efficiency while offering unique possibilities for enhancing their robustness.

One of the key contributions is the *complete design flow for optimizing the CapsNets' execution*. Unlike traditional DNNs, CapsNets involve more complex operations like squash and dynamic routing that execute inefficiently on standard DL accelerators. Hence, specialized designs are required to enable their efficient execution. The proposed optimization flow includes a fast training framework, hardware designs of the computation units and memory organizations, and post-training quantization and approximations. When exploring the design space, heuristic algorithms are employed to leverage the tradeoffs between energy consumption, latency, area, and memory while monitoring the accuracy. *Such an end-to-end flow of designs and set of optimizations enable the deployment of CapsNets on embedded devices with limited hardware resources.*

Various security analyses have been conducted toward the deployment of CapsNets in safety-critical applications. The robustness against affine transformations and adversarial attacks for CapsNets and DNNs has been investigated and compared. Moreover, *novel techniques for generating adversarial attacks have been proposed*. The evaluations have shown that CapsNets tend to be more robust than traditional DNNs

DOI: 10.1201/9781003530459-8

with similar sizes, while, in some cases, CapsNets also achieve higher robustness than deeper CNN models like the ResNet.

The emergence of NAS methodologies led to creating high-accurate DNNs for a given task with minimal design effort. However, high accuracy does not automatically translate into high energy efficiency or robustness. Toward this, *the proposed flow also integrates hardware efficiency and robustness as optimization objectives of the NAS algorithm.* Hence, such a multi-objective NAS shapes the DNN architectural and model parameters to leverage the tradeoffs between accuracy, robustness, and hardware efficiency when executed on specialized hardware accelerators.

SNNs represent another cutting-edge research direction for advanced ML models. They are biologically plausible models that exhibit lower power consumption than traditional DNNs when implemented on neuromorphic devices connected to DVS cameras. However, their deployment in various application domains and trustworthiness are still underexplored. Toward this, *a set of optimizations and implementations of SNNs on the Loihi neuromorphic hardware chip is devised.* Knowing the target hardware platform's specifications and resource constraints makes it possible to shape the architectural SNN models, their training rules, and the pre-processing mechanisms to implement low-latency and energy-efficient SNNs for various applications. Moreover, SNNs' vulnerability threats have been investigated. A defense mechanism that tunes the SNNs' inherent structural parameters is leveraged to increase their robustness. Noise filters represent successful defenses against attacks in the event-based domain, but specifically designed attacks can bypass such filters in specific settings. Considering that their high robustness couples with the low energy consumption of their implementation onto neuromorphic devices, *SNNs represent promising computing infrastructures for energy-efficient and robust DL systems.*

8.2 ROLE OF THE PROPOSED TECHNIQUES IN THE EVOLVING FIELD OF ML

The proposed techniques have been demonstrated to optimize the energy efficiency and robustness of advanced DL models. However, in the fast-evolving field of ML, where thousands or billions of researchers worldwide are working on similar topics, it is challenging to keep pace with recent advancements. Without the due precautions, a cutting-edge method could quickly become outdated when a new technique outperforms it or tackles the same problem from a different perspective more efficiently. To mitigate these issues and to maintain crucial roles in the evolving field of ML, our techniques have the following properties.

- *Orthogonality to other optimization techniques*: Our optimization methodologies are orthogonal to other optimization techniques. In this way, if a new method is proposed, it can be integrated into the optimization flow. An example of this property is that the quantization method is orthogonal to other compression techniques, e.g., pruning. Hence, if a new pruning methodology is proposed, it can be applied alongside our quantization method to further improve the energy efficiency.

- *Modularity*: Our frameworks are designed with modular building blocks that can be easily extended with newly introduced algorithms and techniques. For instance, our multi-objective NAS framework has modular layer descriptors. Therefore, the search space can be easily extended with new types of layers.

- *Black-box relations with the DL model*: Our techniques do not depend on the architectural model of the DNN, CapsNet, or SNN under investigation. This property allows the possibility to apply our methods to new types of DL models. For example, our proposed black-box adversarial attack methodologies can be deployed for the new DL models proposed in the literature and adapted for different applications and datasets.

- *Open-source*: Our frameworks are publicly available in online repositories. This allows other researchers to use our codes to reproduce the experiments and directly modify our methodologies to align them with the newest research directions.

8.3   FUTURE WORKS

The investigations, evaluations for various experiment conditions, and comparisons with relevant state-of-the-art works in this book demonstrate a dire need to mitigate energy and security-related issues for DL architectures. Moreover, the next generation computing infrastructures must support complex operations with limited resources and guarantee high robustness in various adverse conditions. The valuable contributions and outcomes of this research work open new avenues for energy-aware and cost-effective robustness for DL applications, summarized in the following list.

- **Energy-Efficiency Optimizations**
  The proposed designs have shown that advanced DNNs strongly tolerate low precision and compression techniques. However, the limit of such a tolerance remains an open research question. How much can we compress and approximate without compromising accuracy and robustness? Toward this, fine-grained pruning and quantization can push the energy consumption closer to the lower boundary.

  Another exciting research direction consists of extending the NAS framework by exploring the space of the solutions of the hardware architectural parameters and memory configurations. In this way, the optimization problem would jointly co-search the neural model and hardware architecture for extra energy savings.

  With the emergence of other classes of advanced ML models, such as Transformers, a specialized set of hardware and software optimizations for minimizing their energy consumption is required. For instance, the hardware execution support could be extended by designing specialized hardware modules that execute advanced layers and operations (e.g., attention), and extending the NAS operation to include these operations in the search space.

Moreover, the conventional computing paradigm in which logic and memory are separated entities may be quickly outscored by the emerging in-memory computing paradigm, where the computations are conducted inside specific memory cells. This strategy can significantly reduce the memory accesses and largely impact the energy efficiency of the complete system.

- **Algorithms and Applications for Event-Based Neuromorphic Computing**

  The proposed designs implemented on neuromorphic hardware have demonstrated fast performance and high energy efficiency on various tasks. On the other hand, the security analyses have highlighted their weaknesses and robustness. These results are promising for deploying event-based SNNs for safety-critical domains. However, their implementations in various applications are still unexplored and immature. All ranges of control and autonomous systems, like vehicles, robots, and drones, can benefit if they are deployed in event-based platforms.

  Another promising research direction consists of revisiting the basic functionality of SNNs, by designing more efficient neurons, synapses, and specialized spike encoding mechanisms. These types of investigations might lead to more efficient computing and learning engines that can shape the future of our everyday life.

  Moreover, the continuous learning paradigm, in which the networks' weights are progressively updated to adjust for the new input distribution, might potentially improve the SNNs' accuracy and robustness while maintaining low power consumption.

- **Robustness and Security-Oriented Optimizations**

  As demonstrated in this book, various attack threats can be envisioned. The creativity of adversary agents in creating new and efficient attack methodologies is constantly evolving. The defense techniques should rapidly adapt to mitigate against new attacks.

  Moreover, robust defenses should protect against multiple vulnerability threats without affecting the system's performance. Toward this, the robustness methodologies can be extended by including in the optimization goals not only adversarial robustness but also fault tolerance, privacy, hardware security, and other classes of protection mechanisms based on the systems' requirements.

  Another crucial area of investigation is the impact of energy-aware optimizations on DL systems' robustness. For example, investigating the impact of approximations on the systems' robustness might lead to designing specialized approximate components that enhance the robustness.

- **Further Cross-Layer Optimizations**

  While the proposed multi-objective NAS methodologies are based on evolutionary algorithms, another promising research direction for determining the architectural parameters is represented by differentiable NAS.

  Moreover, the outlook for privacy-preserving DL is shifting toward encryption and decryption mechanisms that do not reveal sensitive content. Toward this, there is a dire need for designing specialized accelerators for encrypted DL systems since their computational complexity is prohibited. The encryption property can also be included in the NAS framework for securing DL systems.

Bibliography

[1] Martín Abadi, Paul Barham, Jianmin Chen, Zhifeng Chen, Andy Davis, Jeffrey Dean, Matthieu Devin, Sanjay Ghemawat, Geoffrey Irving, Michael Isard, Manjunath Kudlur, Josh Levenberg, Rajat Monga, Sherry Moore, Derek Gordon Murray, Benoit Steiner, Paul A. Tucker, Vijay Vasudevan, Pete Warden, Martin Wicke, Yuan Yu, and Xiaoqiang Zheng. Tensorflow: A system for large-scale machine learning. In Kimberly Keeton and Timothy Roscoe, editors, *12th USENIX Symposium on Operating Systems Design and Implementation, OSDI 2016, Savannah, GA, USA, November 2-4, 2016*, pages 265–283. USENIX Association, 2016.

[2] Martín Abadi, Andy Chu, Ian J. Goodfellow, H. Brendan McMahan, Ilya Mironov, Kunal Talwar, and Li Zhang. Deep learning with differential privacy. In Edgar R. Weippl, Stefan Katzenbeisser, Christopher Kruegel, Andrew C. Myers, and Shai Halevi, editors, *Proceedings of the 2016 ACM SIGSAC Conference on Computer and Communications Security, Vienna, Austria, October 24-28, 2016*, pages 308–318. ACM, 2016.

[3] Imran Hafeez Abbassi, Faiq Khalid, Semeen Rehman, Awais Mehmood Kamboh, Axel Jantsch, Siddharth Garg, and Muhammad Shafique. Trojanzero: Switching activity-aware design of undetectable hardware trojans with zero power and area footprint. In Jürgen Teich and Franco Fummi, editors, *Design, Automation & Test in Europe Conference & Exhibition, DATE 2019, Florence, Italy, March 25-29, 2019*, pages 914–919. IEEE, 2019.

[4] Paniti Achararit, Muhammad Abdullah Hanif, Rachmad Vidya Wicaksana Putra, Muhammad Shafique, and Yuko Hara-Azumi. APNAS: accuracy-and-performance-aware neural architecture search for neural hardware accelerators. *IEEE Access*, 8:165319–165334, 2020.

[5] Michel Agoyan, Jean-Max Dutertre, Amir-Pasha Mirbaha, David Naccache, Anne-Lise Ribotta, and Assia Tria. How to flip a bit? In *16th IEEE International On-Line Testing Symposium (IOLTS 2010), 5-7 July, 2010, Corfu, Greece*, pages 235–239. IEEE Computer Society, 2010.

[6] Hassan Ali, Faiq Khalid, Hammad Tariq, Muhammad Abdullah Hanif, Rehan Ahmed, and Semeen Rehman. Sscnets: Robustifying dnns using secure selective convolutional filters. *IEEE Des. Test*, 37(2):58–65, 2020.

[7] H. Amin, K.M. Curtis, and B.R. Hayes-Gill. Piecewise linear approximation applied to nonlinear function of a neural network. *IEE Proceedings - Circuits, Devices and Systems*, 144(6):313–317, 1997.

[8] Arnon Amir, Brian Taba, David J. Berg, Timothy Melano, Jeffrey L. McKinstry, Carmelo di Nolfo, Tapan K. Nayak, Alexander Andreopoulos, Guillaume Garreau, Marcela Mendoza, Jeff Kusnitz, Michael DeBole, Steven K. Esser, Tobi Delbrück, Myron Flickner, and Dharmendra S. Modha. A low power, fully event-based gesture recognition system. In *2017 IEEE Conference on Computer Vision and Pattern Recognition, CVPR 2017, Honolulu, HI, USA, July 21-26, 2017*, pages 7388–7397. IEEE Computer Society, 2017.

[9] Kevin Bache, Dennis DeCoste, and Padhraic Smyth. Hot swapping for online adaptation of optimization hyperparameters. In Yoshua Bengio and Yann LeCun, editors, *3rd International Conference on Learning Representations, ICLR 2015, San Diego, CA, USA, May 7-9, 2015, Workshop Track Proceedings*, 2015.

[10] Alireza Bagheri, Osvaldo Simeone, and Bipin Rajendran. Adversarial training for probabilistic spiking neural networks. In *19th IEEE International Workshop on Signal Processing Advances in Wireless Communications, SPAWC 2018, Kalamata, Greece, June 25-28, 2018*, pages 1–5. IEEE, 2018.

[11] R.C. Baumann. Radiation-induced soft errors in advanced semiconductor technologies. *IEEE Transactions on Device and Materials Reliability*, 5(3):305–316, 2005.

[12] Trevor Bekolay, James Bergstra, Eric Hunsberger, Travis DeWolf, Terrence C. Stewart, Daniel Rasmussen, Feng-Xuan Choo, Aaron Voelker, and Chris Eliasmith. Nengo: a python tool for building large-scale functional brain models. *Frontiers Neuroinformatics*, 7:48, 2013.

[13] Yoshua Bengio. Learning deep architectures for AI. *Foundations and Trends in Machine Learning*, 2(1):1–127, 2009.

[14] Yoshua Bengio. Practical recommendations for gradient-based training of deep architectures. In Grégoire Montavon, Genevieve B. Orr, and Klaus-Robert Müller, editors, *Neural Networks: Tricks of the Trade - Second Edition*, volume 7700 of *Lecture Notes in Computer Science*, pages 437–478. Springer, 2012.

[15] Yoshua Bengio, Pascal Lamblin, Dan Popovici, and Hugo Larochelle. Greedy layer-wise training of deep networks. In Bernhard Schölkopf, John C. Platt, and Thomas Hofmann, editors, *Advances in Neural Information Processing Systems 19, Proceedings of the Twentieth Annual Conference on Neural Information Processing Systems, Vancouver, British Columbia, Canada, December 4-7, 2006*, pages 153–160. MIT Press, 2006.

[16] Ben Varkey Benjamin, Peiran Gao, Emmett McQuinn, Swadesh Choudhary, Anand Chandrasekaran, Jean-Marie Bussat, Rodrigo Alvarez-Icaza, John V. Arthur, Paul Merolla, and Kwabena Boahen. Neurogrid: A mixed-analog-digital multichip system for large-scale neural simulations. *Proc. IEEE*, 102(5):699–716, 2014.

[17] Alan C. Bovik, Marianna Clark, and Wilson S. Geisler. Multichannel texture analysis using localized spatial filters. *IEEE Trans. Pattern Anal. Mach. Intell.*, 12(1):55–73, 1990.

[18] Christian Brandli, Raphael Berner, Minhao Yang, Shih-Chii Liu, and Tobi Delbrück. A 240 × 180 130 db 3 μs latency global shutter spatiotemporal vision sensor. *IEEE J. Solid State Circuits*, 49(10):2333–2341, 2014.

[19] Jakub Breier, Xiaolu Hou, Dirmanto Jap, Lei Ma, Shivam Bhasin, and Yang Liu. Practical fault attack on deep neural networks. In David Lie, Mohammad Mannan, Michael Backes, and XiaoFeng Wang, editors, *Proceedings of the 2018 ACM SIGSAC Conference on Computer and Communications Security, CCS 2018, Toronto, ON, Canada, October 15-19, 2018*, pages 2204–2206. ACM, 2018.

[20] Wieland Brendel, Jonas Rauber, and Matthias Bethge. Decision-based adversarial attacks: Reliable attacks against black-box machine learning models. In the *6th International Conference on Learning Representations, ICLR 2018, Vancouver, BC, Canada, April 30—May 3, 2018, Conference Track Proceedings*. OpenReview.net, 2018.

[21] Julian Büchel, Gregor Lenz, Yalun Hu, Sadique Sheik, and Martino Sorbaro. Adversarial attacks on spiking convolutional networks for event-based vision. *CoRR*, abs/2110.02929, 2021.

[22] Maurizio Capra, Beatrice Bussolino, Alberto Marchisio, Guido Masera, Maurizio Martina, and Muhammad Shafique. Hardware and software optimizations for accelerating deep neural networks: Survey of current trends, challenges, and the road ahead. *IEEE Access*, 8:225134–225180, 2020.

[23] Maurizio Capra, Beatrice Bussolino, Alberto Marchisio, Muhammad Shafique, Guido Masera, and Maurizio Martina. An updated survey of efficient hardware architectures for accelerating deep convolutional neural networks. *Future Internet*, 12(7):113, 2020.

[24] Nicholas Carlini and David A. Wagner. Towards evaluating the robustness of neural networks. In *2017 IEEE Symposium on Security and Privacy, SP 2017, San Jose, CA, USA, May 22-26, 2017*, pages 39–57. IEEE Computer Society, 2017.

[25] M. Emre Celebi, Fatih Celiker, and Hassan A. Kingravi. On euclidean norm approximations. *Pattern Recognit.*, 44(2):278–283, 2011.

[26] Chia-Yu Chen, Jungwook Choi, Kailash Gopalakrishnan, Viji Srinivasan, and Swagath Venkataramani. Exploiting approximate computing for deep learning acceleration. In Jan Madsen and Ayse K. Coskun, editors, *2018 Design, Automation & Test in Europe Conference & Exhibition, DATE 2018, Dresden, Germany, March 19-23, 2018*, pages 821–826. IEEE, 2018.

[27] Liang-Chieh Chen, George Papandreou, Florian Schroff, and Hartwig Adam. Rethinking atrous convolution for semantic image segmentation. *CoRR*, abs/1706.05587, 2017.

[28] Shoushun Chen and Menghan Guo. Live demonstration: Celex-v: A 1m pixel multi-mode event-based sensor. In the *IEEE Conference on Computer Vision and Pattern Recognition Workshops, CVPR Workshops 2019, Long Beach, CA, USA, June 16-20, 2019*, pages 1682–1683. Computer Vision Foundation/IEEE, 2019.

[29] Yu-Hsin Chen, Joel S. Emer, and Vivienne Sze. Eyeriss: A spatial architecture for energy-efficient dataflow for convolutional neural networks. In *43rd ACM/IEEE Annual International Symposium on Computer Architecture, ISCA 2016, Seoul, South Korea, June 18-22, 2016*, pages 367–379. IEEE Computer Society, 2016.

[30] Yu-Hsin Chen, Joel S. Emer, and Vivienne Sze. Using dataflow to optimize energy efficiency of deep neural network accelerators. *IEEE Micro*, 37(3):12–21, 2017.

[31] Yu-Hsin Chen, Tien-Ju Yang, Joel S. Emer, and Vivienne Sze. Eyeriss v2: A flexible accelerator for emerging deep neural networks on mobile devices. *IEEE J. Emerg. Sel. Topics Circuits Syst.*, 9(2):292–308, 2019.

[32] Zitao Chen, Guanpeng Li, and Karthik Pattabiraman. Ranger: Boosting error resilience of deep neural networks through range restriction. *CoRR*, abs/2003.13874, 2020.

[33] Wensheng Cheng, Hao Luo, Wen Yang, Lei Yu, Shoushun Chen, and Wei Li. DET: A high-resolution DVS dataset for lane extraction. In *IEEE Conference on Computer Vision and Pattern Recognition Workshops, CVPR Workshops 2019, Long Beach, CA, USA, June 16-20, 2019*, pages 1666–1675. Computer Vision Foundation/IEEE, 2019.

[34] Sharan Chetlur, Cliff Woolley, Philippe Vandermersch, Jonathan Cohen, John Tran, Bryan Catanzaro, and Evan Shelhamer. cudnn: Efficient primitives for deep learning. *CoRR*, abs/1410.0759, 2014.

[35] Shriyash Chougule, Nora Kozonek, Asad Ismail, Ganesh Adam, Vikram Narayan, and Matthias Schulze. Reliable multilane detection and classification by utilizing CNN as a regression network. In Laura Leal-Taixé and Stefan Roth, editors, *Computer Vision - ECCV 2018 Workshops - Munich, Germany,*

September 8-14, 2018, Proceedings, Part V, volume 11133 of *Lecture Notes in Computer Science*, pages 740–752. Springer, 2018.

[36] Joseph Clements and Yingjie Lao. Hardware trojan design on neural networks. In *IEEE International Symposium on Circuits and Systems, ISCAS 2019, Sapporo, Japan, May 26-29, 2019*, pages 1–5. IEEE, 2019.

[37] Jeremy M. Cohen, Elan Rosenfeld, and J. Zico Kolter. Certified adversarial robustness via randomized smoothing. In Kamalika Chaudhuri and Ruslan Salakhutdinov, editors, *Proceedings of the 36th International Conference on Machine Learning, ICML 2019, 9-15 June 2019, Long Beach, California, USA*, volume 97 of *Proceedings of Machine Learning Research*, pages 1310–1320. PMLR, 2019.

[38] Alessio Colucci, Andreas Steininger, and Muhammad Shafique. enpheeph: A fault injection framework for spiking and compressed deep neural networks. *CoRR*, abs/2208.00328, 2022.

[39] Jonathan Cook and Vikram Ramadas. When to consult precision-recall curves. *The Stata Journal*, 20(1):131–148, 2020.

[40] Mike Davies, Narayan Srinivasa, Tsung-Han Lin, Gautham N. Chinya, Yongqiang Cao, Sri Harsha Choday, Georgios D. Dimou, Prasad Joshi, Nabil Imam, Shweta Jain, Yuyun Liao, Chit-Kwan Lin, Andrew Lines, Ruokun Liu, Deepak Mathaikutty, Steven McCoy, Arnab Paul, Jonathan Tse, Guruguhanathan Venkataramanan, Yi-Hsin Weng, Andreas Wild, Yoonseok Yang, and Hong Wang. Loihi: A neuromorphic manycore processor with on-chip learning. *IEEE Micro*, 38(1):82–99, 2018.

[41] Andrew P. Davison, Daniel Brüderle, Jochen M. Eppler, Jens Kremkow, Eilif B. Müller, Dejan Pecevski, Laurent U. Perrinet, and Pierre Yger. Pynn: a common interface for neuronal network simulators. *Frontiers Neuroinformatics*, 2:11, 2008.

[42] Kalyanmoy Deb, Samir Agrawal, Amrit Pratap, and T. Meyarivan. A fast and elitist multiobjective genetic algorithm: NSGA-II. *IEEE Trans. Evol. Comput.*, 6(2):182–197, 2002.

[43] Jia Deng, Wei Dong, Richard Socher, Li-Jia Li, Kai Li, and Li Fei-Fei. Imagenet: A large-scale hierarchical image database. In *2009 IEEE Computer Society Conference on Computer Vision and Pattern Recognition (CVPR 2009), 20-25 June 2009, Miami, Florida, USA*, pages 248–255. IEEE Computer Society, 2009.

[44] Aditya Devarakonda, Maxim Naumov, and Michael Garland. Adabatch: Adaptive batch sizes for training deep neural networks. *CoRR*, abs/1712.02029, 2017.

[45] Peter U. Diehl, Daniel Neil, Jonathan Binas, Matthew Cook, Shih-Chii Liu, and Michael Pfeiffer. Fast-classifying, high-accuracy spiking deep networks through weight and threshold balancing. In *2015 International Joint Conference on Neural Networks, IJCNN 2015, Killarney, Ireland, July 12-17, 2015*, pages 1–8. IEEE, 2015.

[46] Zidong Du, Robert Fasthuber, Tianshi Chen, Paolo Ienne, Ling Li, Tao Luo, Xiaobing Feng, Yunji Chen, and Olivier Temam. Shidiannao: shifting vision processing closer to the sensor. In Deborah T. Marr and David H. Albonesi, editors, *Proceedings of the 42nd Annual International Symposium on Computer Architecture, Portland, OR, USA, June 13-17, 2015*, pages 92–104. ACM, 2015.

[47] Rida El-Allami, Alberto Marchisio, Muhammad Shafique, and Ihsen Alouani. Securing deep spiking neural networks against adversarial attacks through inherent structural parameters. In *Design, Automation & Test in Europe Conference & Exhibition, DATE 2021, Grenoble, France, February 1-5, 2021*, pages 774–779. IEEE, 2021.

[48] Kevin Eykholt, Ivan Evtimov, Earlence Fernandes, Bo Li, Amir Rahmati, Chaowei Xiao, Atul Prakash, Tadayoshi Kohno, and Dawn Song. Robust physical-world attacks on deep learning visual classification. In *2018 IEEE Conference on Computer Vision and Pattern Recognition, CVPR 2018, Salt Lake City, UT, USA, June 18-22, 2018*, pages 1625–1634. Computer Vision Foundation/IEEE Computer Society, 2018.

[49] Reza Fani and Morteza Saheb Zamani. Runtime hardware trojan detection by reconfigurable monitoring circuits. *The Journal of Supercomputing*, 2022.

[50] Thomas Finateu, Atsumi Niwa, Daniel Matolin, Koya Tsuchimoto, Andrea Mascheroni, Etienne Reynaud, Pooria Mostafalu, Frederick T. Brady, Ludovic Chotard, Florian LeGoff, Hirotsugu Takahashi, Hayato Wakabayashi, Yusuke Oike, and Christoph Posch. 5.10 A 1280×720 back-illuminated stacked temporal contrast event-based vision sensor with $4.86\mu m$ pixels, 1.066geps readout, programmable event-rate controller and compressive data-formatting pipeline. In *2020 IEEE International Solid- State Circuits Conference, ISSCC 2020, San Francisco, CA, USA, February 16-20, 2020*, pages 112–114. IEEE, 2020.

[51] Jonathan Frankle and Michael Carbin. The lottery ticket hypothesis: Finding sparse, trainable neural networks. In *7th International Conference on Learning Representations, ICLR 2019, New Orleans, LA, USA, May 6-9, 2019*. OpenReview.net, 2019.

[52] Scott Freeman and Healy Hamilton. *Biological Science*, 2005.

[53] Charlotte Frenkel, Martin Lefebvre, Jean-Didier Legat, and David Bol. A 0.086-mm^2 12.7-pj/sop 64k-synapse 256-neuron online-learning digital spiking

neuromorphic processor in 28-nm CMOS. *IEEE Trans. Biomed. Circuits Syst.*, 13(1):145–158, 2019.

[54] Nicholas Frosst, Sara Sabour, and Geoffrey E. Hinton. DARCCC: detecting adversaries by reconstruction from class conditional capsules. *CoRR*, abs/1811.06969, 2018.

[55] Steve B. Furber, Francesco Galluppi, Steve Temple, and Luis A. Plana. The spinnaker project. *Proc. IEEE*, 102(5):652–665, 2014.

[56] Stefano Fusi, Mario Annunziato, Davide Badoni, Andrea Salamon, and Daniel J. Amit. Spike-driven synaptic plasticity: Theory, simulation, VLSI implementation. *Neural Comput.*, 12(10):2227–2258, 2000.

[57] Guillermo Gallego, Tobi Delbrück, Garrick Orchard, Chiara Bartolozzi, Brian Taba, Andrea Censi, Stefan Leutenegger, Andrew J. Davison, Jörg Conradt, Kostas Daniilidis, and Davide Scaramuzza. Event-based vision: A survey. *IEEE Trans. Pattern Anal. Mach. Intell.*, 44(1):154–180, 2022.

[58] Karan Ganju, Qi Wang, Wei Yang, Carl A. Gunter, and Nikita Borisov. Property inference attacks on fully connected neural networks using permutation invariant representations. In David Lie, Mohammad Mannan, Michael Backes, and XiaoFeng Wang, editors, *Proceedings of the 2018 ACM SIGSAC Conference on Computer and Communications Security, CCS 2018, Toronto, ON, Canada, October 15-19, 2018*, pages 619–633. ACM, 2018.

[59] Yue Gao, Weiqiang Liu, and Fabrizio Lombardi. Design and implementation of an approximate softmax layer for deep neural networks. In *IEEE International Symposium on Circuits and Systems, ISCAS 2020, Sevilla, Spain, October 10-21, 2020*, pages 1–5. IEEE, 2020.

[60] Craig Gentry. Fully homomorphic encryption using ideal lattices. In Michael Mitzenmacher, editor, *Proceedings of the 41st Annual ACM Symposium on Theory of Computing, STOC 2009, Bethesda, MD, USA, May 31 - June 2, 2009*, pages 169–178. ACM, 2009.

[61] Wulfram Gerstner and Werner M. Kistler. *Spiking Neuron Models: Single Neurons, Populations, Plasticity*. Cambridge University Press, 2002.

[62] Ran Gilad-Bachrach, Nathan Dowlin, Kim Laine, Kristin E. Lauter, Michael Naehrig, and John Wernsing. Cryptonets: Applying neural networks to encrypted data with high throughput and accuracy. In Maria-Florina Balcan and Kilian Q. Weinberger, editors, *Proceedings of the 33nd International Conference on Machine Learning, ICML 2016, New York City, NY, USA, June 19-24, 2016*, volume 48 of *JMLR Workshop and Conference Proceedings*, pages 201–210. JMLR.org, 2016.

[63] G. A. Gillani, Muhammad Abdullah Hanif, M. Krone, Sabih H. Gerez, Muhammad Shafique, and André B. J. Kokkeler. Squash: Approximate square-accumulate with self-healing. *IEEE Access*, 6:49112–49128, 2018.

[64] Tobias Glasmachers. A fast incremental BSP tree archive for non-dominated points. In Heike Trautmann, Günter Rudolph, Kathrin Klamroth, Oliver Schütze, Margaret M. Wiecek, Yaochu Jin, and Christian Grimme, editors, *Evolutionary Multi-Criterion Optimization - 9th International Conference, EMO 2017, Münster, Germany, March 19-22, 2017, Proceedings*, volume 10173 of *Lecture Notes in Computer Science*, pages 252–266. Springer, 2017.

[65] Ian J. Goodfellow, Nicolas Papernot, and Patrick D. McDaniel. cleverhans v0.1: an adversarial machine learning library. *CoRR*, abs/1610.00768, 2016.

[66] Ian J. Goodfellow, Jean Pouget-Abadie, Mehdi Mirza, Bing Xu, David Warde-Farley, Sherjil Ozair, Aaron C. Courville, and Yoshua Bengio. Generative adversarial networks. *CoRR*, abs/1406.2661, 2014.

[67] Ian J. Goodfellow, Jonathon Shlens, and Christian Szegedy. Explaining and harnessing adversarial examples. In Yoshua Bengio and Yann LeCun, editors, *3rd International Conference on Learning Representations, ICLR 2015, San Diego, CA, USA, May 7-9, 2015, Conference Track Proceedings*, 2015.

[68] Jindong Gu and Volker Tresp. Improving the robustness of capsule networks to image affine transformations. In *2020 IEEE/CVF Conference on Computer Vision and Pattern Recognition, CVPR 2020, Seattle, WA, USA, June 13-19, 2020*, pages 7283–7291. Computer Vision Foundation/IEEE, 2020.

[69] Jindong Gu, Volker Tresp, and Han Hu. Capsule network is not more robust than convolutional network. In *IEEE Conference on Computer Vision and Pattern Recognition, CVPR 2021, virtual, June 19-25, 2021*, pages 14309–14317. Computer Vision Foundation/IEEE, 2021.

[70] Jindong Gu, Baoyuan Wu, and Volker Tresp. Effective and efficient vote attack on capsule networks. In *9th International Conference on Learning Representations, ICLR 2021, Virtual Event, Austria, May 3-7, 2021*. OpenReview.net, 2021.

[71] Tianyu Gu, Kang Liu, Brendan Dolan-Gavitt, and Siddharth Garg. Badnets: Evaluating backdooring attacks on deep neural networks. *IEEE Access*, 7:47230–47244, 2019.

[72] Amira Guesmi, Ihsen Alouani, Khaled N. Khasawneh, Mouna Baklouti, Tarek Frikha, Mohamed Abid, and Nael B. Abu-Ghazaleh. Defensive approximation: securing cnns using approximate computing. In Tim Sherwood, Emery D. Berger, and Christos Kozyrakis, editors, *ASPLOS '21: 26th ACM International Conference on Architectural Support for Programming Languages and Operating Systems, Virtual Event, USA, April 19-23, 2021*, pages 990–1003. ACM, 2021.

[73] Josef Gugglberger, David Peer, and Antonio Jose Rodríguez-Sánchez. Training deep capsule networks with residual connections. In Igor Farkas, Paolo Masulli, Sebastian Otte, and Stefan Wermter, editors, *Artificial Neural Networks and Machine Learning - ICANN 2021 - 30th International Conference on Artificial Neural Networks, Bratislava, Slovakia, September 14-17, 2021, Proceedings, Part I*, volume 12891 of *Lecture Notes in Computer Science*, pages 541–552. Springer, 2021.

[74] Wenzhe Guo, Mohammed E. Fouda, Ahmed M. Eltawil, and Khaled Nabil Salama. Neural coding in spiking neural networks: A comparative study for robust neuromorphic systems. *Frontiers in Neuroscience*, 15, 2021.

[75] Suyog Gupta, Ankur Agrawal, Kailash Gopalakrishnan, and Pritish Narayanan. Deep learning with limited numerical precision. In Francis R. Bach and David M. Blei, editors, *Proceedings of the 32nd International Conference on Machine Learning, ICML 2015, Lille, France, 6-11 July 2015*, volume 37 of *JMLR Workshop and Conference Proceedings*, pages 1737–1746. JMLR.org, 2015.

[76] Rehan Hameed, Wajahat Qadeer, Megan Wachs, Omid Azizi, Alex Solomatnikov, Benjamin C. Lee, Stephen Richardson, Christos Kozyrakis, and Mark Horowitz. Understanding sources of inefficiency in general-purpose chips. In André Seznec, Uri C. Weiser, and Ronny Ronen, editors, *37th International Symposium on Computer Architecture (ISCA 2010), June 19-23, 2010, Saint-Malo, France*, pages 37–47. ACM, 2010.

[77] Song Han, Xingyu Liu, Huizi Mao, Jing Pu, Ardavan Pedram, Mark A. Horowitz, and William J. Dally. EIE: efficient inference engine on compressed deep neural network. In *43rd ACM/IEEE Annual International Symposium on Computer Architecture, ISCA 2016, Seoul, South Korea, June 18-22, 2016*, pages 243–254. IEEE Computer Society, 2016.

[78] Song Han, Huizi Mao, and William J. Dally. Deep compression: Compressing deep neural network with pruning, trained quantization and huffman coding. In Yoshua Bengio and Yann LeCun, editors, *4th International Conference on Learning Representations, ICLR 2016, San Juan, Puerto Rico, May 2-4, 2016, Conference Track Proceedings*, 2016.

[79] Song Han, Jeff Pool, John Tran, and William J. Dally. Learning both weights and connections for efficient neural network. In Corinna Cortes, Neil D. Lawrence, Daniel D. Lee, Masashi Sugiyama, and Roman Garnett, editors, *Advances in Neural Information Processing Systems 28: Annual Conference on Neural Information Processing Systems 2015, December 7-12, 2015, Montreal, Quebec, Canada*, pages 1135–1143, 2015.

[80] Muhammad Abdullah Hanif, Rehan Hafiz, and Muhammad Shafique. Error resilience analysis for systematically employing approximate computing in

convolutional neural networks. In Jan Madsen and Ayse K. Coskun, editors, *2018 Design, Automation & Test in Europe Conference & Exhibition, DATE 2018, Dresden, Germany, March 19-23, 2018*, pages 913–916. IEEE, 2018.

[81] Muhammad Abdullah Hanif, Giuseppe Maria Sarda, Alberto Marchisio, Guido Masera, Maurizio Martina, and Muhammad Shafique. Conlocnn: Exploiting correlation and non-uniform quantization for energy-efficient low-precision deep convolutional neural networks. In *2022 International Joint Conference on Neural Networks, IJCNN 2022*. IEEE, 2022.

[82] Muhammad Abdullah Hanif and Muhammad Shafique. Salvagednn: salvaging deep neural network accelerators with permanent faults through saliency-driven fault-aware mapping. *Philosophical Transactions of the Royal Society A*, 378(2164), 2020.

[83] Muhammad Abdullah Hanif and Muhammad Shafique. Dnn-life: An energy-efficient aging mitigation framework for improving the lifetime of on-chip weight memories in deep neural network hardware architectures. In *Design, Automation & Test in Europe Conference & Exhibition, DATE 2021, Grenoble, France, February 1-5, 2021*, pages 729–734. IEEE, 2021.

[84] Kaiming He, Xiangyu Zhang, Shaoqing Ren, and Jian Sun. Deep residual learning for image recognition. In *2016 IEEE Conference on Computer Vision and Pattern Recognition, CVPR 2016, Las Vegas, NV, USA, June 27-30, 2016*, pages 770–778. IEEE Computer Society, 2016.

[85] G. E. Hinton and R. R. Salakhutdinov. Reducing the dimensionality of data with neural networks. *Science*, 313(5786):504–507, 2006.

[86] Geoffrey E. Hinton, Alex Krizhevsky, and Sida D. Wang. Transforming auto-encoders. In Timo Honkela, Wlodzislaw Duch, Mark A. Girolami, and Samuel Kaski, editors, *Artificial Neural Networks and Machine Learning - ICANN 2011 - 21st International Conference on Artificial Neural Networks, Espoo, Finland, June 14-17, 2011, Proceedings, Part I*, volume 6791 of *Lecture Notes in Computer Science*, pages 44–51. Springer, 2011.

[87] Geoffrey E. Hinton, Simon Osindero, and Yee Whye Teh. A fast learning algorithm for deep belief nets. *Neural Comput.*, 18(7):1527–1554, 2006.

[88] Yaoshiang Ho and Samuel Wookey. The real-world-weight cross-entropy loss function: Modeling the costs of mislabeling. *IEEE Access*, 8:4806–4813, 2020.

[89] Le Ha Hoang, Muhammad Abdullah Hanif, and Muhammad Shafique. Ft-clipact: Resilience analysis of deep neural networks and improving their fault tolerance using clipped activation. In *2020 Design, Automation & Test in Europe Conference & Exhibition, DATE 2020, Grenoble, France, March 9-13, 2020*, pages 1241–1246. IEEE, 2020.

[90] A. L. Hodgkin and A. F. Huxley. A quantitative description of membrane current and its application to conduction and excitation in nerve. *The Journal of Physiology*, 117(4):500–544, 1952.

[91] Lasse Holmström and Petri Koistinen. Using additive noise in back-propagation training. *IEEE Trans. Neural Networks*, 3(1):24–38, 1992.

[92] Sebastian Houben, Johannes Stallkamp, Jan Salmen, Marc Schlipsing, and Christian Igel. Detection of traffic signs in real-world images: The german traffic sign detection benchmark. In *The 2013 International Joint Conference on Neural Networks, IJCNN 2013, Dallas, TX, USA, August 4-9, 2013*, pages 1–8. IEEE, 2013.

[93] Andrew G. Howard, Menglong Zhu, Bo Chen, Dmitry Kalenichenko, Weijun Wang, Tobias Weyand, Marco Andreetto, and Hartwig Adam. Mobilenets: Efficient convolutional neural networks for mobile vision applications. *CoRR*, abs/1704.04861, 2017.

[94] Sergey Ioffe and Christian Szegedy. Batch normalization: Accelerating deep network training by reducing internal covariate shift. In Francis Bach and David Blei, editors, *Proceedings of the 32nd International Conference on Machine Learning*, volume 37 of *Proceedings of Machine Learning Research*, pages 448–456, Lille, France, 07–09 Jul 2015. PMLR.

[95] Eugene M. Izhikevich. Simple model of spiking neurons. *IEEE Trans. Neural Networks*, 14(6):1569–1572, 2003.

[96] Benoit Jacob, Skirmantas Kligys, Bo Chen, Menglong Zhu, Matthew Tang, Andrew G. Howard, Hartwig Adam, and Dmitry Kalenichenko. Quantization and training of neural networks for efficient integer-arithmetic-only inference. In *2018 IEEE Conference on Computer Vision and Pattern Recognition, CVPR 2018, Salt Lake City, UT, USA, June 18-22, 2018*, pages 2704–2713. Computer Vision Foundation / IEEE Computer Society, 2018.

[97] Shruti Jadon. A survey of loss functions for semantic segmentation. In *IEEE Conference on Computational Intelligence in Bioinformatics and Computational Biology, CIBCB 2020, Viña del Mar, Chile, October 27-29, 2020*, pages 1–7. IEEE, 2020.

[98] Weiwen Jiang, Lei Yang, Sakyasingha Dasgupta, Jingtong Hu, and Yiyu Shi. Standing on the shoulders of giants: Hardware and neural architecture co-search with hot start. *IEEE Trans. Comput. Aided Des. Integr. Circuits Syst.*, 39(11):4154–4165, 2020.

[99] Jianhao Jiao, Huaiyang Huang, Liang Li, Zhijian He, Yilong Zhu, and Ming Liu. Comparing representations in tracking for event camera-based SLAM. In *IEEE Conference on Computer Vision and Pattern Recognition Workshops, CVPR Workshops 2021, virtual, June 19-25, 2021*, pages 1369–1376. Computer Vision Foundation/IEEE, 2021.

[100] Norman P. Jouppi, Cliff Young, Nishant Patil, David A. Patterson, Gaurav Agrawal, Raminder Bajwa, Sarah Bates, Suresh Bhatia, Nan Boden, Al Borchers, Rick Boyle, Pierre-luc Cantin, Clifford Chao, Chris Clark, Jeremy Coriell, Mike Daley, Matt Dau, Jeffrey Dean, Ben Gelb, Tara Vazir Ghaemmaghami, Rajendra Gottipati, William Gulland, Robert Hagmann, C. Richard Ho, Doug Hogberg, John Hu, Robert Hundt, Dan Hurt, Julian Ibarz, Aaron Jaffey, Alek Jaworski, Alexander Kaplan, Harshit Khaitan, Daniel Killebrew, Andy Koch, Naveen Kumar, Steve Lacy, James Laudon, James Law, Diemthu Le, Chris Leary, Zhuyuan Liu, Kyle Lucke, Alan Lundin, Gordon MacKean, Adriana Maggiore, Maire Mahony, Kieran Miller, Rahul Nagarajan, Ravi Narayanaswami, Ray Ni, Kathy Nix, Thomas Norrie, Mark Omernick, Narayana Penukonda, Andy Phelps, Jonathan Ross, Matt Ross, Amir Salek, Emad Samadiani, Chris Severn, Gregory Sizikov, Matthew Snelham, Jed Souter, Dan Steinberg, Andy Swing, Mercedes Tan, Gregory Thorson, Bo Tian, Horia Toma, Erick Tuttle, Vijay Vasudevan, Richard Walter, Walter Wang, Eric Wilcox, and Doe Hyun Yoon. In-datacenter performance analysis of a tensor processing unit. In *Proceedings of the 44th Annual International Symposium on Computer Architecture, ISCA 2017, Toronto, ON, Canada, June 24-28, 2017*, pages 1–12. ACM, 2017.

[101] Chiraag Juvekar, Vinod Vaikuntanathan, and Anantha P. Chandrakasan. GAZELLE: A low latency framework for secure neural network inference. In William Enck and Adrienne Porter Felt, editors, *27th USENIX Security Symposium, USENIX Security 2018, Baltimore, MD, USA, August 15-17, 2018*, pages 1651–1669. USENIX Association, 2018.

[102] Jacques Kaiser, Alexander Friedrich, Juan Camilo Vasquez Tieck, Daniel Reichard, Arne Roennau, Emre Neftci, and Rüdiger Dillmann. Embodied event-driven random backpropagation. *CoRR*, abs/1904.04805, 2019.

[103] Kunhyuk Kang, Saakshi Gangwal, Sang Phill Park, and Kaushik Roy. NBTI induced performance degradation in logic and memory circuits: how effectively can we approach a reliability solution? In Chong-Min Kyung, Kiyoung Choi, and Soonhoi Ha, editors, *Proceedings of the 13th Asia South Pacific Design Automation Conference, ASP-DAC 2008, Seoul, Korea, January 21-24, 2008*, pages 726–731. IEEE, 2008.

[104] Faiq Khalid, Hassan Ali, Muhammad Abdullah Hanif, Semeen Rehman, Rehan Ahmed, and Muhammad Shafique. Fadec: A fast decision-based attack for adversarial machine learning. In *2020 International Joint Conference on Neural Networks, IJCNN 2020, Glasgow, United Kingdom, July 19-24, 2020*, pages 1–8. IEEE, 2020.

[105] Faiq Khalid, Hassan Ali, Hammad Tariq, Muhammad Abdullah Hanif, Semeen Rehman, Rehan Ahmed, and Muhammad Shafique. Qusecnets: Quantization-based defense mechanism for securing deep neural network against adversarial attacks. In Dimitris Gizopoulos, Dan Alexandrescu, Panagiota Papavramidou,

and Michail Maniatakos, editors, *25th IEEE International Symposium on On-Line Testing and Robust System Design, IOLTS 2019, Rhodes, Greece, July 1-3, 2019*, pages 182–187. IEEE, 2019.

[106] Jihun Kim and Minho Lee. Robust lane detection based on convolutional neural network and random sample consensus. In Chu Kiong Loo, Keem Siah Yap, Kok Wai Wong, Andrew Teoh Beng Jin, and Kaizhu Huang, editors, *Neural Information Processing - 21st International Conference, ICONIP 2014, Kuching, Malaysia, November 3-6, 2014. Proceedings, Part I*, volume 8834 of *Lecture Notes in Computer Science*, pages 454–461. Springer, 2014.

[107] Yoongu Kim, Ross Daly, Jeremie S. Kim, Chris Fallin, Ji-Hye Lee, Donghyuk Lee, Chris Wilkerson, Konrad Lai, and Onur Mutlu. Flipping bits in memory without accessing them: An experimental study of DRAM disturbance errors. In *ACM/IEEE 41st International Symposium on Computer Architecture, ISCA 2014, Minneapolis, MN, USA, June 14-18, 2014*, pages 361–372. IEEE Computer Society, 2014.

[108] Youngeun Kim, Hyoungseob Park, Abhishek Moitra, Abhiroop Bhattacharjee, Yeshwanth Venkatesha, and Priyadarshini Panda. Rate coding or direct coding: Which one is better for accurate, robust, and energy-efficient spiking neural networks? In *IEEE International Conference on Acoustics, Speech and Signal Processing, ICASSP 2022, Virtual and Singapore, 23-27 May 2022*, pages 71–75. IEEE, 2022.

[109] Youngeun Kim, Yeshwanth Venkatesha, and Priyadarshini Panda. Privatesnn: Privacy-preserving spiking neural networks. In *Thirty-Sixth AAAI Conference on Artificial Intelligence, AAAI 2022, Thirty-Fourth Conference on Innovative Applications of Artificial Intelligence, IAAI 2022, The Twelveth Symposium on Educational Advances in Artificial Intelligence, EAAI 2022 Virtual Event, February 22–March 1, 2022*, pages 1192–1200. AAAI Press, 2022.

[110] Diederik P. Kingma and Jimmy Ba. Adam: A method for stochastic optimization. In Yoshua Bengio and Yann LeCun, editors, *3rd International Conference on Learning Representations, ICLR 2015, San Diego, CA, USA, May 7-9, 2015, Conference Track Proceedings*, 2015.

[111] Sarada Krithivasan, Sanchari Sen, Nitin Rathi, Kaushik Roy, and Anand Raghunathan. Efficiency attacks on spiking neural networks. In Rob Oshana, editor, *DAC '22: 59th ACM/IEEE Design Automation Conference, San Francisco, California, USA, July 10-14, 2022*, pages 373–378. ACM, 2022.

[112] Alex Krizhevsky, Vinod Nair, and Geoffrey Hinton. Cifar-10 (canadian institute for advanced research). 2009.

[113] Alex Krizhevsky, Ilya Sutskever, and Geoffrey E. Hinton. Imagenet classification with deep convolutional neural networks. In Peter L. Bartlett, Fernando C. N. Pereira, Christopher J. C. Burges, Léon Bottou, and Kilian Q.

Weinberger, editors, *Advances in Neural Information Processing Systems 25: 26th Annual Conference on Neural Information Processing Systems 2012. Proceedings of a meeting held December 3-6, 2012, Lake Tahoe, Nevada, United States*, pages 1106–1114, 2012.

[114] Souvik Kundu, Massoud Pedram, and Peter A. Beerel. HIRE-SNN: harnessing the inherent robustness of energy-efficient deep spiking neural networks by training with crafted input noise. In *2021 IEEE/CVF International Conference on Computer Vision, ICCV 2021, Montreal, QC, Canada, October 10-17, 2021*, pages 5189–5198. IEEE, 2021.

[115] Alexey Kurakin, Ian J. Goodfellow, and Samy Bengio. Adversarial examples in the physical world. In *5th International Conference on Learning Representations, ICLR 2017, Toulon, France, April 24-26, 2017, Workshop Track Proceedings*. OpenReview.net, 2017.

[116] Hyoukjun Kwon, Ananda Samajdar, and Tushar Krishna. MAERI: enabling flexible dataflow mapping over DNN accelerators via reconfigurable interconnects. In Xipeng Shen, James Tuck, Ricardo Bianchini, and Vivek Sarkar, editors, *Proceedings of the Twenty-Third International Conference on Architectural Support for Programming Languages and Operating Systems, ASPLOS 2018, Williamsburg, VA, USA, March 24-28, 2018*, pages 461–475. ACM, 2018.

[117] Xavier Lagorce, Garrick Orchard, Francesco Galluppi, Bertram E. Shi, and Ryad Benosman. HOTS: A hierarchy of event-based time-surfaces for pattern recognition. *IEEE Trans. Pattern Anal. Mach. Intell.*, 39(7):1346–1359, 2017.

[118] Yann Lecun, Leon Bottou, Y. Bengio, and Patrick Haffner. Gradient-based learning applied to document recognition. *Proceedings of the IEEE*, 86:2278 – 2324, 12 1998.

[119] Seokju Lee, Junsik Kim, Jae Shin Yoon, Seunghak Shin, Oleksandr Bailo, Namil Kim, Tae-Hee Lee, Hyun Seok Hong, Seung-Hoon Han, and In So Kweon. Vpgnet: Vanishing point guided network for lane and road marking detection and recognition. In *IEEE International Conference on Computer Vision, ICCV 2017, Venice, Italy, October 22-29, 2017*, pages 1965–1973. IEEE Computer Society, 2017.

[120] Wooju Lee and Hyun Myung. Adversarial attack for asynchronous event-based data. In *Thirty-Sixth AAAI Conference on Artificial Intelligence, AAAI 2022, Thirty-Fourth Conference on Innovative Applications of Artificial Intelligence, IAAI 2022, The Twelveth Symposium on Educational Advances in Artificial Intelligence, EAAI 2022 Virtual Event, February 22 - March 1, 2022*, pages 1237–1244. AAAI Press, 2022.

[121] Gilbert N. Lewis, Nancy J. Boynton, and F. Warren Burton. Expected complexity of fast search with uniformly distributed data. *Information Processing Letters*, 13(1):4–7, 1981.

[122] Haitong Li, Mudit Bhargava, Paul N. Whatmough, and H.-S. Philip Wong. On-chip memory technology design space explorations for mobile deep neural network accelerators. In *Proceedings of the 56th Annual Design Automation Conference 2019, DAC 2019, Las Vegas, NV, USA, June 02-06, 2019*, page 131. ACM, 2019.

[123] Jingtao Li, Adnan Siraj Rakin, Yan Xiong, Liangliang Chang, Zhezhi He, Deliang Fan, and Chaitali Chakrabarti. Defending bit-flip attack through DNN weight reconstruction. In *57th ACM/IEEE Design Automation Conference, DAC 2020, San Francisco, CA, USA, July 20-24, 2020*, pages 1–6. IEEE, 2020.

[124] Sheng Li, Ke Chen, Jung Ho Ahn, Jay B. Brockman, and Norman P. Jouppi. CACTI-P: architecture-level modeling for sram-based structures with advanced leakage reduction techniques. In Joel R. Phillips, Alan J. Hu, and Helmut Graeb, editors, *2011 IEEE/ACM International Conference on Computer-Aided Design, ICCAD 2011, San Jose, California, USA, November 7-10, 2011*, pages 694–701. IEEE Computer Society, 2011.

[125] Bin Liang, Hongcheng Li, Miaoqiang Su, Xirong Li, Wenchang Shi, and Xiaofeng Wang. Detecting adversarial image examples in deep neural networks with adaptive noise reduction. *IEEE Transactions on Dependable and Secure Computing*, 18(1):72–85, 2021.

[126] Ling Liang, Xing Hu, Lei Deng, Yujie Wu, Guoqi Li, Yufei Ding, Peng Li, and Yuan Xie. Exploring adversarial attack in spiking neural networks with spike-compatible gradient. *CoRR*, abs/2001.01587, 2020.

[127] Ling Liang, Kaidi Xu, Xing Hu, Lei Deng, and Yuan Xie. Toward robust spiking neural network against adversarial perturbation. *CoRR*, abs/2205.01625, 2022.

[128] Patrick Lichtsteiner, Christoph Posch, and Tobi Delbrück. A 128×128 120 db 15 μs latency asynchronous temporal contrast vision sensor. *IEEE Journal of Solid-State Circuits*, 43(2):566–576, 2008.

[129] Chit-Kwan Lin, Andreas Wild, Gautham N. Chinya, Yongqiang Cao, Mike Davies, Daniel M. Lavery, and Hong Wang. Programming spiking neural networks on intel's loihi. *Computer*, 51(3):52–61, 2018.

[130] Chit-Kwan Lin, Andreas Wild, Gautham N. Chinya, Tsung-Han Lin, Mike Davies, and Hong Wang. Mapping spiking neural networks onto a manycore neuromorphic architecture. In Jeffrey S. Foster and Dan Grossman, editors, *Proceedings of the 39th ACM SIGPLAN Conference on Programming Language Design and Implementation, PLDI 2018, Philadelphia, PA, USA, June 18-22, 2018*, pages 78–89. ACM, 2018.

[131] Guosheng Lin, Anton Milan, Chunhua Shen, and Ian D. Reid. Refinenet: Multi-path refinement networks for high-resolution semantic segmentation. In *2017 IEEE Conference on Computer Vision and Pattern Recognition, CVPR*

2017, Honolulu, HI, USA, July 21-26, 2017, pages 5168–5177. IEEE Computer Society, 2017.

[132] Ji Lin, Chuang Gan, and Song Han. Defensive quantization: When efficiency meets robustness. In *7th International Conference on Learning Representations, ICLR 2019, New Orleans, LA, USA, May 6-9, 2019*. OpenReview.net, 2019.

[133] Alejandro Linares-Barranco, Fernando Perez-Peña, Diederik Paul Moeys, Francisco Gomez-Rodriguez, Gabriel Jiménez-Moreno, Shih-Chii Liu, and Tobi Delbrück. Low latency event-based filtering and feature extraction for dynamic vision sensors in real-time FPGA applications. *IEEE Access*, 7:134926–134942, 2019.

[134] Chen Liu, Guillaume Bellec, Bernhard Vogginger, David Kappel, Johannes Partzsch, Felix Neumärker, Sebastian Höppner, Wolfgang Maass, Steve B. Furber, Robert Legenstein, and Christian G. Mayr. Memory-efficient deep learning on a spinnaker 2 prototype. *Frontiers in Neuroscience*, 12, 2018.

[135] Jian Liu, Mika Juuti, Yao Lu, and N. Asokan. Oblivious neural network predictions via minionn transformations. In Bhavani M. Thuraisingham, David Evans, Tal Malkin, and Dongyan Xu, editors, *Proceedings of the 2017 ACM SIGSAC Conference on Computer and Communications Security, CCS 2017, Dallas, TX, USA, October 30–November 03, 2017*, pages 619–631. ACM, 2017.

[136] Kang Liu, Brendan Dolan-Gavitt, and Siddharth Garg. Fine-pruning: Defending against backdooring attacks on deep neural networks. In Michael Bailey, Thorsten Holz, Manolis Stamatogiannakis, and Sotiris Ioannidis, editors, *Research in Attacks, Intrusions, and Defenses - 21st International Symposium, RAID 2018, Heraklion, Crete, Greece, September 10-12, 2018, Proceedings*, volume 11050 of *Lecture Notes in Computer Science*, pages 273–294. Springer, 2018.

[137] Ximeng Liu, Robert H. Deng, Pengfei Wu, and Yang Yang. Lightning-fast and privacy-preserving outsourced computation in the cloud. *Cybersecurity*, 3(1):17, 2020.

[138] Yannan Liu, Lingxiao Wei, Bo Luo, and Qiang Xu. Fault injection attack on deep neural network. In Sri Parameswaran, editor, *2017 IEEE/ACM International Conference on Computer-Aided Design, ICCAD 2017, Irvine, CA, USA, November 13-16, 2017*, pages 131–138. IEEE, 2017.

[139] Yingqi Liu, Shiqing Ma, Yousra Aafer, Wen-Chuan Lee, Juan Zhai, Weihang Wang, and Xiangyu Zhang. Trojaning attack on neural networks. In *25th Annual Network and Distributed System Security Symposium, NDSS 2018, San Diego, California, USA, February 18-21, 2018*. The Internet Society, 2018.

[140] Jonathan Long, Evan Shelhamer, and Trevor Darrell. Fully convolutional networks for semantic segmentation. In *IEEE Conference on Computer Vision*

and Pattern Recognition, CVPR 2015, Boston, MA, USA, June 7-12, 2015, pages 3431–3440. IEEE Computer Society, 2015.

[141] Ilya Loshchilov and Frank Hutter. SGDR: stochastic gradient descent with warm restarts. In *5th International Conference on Learning Representations, ICLR 2017, Toulon, France, April 24-26, 2017, Conference Track Proceedings*. OpenReview.net, 2017.

[142] Ilya Loshchilov and Frank Hutter. Decoupled weight decay regularization. In *7th International Conference on Learning Representations, ICLR 2019, New Orleans, LA, USA, May 6-9, 2019*. OpenReview.net, 2019.

[143] Sheng Lu, Zhaojie Luo, Feng Gao, Mingjie Liu, KyungHi Chang, and Chang Hao Piao. A fast and robust lane detection method based on semantic segmentation and optical flow estimation. *Sensors*, 21(2):400, 2021.

[144] Wenyan Lu, Guihai Yan, Jiajun Li, Shijun Gong, Yinhe Han, and Xiaowei Li. Flexflow: A flexible dataflow accelerator architecture for convolutional neural networks. In *2017 IEEE International Symposium on High Performance Computer Architecture, HPCA 2017, Austin, TX, USA, February 4-8, 2017*, pages 553–564. IEEE Computer Society, 2017.

[145] Bo Luo, Yannan Liu, Lingxiao Wei, and Qiang Xu. Towards imperceptible and robust adversarial example attacks against neural networks. In Sheila A. McIlraith and Kilian Q. Weinberger, editors, *Proceedings of the Thirty-Second AAAI Conference on Artificial Intelligence, (AAAI-18), the 30th innovative Applications of Artificial Intelligence (IAAI-18), and the 8th AAAI Symposium on Educational Advances in Artificial Intelligence (EAAI-18), New Orleans, Louisiana, USA, February 2-7, 2018*, pages 1652–1659. AAAI Press, 2018.

[146] Robert E. Lyons and Wouter Vanderkulk. The use of triple-modular redundancy to improve computer reliability. *IBM Journal of Research and Development*, 6(2):200–209, 1962.

[147] Wolfgang Maass. Networks of spiking neurons: The third generation of neural network models. *Neural Networks*, 10(9):1659–1671, 1997.

[148] Aleksander Madry, Aleksandar Makelov, Ludwig Schmidt, Dimitris Tsipras, and Adrian Vladu. Towards deep learning models resistant to adversarial attacks. In *6th International Conference on Learning Representations, ICLR 2018, Vancouver, BC, Canada, April 30–May 3, 2018, Conference Track Proceedings*. OpenReview.net, 2018.

[149] Alberto Marchisio, Beatrice Bussolino, Alessio Colucci, Muhammad Abdullah Hanif, Maurizio Martina, Guido Masera, and Muhammad Shafique. Fastrcaps: An integrated framework for fast yet accurate training of capsule networks. In *2020 International Joint Conference on Neural Networks, IJCNN 2020, Glasgow, United Kingdom, July 19-24, 2020*, pages 1–8. IEEE, 2020.

[150] Alberto Marchisio, Beatrice Bussolino, Alessio Colucci, Maurizio Martina, Guido Masera, and Muhammad Shafique. Q-capsnets: A specialized framework for quantizing capsule networks. In *57th ACM/IEEE Design Automation Conference, DAC 2020, San Francisco, CA, USA, July 20-24, 2020*, pages 1–6. IEEE, 2020.

[151] Alberto Marchisio, Beatrice Bussolino, Edoardo Salvati, Maurizio Martina, Guido Masera, and Muhammad Shafique. Enabling capsule networks at the edge through approximate softmax and squash operations. In Hai Helen Li, Charles Augustine, Ayse Kivilcim Coskun, and Swaroop Ghosh, editors, *ISLPED '22: ACM/IEEE International Symposium on Low Power Electronics and Design, Boston, MA, USA, August 1-3, 2022*, pages 27:1–27:6. ACM, 2022.

[152] Alberto Marchisio, Giovanni Caramia, Maurizio Martina, and Muhammad Shafique. fakeweather: Adversarial attacks for deep neural networks emulating weather conditions on the camera lens of autonomous systems. In *International Joint Conference on Neural Networks, IJCNN 2022, Padua, Italy, July 18-23, 2022*, pages 1–9. IEEE, 2022.

[153] Alberto Marchisio, Antonio De Marco, Alessio Colucci, Maurizio Martina, and Muhammad Shafique. RobCaps: Evaluating the Robustness of Capsule Networks against Affine Transformations and Adversarial Attacks. In *International Joint Conference on Neural Networks (IJCNN)*, 2023.

[154] Alberto Marchisio, Muhammad Abdullah Hanif, Maurizio Martina, and Muhammad Shafique. Prunet: Class-blind pruning method for deep neural networks. In *2018 International Joint Conference on Neural Networks, IJCNN 2018, Rio de Janeiro, Brazil, July 8-13, 2018*, pages 1–8. IEEE, 2018.

[155] Alberto Marchisio, Muhammad Abdullah Hanif, and Muhammad Shafique. Capsacc: An efficient hardware accelerator for capsulenets with data reuse. In Jürgen Teich and Franco Fummi, editors, *Design, Automation & Test in Europe Conference & Exhibition, DATE 2019, Florence, Italy, March 25-29, 2019*, pages 964–967. IEEE, 2019.

[156] Alberto Marchisio, Andrea Massa, Vojtech Mrazek, Beatrice Bussolino, Maurizio Martina, and Muhammad Shafique. Nascaps: A framework for neural architecture search to optimize the accuracy and hardware efficiency of convolutional capsule networks. In *IEEE/ACM International Conference On Computer Aided Design, ICCAD 2020, San Diego, CA, USA, November 2-5, 2020*, pages 114:1–114:9. IEEE, 2020.

[157] Alberto Marchisio, Vojtech Mrazek, Muhammad Abdullah Hanif, and Muhammad Shafique. Red-cane: A systematic methodology for resilience analysis and design of capsule networks under approximations. In *2020 Design, Automation & Test in Europe Conference & Exhibition, DATE 2020, Grenoble, France, March 9-13, 2020*, pages 1205–1210. IEEE, 2020.

[158] Alberto Marchisio, Vojtech Mrazek, Muhammad Abdullah Hanif, and Muhammad Shafique. Descnet: Developing efficient scratchpad memories for capsule network hardware. *IEEE Transactions on Computer-Aided Design of Integrated Circuits and Systems*, 40(9):1768–1781, 2021.

[159] Alberto Marchisio, Vojtech Mrazek, Muhammad Abdullah Hanif, and Muhammad Shafique. FEECA: design space exploration for low-latency and energy-efficient capsule network accelerators. *IEEE Transactions on Very Large Scale Integration Systems*, 29(4):716–729, 2021.

[160] Alberto Marchisio, Vojtech Mrazek, Andrea Massa, Beatrice Bussolino, Maurizio Martina, and Muhammad Shafique. HARNAS: Neural Architecture Search Jointly Optimizing for Hardware Efficiency and Adversarial Robustness of Convolutional and Capsule Networks. *ICML Workshop on Dynamic Neural Networks (DyNN)*, 2022.

[161] Alberto Marchisio, Vojtech Mrazek, Andrea Massa, Beatrice Bussolino, Maurizio Martina, and Muhammad Shafique. Rohnas: A neural architecture search framework with conjoint optimization for adversarial robustness and hardware efficiency of convolutional and capsule networks. *IEEE Access*, 10:109043–109055, 2022.

[162] Alberto Marchisio, Giorgio Nanfa, Faiq Khalid, Muhammad Abdullah Hanif, Maurizio Martina, and Muhammad Shafique. CapsAttacks: Robust and Imperceptible Adversarial Attacks on Capsule Networks. *ICML Workshop on Uncertainty & Robustness in Deep Learning. UDL 2019, Long Beach, CA, USA, July 9-15*, 2019.

[163] Alberto Marchisio, Giorgio Nanfa, Faiq Khalid, Muhammad Abdullah Hanif, Maurizio Martina, and Muhammad Shafique. Is spiking secure? A comparative study on the security vulnerabilities of spiking and deep neural networks. In *2020 International Joint Conference on Neural Networks, IJCNN 2020, Glasgow, United Kingdom, July 19-24, 2020*, pages 1–8. IEEE, 2020.

[164] Alberto Marchisio, Giorgio Nanfa, Faiq Khalid, Muhammad Abdullah Hanif, Maurizio Martina, and Muhammad Shafique. SeVuC: A Study on the Security Vulnerabilities of Capsule Networks against Adversarial Attacks. *Microprocessors and Microsystems (MICPRO)*, 2023.

[165] Alberto Marchisio, Giacomo Pira, Maurizio Martina, Guido Masera, and Muhammad Shafique. Dvs-attacks: Adversarial attacks on dynamic vision sensors for spiking neural networks. In *International Joint Conference on Neural Networks, IJCNN 2021, Shenzhen, China, July 18-22, 2021*, pages 1–9. IEEE, 2021.

[166] Alberto Marchisio, Giacomo Pira, Maurizio Martina, Guido Masera, and Muhammad Shafique. R-SNN: an analysis and design methodology for robustifying spiking neural networks against adversarial attacks through noise

filters for dynamic vision sensors. In *IEEE/RSJ International Conference on Intelligent Robots and Systems, IROS 2021, Prague, Czech Republic, September 27 - Oct. 1, 2021*, pages 6315–6321. IEEE, 2021.

[167] Stefano Markidis, Steven Wei Der Chien, Erwin Laure, Ivy Bo Peng, and Jeffrey S. Vetter. NVIDIA tensor core programmability, performance & precision. In *2018 IEEE International Parallel and Distributed Processing Symposium Workshops, IPDPS Workshops 2018, Vancouver, BC, Canada, May 21-25, 2018*, pages 522–531. IEEE Computer Society, 2018.

[168] Riccardo Massa, Alberto Marchisio, Maurizio Martina, and Muhammad Shafique. An efficient spiking neural network for recognizing gestures with a DVS camera on the loihi neuromorphic processor. In *2020 International Joint Conference on Neural Networks, IJCNN 2020, Glasgow, United Kingdom, July 19-24, 2020*, pages 1–9. IEEE, 2020.

[169] Warren S. McCulloch and Walter H. Pitts. A logical calculus of the ideas immanent in nervous activity. In Margaret A. Boden, editor, *The Philosophy of Artificial Intelligence*, Oxford readings in philosophy, pages 22–39. Oxford University Press, 1990.

[170] Paul A. Merolla, John V. Arthur, Rodrigo Alvarez-Icaza, Andrew S. Cassidy, Jun Sawada, Filipp Akopyan, Bryan L. Jackson, Nabil Imam, Chen Guo, Yutaka Nakamura, Bernard Brezzo, Ivan Vo, Steven K. Esser, Rathinakumar Appuswamy, Brian Taba, Arnon Amir, Myron D. Flickner, William P. Risk, Rajit Manohar, and Dharmendra S. Modha. A million spiking-neuron integrated circuit with a scalable communication network and interface. *Science*, 345(6197):668–673, 2014.

[171] Carlo Michaelis, Andrew B. Lehr, Winfried Oed, and Christian Tetzlaff. Brian2loihi: An emulator for the neuromorphic chip loihi using the spiking neural network simulator brian. *CoRR*, abs/2109.12308, 2021.

[172] Felix Michels, Tobias Uelwer, Eric Upschulte, and Stefan Harmeling. On the vulnerability of capsule networks to adversarial attacks. *CoRR*, abs/1906.03612, 2019.

[173] Payman Mohassel and Yupeng Zhang. Secureml: A system for scalable privacy-preserving machine learning. In *2017 IEEE Symposium on Security and Privacy, SP 2017, San Jose, CA, USA, May 22-26, 2017*, pages 19–38. IEEE Computer Society, 2017.

[174] Martin Fodslette Møller. A scaled conjugate gradient algorithm for fast supervised learning. *Neural Networks*, 6(4):525–533, 1993.

[175] Happy Nkanta Monday, Jianping Li, Grace Ugochi Nneji, Saifun Nahar, Md Altab Hossin, and Jehoiada Jackson. Covid-19 pneumonia classification based on neurowavelet capsule network. *Healthcare*, 10(3), 2022.

[176] Seyed-Mohsen Moosavi-Dezfooli, Alhussein Fawzi, Omar Fawzi, and Pascal Frossard. Universal adversarial perturbations. In *2017 IEEE Conference on Computer Vision and Pattern Recognition, CVPR 2017, Honolulu, HI, USA, July 21-26, 2017*, pages 86–94. IEEE Computer Society, 2017.

[177] Seyed-Mohsen Moosavi-Dezfooli, Alhussein Fawzi, and Pascal Frossard. Deepfool: A simple and accurate method to fool deep neural networks. In *2016 IEEE Conference on Computer Vision and Pattern Recognition, CVPR 2016, Las Vegas, NV, USA, June 27-30, 2016*, pages 2574–2582. IEEE Computer Society, 2016.

[178] Saber Moradi, Qiao Ning, Fabio Stefanini, and Giacomo Indiveri. A scalable multicore architecture with heterogeneous memory structures for dynamic neuromorphic asynchronous processors (dynaps). *IEEE Transactions on Biomedical Circuits and Systems*, 12(1):106–122, 2018.

[179] Vojtech Mrazek, Radek Hrbacek, Zdenek Vasícek, and Lukás Sekanina. Evoapproxsb: Library of approximate adders and multipliers for circuit design and benchmarking of approximation methods. In David Atienza and Giorgio Di Natale, editors, *Design, Automation & Test in Europe Conference & Exhibition, DATE 2017, Lausanne, Switzerland, March 27-31, 2017*, pages 258–261. IEEE, 2017.

[180] Vojtech Mrazek, Zdenek Vasícek, Lukás Sekanina, Muhammad Abdullah Hanif, and Muhammad Shafique. ALWANN: automatic layer-wise approximation of deep neural network accelerators without retraining. In David Z. Pan, editor, *Proceedings of the International Conference on Computer-Aided Design, ICCAD 2019, Westminster, CO, USA, November 4-7, 2019*, pages 1–8. ACM, 2019.

[181] Farzeen Munir, Shoaib Azam, Moongu Jeon, Byung-Geun Lee, and Witold Pedrycz. Ldnet: End-to-end lane marking detection approach using a dynamic vision sensor. *IEEE Transactions on Intelligent Transportation Systems*, 23(7):9318–9334, 2022.

[182] Karthikeyan Nagarajan, Junde Li, Sina Sayyah Ensan, Mohammad Nasim Imtiaz Khan, Sachhidh Kannan, and Swaroop Ghosh. Analysis of power-oriented fault injection attacks on spiking neural networks. In Cristiana Bolchini, Ingrid Verbauwhede, and Ioana Vatajelu, editors, *2022 Design, Automation & Test in Europe Conference & Exhibition, DATE 2022, Antwerp, Belgium, March 14-23, 2022*, pages 861–866. IEEE, 2022.

[183] Vinod Nair and Geoffrey E. Hinton. Rectified linear units improve restricted boltzmann machines. In Johannes Fürnkranz and Thorsten Joachims, editors, *Proceedings of the 27th International Conference on Machine Learning (ICML-10), June 21-24, 2010, Haifa, Israel*, pages 807–814. Omnipress, 2010.

[184] Karthik Nandakumar, Nalini K. Ratha, Sharath Pankanti, and Shai Halevi. Towards deep neural network training on encrypted data. In *IEEE Conference on Computer Vision and Pattern Recognition Workshops, CVPR Workshops 2019, Long Beach, CA, USA, June 16-20, 2019*, pages 40–48. Computer Vision Foundation/IEEE, 2019.

[185] Emre O. Neftci, Hesham Mostafa, and Friedemann Zenke. Surrogate gradient learning in spiking neural networks: Bringing the power of gradient-based optimization to spiking neural networks. *IEEE Signal Processing Magazine*, 36(6):51–63, 2019.

[186] Yuval Netzer, Tao Wang, Adam Coates, Alessandro Bissacco, Bo Wu, and Andrew Y. Ng. Reading digits in natural images with unsupervised feature learning. In *NIPS Workshop on Deep Learning and Unsupervised Feature Learning*, 2011.

[187] Davy Neven, Bert De Brabandere, Stamatios Georgoulis, Marc Proesmans, and Luc Van Gool. Towards end-to-end lane detection: an instance segmentation approach. In *2018 IEEE Intelligent Vehicles Symposium, IV 2018, Changshu, Suzhou, China, June 26-30, 2018*, pages 286–291. IEEE, 2018.

[188] Andrew Y. Ng. Feature selection, l1 vs. l2 regularization, and rotational invariance. In *Proceedings of the Twenty-First International Conference on Machine Learning*, ICML '04, page 78, New York, NY, USA, 2004. Association for Computing Machinery.

[189] Farzad Nikfam, Alberto Marchisio, Maurizio Martina, and Muhammad Shafique. Accelat: A framework for accelerating the adversarial training of deep neural networks through accuracy gradient. *IEEE Access*, 10:108997–109007, 2022.

[190] Osamu Nomura, Yusuke Sakemi, Takeo Hosomi, and Takashi Morie. Robustness of spiking neural networks based on time-to-first-spike encoding against adversarial attacks. *IEEE Transactions on Circuits and Systems II: Express Briefs*, pages 1–1, 2022.

[191] Yuji Nozaki and Tobi Delbruck. Temperature and parasitic photocurrent effects in dynamic vision sensors. *IEEE Transactions on Electron Devices*, 64(8):3239–3245, 2017.

[192] Peter O'Connor, Daniel Neil, Shih-Chii Liu, Tobi Delbruck, and Michael Pfeiffer. Real-time classification and sensor fusion with a spiking deep belief network. *Frontiers in Neuroscience*, 7:178, 2013.

[193] Garrick Orchard, Ajinkya Jayawant, Gregory Cohen, and Nitish V. Thakor. Converting static image datasets to spiking neuromorphic datasets using saccades. *CoRR*, abs/1507.07629, 2015.

[194] Elbruz Ozen and Alex Orailoglu. Sanity-check: Boosting the reliability of safety-critical deep neural network applications. In *28th IEEE Asian Test Symposium, ATS 2019, Kolkata, India, December 10-13, 2019*, pages 7–12. IEEE, 2019.

[195] Elbruz Ozen and Alex Orailoglu. Boosting bit-error resilience of DNN accelerators through median feature selection. *IEEE Transactions on Computer-Aided Design of Integrated Circuits and Systems*, 39(11):3250–3262, 2020.

[196] Pascal Paillier. Public-key cryptosystems based on composite degree residuosity classes. In Jacques Stern, editor, *Advances in Cryptology - EUROCRYPT '99, International Conference on the Theory and Application of Cryptographic Techniques, Prague, Czech Republic, May 2-6, 1999, Proceeding*, volume 1592 of *Lecture Notes in Computer Science*, pages 223–238. Springer, 1999.

[197] Xingang Pan, Jianping Shi, Ping Luo, Xiaogang Wang, and Xiaoou Tang. Spatial as deep: Spatial CNN for traffic scene understanding. In Sheila A. McIlraith and Kilian Q. Weinberger, editors, *Proceedings of the Thirty-Second AAAI Conference on Artificial Intelligence, (AAAI-18), the 30th innovative Applications of Artificial Intelligence (IAAI-18), and the 8th AAAI Symposium on Educational Advances in Artificial Intelligence (EAAI-18), New Orleans, Louisiana, USA, February 2-7, 2018*, pages 7276–7283. AAAI Press, 2018.

[198] Xingang Pan, Jianping Shi, Ping Luo, Xiaogang Wang, and Xiaoou Tang. Spatial as deep: Spatial CNN for traffic scene understanding. In Sheila A. McIlraith and Kilian Q. Weinberger, editors, *Proceedings of the Thirty-Second AAAI Conference on Artificial Intelligence, (AAAI-18), the 30th innovative Applications of Artificial Intelligence (IAAI-18), and the 8th AAAI Symposium on Educational Advances in Artificial Intelligence (EAAI-18), New Orleans, Louisiana, USA, February 2-7, 2018*, pages 7276–7283. AAAI Press, 2018.

[199] Zihan Pan, Jibin Wu, Malu Zhang, Haizhou Li, and Yansong Chua. Neural population coding for effective temporal classification. In *International Joint Conference on Neural Networks, IJCNN 2019 Budapest, Hungary, July 14-19, 2019*, pages 1–8. IEEE, 2019.

[200] Preeti Ranjan Panda, Nikil D. Dutt, and Alexandru Nicolau. On-chip vs. off-chip memory: the data partitioning problem in embedded processor-based systems. *ACM Transactions on Design Automation of Electronic Systems*, 5(3):682–704, 2000.

[201] Pramesh Pandey, Prabal Basu, Koushik Chakraborty, and Sanghamitra Roy. Greentpu: Predictive design paradigm for improving timing error resilience of a near-threshold tensor processing unit. *IEEE Transactions on Very Large Scale Integration Systems*, 28(7):1557–1566, 2020.

[202] Nicolas Papernot, Shuang Song, Ilya Mironov, Ananth Raghunathan, Kunal Talwar, and Úlfar Erlingsson. Scalable private learning with PATE. In

6th International Conference on Learning Representations, ICLR 2018, Vancouver, BC, Canada, April 30–May 3, 2018, Conference Track Proceedings. OpenReview.net, 2018.

[203] Angshuman Parashar, Minsoo Rhu, Anurag Mukkara, Antonio Puglielli, Rangharajan Venkatesan, Brucek Khailany, Joel S. Emer, Stephen W. Keckler, and William J. Dally. SCNN: an accelerator for compressed-sparse convolutional neural networks. In *Proceedings of the 44th Annual International Symposium on Computer Architecture, ISCA 2017, Toronto, ON, Canada, June 24-28, 2017*, pages 27–40. ACM, 2017.

[204] Adam Paszke, Sam Gross, Francisco Massa, Adam Lerer, James Bradbury, Gregory Chanan, Trevor Killeen, Zeming Lin, Natalia Gimelshein, Luca Antiga, Alban Desmaison, Andreas Köpf, Edward Z. Yang, Zachary DeVito, Martin Raison, Alykhan Tejani, Sasank Chilamkurthy, Benoit Steiner, Lu Fang, Junjie Bai, and Soumith Chintala. Pytorch: An imperative style, high-performance deep learning library. In Hanna M. Wallach, Hugo Larochelle, Alina Beygelzimer, Florence d'Alché-Buc, Emily B. Fox, and Roman Garnett, editors, *Advances in Neural Information Processing Systems 32: Annual Conference on Neural Information Processing Systems 2019, NeurIPS 2019, December 8-14, 2019, Vancouver, BC, Canada*, pages 8024–8035, 2019.

[205] Bijaya Paudel, Aashish Itani, and Spyros Tragoudas. Resiliency of SNN on black-box adversarial attacks. In M. Arif Wani, Ishwar K. Sethi, Weisong Shi, Guangzhi Qu, Daniela Stan Raicu, and Ruoming Jin, editors, *20th IEEE International Conference on Machine Learning and Applications, ICMLA 2021, Pasadena, CA, USA, December 13-16, 2021*, pages 799–806. IEEE, 2021.

[206] Andrea Paudice, Luis Muñoz-González, András György, and Emil C. Lupu. Detection of adversarial training examples in poisoning attacks through anomaly detection. *CoRR*, abs/1802.03041, 2018.

[207] Hélène Paugam-Moisy and Sander M. Bohté. Computing with spiking neuron networks. In Grzegorz Rozenberg, Thomas Bäck, and Joost N. Kok, editors, *Handbook of Natural Computing*, pages 335–376. Springer, 2012.

[208] Karl Pearson. Note on regression and inheritance in the case of two parents. *Proceedings of the Royal Society of London*, 58:240–242, 1895.

[209] Christian Pehle and Jens Egholm Pedersen. Norse - A deep learning library for spiking neural networks, January 2021. Documentation: https://norse.ai/docs/.

[210] Filip Ponulak and Andrzej J. Kasinski. Introduction to spiking neural networks: Information processing, learning and applications. *Acta neurobiologiae experimentalis*, 71 4:409–33, 2011.

[211] Christoph Posch, Daniel Matolin, and Rainer Wohlgenannt. A QVGA 143 db dynamic range frame-free PWM image sensor with lossless pixel-level video

compression and time-domain CDS. *IEEE J. Solid State Circuits*, 46(1):259–275, 2011.

[212] V. Prasanth, Virendra Singh, and Rubin A. Parekhji. Reduced overhead soft error mitigation using error control coding techniques. In *17th IEEE International On-Line Testing Symposium (IOLTS 2011), 13-15 July, 2011, Athens, Greece*, pages 163–168. IEEE Computer Society, 2011.

[213] Rachmad Vidya Wicaksana Putra, Muhammad Abdullah Hanif, and Muhammad Shafique. Drmap: A generic DRAM data mapping policy for energy-efficient processing of convolutional neural networks. In *57th ACM/IEEE Design Automation Conference, DAC 2020, San Francisco, CA, USA, July 20-24, 2020*, pages 1–6. IEEE, 2020.

[214] Rachmad Vidya Wicaksana Putra, Muhammad Abdullah Hanif, and Muhammad Shafique. Respawn: Energy-efficient fault-tolerance for spiking neural networks considering unreliable memories. In *IEEE/ACM International Conference On Computer Aided Design, ICCAD 2021, Munich, Germany, November 1-4, 2021*, pages 1–9. IEEE, 2021.

[215] Rachmad Vidya Wicaksana Putra, Muhammad Abdullah Hanif, and Muhammad Shafique. Softsnn: Low-cost fault tolerance for spiking neural network accelerators under soft errors. *CoRR*, abs/2203.05523, 2022.

[216] Yao Qin, Nicholas Frosst, Colin Raffel, Garrison W. Cottrell, and Geoffrey E. Hinton. Deflecting adversarial attacks. *CoRR*, abs/2002.07405, 2020.

[217] Yao Qin, Nicholas Frosst, Sara Sabour, Colin Raffel, Garrison W. Cottrell, and Geoffrey E. Hinton. Detecting and diagnosing adversarial images with class-conditional capsule reconstructions. In *8th International Conference on Learning Representations, ICLR 2020, Addis Ababa, Ethiopia, April 26-30, 2020*. OpenReview.net, 2020.

[218] Maithra Raghu, Ben Poole, Jon M. Kleinberg, Surya Ganguli, and Jascha Sohl-Dickstein. On the expressive power of deep neural networks. In Doina Precup and Yee Whye Teh, editors, *Proceedings of the 34th International Conference on Machine Learning, ICML 2017, Sydney, NSW, Australia, 6-11 August 2017*, volume 70 of *Proceedings of Machine Learning Research*, pages 2847–2854. PMLR, 2017.

[219] Bharathwaj Raghunathan, Yatish Turakhia, Siddharth Garg, and Diana Marculescu. Cherry-picking: exploiting process variations in dark-silicon homogeneous chip multi-processors. In Enrico Macii, editor, *Design, Automation and Test in Europe, DATE 13, Grenoble, France, March 18-22, 2013*, pages 39–44. EDA Consortium San Jose, CA, USA/ACM DL, 2013.

[220] Jathushan Rajasegaran, Vinoj Jayasundara, Sandaru Jayasekara, Hirunima Jayasekara, Suranga Seneviratne, and Ranga Rodrigo. Deepcaps: Going deeper

with capsule networks. In *IEEE Conference on Computer Vision and Pattern Recognition, CVPR 2019, Long Beach, CA, USA, June 16-20, 2019*, pages 10725–10733. Computer Vision Foundation/IEEE, 2019.

[221] Adnan Siraj Rakin, Zhezhi He, and Deliang Fan. Bit-flip attack: Crushing neural network with progressive bit search. In *2019 IEEE/CVF International Conference on Computer Vision, ICCV 2019, Seoul, Korea (South), October 27 - November 2, 2019*, pages 1211–1220. IEEE, 2019.

[222] Daniel Rasmussen. Nengodl: Combining deep learning and neuromorphic modelling methods. *CoRR*, abs/1805.11144, 2018.

[223] Nitin Rathi, Gopalakrishnan Srinivasan, Priyadarshini Panda, and Kaushik Roy. Enabling deep spiking neural networks with hybrid conversion and spike timing dependent backpropagation. In *8th International Conference on Learning Representations, ICLR 2020, Addis Ababa, Ethiopia, April 26-30, 2020*. OpenReview.net, 2020.

[224] Jonas Rauber, Wieland Brendel, and Matthias Bethge. Foolbox v0.8.0: A python toolbox to benchmark the robustness of machine learning models. *CoRR*, abs/1707.04131, 2017.

[225] Raimundo Real and J. Vargas. The probabilistic basis of jaccard's index of similarity. *Systematic Biology - SYST BIOL*, 45:380–385, 09 1996.

[226] Joseph Redmon and Ali Farhadi. YOLO9000: better, faster, stronger. In *2017 IEEE Conference on Computer Vision and Pattern Recognition, CVPR 2017, Honolulu, HI, USA, July 21-26, 2017*, pages 6517–6525. IEEE Computer Society, 2017.

[227] Alpha Renner, Forrest Sheldon, Anatoly Zlotnik, Louis Tao, and Andrew T. Sornborger. The backpropagation algorithm implemented on spiking neuromorphic hardware. *CoRR*, abs/2106.07030, 2021.

[228] Frank Rhodes. On the metrics of chaudhuri, murthy and chaudhuri. *Pattern Recognition*, 28(5):745–752, 1995.

[229] Enrique Romero, Ferran Mazzanti, Jordi Delgado, and David Buchaca Prats. Weighted contrastive divergence. *Neural Networks*, 114:147–156, 2019.

[230] Frank Rosenblatt. The perceptron: a probabilistic model for information storage and organization in the brain. *Psychological review*, 65 6:386–408, 1958.

[231] Bita Darvish Rouhani, M. Sadegh Riazi, and Farinaz Koushanfar. Deepsecure: scalable provably-secure deep learning. In *Proceedings of the 55th Annual Design Automation Conference, DAC 2018, San Francisco, CA, USA, June 24-29, 2018*, pages 2:1–2:6. ACM, 2018.

[232] Bodo Rückauer, Nicolas Känzig, Shih-Chii Liu, Tobi Delbrück, and Yulia Sandamirskaya. Closing the accuracy gap in an event-based visual recognition task. *CoRR*, abs/1906.08859, 2019.

[233] Bodo Rueckauer, Connor Bybee, Ralf Goettsche, Yashwardhan Singh, Joyesh Mishra, and Andreas Wild. Nxtf: An API and compiler for deep spiking neural networks on intel loihi. *CoRR*, abs/2101.04261, 2021.

[234] Bodo Rueckauer, Iulia-Alexandra Lungu, Yuhuang Hu, Michael Pfeiffer, and Shih-Chii Liu. Conversion of continuous-valued deep networks to efficient event-driven networks for image classification. *Frontiers in Neuroscience*, 11, 2017.

[235] Berthold Ruf and Michael Schmitt. Hebbian learning in networks of spiking neurons using temporal coding. In José Mira, Roberto Moreno-Díaz, and Joan Cabestany, editors, *Biological and Artificial Computation: From Neuroscience to Technology, International Work-Conference on Artificial and Natural Neural Networks, IWANN '97, Lanzarote, Canary Islands, Spain, June 4-6, 1997, Proceedings*, volume 1240 of *Lecture Notes in Computer Science*, pages 380–389. Springer, 1997.

[236] Sara Sabour, Nicholas Frosst, and Geoffrey E. Hinton. Dynamic routing between capsules. In Isabelle Guyon, Ulrike von Luxburg, Samy Bengio, Hanna M. Wallach, Rob Fergus, S. V. N. Vishwanathan, and Roman Garnett, editors, *Advances in Neural Information Processing Systems 30: Annual Conference on Neural Information Processing Systems 2017, December 4-9, 2017, Long Beach, CA, USA*, pages 3856–3866, 2017.

[237] Sebastian Schmitt, Johann Klähn, Guillaume Bellec, Andreas Grübl, Maurice Güttler, Andreas Hartel, Stephan Hartmann, Dan Husmann de Oliveira, Kai Husmann, Sebastian Jeltsch, Vitali Karasenko, Mitja Kleider, Christoph Koke, Alexander Kononov, Christian Mauch, Eric Müller, Paul Müller, Johannes Partzsch, Mihai A. Petrovici, Stefan Schiefer, Stefan Scholze, Vasilis N. Thanasoulis, Bernhard Vogginger, Robert Legenstein, Wolfgang Maass, Christian Mayr, René Schüffny, Johannes Schemmel, and Karlheinz Meier. Neuromorphic hardware in the loop: Training a deep spiking network on the brainscales wafer-scale system. In *2017 International Joint Conference on Neural Networks, IJCNN 2017, Anchorage, AK, USA, May 14-19, 2017*, pages 2227–2234. IEEE, 2017.

[238] Christoph Schorn, Thomas Elsken, Sebastian Vogel, Armin Runge, Andre Guntoro, and Gerd Ascheid. Automated design of error-resilient and hardware-efficient deep neural networks. *Neural Comput. Appl.*, 32(24):18327–18345, 2020.

[239] Lukás Sekanina. Neural architecture search and hardware accelerator co-search: A survey. *IEEE Access*, 9:151337–151362, 2021.

[240] Ali Shafahi, W. Ronny Huang, Mahyar Najibi, Octavian Suciu, Christoph Studer, Tudor Dumitras, and Tom Goldstein. Poison frogs! targeted clean-label poisoning attacks on neural networks. In Samy Bengio, Hanna M. Wallach, Hugo Larochelle, Kristen Grauman, Nicolò Cesa-Bianchi, and Roman Garnett, editors, *Advances in Neural Information Processing Systems 31: Annual Conference on Neural Information Processing Systems 2018, NeurIPS 2018, December 3-8, 2018, Montréal, Canada*, pages 6106–6116, 2018.

[241] Muhammad Shafique, Alberto Marchisio, Rachmad Vidya Wicaksana Putra, and Muhammad Abdullah Hanif. Towards energy-efficient and secure edge AI: A cross-layer framework ICCAD special session paper. In *IEEE/ACM International Conference On Computer Aided Design, ICCAD 2021, Munich, Germany, November 1-4, 2021*, pages 1–9. IEEE, 2021.

[242] Muhammad Shafique, Mahum Naseer, Theocharis Theocharides, Christos Kyrkou, Onur Mutlu, Lois Orosa, and Jungwook Choi. Robust machine learning systems: Challenges, current trends, perspectives, and the road ahead. *IEEE Des. Test*, 37(2):30–57, 2020.

[243] Mahmood Sharif, Sruti Bhagavatula, Lujo Bauer, and Michael K. Reiter. Accessorize to a crime: Real and stealthy attacks on state-of-the-art face recognition. In Edgar R. Weippl, Stefan Katzenbeisser, Christopher Kruegel, Andrew C. Myers, and Shai Halevi, editors, *Proceedings of the 2016 ACM SIGSAC Conference on Computer and Communications Security, Vienna, Austria, October 24-28, 2016*, pages 1528–1540. ACM, 2016.

[244] Hardik Sharma, Jongse Park, Naveen Suda, Liangzhen Lai, Benson Chau, Vikas Chandra, and Hadi Esmaeilzadeh. Bit fusion: Bit-level dynamically composable architecture for accelerating deep neural network. In Murali Annavaram, Timothy Mark Pinkston, and Babak Falsafi, editors, *45th ACM/IEEE Annual International Symposium on Computer Architecture, ISCA 2018, Los Angeles, CA, USA, June 1-6, 2018*, pages 764–775. IEEE Computer Society, 2018.

[245] Saima Sharmin, Priyadarshini Panda, Syed Shakib Sarwar, Chankyu Lee, Wachirawit Ponghiran, and Kaushik Roy. A comprehensive analysis on adversarial robustness of spiking neural networks. In *International Joint Conference on Neural Networks, IJCNN 2019 Budapest, Hungary, July 14-19, 2019*, pages 1–8. IEEE, 2019.

[246] Saima Sharmin, Nitin Rathi, Priyadarshini Panda, and Kaushik Roy. Inherent adversarial robustness of deep spiking neural networks: Effects of discrete input encoding and non-linear activations. In *Computer Vision - ECCV 2020 - 16th European Conference, Glasgow, UK, August 23-28, 2020, Proceedings, Part XXIX*, volume 12374 of *Lecture Notes in Computer Science*, pages 399–414. Springer, 2020.

[247] Reza Shokri, Marco Stronati, Congzheng Song, and Vitaly Shmatikov. Membership inference attacks against machine learning models. In *2017 IEEE*

Symposium on Security and Privacy, SP 2017, San Jose, CA, USA, May 22-26, 2017, pages 3–18. IEEE Computer Society, 2017.

[248] Sumit Bam Shrestha and Garrick Orchard. SLAYER: spike layer error reassignment in time. In Samy Bengio, Hanna M. Wallach, Hugo Larochelle, Kristen Grauman, Nicolò Cesa-Bianchi, and Roman Garnett, editors, *Advances in Neural Information Processing Systems 31: Annual Conference on Neural Information Processing Systems 2018, NeurIPS 2018, December 3-8, 2018, Montréal, Canada*, pages 1419–1428, 2018.

[249] Ayesha Siddique and Khaza Anuarul Hoque. Is approximation universally defensive against adversarial attacks in deep neural networks? In Cristiana Bolchini, Ingrid Verbauwhede, and Ioana Vatajelu, editors, *2022 Design, Automation & Test in Europe Conference & Exhibition, DATE 2022, Antwerp, Belgium, March 14-23, 2022*, pages 364–369. IEEE, 2022.

[250] Arnold J. F. Siegert. On the first passage time probability problem. *Phys. Rev.*, 81:617–623, 1951.

[251] Karen Simonyan and Andrew Zisserman. Very deep convolutional networks for large-scale image recognition. In Yoshua Bengio and Yann LeCun, editors, *3rd International Conference on Learning Representations, ICLR 2015, San Diego, CA, USA, May 7-9, 2015, Conference Track Proceedings*, 2015.

[252] Amos Sironi, Manuele Brambilla, Nicolas Bourdis, Xavier Lagorce, and Ryad Benosman. HATS: histograms of averaged time surfaces for robust event-based object classification. In *2018 IEEE Conference on Computer Vision and Pattern Recognition, CVPR 2018, Salt Lake City, UT, USA, June 18-22, 2018*, pages 1731–1740. Computer Vision Foundation/IEEE Computer Society, 2018.

[253] Leslie N. Smith and Nicholay Topin. Super-convergence: Very fast training of residual networks using large learning rates. *CoRR*, abs/1708.07120, 2017.

[254] Theofilos Spyrou, Sarah A. El-Sayed, Engin Afacan, Luis A. Camuñas-Mesa, Bernabé Linares-Barranco, and Haralampos-G. Stratigopoulos. Neuron fault tolerance in spiking neural networks. In *Design, Automation & Test in Europe Conference & Exhibition, DATE 2021, Grenoble, France, February 1-5, 2021*, pages 743–748. IEEE, 2021.

[255] Gopalakrishnan Srinivasan, Priyadarshini Panda, and Kaushik Roy. Stdp-based unsupervised feature learning using convolution-over-time in spiking neural networks for energy-efficient neuromorphic computing. *ACM Journal on Emerging Technologies in Computing Systems*, 14(4):44:1–44:12, 2018.

[256] Nitish Srivastava, Geoffrey Hinton, Alex Krizhevsky, Ilya Sutskever, and Ruslan Salakhutdinov. Dropout: A simple way to prevent neural networks from overfitting. *Journal of Machine Learning Research*, 15(56):1929–1958, 2014.

[257] Kenneth Stewart, Garrick Orchard, Sumit Bam Shrestha, and Emre Neftci. Online few-shot gesture learning on a neuromorphic processor. *IEEE Journal on Emerging and Selected Topics in Circuits and Systems*, 10(4):512–521, 2020.

[258] Marcel Stimberg, Romain Brette, and Dan FM Goodman. Brian 2, an intuitive and efficient neural simulator. *eLife*, 8:e47314, aug 2019.

[259] Jan Stuijt, Manolis Sifalakis, Amirreza Yousefzadeh, and Federico Corradi. μbrain: An event-driven and fully synthesizable architecture for spiking neural networks. *Frontiers in Neuroscience*, 15, 2021.

[260] Jiawei Su, Danilo Vasconcellos Vargas, and Kouichi Sakurai. One pixel attack for fooling deep neural networks. *IEEE Transactions on Evolutionary Computation*, 23(5):828–841, 2019.

[261] Yunjae Suh, Seungnam Choi, Masamichi Ito, Jeongseok Kim, Youngho Lee, Jongseok Seo, Heejae Jung, Dong-Hee Yeo, Seol Namgung, Jongwoo Bong, Sehoon Yoo, Seung-Hun Shin, Doowon Kwon, Pilkyu Kang, Seokho Kim, Hoonjoo Na, Kihyun Hwang, Chang-Woo Shin, Jun-Seok Kim, Paul K. J. Park, Joonseok Kim, Hyunsurk Ryu, and Yongin Park. A 1280×960 dynamic vision sensor with a 4.95-μm pixel pitch and motion artifact minimization. In *IEEE International Symposium on Circuits and Systems, ISCAS 2020, Sevilla, Spain, October 10-21, 2020*, pages 1–5. IEEE, 2020.

[262] Vivienne Sze, Yu-Hsin Chen, Tien-Ju Yang, and Joel S. Emer. Efficient processing of deep neural networks: A tutorial and survey. *Proceedings of the IEEE*, 105(12):2295–2329, 2017.

[263] Mingxing Tan, Bo Chen, Ruoming Pang, Vijay Vasudevan, Mark Sandler, Andrew Howard, and Quoc V. Le. Mnasnet: Platform-aware neural architecture search for mobile. In *IEEE Conference on Computer Vision and Pattern Recognition, CVPR 2019, Long Beach, CA, USA, June 16-20, 2019*, pages 2820–2828. Computer Vision Foundation/IEEE, 2019.

[264] Jigang Tang, Songbin Li, and Peng Liu. A review of lane detection methods based on deep learning. *Pattern Recognition*, 111:107623, 2021.

[265] Simen Thys, Wiebe Van Ranst, and Toon Goedemé. Fooling automated surveillance cameras: Adversarial patches to attack person detection. In *IEEE Conference on Computer Vision and Pattern Recognition Workshops, CVPR Workshops 2019, Long Beach, CA, USA, June 16-20, 2019*, pages 49–55. Computer Vision Foundation/IEEE, 2019.

[266] Tijmen Tieleman. The affnist dataset. *cs.toronto.edu*, 2013.

[267] Florian Tramèr, Fan Zhang, Ari Juels, Michael K. Reiter, and Thomas Ristenpart. Stealing machine learning models via prediction apis. In Thorsten Holz and Stefan Savage, editors, *25th USENIX Security Symposium, USENIX*

Security 16, Austin, TX, USA, August 10-12, 2016, pages 601–618. USENIX Association, 2016.

[268] Frederick Tung and Greg Mori. CLIP-Q: deep network compression learning by in-parallel pruning-quantization. In *2018 IEEE Conference on Computer Vision and Pattern Recognition, CVPR 2018, Salt Lake City, UT, USA, June 18-22, 2018*, pages 7873–7882. Computer Vision Foundation/IEEE Computer Society, 2018.

[269] Ramakrishna Vadlamani, Jia Zhao, Wayne P. Burleson, and Russell Tessier. Multicore soft error rate stabilization using adaptive dual modular redundancy. In Giovanni De Micheli, Bashir M. Al-Hashimi, Wolfgang Müller, and Enrico Macii, editors, *Design, Automation and Test in Europe, DATE 2010, Dresden, Germany, March 8-12, 2010*, pages 27–32. IEEE Computer Society, 2010.

[270] Valerio Venceslai, Alberto Marchisio, Ihsen Alouani, Maurizio Martina, and Muhammad Shafique. Neuroattack: Undermining spiking neural networks security through externally triggered bit-flips. In *2020 International Joint Conference on Neural Networks, IJCNN 2020, Glasgow, United Kingdom, July 19-24, 2020*, pages 1–8. IEEE, 2020.

[271] Alberto Viale, Alberto Marchisio, Maurizio Martina, Guido Masera, and Muhammad Shafique. Carsnn: An efficient spiking neural network for event-based autonomous cars on the loihi neuromorphic research processor. In *International Joint Conference on Neural Networks, IJCNN 2021, Shenzhen, China, July 18-22, 2021*, pages 1–10. IEEE, 2021.

[272] Alberto Viale, Alberto Marchisio, Maurizio Martina, Guido Masera, and Muhammad Shafique. Lanesnns: Spiking neural networks for lane detection on the loihi neuromorphic processor. In *IEEE/RSJ International Conference on Intelligent Robots and Systems, IROS 2022, Kyoto, Japan, October 23-27, 2022*, pages 79–86. IEEE, 2022.

[273] Sameer Wagh, Divya Gupta, and Nishanth Chandran. Securenn: 3-party secure computation for neural network training. *Proc. Priv. Enhancing Technol.*, 2019(3):26–49, 2019.

[274] Binghui Wang and Neil Zhenqiang Gong. Stealing hyperparameters in machine learning. In *2018 IEEE Symposium on Security and Privacy, SP 2018, Proceedings, 21-23 May 2018, San Francisco, California, USA*, pages 36–52. IEEE Computer Society, 2018.

[275] Kuan Wang, Zhijian Liu, Yujun Lin, Ji Lin, and Song Han. HAQ: hardware-aware automated quantization with mixed precision. In *IEEE Conference on Computer Vision and Pattern Recognition, CVPR 2019, Long Beach, CA, USA, June 16-20, 2019*, pages 8612–8620. Computer Vision Foundation / IEEE, 2019.

[276] Limin Wang, Sheng Guo, Weilin Huang, and Yu Qiao. Places205-vggnet models for scene recognition. *CoRR*, abs/1508.01667, 2015.

[277] Meiqi Wang, Siyuan Lu, Danyang Zhu, Jun Lin, and Zhongfeng Wang. A high-speed and low-complexity architecture for softmax function in deep learning. In *2018 IEEE Asia Pacific Conference on Circuits and Systems, APCCAS 2018, Chengdu, China, October 26-30, 2018*, pages 223–226. IEEE, 2018.

[278] Zhenzhong Wang, Lilin Guo, and Malek Adjouadi. A biological plausible generalized leaky integrate-and-fire neuron model. In *36th Annual International Conference of the IEEE Engineering in Medicine and Biology Society, EMBC 2014, Chicago, IL, USA, August 26-30, 2014*, pages 6810–6813. IEEE, 2014.

[279] Devin Willmott et al. You only query once: Effective black box adversarial attacks with minimal repeated queries. *arXiv*, 2021.

[280] Bichen Wu, Xiaoliang Dai, Peizhao Zhang, Yanghan Wang, Fei Sun, Yiming Wu, Yuandong Tian, Peter Vajda, Yangqing Jia, and Kurt Keutzer. Fbnet: Hardware-aware efficient convnet design via differentiable neural architecture search. In *IEEE Conference on Computer Vision and Pattern Recognition, CVPR 2019, Long Beach, CA, USA, June 16-20, 2019*, pages 10734–10742. Computer Vision Foundation/IEEE, 2019.

[281] Xixin Wu, Yuewen Cao, Hui Lu, Songxiang Liu, Disong Wang, Zhiyong Wu, Xunying Liu, and Helen Meng. Speech emotion recognition using sequential capsule networks. *IEEE/ACM Transactions on Audio, Speech, and Language Processing*, 29:3280–3291, 2021.

[282] Yanzhao Wu, Ling Liu, Juhyun Bae, Ka Ho Chow, Arun Iyengar, Calton Pu, Wenqi Wei, Lei Yu, and Qi Zhang. Demystifying learning rate polices for high accuracy training of deep neural networks. *CoRR*, abs/1908.06477, 2019.

[283] Yujie Wu, Lei Deng, Guoqi Li, Jun Zhu, and Luping Shi. Spatio-temporal backpropagation for training high-performance spiking neural networks. *Frontiers in Neuroscience*, 12, 2018.

[284] Han Xiao, Kashif Rasul, and Roland Vollgraf. Fashion-mnist: a novel image dataset for benchmarking machine learning algorithms. *CoRR*, abs/1708.07747, 2017.

[285] Chen Zhang, Peng Li, Guangyu Sun, Yijin Guan, Bingjun Xiao, and Jason Cong. Optimizing fpga-based accelerator design for deep convolutional neural networks. In George A. Constantinides and Deming Chen, editors, *Proceedings of the 2015 ACM/SIGDA International Symposium on Field-Programmable Gate Arrays, Monterey, CA, USA, February 22-24, 2015*, pages 161–170. ACM, 2015.

[286] Jeff Zhang, Kartheek Rangineni, Zahra Ghodsi, and Siddharth Garg. Thundervolt: enabling aggressive voltage underscaling and timing error resilience for energy efficient deep learning accelerators. In *Proceedings of the 55th Annual Design Automation Conference, DAC 2018, San Francisco, CA, USA, June 24-29, 2018*, pages 19:1–19:6. ACM, 2018.

[287] Jeff Jun Zhang, Tianyu Gu, Kanad Basu, and Siddharth Garg. Analyzing and mitigating the impact of permanent faults on a systolic array based neural network accelerator. In *36th IEEE VLSI Test Symposium, VTS 2018, San Francisco, CA, USA, April 22-25, 2018*, pages 1–6. IEEE Computer Society, 2018.

[288] Qian Zhang, Ting Wang, Ye Tian, Feng Yuan, and Qiang Xu. Approxann: an approximate computing framework for artificial neural network. In Wolfgang Nebel and David Atienza, editors, *Proceedings of the 2015 Design, Automation & Test in Europe Conference & Exhibition, DATE 2015, Grenoble, France, March 9-13, 2015*, pages 701–706. ACM, 2015.

[289] Kai Zhao, Sheng Di, Sihuan Li, Xin Liang, Yujia Zhai, Jieyang Chen, Kaiming Ouyang, Franck Cappello, and Zizhong Chen. FT-CNN: algorithm-based fault tolerance for convolutional neural networks. *IEEE Trans. Parallel Distributed Syst.*, 32(7):1677–1689, 2021.

[290] Wei Zhao, Haiyun Peng, Steffen Eger, Erik Cambria, and Min Yang. Towards scalable and reliable capsule networks for challenging NLP applications. In Anna Korhonen, David R. Traum, and Lluís Màrquez, editors, *Proceedings of the 57th Conference of the Association for Computational Linguistics, ACL 2019, Florence, Italy, July 28- August 2, 2019, Volume 1: Long Papers*, pages 1549–1559. Association for Computational Linguistics, 2019.

[291] Barret Zoph, Vijay Vasudevan, Jonathon Shlens, and Quoc V. Le. Learning transferable architectures for scalable image recognition. In *2018 IEEE Conference on Computer Vision and Pattern Recognition, CVPR 2018, Salt Lake City, UT, USA, June 18-22, 2018*, pages 8697–8710. Computer Vision Foundation/IEEE Computer Society, 2018.

Index